Oh, the doors you will open!

Dive Right In

Senior Authors
Isabel L. Beck • Roger C. Farr • Dorothy S. Strickland

Authors
Alma Flor Ada • Roxanne F. Hudson • Margaret G. McKeown
Robin C. Scarcella • Julie A. Washington

Consultants
F. Isabel Campoy • Tyrone C. Howard • David A. Monti

Harcourt
SCHOOL PUBLISHERS

www.harcourtschool.com

HARCOURT SCHOOL PUBLISHERS

STORYtown

Dive Right In

Harcourt

SCHOOL PUBLISHERS

www.harcourtschool.com

Theme 1
Personal Triumphs

Contents

4

Theme 2
Joining Forces

Contents

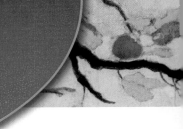

Theme ③
A Changing Planet

Contents

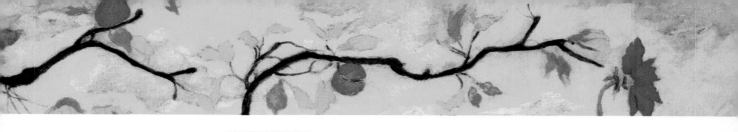

Theme 4

Unique Perspectives

Contents

Theme **5**
Ancient Wisdom

Contents

Theme 6
The Outer Limits

Contents

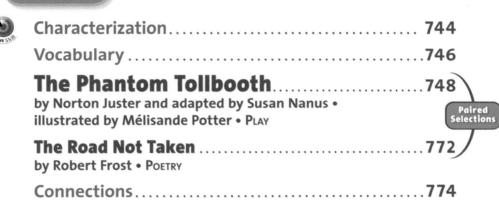

Comprehension Strategies

Strategies for Reading

A **strategy** is a plan for doing something well. You can use strategies before, during, and after reading.

Before You Read
- **Preview the text** by looking at the title, headings, and photographs or illustrations.
- **Access prior knowledge** by thinking about what you already know about the topic or genre.
- **Predict** what the text will be about and what you might learn from reading it. Then **set a purpose** for reading.

While You Read
Think about what you understand and do not understand. Use the comprehension strategies on page 17 to help you understand the text and remember it later.

After You Read
Talk with a classmate about which strategies you used and why you used them.

Strategies to Use When Reading

- **Use Story Structure** Keep track of the characters, setting, and plot events to help you understand how a story is organized.

- **Summarize** Pause as you read to identify the most important ideas in the text.

- **Ask and Answer Questions** Ask yourself questions about what you do not understand in the text. Look for answers to questions as you read.

- **Use Graphic Organizers** Make charts and diagrams as you read to show how important ideas in the text are related.

- **Monitor Comprehension** When you do not understand a section of text, use one of these strategies to clarify the information.
  - **Reread**
  - **Read Ahead**
  - **Adjust Reading Rate**
  - **Self-Correct**

Theme 1 Personal Triumphs

▸ *Woman in Hot Air Balloon*, Larry Moore

19

CONTENTS

Lesson 1

Genre: Realistic Fiction

MAXX COMEDY

Funniest Kid in America

GORDON KORMAN

Genre: Personal Narrative

ARE YOU LAUGHING AT ME?

I hope so!
Stand-up comedy is my life.

by Michael Witzer, as told to Laura Daily
photographs by Peter McBride

21

Focus Skill

Plot and Setting

Plot is the series of events that make up a story. The plot contains a **conflict,** or problem, and events that lead to a **resolution,** or solution to the problem. The **setting** of a story is where and when the events take place. As you read a story, think about how the setting affects the conflict and resolution in the plot. Why is the setting important to the plot? Does the setting create challenges for the characters?

Characters	Setting

Conflict

Plot Events

Resolution

Tip

To figure out the conflict in a story, ask yourself what challenge the main character is facing.

Read the paragraph. Then look at the story map below to see how the plot conflict and the setting are related. The story takes place in summer, and the heat from the highway probably caused the flat tire.

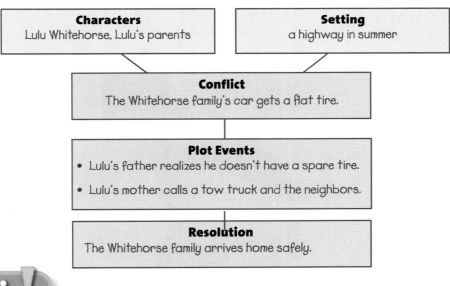

Lulu Whitehorse and her parents were driving home after a summer camping trip. Heat from the highway rose in waves before them. Suddenly, there was a sharp popping sound, and the car swerved. Lulu's father pumped the brakes and pulled over. Then he said, "I took out that spare tire to make room for our tent!" Lulu's mother used her cellular phone to call a tow truck and the neighbors to pick them up. Eventually, they all arrived home safely.

Characters	Setting
Lulu Whitehorse, Lulu's parents	a highway in summer

Conflict
The Whitehorse family's car gets a flat tire.

Plot Events
- Lulu's father realizes he doesn't have a spare tire.
- Lulu's mother calls a tow truck and the neighbors.

Resolution
The Whitehorse family arrives home safely.

Try This!

Look back at the paragraph. How did the setting affect the resolution?

Vocabulary

Build Robust Vocabulary

- ricocheted
- hysterical
- crestfallen
- ecstatic
- incapacitated
- lamented
- mirth
- perishable

Cougars Win, Eggs Lose

Fall Field Day at Susan B. Anthony Middle School was full of surprises. First, the Cougars won the softball cup in an upset. When Ruby Jones scored the winning run, cheers **ricocheted** around the ball field. Her mother was so **hysterical** with excitement that she ran out and hugged the coach!

Of course, the news was not greeted with joy by the Sharks. Their **crestfallen** captain said the loss meant an end to a three-semester winning streak.

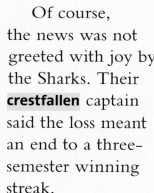

Ruby Jones was **ecstatic** when she hit the winning run off the Sharks' substitute pitcher.

"Our best pitcher was **incapacitated** last week by a knee injury," he **lamented**. "If she'd been available, we might have won today."

The second surprise of the day came when it was discovered that the eggs reserved for the egg toss were rotten. Participants and spectators alike fled the field after several eggs were broken. There was no **mirth** in Principal Donley's voice when she said, "As you know, eggs are highly **perishable**." Sadly, the supermarket was closed, so the egg toss was canceled.

 www.harcourtschool.com/storytown

GO online www.harcourtschool.com/storytown

Word Scribe

This week, your task is to use the Vocabulary Words in your writing. In your vocabulary journal, write sentences that show the meanings of the words. For example, you could write about an experience that made you feel ecstatic or one that made you feel crestfallen. Use as many Vocabulary Words as you can. Share your writing with your classmates.

Realistic Fiction

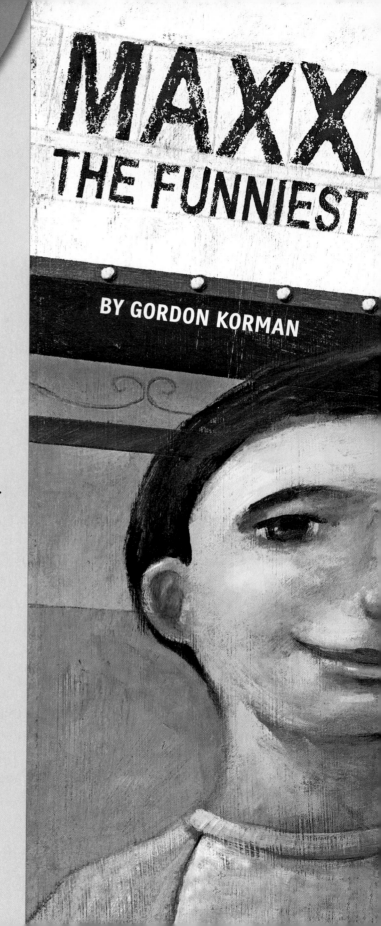

MAXX THE FUNNIEST

BY GORDON KORMAN

Genre Study

Realistic fiction has characters and events that are like people and events in real life. As you read, look for

- a setting based on a real place.

- characters who face a problem.

Characters — Setting
Conflict
Plot Events
Resolution

Comprehension Strategy

Use story structure to identify and understand the story's conflict and resolution.

COMEDY
KID IN AMERICA

ILLUSTRATED BY STEVE ADAMS

Max Carmody wants to enter a contest in which the funniest kid in America will be chosen. He calls himself Maxx Comedy and makes an audition video that includes a laugh track—or so he thinks....

Weeks later, Max is invited to audition live for the competition in Chicago. His stepfather, Mario, a big rig driver, is unable to take him to the contest. Instead, Dr. Carmody and Ellen Plunkett, Max's parents, take him. His stepsister, Olivia, and his best friend, Maude, go along to support Max. The group has gotten lost and is running very late on the way from Bartonville, Ohio, to Chicago. Max wonders if they'll make it in time for his scheduled performance.

"The highway!" cried Max.

Filthy and sopping wet, his father jumped back behind the wheel and threw the car in gear. "Hang in there, kid! I told you we'd make it!"

As they jounced along the dirt road, the Volvo became the scene of the kind of mathematical calculations that normally took place only in physics labs. It was eleven o'clock. The Balsam Auditorium was 240 miles away.

"Which means," Max concluded excitedly, "if we go eighty, we'll make it just in time for the two o'clock start!"

"You can't go eighty on a dirt road," Dr. Carmody called back from the driver's seat.

"You can't go eighty on *any* road," amended his ex-wife sternly.

"We can slow to fifty on the unpaved portion," Maude agreed, expertly crunching numbers in her head, "if we bump it up to eighty-five once we hit the Interstate." At that moment, the Volvo's tires jumped from the rutted mud and stones onto a bumpy but paved two-lane farm route. "This is better. How fast can we go here?"

"At least seventy," put in Max.

"No!" stormed Ellen Plunkett. "We'll drive the speed limit and get there late, but in one piece."

"Come on, Ellen," coaxed Dr. Carmody. "This is a big day for Max. We've got a chance to make it!"

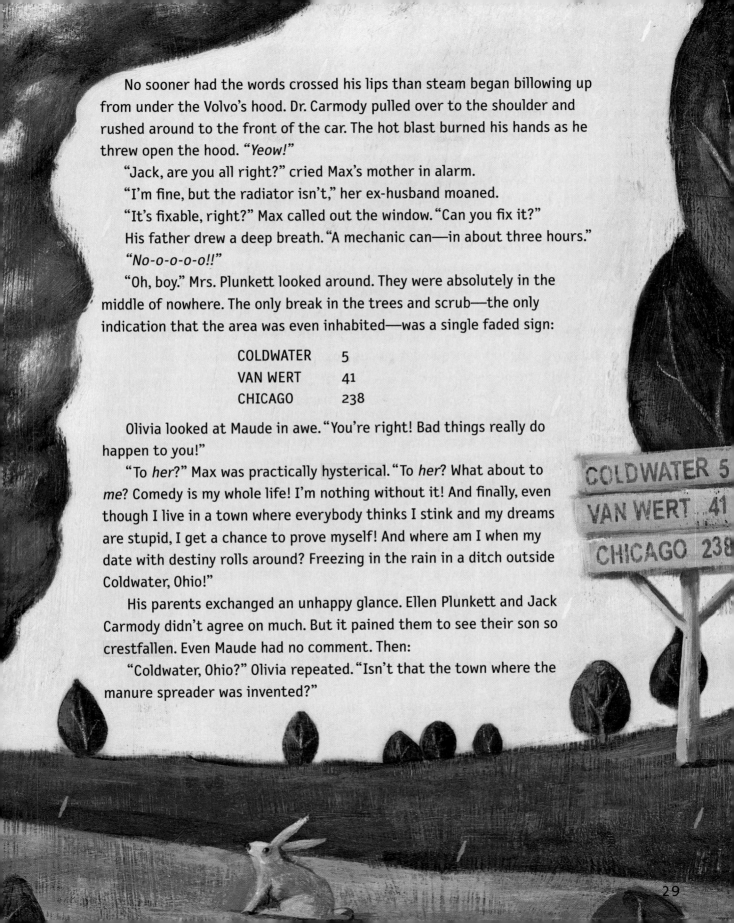

No sooner had the words crossed his lips than steam began billowing up from under the Volvo's hood. Dr. Carmody pulled over to the shoulder and rushed around to the front of the car. The hot blast burned his hands as he threw open the hood. "*Yeow!*"

"Jack, are you all right?" cried Max's mother in alarm.

"I'm fine, but the radiator isn't," her ex-husband moaned.

"It's fixable, right?" Max called out the window. "Can you fix it?"

His father drew a deep breath. "A mechanic can—in about three hours."

"*No-o-o-o-o!!*"

"Oh, boy." Mrs. Plunkett looked around. They were absolutely in the middle of nowhere. The only break in the trees and scrub—the only indication that the area was even inhabited—was a single faded sign:

COLDWATER	5
VAN WERT	41
CHICAGO	238

Olivia looked at Maude in awe. "You're right! Bad things really do happen to you!"

"To *her*?" Max was practically hysterical. "To *her*? What about to *me*? Comedy is my whole life! I'm nothing without it! And finally, even though I live in a town where everybody thinks I stink and my dreams are stupid, I get a chance to prove myself! And where am I when my date with destiny rolls around? Freezing in the rain in a ditch outside Coldwater, Ohio!"

His parents exchanged an unhappy glance. Ellen Plunkett and Jack Carmody didn't agree on much. But it pained them to see their son so crestfallen. Even Maude had no comment. Then:

"Coldwater, Ohio?" Olivia repeated. "Isn't that the town where the manure spreader was invented?"

"That's right!" Max grasped at the information like a drowning man clinging to a life preserver. "Mario passes here all the time! Wasn't he supposed to come through today?"

There was a frantic cell phone conversation, and Mrs. Plunkett delivered the news. "He'll be here in forty-five minutes."

Max jumped up and down like a madman, pumping his fist in the air. "Yes! Yes! Yes! Way to go, Mario! You're my man!" To his father, he added, embarrassed, "And you too, Dad. Thanks for—uh—getting us this far."

Dr. Carmody ruffled his son's unruly hair. "I hope you make it, Max."

It was going to be close. They would be late—there was no question about that. And a big rig like Mario's wouldn't be able to drive as fast as Dr. Carmody's Volvo. But if they could just get to the Balsam Auditorium before the contest ended at five o'clock, Max could explain what had happened, and maybe the judges would let him go on last. It was a slim chance, but the only one he had.

It was after one when Mario's eighteen-wheeler roared up the two-lane farm road to the incapacitated Volvo. Dr. Carmody had to stay to wait for the tow truck. Mrs. Plunkett, Max, Maude, and Olivia wished him good-bye and good luck.

There wasn't enough room in the cab for all five of them, so it was decided that Mrs. Plunkett and Olivia would ride up front with Mario. Max and Maude were relegated to the cheap seats in the refrigerated trailer with the cargo.

Mario led them around the back and opened the big cargo door. The container was piled high with boxes.

"There's no room," Max protested.

"Just wedge yourself between the cartons and hold on tight," Mario advised cheerfully. He tossed his stepson a flashlight. "It's dark with the door closed."

"It's freezing back here," Maude complained. "By the time we get to Chicago, we'll be in suspended animation!"

"There's no extra charge for the air-conditioning," grinned Mario. And he slammed the door and latched it, leaving them in the chilly blackness. A moment later, they heard the roar of the motor, and the truck began to move.

Max switched on the flashlight and played the beam over the piled cartons. "I wonder what this stuff is. It just says 'perishable' on the side."

"I hope that doesn't mean us," sniffed Maude. "I feel like I'm going to perish any minute."

They found a stack of tarpaulins and each took one to use as a blanket against the chill air. "Mario drives me nuts," Max confessed. "But I don't think I've ever been so happy to see anybody!" He closed his eyes and concentrated on the motion of the trailer, trying to estimate their speed. Could the eighteen-wheeler go fast enough? It would be a tragedy beyond words to go through all this and *still* miss the contest.

Max wasn't a very patient car passenger in the best of circumstances. His nervousness and the cold and discomfort of the truck combined to make the time creep along agonizingly slowly. His act played itself out again and again in his head, the jokes rattling painfully around his brain. And it didn't help to have to listen to the rustling and shuffling of Maude fidgeting under her tarpaulin.

"Quit it," Max complained. "I'm uncomfortable too, okay? This isn't exactly my idea of first-class travel."

Her jerky movements only grew more exaggerated. "That's not it. I'm itchy!"

"It's all in your head," Max explained patiently.

"No! I itch all over!"

"Cut it *out*—" But when Max shone his flashlight beam at his best friend, he saw that her face was covered in bright red blotches. "Maude—you're breaking out!"

"Oh no," she cried, "I'm allergic to the truck!"

"No one can be allergic to a truck," argued Max. "Not even you."

"But—" Maude leaped to her feet. "What's in these boxes?"

She ripped the nearest one open. It was packed with—

"*Cherries!!*"

Max stared. There must have been a thousand cherries in that one case alone. He looked around, mentally multiplying by the dozens, no, hundreds of cartons.

"I'm allergic to cherries! I've got to get out of here!" Crawling over the cargo, Maude made her frantic way to the back and yanked on the latch to the cargo door.

Max grabbed her from behind and wrestled her away. "Are you crazy? What are you going to do, jump out of a speeding truck into four lanes of oncoming traffic?"

"But there's enough cherries in here to kill me fifty times!" She pushed her way to the front of the container and began pounding against the wall. "Stop the truck!"

Out of options, Max joined her. "Mario!" he yelled. "Mom! We've got a problem!"

"They can't hear us!" lamented Maude. She picked a crowbar up off the floor and started banging with that.

"Careful!" Max admonished. "If you dent the trailer, they might make Mario pay for the damage!"

"Who's going to pay for the damage to *me*?" wailed Maude. "Help! Help!" She reared back for one monster blow, but instead delivered the homerun swing to the container's refrigeration unit.

Thwack!

The heavy metal ripped the hose clear off the compressor. Dense white mist hissed out of it, filling up the trailer like a fog.

Up front in the cab, Olivia was the first to notice the blinking red warning light on the dashboard. "What's that, Daddy?"

"Uh-oh," said Mario. "Refrigeration failure." He pulled over to the shoulder and jumped out, hurrying to the passenger side to help his wife and daughter down from the big rig. The three rushed to the back of the trailer. Mario unhooked the latch and rolled up the cargo door.

A dense cloud of escaped refrigerant billowed out, followed by two coughing sixth graders.

"Maude!" cried Olivia with relief. "You're okay!"

"I'm fine too, thanks," muttered Max, jumping to the road. "Remember me, your brother?"

Mario helped Maude out of the truck.

Mrs. Plunkett stared in alarm at the fire-engine red rash on Maude's face. "Maude, what happened to you?"

"Cherries!" Maude spat. "Millions of them! I'm lucky to be alive."

Waving his arms to dispel the mist, Mario climbed into the trailer and snaked his way back between the stacks of boxes. "No wonder the cooler's leaking. The hose is detached. Did it just pop clean off like that?"

"Kind of," admitted Max. "When Maude hit it with a crowbar."

"Well, I had to get your attention," Maude explained to Mario. "I was trying to bang on the wall but I missed."

Mario squinted through the fog at the blotches on Maude's face. "It could happen to anybody," he said dubiously.

"Not anybody," Olivia corrected proudly. "Just Maude."

Her father swallowed hard. "We're just glad you're okay."

"What about the cherries?" Max's mother asked in concern. "With the refrigeration unit on the fritz, won't they go bad?"

Her husband looked thoughtful. "Not necessarily . . ."

It was a quiet moment in the hectic weekend schedule of downtown Chicago. The day-trippers had already left, but the dinner and theater crowd had not yet arrived.

That calm was shattered at precisely two minutes to five o'clock, when a massive tractor-trailer came barreling up State Street at breakneck speed. The cargo door was wide open, exposing eighty-seven large cartons of Bing cherries to the crisp November air.

The eighteen-wheeler squealed to a halt in front of the Balsam Auditorium, and out of the back leaped Max Carmody. His normally messy hair had been so blown around by the wind that it stood on end as if he had been filled with static electricity.

He hit the ground running. *"I'm he-e-e-ere!"*

Maude jumped out of the cab in hot pursuit, her red allergic rash slightly faded. "I'm right behind you, Max!"

Olivia was next. "Maude—wait for me!"

"Livy—come back!" Mrs. Plunkett tried in vain to rein in her young daughter. She

gave her husband a quick kiss. "You were a real hero today, Mario. Sorry about the truck. I hope the cherries don't spoil."

"They'll be fine," he assured her. "I'll take the northern route. There's a cold front dipping down from Canada." He hopped back up to the cab and called, "Break a leg, Max!"

Right before the heavy brass doors of the Balsam Auditorium, Max froze. The time pressure was unbelievable—it was ninety seconds to five. Yet there was something that had to be said.

It was probably too late anyway. But Max wouldn't have made it here, would have had no chance at all, had it not been for his stepfather. The guy had driven hours out of his way, and risked an expensive perishable cargo, just to get Max to Chicago. It was more loyalty than Max could have expected from anybody, and a heck of a lot more than he had the right to expect from Mario—someone he'd never been very nice to.

He turned to face his stepfather, who was just about to pull away from the curb. "Hey, Mario—do the Voles have any home games coming up?"

Mario grinned. "Next Wednesday. A grudge match with Caveman Ogrodnick and the Mansfield Mayhem."

"Save me a ticket!" yelled Max, and blasted through the auditorium doors.

He didn't even hear the "Can I help you, son?" from the man in the glass booth. It was five o'clock on the nose, but these things never finished on time, right? There was still a chance! There had to be!

He plowed blindly through the velvet curtain and pounded down the aisle between the packed rows of seats toward the spotlit stage.

"And now, the moment we've all been waiting for," the emcee was announcing. "The judges have reached their decision. The Funniest Kid in America is—" Kettledrums built to a dramatic crescendo—"Barry Robson!"

All the steam went out of Max, and he coasted to a stop on the red carpet. He was amazed he didn't fall flat on his face.

Barry Robson.

The name ricocheted around his head like an accelerated particle as his stomach tied itself into a knot worthy of an eagle scout.

Barry Robson, The Funniest Kid in America.

Not Maxx Comedy. Not Max Carmody.

He watched through eyes filling up with tears as an ecstatic young teen ran onstage to accept a large trophy featuring a gleaming silver microphone. His disbelief melted into despair. They had gone through so much today—getting lost, the breakdown, Maude's allergy attack, Mario's busted cooling unit. Yet, against all odds, they had made it to Chicago and the Balsam Auditorium.

But not in time.

The contest was over.

Their motel was a pleasant little roadside inn on the outskirts of Chicago. But not even the cheery rooms and 140 cable channels could brighten the deep, dark depression that had settled over Max Carmody.

One at a time, his traveling companions tried to lighten his mood.

"I'll watch you do your act any time you want," Olivia offered generously. "You can even make fun of Barney."

"Forget it, kid," her brother muttered. "After today, I'm through with the comedy business. I'm never going to tell another joke as long as I live."

Mrs. Plunkett was next. "Well, the cherries are safe and the truck is fixed," she reported. "Mario just called in from Montague, Iowa. Did you know that's the home of the world's largest fire hydrant?"

"Uh-huh."

His mother regarded him expectantly. "Don't you have anything to add to that, Maxie?"

"If I still made jokes, which I don't," Max replied, "then I might say that I hope the dogs in that town are all ten feet tall. But that would be funny, and there's nothing funny about my life right now."

Last came Maude. She waited until Mrs. Plunkett and Olivia had retired to the girls' room next door. "You think this is bad?" she challenged. "This is *nothing*. Try walking a mile in my shoes, and I don't mean just because of the orthotic insoles for flat feet. *I'm* the world's largest fire hydrant, pal. And there are a lot of dogs out there— of all sizes."

Max looked daggers at her. "It's reassuring to know that, after everything that happened today, this is really all about *you*." He pointed to the door. "Get out of here. I want to be alone."

"What about TV?" Maude switched on the set and deposited herself on one of the beds. "Your mom would never let me watch Chicago news in front of Olivia. The big-city crime is way better than the wimpy stuff that happens at home. In Bartonville, breaking news is Katie Kates sobbing because somebody backed over a caterpillar."

As Maude drank in stories of fires, armed robberies, and high-speed police chases, Max barely heard a word. For two whole months, every fiber of his being had been focused on this contest. Now it was over, and without his firing off so much as a single punch line. It was like losing a war before you could pick up a peashooter in your own defense. And on top of it all, Max now had a date with Mario to see Caveman Ogrodnick and his merry Neanderthals. It was the end. It was more than he could bear.

"Hey, look." Maude pointed at the screen. "They're talking about your contest."

Max picked up the remote and hit MUTE. "I'm not listening."

"There's the guy who won," she went on. "Hey, that's a nice trophy." She reached for the clicker. "Come on, let's listen to the acceptance speech."

"No."

Max tried to yank the remote away, but Maude grabbed on. There was a brief tug-of-war, and then the sound returned—the winner's standing ovation. For Max it was a hammer blow to the heart.

The applause died away and the anchor returned. "There was one additional award, although for some reason, this young comic never got to perform. The chief judge explains...."

Onscreen, the contest official was being interviewed backstage. "We didn't plan on this, but we got a video that you just can't ignore. The whole committee made copies because it's something you want to keep forever. It's the funniest bit I've ever seen.

MOOO! MOOO! MOOO!

If you're out there, Maxx Comedy, you've got a great future."

Max froze as his audition video began to play right there on the Chicago news.

There was Max, larger than life, on the stage of the Bartonville Middle School gym, as Big Byrd had filmed him a month earlier. "In our school cafeteria," he began his routine, "the black-bean burrito has been designated a weapon of mass destruction."

Holding his breath, Max waited for his laugh track to kick in. And, yes, there was a huge reaction. But it was not the howls of mirth he had taped at the Locke party. The sound that swelled through the TV's small speaker was horrible, violent, *animal*....

Maude's jaw fell open. "What's *that*?"

How *would* you describe it? A frantic, agonized combination of moaning, howling, and shrieking. Almost—

"*Mooing?*" Max exclaimed in disbelief.

"Yeah!" Maude snapped her fingers in sudden recognition. "I haven't heard anything like that since your dad gave birth to that cow!"

Strictly speaking, Dad had *delivered* the calf. He was the vet, not the mother. But Max never said this out loud. Because at that instant, everything became crystal clear to him in a flash of sudden, amazing, and terrible understanding.

"It *is* that cow!" Max rasped, awestruck. "Somehow, in the Plandome barn that crazy night, I must have turned on my tape machine by mistake and recorded Madonna giving birth over my laugh track!"

Maude was bewildered. "But why didn't you listen to it before dubbing it onto the audition tape?"

"I couldn't!" Max lamented. "My dad lost the tape machine before I woke up the next morning. And by the time I got it back, Mario was leaving, and the computer's speakers were broken, and—I can't believe it!"

They watched as Max went through his entire act, with each joke being greeted by wild mooing. He had timed it perfectly on the computer. Every blast of bovine labor came exactly where the audience response should have been. Given a real laugh track, and not a recording of a livestock blessed event, he would have succeeded one hundred percent.

He cradled his head in trembling hands. "This is bad. This is worse than bad. I'd need a million percent improvement to get this up to bad!"

"What are you talking about?" asked Maude, listening intently. "You're a smash!"

As the audition tape played, the news anchor, sports reporter, weatherman, and the entire studio crew could be heard howling in the background.

"I'm a joke," Max amended miserably. "The audience is supposed to laugh *with* you, not *at* you."

When it was finally over, the anchor was wiping tears from her eyes as she struggled to regain her composure for the rest of the broadcast. "Maxx Comedy, ladies and gentlemen," she managed. "Remember that name. Coming soon to a barnyard near you."

"See?" moaned Max. "I'm a laughingstock."

"At least it's just in Chicago," Maude offered in consolation. "Nobody knows you around here, anyway."

The phone rang.

Max answered it. "Oh, hi, Dad," he said listlessly. "How's the car?"

Dr. Carmody was in a state of excitement. "I got home an hour ago. But never mind that. Listen, Max, what went on at the contest? I just took a call from a guy named Frank Lugnitz who saw you on TV!"

"Really?" Max was confused. "How does Mr. Lugnitz get Chicago TV all the way in Bartonville?"

"He says he saw you on CNN! According to him, your tape is on all the comedy channels too! What happened? Did you win that contest?"

"Not exactly," Max said shakily. "But I guess people kind of like my audition video."

"*Like it?*" Max's father was almost shouting now. "The man wouldn't shut up about how great you are! He owns the Giggle Factory, and he wants to hire you to perform! He says you're the funniest kid in America!"

THINK CRITICALLY

1 Why do Max and Maude ride in the back of a big rig? CAUSE AND EFFECT

2 How does the setting affect the conflict in the story?
PLOT AND SETTING

3 What is surprising about the end of the story? AUTHOR'S CRAFT

4 In your opinion, are stories with surprise endings or stories with predictable endings more enjoyable to read? Explain. PERSONAL RESPONSE

5 **WRITE** How do Max's feelings toward his stepfather change? Use details and information from the story to support your answer.
SHORT RESPONSE

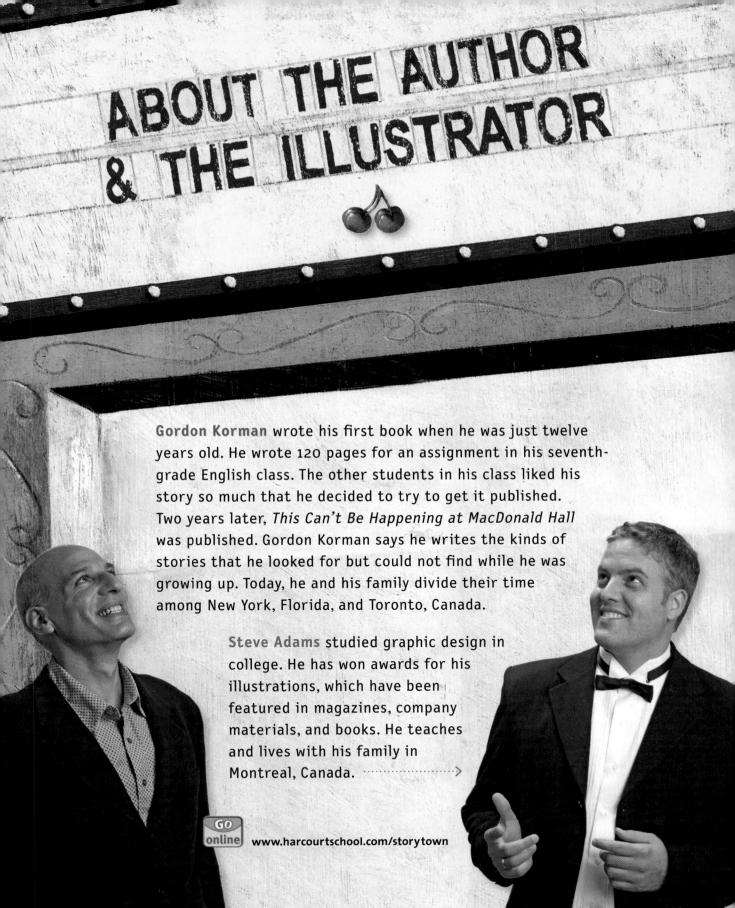

ABOUT THE AUTHOR & THE ILLUSTRATOR

Gordon Korman wrote his first book when he was just twelve years old. He wrote 120 pages for an assignment in his seventh-grade English class. The other students in his class liked his story so much that he decided to try to get it published. Two years later, *This Can't Be Happening at MacDonald Hall* was published. Gordon Korman says he writes the kinds of stories that he looked for but could not find while he was growing up. Today, he and his family divide their time among New York, Florida, and Toronto, Canada.

Steve Adams studied graphic design in college. He has won awards for his illustrations, which have been featured in magazines, company materials, and books. He teaches and lives with his family in Montreal, Canada. ························>

GO online www.harcourtschool.com/storytown

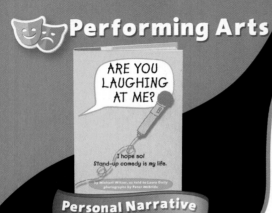

ARE YOU LAUGHING AT ME?

I hope so!
Stand-up comedy is my life.

Personal Narrative

ARE YOU LAUGHING AT ME?

I hope so! Stand-up comedy is my life.

by Michael Witzer, as told to Laura Daily
photographs by Peter McBride

So, I went for my back-to-school checkup last year. How about that tongue depressor? That's a good name for it, because it's pretty depressing having a wooden stick shoved down your throat—especially when it doesn't even have ice cream on it!

To me everything is funny, even a visit to the doctor. That's why three years ago I joined Kids 'N Comedy, a group of young stand-up comedians who go onstage and tell jokes to live audiences. Now I'm 12, and I stand up and perform once a month at the Gotham Comedy Club in New York City.

I make up my own routines. Finding fresh material isn't hard if you pay attention to everyday stuff: riding the school bus, news stories, even cereal.

My secret to cracking crowds up? I try not to borrow jokes. I want my routines to be Michael Witzer originals.

MICHAEL WITZER'S
COMEDY FOR DUMMIES

Don't bother picturing the audience in their underwear. It's better to imagine them laughing hysterically!

The beginning of your joke should always be believable. State the facts and then get silly: "I think the dentist is scary because he wears a mask and gloves. I'm afraid he doesn't want to be recognized or leave his fingerprints behind!"

Involve the audience. Ask a question and wait for an answer. "Do you like going to the doctor? Me neither!" Then get into your best doctor joke.

I was watching a cereal commercial just the other day. They claim it's now "better tasting . . . new and improved." Better? Improved? Is that the best they could say? "We're not quite good yet, but we're getting there." That's why these companies stand behind their products 100 percent: They're all hiding!

Doing stand-up is easy if you're prepared. Knowing your routine, that's what gives you confidence. It's just like studying for a test so you know you'll do well. I usually start practicing two weeks before a show and try to add new material to every show.

Being onstage is weird. The spotlight is blinding, and you can't see the audience. But as long as I've got a microphone in my hand and hear laughter, it feels like home. Speaking of home, mine's in Dix Hills, New York, and I take the bus to school. The bus driver is so strict: no talking, no standing, no jumping . . . out the windows!

Audiences don't always think I'm funny. At my third show, no one laughed at any of the comics. That really freaked me out. But all the kids at the club are really good friends, so when a crowd isn't revved up, we applaud each other.

Outrageous stuff happens all the time. Once I went totally blank and couldn't remember my next line. So I just started walking and talking like a robot, saying "Information overload . . . brain not functioning . . . will self-destruct in 10, 9, 8 . . ." It gave me a chance to collect my thoughts, and it gave the audience something to laugh at. I jumped right back into the routine, and the crowd never knew the difference!

Since I started stand-up, I think I've really matured. I'm more comfortable around people, both on and off stage.

Connections

Comparing Texts

1. How might Max's experiences help you see the bright side of a difficult situation in your own life?

2. How is Michael Witzer in "Are You Laughing at Me?" like Max?

3. Max's family encourages him to follow his dream. What advice would you give to people you know who face setbacks on the path to reaching their dreams?

Vocabulary Review

Rate a Situation

With a partner, read each sentence aloud. Point to the place on the word line that shows how happy you would feel in each situation. Explain your choices.

Least Happy •————————————• **Most Happy**

- You see a bee and become hysterical.
- Your star shortstop is incapacitated.
- A lost item you lamented is recovered.
- People respond to your joke with mirth.
- You left some perishable foods in the car.

ricocheted

hysterical

crestfallen

ecstatic

incapacitated

lamented

mirth

perishable

Partner Reading

When you read with accuracy, you recognize the words in a passage, and you read them without any mistakes. Work with a partner. Choose four paragraphs from "Maxx Comedy: The Funniest Kid in America." Read the passage aloud as your partner follows along. Ask your partner to tell you if you misread any words. Then trade roles, and follow along as your partner reads aloud. Reread the passage until both of you can read it with accuracy.

Writing

Write a Star Story

Imagine you are a star like Maxx Comedy. Write a story about the challenges you have faced on your path to success.

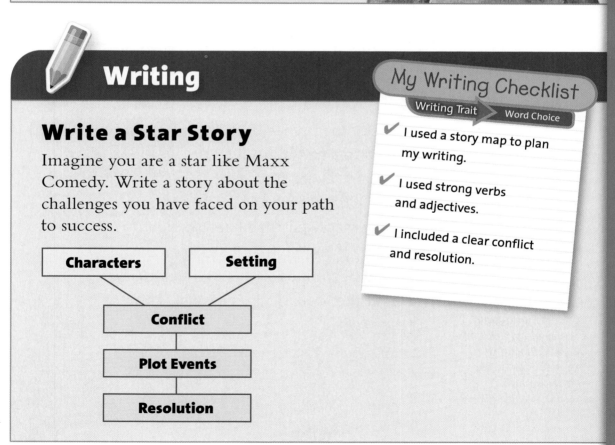

My Writing Checklist

Writing Trait → Word Choice

✓ I used a story map to plan my writing.

✓ I used strong verbs and adjectives.

✓ I included a clear conflict and resolution.

```
Characters        Setting

        Conflict

      Plot Events

      Resolution
```

Reading-Writing Connection

Analyze Writer's Craft: Narrative

A narrative tells a story. It has **characters**, a **setting**, and **events** that move the **plot** forward. Narrative authors use sensory details and concrete language to make characters and events seem real.

When you write narratives, you can use the works of authors such as Gordon Korman as writing models. Read the passage below from "Maxx Comedy," and notice how the author's **word choices** make the characters and events come to life.

Writing Trait

WORD CHOICE
Sensory words, such as *squealed*, help the reader hear, see, and feel the details of the scene.

Writing Trait

WORD CHOICE
Concrete language, such as *blown around by the wind*, helps the reader visualize specific images.

The eighteen-wheeler squealed to a halt in front of the Balsam Auditorium, and out of the back leaped Max Carmody. His normally messy hair had been so blown around by the wind that it stood on end as if he had been filled with static electricity.

He hit the ground running. *"I'm he-e-e-ere!"*

Fictional Narrative

In a **fictional narrative,** the people, places, and events are like the people, places, and events in real life. As you read this fictional narrative written by a student named LaShanti, notice the **word choices** LaShanti made to give the story a rich, colorful flavor.

The Case of the Missing Poodle
by LaShanti C.

WORD CHOICE
One way to write colorfully is to use **strong adjectives** and **vivid descriptions**. LaShanti describes the carrot baby food as *neon orange cream* and *flaming orange debris* at different places in the story.

The use of **vivid verbs** moves the story along. LaShanti uses the verbs *snatched, flung,* and *scattered.*

It was a night like any other at the Fong house. Mimi and Grandpa were munching their chow mein. Hugo, the toy poodle, begged shamelessly at their feet. Mom tried to spoon some neon orange cream into Baby Zan's mouth.

"I thought he'd love these carrots," Mom said. She flew the spoon through the air in looping circles, buzzing loudly like an airplane.

Baby Zan did *not* love carrots. He snatched the flying "airplane" and flung it across the table, knocking over Mimi's bowl. Chow mein and flaming orange debris scattered across the table.

49

Mimi and Grandpa cleaned up while Baby Zan laughed with glee. Grandpa opened the door under the sink. He threw the soggy remains into the trash bin and closed the door.

"I guess it's homework time!" said Mimi. "Come on, Hugo. Let's go to my room."

But Hugo did not come. Mimi called him again.

"Hugo, COME! Hugo, COME!" she shouted. Mom joined the search. Baby Zan added his shrieks to the chorus.

"I'm going to look outside!" said Mimi. She knew Hugo. If he wanted to get out, he would find a way. Mimi ran to the front door, trying not to panic.

"Wait, Mimi!" said Grandpa. "I have an idea!" He walked over to the sink and opened the door under it.

Hugo was very busy. Half of his furry black body was inside the overturned trash bin.

"HUGO, you sneaky dog! Why didn't you say anything when I called you?" asked Mimi.

As if to answer her question, Hugo backed out of the trash bin. His happy face was covered in a shocking orange mask of slippery mush.

"Well at least *someone* liked my carrots!" said Mom.

Now look at what LaShanti did to prepare to write her fictional narrative.

Brainstorm Ideas

One way to develop an idea for a fictional narrative is to think about your own life. LaShanti wrote down the funny things that had happened to her and her friends.

Story Ideas
• forgot to bring music to band concert
• found missing dog under the sink
• accidentally sent e-mail to all friends
• wore shirt inside out all day

Choose One Idea

LaShanti decided that the time she found her missing dog under the sink would make the best idea for a story. She laid out the basic story elements of setting, characters, and plot in a story map.

Develop the Idea

LaShanti made up some characters and events that hadn't been in the real story. For example, she made up a very active baby brother to propel the events of the story forward. LaShanti used a "tip sheet" to keep her on track as she wrote.

Tip Sheet

• **Colorful Characters!** Make them stand out as individuals.

• **Entertaining Events and Plenty of Plot!** A shrieking baby, flung food, and a big cleanup are parts of the problem. Keep the excitement going all the way to the end.

• **Wonderful Word Choices!** Use vivid verbs, awesome adjectives, and delightful descriptions. Keep the details fresh and funny!

CONTENTS

Lesson 2

LYNN JOSEPH

The
COLOR
of My
WORDS

"An achingly beautiful story." —*Kirkus Reviews* (starred review)

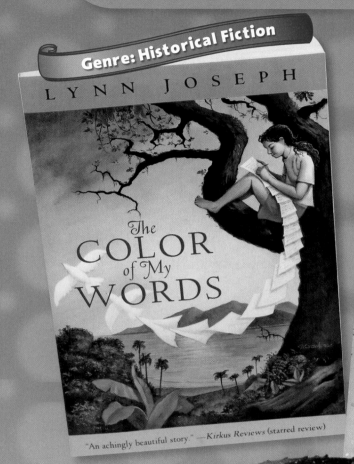

Words Free as
Confetti
by
Pat Mora

Focus Skill

Plot and Setting

You have learned that **plot** is the series of events that make up a story and **setting** is where and when the events happen. The setting may affect the main conflict in the story.

Often, the conflict in a plot builds up to a point called a climax. The **climax** is the most exciting moment in the plot. The action leading up to the climax is called **rising action**. The events that occur after the climax and lead to the resolution are called **falling action**.

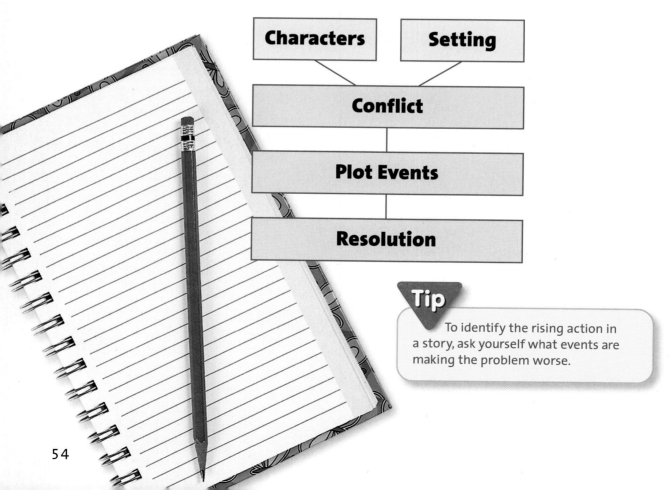

Characters		Setting
	Conflict	
	Plot Events	
	Resolution	

Tip

To identify the rising action in a story, ask yourself what events are making the problem worse.

Read the story. Then look at the story map below. The setting, Pao's bedroom at night, directly affects the conflict. Pao falls asleep while trying to think of ideas for a story.

Pao lay on his bed. He had no ideas for the short story due the next day at school. Pao leaned back and closed his eyes to think. Sometime later, Pao awoke with a start. The bedside clock read 2 A.M. Pao quickly opened his notebook, and his words flowed effortlessly across the page. His slip-up that day became the perfect plot for a story.

Characters	**Setting**
Pao	Pao's bedroom at night

Conflict

Pao doesn't have ideas for a short story.

Plot Events

• Pao falls asleep thinking about his story.
• He awakes suddenly at 2 A.M.
• Pao begins to write.

Resolution

Pao uses his experience as the plot for a story.

Try This!

Look back at the story. What is the climax? How does the setting affect the resolution?

 www.harcourtschool.com/storytown

Vocabulary

Build Robust Vocabulary

- meandering
- emerged
- survey
- frolicked
- hovered
- tormented
- inquire
- subtle

Whale Watching

Monday, September 13   I spent today **meandering** along the cliff trail, in hopes of spotting a whale. Last year, I saw three humpbacks migrating to their summer home. One **emerged** from the water right below the cliff where I was standing! I didn't see any whales today, though.

Wednesday, September 15   Today, I went to the ocean again. I sat down to **survey** the water. Sea otters **frolicked** in the waves, and some kind of seabird **hovered** over the water, but there were no signs of whales.

Sea otters are social animals. They are often found in groups.

Thursday, September 16 I must have touched some poison oak on my way back from the ocean yesterday. Last night, my itching legs **tormented** me! Mom went to the pharmacy to **inquire** about a cream to use. She bought one that seems to be helping.

Friday, September 17
Today, my rash is a **subtle** pink rather than fire-engine red. When I told Dad that I brushed against poison oak while I was whale watching, he laughed and said, "You got one whale of a rash!" I gave him my best "that's not funny" look. I felt better when Dad promised to take me whale watching in a boat.

Poison oak grows as a bush or vine. The leaves are divided into three leaflets.

GO online www.harcourtschool.com/storytown

Word Champion

Your challenge this week is to use the Vocabulary Words in conversations outside the classroom. Post the words where you will see them often. Use as many of the words as you can. For example, you might describe a subtle change in the air temperature. At the end of each day, write in your vocabulary journal the words you used. Tell how you used them.

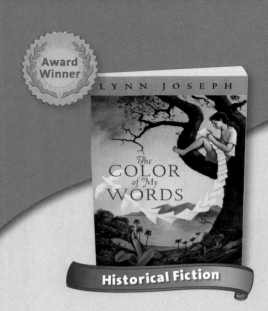

LYNN JOSEPH

The COLOR *of My* WORDS

Historical Fiction

Genre Study

Historical fiction is about people, places, and events from the past. As you read, look for

- a setting that is a real time and place in the past.

- events that are made up but could have really happened.

Characters	Setting
Conflict	
Plot Events	
Resolution	

Comprehension Strategy

Use story structure to identify and understand the story's conflict and resolution.

THE COLOR OF MY WORDS

BY LYNN JOSEPH
ILLUSTRATED BY JOE CEPEDA

Twelve-year-old Ana Rosa lives in the Dominican Republic at a time when free speech is censored by the government. Ana Rosa's only notebook is used for school, so she secretly writes her own stories and poems on any paper she can find—paper bags, napkins, and even her brother Guario's notepad for taking orders at a restaurant. Her mother is the one person in the village who knows about her dream of becoming a writer, until one day everything changes.

THE GRI GRI TREE

I like to sit high
in my gri gri tree
where I can survey
all below me.

On top of the gri gri
I'm a strong, dark queen
sitting on a throne
of towering green.

I hold the leaves close
as the wind blows past.
I kiss the rain drops
as the thunder blasts.

I'm the gri gri queen
and I'm in command
protecting my tree
from careless hands.

Alone with a treasure
no one else sees.
Hidden from the world
and all who seek me.

No one had to point out that I was different from everyone else in our village. It was clear from the first day I began climbing the gri gri (GREE GREE) tree and staying up there for hours.

"What's wrong with your daughter?" neighbors asked Mami.

"She's not right in her head," they answered themselves, when Mami only shrugged her shoulders.

Papi would say, "Nothing wrong with sitting in a tree. It's the same as sitting on a porch except it's higher."

Roberto would climb up with me sometimes but he got bored quickly and swung down, yelling like a monkey. Angela shook her head at me and said I would never be a real *chica*,[1] because *chicas* do not climb trees when they are twelve years old.

Not even Guario understood, although he tried. He asked me once what I did up there. That was more than anyone else had ventured to inquire.

I told him I looked around.

He asked if I didn't think I was wasting a lot of time, when I could be doing something to prepare for my future such as studying English.

Guario always had his mind on the future. Sometimes I think that he was tormented by all of us who didn't particularly care what tomorrow was going to bring. And really, what was there to know—either it would rain or it would not. But it was definitely going to be hot and Mami was going to cook and Papi was going to sit on the porch and the radio was going to play *merengues*[2] all day. That was for sure.

Besides, I already knew what I wanted to do in my future. I wanted to be a writer, but only Mami knew that. If I told Guario, he would say I was unreasonable. If I told anyone else, they would laugh. But in my gri gri tree, I could be anything I wanted to be—even a writer with words for everything I saw from my leafy green hideout.

[1]*chica*: girl

[2]*merengues*: a style of music and dance that is popular in the Dominican Republic and other Latin American countries

I could see the ocean glittering silver in the sunlight. I could see people trudging along the dusty road from Sosúa, some balancing buckets of water on their heads. I could see boys playing baseball in the schoolyard with a tree branch bat and a rubber band ball. I could see the river, meandering over rocks, hungry for rain. Far off in Puerto Plata, I could see Mount Isabel de Torres, a green giant with misty white curls dancing 'round her head.

I could see the sleepy lagoon and the sad little homes of the lagoon people. I could see the birds that flew past my gri gri, their ruby-and-gold velvet feathers shimmering on their tiny bodies. I could see the rainbows that glowed in the sea-sky after a rain passed. I could count the sunset roses in Señora Garcia's backyard. I could see my teacher climbing the hill near her house, and I could see Papi sitting on our porch, nodding off to sleep.

Then one day I saw something that I had never seen before and I was so scared that I almost fell out of the tree. There I was looking at the sea when suddenly out of it rose a giant monster, tall and black and covering the sun with its shadow. Before I could scream, the monster fell back into the sea.

I scrambled down the tree quickly and ran toward my house, shouting "Papi, there's a monster in the sea!"

Papi woke up from his siesta. "¿Qué pasa?"[3]

"A monster," I repeated. "A giant sea monster and it's coming this way!"

I shouted inside the house. "Mami, come quick. There's a monster in the sea. I saw it."

Mami came outside and Angela followed her. They were drying their hands from washing the lunch dishes.

Everyone looked at me as if I were crazy.

"It's true," I said, jumping up and down.

Mami made me sit down and describe exactly what I saw.

[3]¿Qué pasa?: What's happening?

62

Before I had finished, Angela shouted my news to her best friend walking by. Then Papi waved over some of his domino-playing *amigos*[4] and told them what I saw from on top of my gri gri tree.

Soon our porch was surrounded with people all asking me to tell my story again.

When I had told it for the fourth time, Señor Garcia, the *colmado*[5] owner, began to laugh.

"You must have fallen asleep in the tree and had a bad dream, *cariño*[6]," he said.

"No," I replied, shaking my head. "I saw it."

But his words had relieved everyone's fears of a sea monster. "Yes," they agreed. "You must have imagined it."

I wanted to shout. "I didn't imagine anything." But I kept quiet because Mami and Papi would not like it if I shouted at the neighbors. That was for sure.

As everyone sat down on the porch to share a drink and talk about my sea monster, I slipped away and ran to my gri gri tree. I heard Mami calling me, but I pretended I didn't hear and climbed up the tree fast. I needed to find out if what I had seen would come back again.

[4]*amigos*: friends
[5]*colmado*: grocery store
[6]*cariño*: darling

I sat down on my usual branch and tucked a few leaves away from my eyes. Then I stared at the sea. I looked so hard and for so long that its blueness filled up my eyeballs and I had to blink a lot so I wouldn't go blind.

The afternoon faded into evening and the sea's blueness turned gray. I watched and waited. My stomach made grumbling noises but I covered them with my hand.

Then, just as I began to think that maybe I had imagined it after all, I saw a splash of white water. The splash of water rose up, up until it was high in the air like a magic fountain.

"It's a volcano," I whispered. I remembered that my teacher had told us how many of the Caribbean islands had been formed by volcanoes that rose out of the sea.

I gasped. Maybe I was seeing the beginning of a brand-new island right next to the República Dominicana. As I kept on looking, a black shape emerged out of the fountain of water. It rose and turned, as if doing a dance, and that's when I saw the gleaming white throat of the sea monster.

It hovered in between heaven and ocean for a few seconds and then fell back into the water with a splash that sprayed salt drops as high as the pearl-pink clouds.

My heart beat furiously and I steadied myself so I wouldn't fall down from the tree. I was right. I had not imagined anything. There really was a sea monster out there. But this time I didn't rush down to tell anyone.

What would the people do, I wondered. Would they try to find it? Or maybe to kill it? Somehow, although I didn't know why, I could tell that the sea monster was not dangerous. It just wanted to swim and splash and jump out of the sea the same way I jumped over the waves.

I climbed down the tree and went home. The first thing I wanted to do was eat, but people were all over the porch talking wildly. "We saw it, Ana Rosa," they shouted. "We saw that big sea monster of yours."

Papi was busy handing out glasses, cups, and small jars. Mami was passing around a plate of *dulces*,[7] the sweet milk candy that I love. She must have just made them because they were still warm and soft.

Children were carrying huge plates filled with different foods that their mothers had made. Angela was directing them to put the food here or there on our big table. I saw plates piled high with *arroz con pollo*,[8] *plátanos fritos*,[9] and *batatas fritas*.[10]

[7]*dulces*: candies
[8]*arroz con pollo*: chicken and rice
[9]*plátanos fritos*: fried plantains
[10]*batatas fritas*: fried sweet potatoes

Señor Garcia apologized over and over to me. About a hundred people were gathered on our porch, in the yard, and along the roadside, talking about the sea monster.

"The tourist high-season is coming," said Señor Rojas, who owned a Jeep that he rented to tourists. "We can't let anyone know we have a sea monster hanging around Sosúa Bay."

"But why not?" asked Señora Perez, who sold paintings on the beach. "It could be a tourist attraction. Plenty people may decide to come here just to see it."

Half the folks whispered, "He's right." And the other half said, "She's the one who's right."

It looked as if we were going to have a big debate on our porch just like the ones that take place when it is a presidential election year. The way everyone was carrying on, soon we would have people writing *merengues* about the sea monster and there would be sea monster fiestas all over the place just like during elections.

I shook my head and just listened to everyone as I ate a plate heaped high with food. That poor sea monster, I thought.

Then the people began to make a Plan. When Dominicans get together and decide to make a plan, watch out, because there are plans, and then there are Plans, and this was definitely a PLAN!

The first thing the people decided was that someone had to keep watch over this sea monster. Well, everyone looked around to see who would volunteer. That's when we knew the PLAN would not work because no one wanted to do something so stupid as to go down to the sea and watch for the sea monster.

It was Angela who got the bright idea that since I saw it first, I could keep watch over it from my gri gri tree. Everyone turned to me and nodded their heads.

"Finally, a good reason for her to be up there all the time," I heard Señora Garcia whisper.

Papi was looking at me and nodding his head, proud that his daughter was selected for such an important job. I said, Okay, I would do it.

Then the PLAN continued. Half the people wanted to make signs and announce that Sosúa Bay had a new visitor and it was a one-of-a-kind sea monster. The other half of the crowd shook their heads and said, No, it was too obvious.

"We must be subtle about a delicate matter like this," said Señora Perez. "We must make up a wonderful story about this sea monster, give it a name, make it a friendly monster, and then tell the world. Otherwise all we will do is scare everyone away from this side of the island."

She had a point. A story about the sea monster was much better than a big billboard with an arrow pointing "This way to Sea Monster of Sosúa Bay!"

The idea of it all made me giggle. Wait until Guario came home and heard all this. I could hardly wait for him to return from the restaurant.

"Well," said Señor Rojas, "what will we name the sea monster?"

"And who knows how to write a story about it, anyway?" asked Señor Garcia.

Señora Perez shrugged her shoulders. "I don't know how to write too good, but we could make up something."

Then Mami, who was usually quiet during these kinds of discussions, spoke up loud and clear. "Ana Rosa would be the best person to write a story about the sea monster."

I was shocked. This wasn't the same Mami who worshiped silence.

People began to shake their heads. "A child to do something so important?" they whispered.

"Yes," said Mami. "Let us give her a notebook to write in and she will write us a story about the sea monster. If we don't like it, someone else can try."

The way Mami said it, so definite and firm, made people nod their heads in agreement. "Well, it doesn't hurt to let her try," they said.

So Señor Garcia went and brought back a notebook from his *colmado*. Mami gave it to me and her hands were cold like the river.

While the grown-ups stayed up late on the porch talking and drinking and eating, I went inside and began to write a story about the sea monster. First I tried to give him a name. But I couldn't think of a good one. So instead I thought about what he looked like. Then I imagined what he must feel like living all alone in the sea, different from all of the other sea creatures.

The fish and animals in the ocean were probably afraid of his huge size and his big nose and long, swishing tail. And they probably didn't want to play with him. Maybe they whispered about how strange he looked. But the sea monster wanted a friend. Deep down, I understood exactly how the sea monster must feel.

I began to write. I wrote page after page in the notebook the people had given to me. When I was finished, it was almost midnight. I went to the porch. Everyone was still there laughing and talking and some were dancing to the music on the radio.

Children were asleep on their mothers' and fathers' laps. Some of the bigger children were sprawled out on a blanket on the floor and the *merengue* music was a background lullaby for them.

When the people saw me, they got quiet. Someone turned off the radio. Some woke the children on their laps. Papi moved from his chair and put his arm around my shoulders. He led me to the front of the porch.

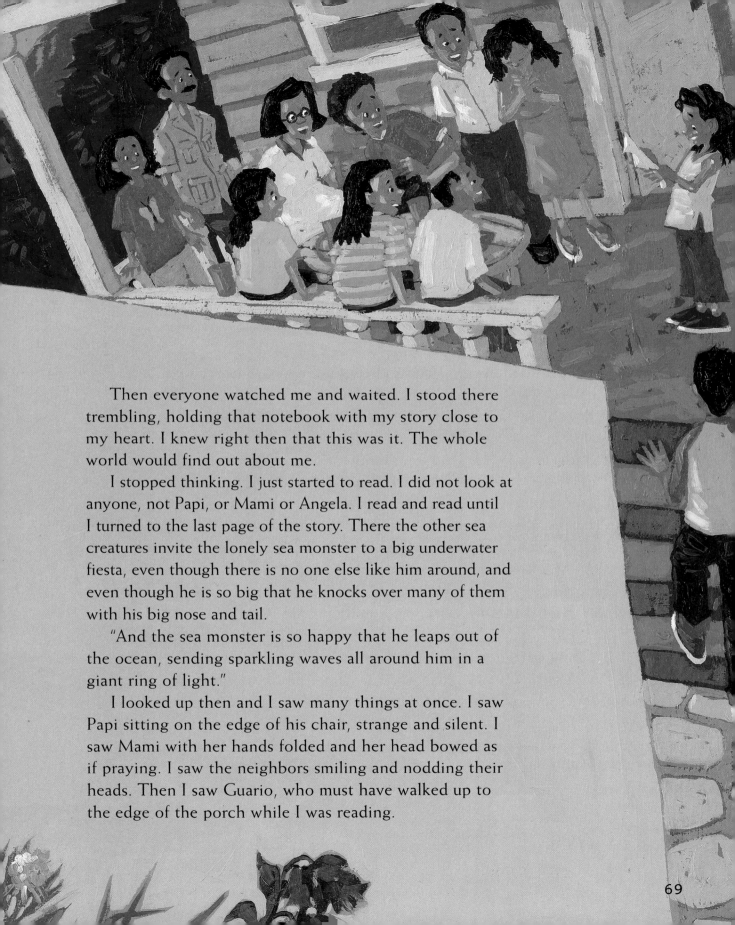

Then everyone watched me and waited. I stood there trembling, holding that notebook with my story close to my heart. I knew right then that this was it. The whole world would find out about me.

I stopped thinking. I just started to read. I did not look at anyone, not Papi, or Mami or Angela. I read and read until I turned to the last page of the story. There the other sea creatures invite the lonely sea monster to a big underwater fiesta, even though there is no one else like him around, and even though he is so big that he knocks over many of them with his big nose and tail.

"And the sea monster is so happy that he leaps out of the ocean, sending sparkling waves all around him in a giant ring of light."

I looked up then and I saw many things at once. I saw Papi sitting on the edge of his chair, strange and silent. I saw Mami with her hands folded and her head bowed as if praying. I saw the neighbors smiling and nodding their heads. Then I saw Guario, who must have walked up to the edge of the porch while I was reading.

It was Guario's face I focused on. He was smiling. My big strong brother who worried about our future, my serious Guario who almost never smiled, suddenly let out a loud whoop and grabbed me up. He spun me around and around.

"Little sister, I am buying you a new notebook every month no matter what!" he shouted.

I closed my eyes so I wouldn't start crying there in front of all the neighbors. Guario always kept his promises. I would be able to write down everything now, everything I thought or dreamed or felt or saw or wondered about. I was so happy I thought I would leap as high as the sea monster.

Then, in the background, I heard clapping. The people had stood up from their chairs and were clapping for me.

I heard shouts of how great my story was and people congratulating Papi and kissing Mami's cheeks telling them how lucky it was that I was so smart. I heard Mami saying it had nothing to do with luck. I grinned and went over to her. She put her arm around me and squeezed my shoulders.

"You're going to write many stories, remember, *cara*[11]?" she whispered in my ear. It was the happiest night in my life.

We all forgot about the sea monster until the next day.

Over the radio, a news broadcast announced that one of the humpback whales making its way to Samaná Bay for the annual winter mating season had gotten sidetracked in Sosúa.

"But Samaná Bay is only a two-hour drive from here," said Papi.

"Well, the poor whale doesn't know how to drive," Mami teased.

For two weeks our humpback whale jumped and frolicked about in Sosúa Bay until finally heading east to Samaná to join the other three thousand humpbacks that go there every winter.

But while he was in Sosúa, I watched him every day from my gri gri tree. The beautiful black-and-white sea monster had helped me to make my dream come true. I loved the whale. And I named him Guario.

[11]*cara*: dear

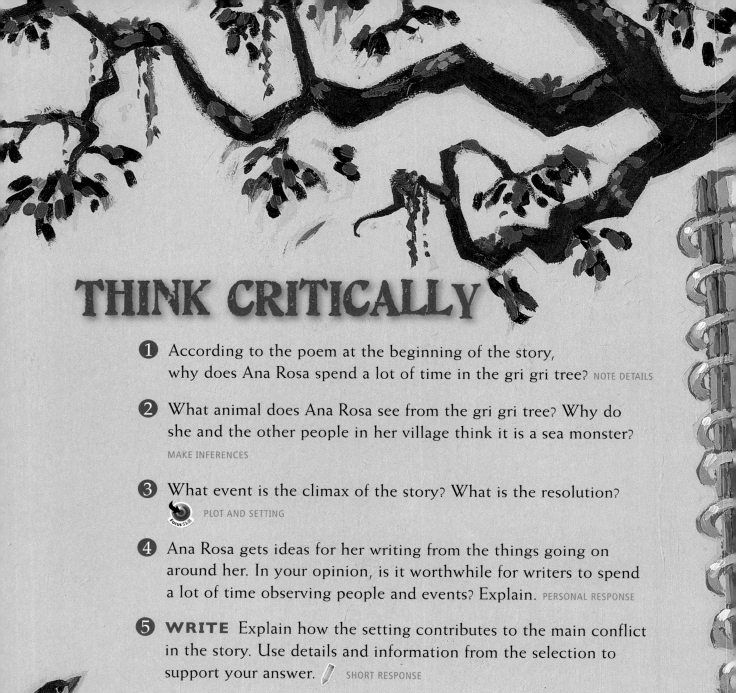

THINK CRITICALLY

1 According to the poem at the beginning of the story, why does Ana Rosa spend a lot of time in the gri gri tree? NOTE DETAILS

2 What animal does Ana Rosa see from the gri gri tree? Why do she and the other people in her village think it is a sea monster? MAKE INFERENCES

3 What event is the climax of the story? What is the resolution? PLOT AND SETTING

4 Ana Rosa gets ideas for her writing from the things going on around her. In your opinion, is it worthwhile for writers to spend a lot of time observing people and events? Explain. PERSONAL RESPONSE

5 **WRITE** Explain how the setting contributes to the main conflict in the story. Use details and information from the selection to support your answer. SHORT RESPONSE

72

ABOUT THE AUTHOR AND THE ILLUSTRATOR

Lynn Joseph

Lynn Joseph grew up in Trinidad, an island located in the Caribbean Sea. She has written several books that are set in Trinidad. She has won the Américas Book Award for Children's and Young Adult Literature. This award is given to writers whose works portray Latin America, the Caribbean, or Latinos in the United States. Lynn Joseph has two children, and she divides her time between New York City and the Dominican Republic.

Joe Cepeda

Joe Cepeda grew up in East Los Angeles, and he still calls southern California home. When he draws, he likes to use bright, strong colors. When he draws people, he likes to make them look like people he knows. He also enjoys making things out of wood. Joe Cepeda says that his son is his inspiration.

 www.harcourtschool.com/storytown

Poetry

Words

Come, words, come in your every color.
I'll toss you in storm or breeze.
I'll say, say, say you,
taste you sweet as plump plums,
bitter as old lemons.
I'll sniff you, words, warm
as almonds or tart as apple-red,
feel you green
and soft as new grass,
lightwhite as dandelion plumes,
or thorngray as cactus,
heavy as black cement,
cold as blue icicles,
warm as *abuelita's* yellowlap.
I'll hear you, words, loud as searoar's
purple crash, hushed
as *gatitos* curled in sleep,
as the last goldlullaby.

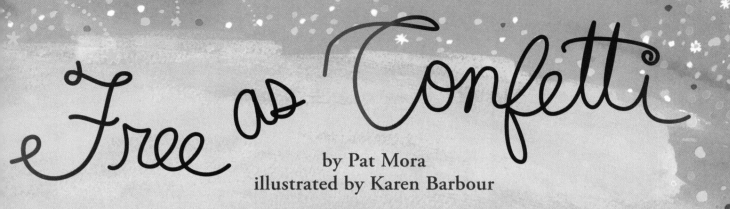

Free as Confetti

by Pat Mora
illustrated by Karen Barbour

I'll see you long and dark as tunnels,
bright as rainbows,
playful as chestnutwind.
I'll watch you, words, rise and dance and spin.
I'll say, say, say you
in English,
in Spanish,
I'll find you.
Hold you.
Toss you.
I'm free too.
I say *yo soy libre*,
I am free
free, free,
free as confetti.

abuelita
(ah-bweh-LEE-tah):
grandmother

gatitos
(gah-TEE-tohs):
kittens

yo soy libre
(YOH SOY LEE-breh):
I am free

75

Connections

Comparing Texts

1. Ana Rosa sits in her special tree to observe the world. What is your favorite place to observe the world? Explain.

2. Why are words important to Ana Rosa and to the speaker in the poem "Words Free as Confetti"?

3. Do you think that free speech is an important freedom? Explain.

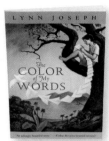

Vocabulary Review

While some birds frolicked in the water, others hovered overhead.

Word Pairs

With a partner, write the Vocabulary Words on separate index cards. Place all the cards face up on a table or desk. Take turns choosing two words to use in one sentence. Write the sentence, and then read it aloud to your partner. Every time you use a word correctly, you get one point. Return the word cards to the table and, in the next round, choose two different words to use in one sentence. The person who uses the most words correctly wins.

meandering

emerged

survey

frolicked

hovered

tormented

inquire

subtle

Fluency Practice

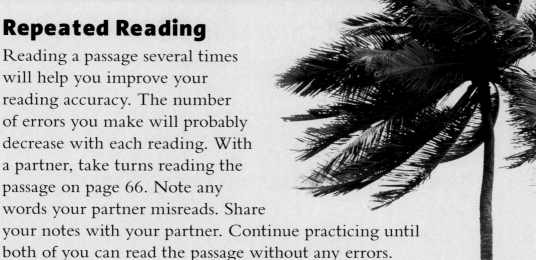

Repeated Reading

Reading a passage several times will help you improve your reading accuracy. The number of errors you make will probably decrease with each reading. With a partner, take turns reading the passage on page 66. Note any words your partner misreads. Share your notes with your partner. Continue practicing until both of you can read the passage without any errors.

Writing

Write a Narrative

Imagine that you are in a natural setting and you encounter a mysterious creature. Write a narrative that tells what you see and what happens.

```
┌──────────────┐      ┌──────────────┐
│  Characters  │      │   Setting    │
└──────────────┘      └──────────────┘
         └──────────┬──────────┘
            ┌──────────────┐
            │   Conflict   │
            └──────────────┘
            ┌──────────────┐
            │  Plot Events │
            └──────────────┘
            ┌──────────────┐
            │  Resolution  │
            └──────────────┘
```

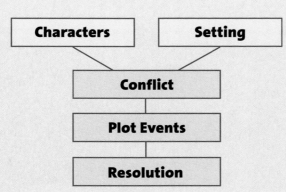

My Writing Checklist

Writing Trait → Word Choice

✔ I used a story map to plan my writing.

✔ I included an interesting conflict and a satisfying resolution.

✔ I used sensory words to help readers see, feel, and hear what happened.

CONTENTS

Lesson 3

Genre: Biography

The Wright Brothers
A Flying Start

KIDS CAN PRESS

Elizabeth MacLeod

From Inspiration to Invention
by Cate Baily

Genre: Magazine Article

Focus Skill

Text Structure: Chronological Order

Authors of nonfiction text organize their ideas in certain ways called text structures. One kind of text structure is **chronological order**. In texts with this structure:

- Events are told in the order in which they happened.
- The author uses clue words such as *first, next, then,* and *finally* to make the sequence of events clear.
- The author may include dates or other information about time to help readers understand the relationship between events in the text.

First
↓
Next
↓
Then
↓
Finally

Tip

Thinking about genre may help you identify a text's structure. For example, biographies and texts about historical events are usually organized in chronological order.

Read the paragraph below. Then look at the graphic organizer. It shows two important events in Chester Greenwood's life in chronological order.

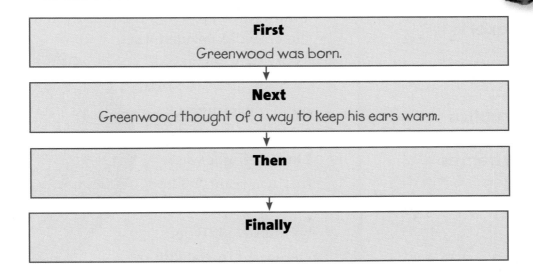

Chester Greenwood was born in Farmington, Maine, in 1858. At the age of fifteen, Greenwood thought of an unusual way to keep his ears warm in the frigid Maine winter. He asked his grandmother to sew two fur patches over a loop of wire. The resulting invention, earmuffs, made Greenwood wealthy. He patented the invention in 1877. This was the first of more than one hundred patents that Greenwood would acquire in his life.

First
Greenwood was born.

↓

Next
Greenwood thought of a way to keep his ears warm.

↓

Then

↓

Finally

Try This!

Reread the paragraph. What other events could you add to the graphic organizer? How do dates and other details help you understand the sequence in which the events happened?

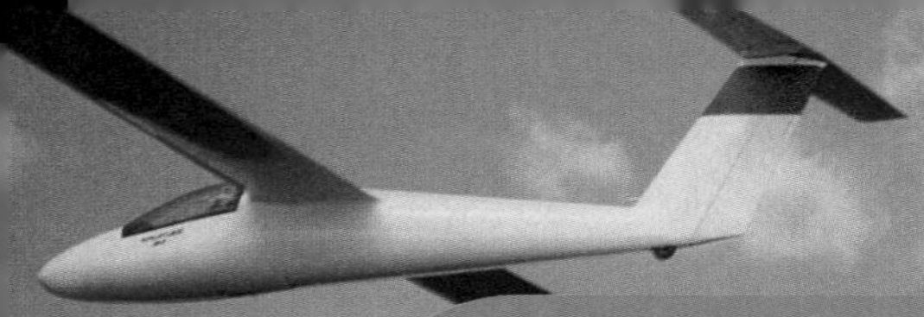

Vocabulary

Build Robust Vocabulary

- astounding
- disbanded
- stabilize
- exerts
- rigged
- replica
- schemes

Airships

In 1783, a crowd gathered near Paris, France, to witness an **astounding** event. Brothers Joseph-Michel and Jacques-Étienne Montgolfier launched the first hot-air balloon to carry passengers. The lucky riders were a duck, a sheep, and a rooster. Even after the crowd **disbanded**, the excitement remained.

Soon after, the first human passengers took to the air. Human flight was finally a reality! The balloons began to be improved. Ropes were used to **stabilize** the baskets. Hydrogen replaced hot air.

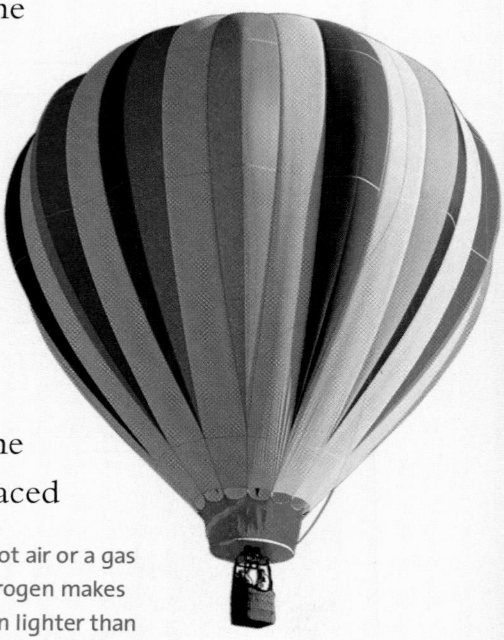

When hot air or a gas like hydrogen makes a balloon lighter than the outside air, that air **exerts** an upward force that lifts the balloon.

Today's blimps are filled with helium.

In 1901, a Brazilian named Alberto Santos-Dumont **rigged** the newly invented gasoline-powered engine to a balloon. He built one **replica** after another, until he had fourteen gas-powered airships. In his **schemes** to promote the Age of Flight, he flew over the streets of Paris, sometimes landing in front of his favorite café for lunch.

As the years went by, experts continued to improve airships. They became safer and easier to control. Today, we call them blimps.

GO online   www.harcourtschool.com/storytown

Word Scribe

This week, your task is to use the Vocabulary Words in your writing. In your vocabulary journal, write sentences to show the meaning of the words. For example, you could write about something astounding that you saw or heard about. Write sentences using as many of the Vocabulary Words as you can. Share your writing with your classmates.

83

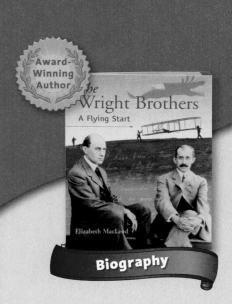

Genre Study

A biography tells about a person's life and is written by another person. As you read, look for

- information telling why the person is important.
- events told in chronological order.

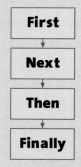

> **First**
> ↓
> **Next**
> ↓
> **Then**
> ↓
> **Finally**

Comprehension Strategy

Use graphic organizers like the one shown above to keep track of the sequence of events.

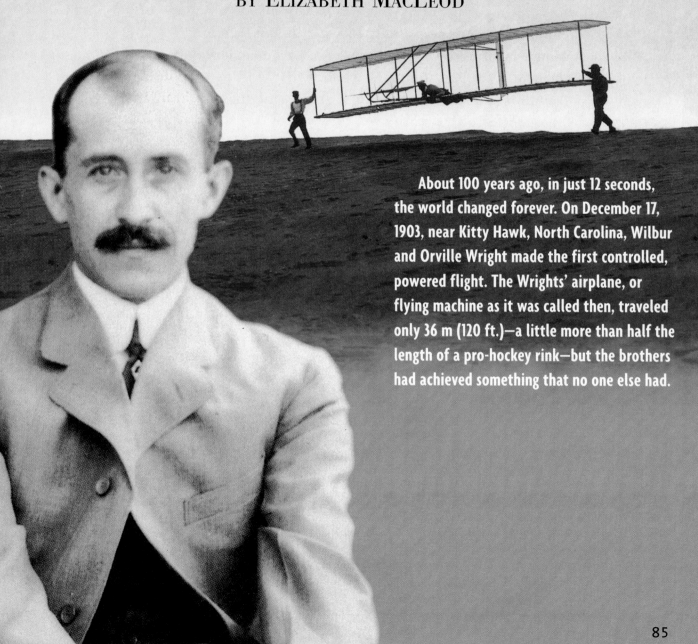

THE WRIGHT BROTHERS
A FLYING START

by Elizabeth MacLeod

About 100 years ago, in just 12 seconds, the world changed forever. On December 17, 1903, near Kitty Hawk, North Carolina, Wilbur and Orville Wright made the first controlled, powered flight. The Wrights' airplane, or flying machine as it was called then, traveled only 36 m (120 ft.)—a little more than half the length of a pro-hockey rink—but the brothers had achieved something that no one else had.

EARLY YEARS

As kids, Wilbur and Orville loved fixing machines and experimenting. To earn extra money, they sold kites to the neighborhood children in Dayton, Ohio. Orville tried other money-making schemes, such as collecting bones for a fertilizer plant, gathering old wood and metal for a junkyard, and even putting on a circus.

The brothers were also interested in printing. When Wilbur was in his teens, he invented a machine to fold papers for mailing. Orville was about 14 when he and a friend set up a small printing firm. To get more experience, Orville worked for a printer for two summers. Then, with Wilbur's help, he built another printing press, using a gravestone for part of it, and opened his own print shop.

Sometimes the brothers' experiments and hobbies got in the way of school. They skipped classes, and once Orville was even expelled.

At 18, Wilbur planned to go to Yale University and become a minister. But one day, while playing hockey, a teammate accidentally hit him and knocked out his front teeth. Surgery and false teeth restored Wilbur's face, but he lost his confidence. During his long recovery, Wilbur gave up the idea of university. Besides, Orville wanted to start a newspaper and would need Wilbur's help.

Wilbur was four years older than Orville. Here's Wilbur at 12 (left) and Orville at 8 (right).

Newspapers and Bicycles ◄ ·······················

Orville's dream of publishing a newspaper came true on March 1, 1889, with Wilbur's help. Wilbur edited the *West Side News*, a weekly paper, while Orville printed and sold it. With the two brothers working together, the paper did so well that after a year they decided to give it a new name and publish it every day. But the new *Evening Item* couldn't compete with other daily papers, and the last issue appeared just four months later.

The print shop was doing well, but the brothers wanted a new challenge. What to do next? Cycling was a growing sport, and Orville often competed in local races. (Wilbur preferred long rides in the country.) Friends were always asking the Wrights to repair their bicycles. So when they were in their early twenties, the brothers opened a bicycle shop called the Wright Cycle Company. They weren't alone. More and more stores opened, and competition got tougher and tougher.

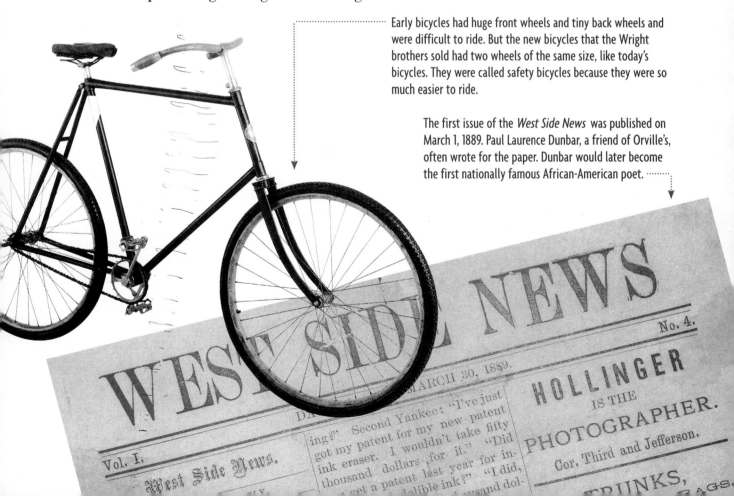

Early bicycles had huge front wheels and tiny back wheels and were difficult to ride. But the new bicycles that the Wright brothers sold had two wheels of the same size, like today's bicycles. They were called safety bicycles because they were so much easier to ride.

The first issue of the *West Side News* was published on March 1, 1889. Paul Laurence Dunbar, a friend of Orville's, often wrote for the paper. Dunbar would later become the first nationally famous African-American poet. ········

WEST SIDE NEWS

No. 4.

MARCH 30, 1889.

ing?" Second Yankee: "I've just got my patent for my new patent ink eraser. I wouldn't take fifty thousand dollars for it." "Did get a patent last year for in-delible ink?" "I did,

HOLLINGER
IS THE
PHOTOGRAPHER.
Cor. Third and Jefferson.

TRUNKS,

Vol. I.

West Side News,

Business was slow. Wilbur thought again about going to college—he'd read and studied a lot while recovering from his accident, and his amazing memory retained most of what he read. But Orville convinced him to stay to help expand the bicycle business. Instead of just selling and repairing bicycles, they would also build them. That was just the kind of challenge Wilbur and Orville loved.

Then in August 1896, Orville suddenly became ill with typhoid fever, a severe illness caused by bacteria. For weeks he lay unconscious, close to death. Wilbur stayed with him, nursing him and reading to him. Finally, in October, Orville's fever broke and he began to get better.

Wilbur read a lot during those long hours by Orville's bed, including an article about an inventor and his flying machines. Life would never be the same for the Wright brothers.

········► UP IN THE AIR

The inventor of flying machines whom Wilbur had read about was Otto Lilienthal. He was a German engineer, famous for his experiments with gliders. But Lilienthal wasn't the first to try to invent a flying machine.

Back in 1500, inventor and artist Leonardo da Vinci sketched airplane-like machines, although he never built them. Then, in 1783, Joseph and Étienne (ay•TYEHN) Montgolfier launched the first hot-air balloon in France. No one knew if it was safe to breathe so far above Earth. To find out, the brothers tied a basket to the balloon and placed a duck, a rooster, and a sheep in it. All three animals survived—although the sheep stepped on the rooster. A few weeks later, two men went up in the balloon. But balloonists could only drift with the wind. What inventors wanted was a machine whose flight could be *controlled*.

Otto Lilienthal based his work on what he'd learned from watching birds. He was the first to pilot a glider successfully and went on to build 16 different types. ·······

All serious inventors knew the work of Daniel Bernoulli, a Swiss scientist. In 1738 he realized that the faster a fluid, such as air, moves, the less pressure it exerts. This is called "Bernoulli's principle," the basis for all flight. For example, a bird's wing is more curved on the top than on the bottom. The air going *over* the wing has to go a little farther than the air going *under* the wing because of that curve. But it has to do it in the same amount of time, so it has to go *faster*, too.

Bernoulli discovered that the faster the air moves, the less pressure it exerts. So the air under the wing pushes up harder than the air on top pushes down. This extra pressure pushes—or lifts—the bird into the air.

Some of the flying machines sketched by inventors look so odd that it's hard to believe anyone really thought they could ever fly.

According to Bernoulli's principle, the air going *over* the curved wing of a bird or airplane goes farther—and faster—than the air going *under* the wing. The faster-moving air exerts less pressure. So the air under the wing pushes up harder than the air on top pushes down, lifting the bird or airplane into the air.

British experimenter Sir George Cayley designed several gliders, using Bernoulli's principle. In 1849 he launched a glider that carried a 10-year-old boy a short distance. Five years later Cayley sent up his carriage driver in a glider—the driver quit when he landed. But Cayley kept working to build a steerable glider. Cayley's work inspired Otto Lilienthal. By 1896 Lilienthal had made about 2,000 glider flights. His next step was to add power. That's what Lilienthal was doing when his glider crashed and he was killed. His death might have scared off most people, but it didn't frighten the Wright brothers. They were ready to tackle the challenge of flight.

THE WRIGHT WAY

Like many other inventors at the time, the Wright brothers wanted to invent a machine capable of powered, controlled flight. They soon realized that such a machine would need three things:

1. Wings strong enough to lift a person into the air.

2. An engine that could move the machine forward fast enough so that air flowing over the wings kept the machine airborne.

3. A way to control its path and direction.

Wilbur and Orville worried most about controlling the flying machine—it was lack of control that had killed Lilienthal. One day, while watching pigeons fly by, Wilbur noticed that one of the birds changed the position of its wing tips to turn. If the brothers could figure out how to change, or "warp," the shape of a machine's wings during flight, they could control its direction.

A little later in the bicycle shop, after fixing a puncture in an inner tube, Wilbur fiddled with the long, narrow cardboard box the inner tube had come in. He twisted the two ends of the box in different directions. When he twisted one way, the top left end of the box and the bottom right were up. When he twisted the other way, the top right and bottom left ends came up. Just like the right and left wings of a bird, he thought. Maybe this was the way to change a flying machine's wings and control flight.

Wilbur and Orville decided to try it. By the summer of 1899, they had built their first model—a double-decker kite—and were ready to test it.

There are three basic movements an airplane can make:

It can **roll**, or dip its wings from side to side.

It can **pitch**, which means its nose goes up and down.

Or it can **yaw**—turn from side to side.

90

GO FLY A KITE! ◄ ·······································

The double-decker kite that Wilbur and Orville built was equipped with cords attached to its wing tips so the brothers could experiment with wing warping.

In the spring of 1900, the Wright brothers began building a glider strong enough to carry a person. With such a heavy load, they knew they'd need high winds to launch it. So they wrote to the National Weather Bureau to find the windiest places in the United States. The brothers also contacted flying-machine inventor Octave Chanute, who recommended sand hills for soft landings. Kitty Hawk, North Carolina, fit the bill—it was windy, with lots of sand dunes nearby.

Finally the weather conditions were just right. On October 3, 1900, with the help of a local man, Bill Tate, the Wrights carried the glider to the highest sand dunes on the island. The area had a threatening name—Kill Devil Hills—but it was the perfect launching point.

Wilbur couldn't resist trying out the glider. With Orville and Tate each holding a wing, and Wilbur in the middle, they ran with the machine into the wind until it began to lift. Then Wilbur scrambled in. But just as the glider lifted him off the ground, he yelled, "Let me down!" Orville yanked the glider down and angrily demanded an explanation. "I promised Pop I'd take care of myself," said his brother.

The brothers flew the glider a few more times before heading home to Dayton on October 23. When they analyzed the glider's flight, they were puzzled. According to Lilienthal's data, it shouldn't have flown the way it did. Wilbur and Orville decided they were incorrect and obviously needed more experience. They would later find out that they were right, and Lilienthal was wrong.

The 1900 glider was made of wooden ribs with a shiny cotton covering. When the brothers were finished with it, Bill Tate took the wing fabric home, and his wife made dresses for their daughters.

THE WRIGHTS GO WRONG

By the summer of 1901, Wilbur and Orville were ready to return to Kill Devil Hills. They'd built a bigger glider, and Octave Chanute had sent two people he'd worked with to help. But everything went wrong: rain poured down, the brothers were sick, mosquitoes buzzed constantly, and one of Chanute's men was useless.

On top of all this, the Wrights' new glider didn't fly very well. Once, with Wilbur aboard, it rose into the air, then almost stopped moving—the same situation that had killed Lilienthal. Luckily, Wilbur was able to land safely. The brothers realized they still had a lot to learn.

A depressed Wilbur and Orville headed home in mid-August. Back in Dayton, the brothers were filled with doubts. Why should they achieve their goal of powered, controlled flight when so many others, better educated and skilled, had failed? Orville decided to recheck the data they'd collected from other inventors' work. He attached small wings of different shapes to a bicycle wheel tipped on its side and turned it to see how the wings reacted.

Orville (back to the camera) and Wilbur tried flying their glider as a kite. The "wing" above Orville's head was attached to the front of the glider to balance it as it climbed and descended.

You can see how big the 1901 glider is compared to Orville. It was the largest glider ever flown up to this point.

Orville soon realized that the data he and Wilbur—and other inventors—had used were wrong, but he didn't know by how much. To find out, he rigged up a wind tunnel in a 46-cm (18-in.) long wooden box. The wind tunnel allowed the Wrights to test how air moves over a wing. It worked well, and Orville spent hours experimenting.

The brothers built a bigger wind tunnel and tested more than 200 wing shapes. Their conclusions were astounding: all the previous data were wrong and the Wrights were right. The brothers finally had the information they needed about wing shape and lift to design a flying machine.

This is a replica of the wind tunnel used by Orville and Wilbur. Their experiments were tedious and slow, but the brothers were making new discoveries.

ADD SOME POWER

By September 1902, the brothers were back at Kill Devil Hills with an even bigger glider. For the first time, they added an immovable, vertical tail. But this one was hard to control, too. One night while lying in bed, Orville figured out that its immovable tail might be the problem. If the tail could move, maybe the pilot could change the glider's position and stabilize it.

Orville knew he'd have to be careful how he suggested this change to Wilbur. As the older brother, Wilbur often seemed to automatically reject Orville's ideas. But Wilbur agreed this time and suggested connecting a tail control to the wing-warping system.

The new movable rudder was a success. It allowed the rudder to turn and to reduce the drag (air resistance) on the glider during wing warping. This was an important breakthrough, and the control system in today's airplanes is based on it.

The brothers went up in their improved glider more than 700 times. The glider could stay airborne for up to 26 seconds and had good lift and control. Finally the Wright brothers felt it was time to add power.

The 1902 glider had a vertical rudder on the back to prevent spins and stalls.

Soon after Wilbur and Orville returned to Dayton in November 1902, they began work in their bicycle shop on a new flying machine. It was so big that when a customer entered the shop, one of the brothers had to scoot out the side door and around to the front to wait on him.

The brothers wrote to motor manufacturers, asking them to build a strong, light engine. Some manufacturers were willing, but no one could do it for the money Wilbur and Orville had. So, as with many other things, the brothers designed an engine themselves.

The Wrights also researched propellers. They investigated ship propellers, but found they were built by trial and error and weren't based on scientific calculations. Once again the brothers had to do their own research. In a few months they had built the two 2.4 m (8 ft.) propellers they needed.

Wilbur and Orville knew that many other inventors were trying to build flying machines. Would someone steal their ideas? They tried to patent the design of their flying machine, but the U.S. Patent Office, tired of seeing "crazy" flying-machine designs, told the Wrights their ideas would never work.

On October 10, 1902, Orville flew the glider with the rudder and wing-warping system. Wilbur (left) and an assistant helped launch it.

Wilbur and Orville designed this engine, and Charlie Taylor, a mechanic in their shop, built it.

THEY'VE DONE IT!

The Wrights left Dayton on September 23, 1903, determined to make at least one powered flight in their new machine. First they practiced in last year's glider. Then they tested the new engine, but ran into the same bad luck that had haunted them the summer before. The engine backfired, the propeller shafts cracked, and the weather grew colder.

It wasn't until December 14 that the brothers were ready to attempt powered flight. The winds were light, so the Wrights decided to use gravity to help them get the *Flyer* into the air. They built a long rail up a nearby hill, and, with the help of local lifeguards, rolled the flying machine up the rail on two bicycle-wheel hubs. The *Flyer* would roll down the rail to get enough speed to become airborne.

By mid-afternoon the Wrights were almost ready. They tossed a coin to decide who would climb into the *Flyer*. Wilbur won— was he about to become the first person to fly?

The lifeguards watched anxiously while Orville tried to steady the flying machine as it zoomed down the rail. He let go and it lifted into the air. Then suddenly it dropped and caught a wing in the sand. The *Flyer* had crashed after only three seconds.

Wilbur climbed out, and the brothers inspected the damage. Luckily it wasn't too bad. Two days later, the flying machine was repaired and it was Orville's turn. But the winds weren't strong enough. The Wrights moved the rail to level ground and waited.

The brothers awoke on December 17 to a windy day. But they knew if they didn't try again soon, they might have to wait until spring. Wilbur and Orville signaled the lifeguards: they were ready. The flying machine was on its launching rail, its engine running smoothly.

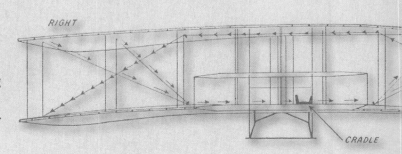

The sketch shows how the wings on the Wrights' airplane could be twisted or warped. If the pilot shifted his hips a little to the left on the cradle, for example, the left wing moved lower than the right one, and the flying machine turned to the left.

RIGHT

CRADLE

Orville eased into the *Flyer* and released the anchor—and he was airborne! The flight lasted only 12 seconds, but the Wright brothers had made history with the first powered and controlled flight. One lifeguard ran into town yelling, "They done it! They done it!"

The brothers made four flights, with Wilbur making the longest—260 m (852 ft.)—and staying airborne for 59 seconds. The Wrights telegraphed their friends and family but told no one else. They wanted to keep their design secret so no one could copy it. But the news leaked out, thanks to the telegraph operators.

December 17—Success at last! Wilbur stands by while Orville becomes the first person to fly.

Orville's name is misspelled in this telegram he sent to his father, and the brothers' longest flight was actually 59 seconds.

LEFT

UNION TELEGRAPH COMPANY.
INCORPORATED
IN AMERICA. CABLE SERVICE TO ALL THE WORLD.

RECEIVED at

176 C KA GS 33 Paid.   Via Norfolk Va
Kitty Hawk N C Dec 17
Bishop M Wright

7 Hawthorne St

Success four flights thursday morning all against twenty one mile wind started from Level with engine power alone average speed through air thirty one miles longest 57 seconds inform Press home Christmas .

Orevelle Wright   525P

UPS AND DOWNS

You'd think that newspapers everywhere would have carried the story of the Wrights' flight. But most outsiders who heard about it didn't realize what the brothers had done. Others didn't believe them—after all, so many inventors, with better educations, had failed.

Wilbur and Orville kept experimenting. They no longer needed the high winds and soft dunes of Kill Devil Hills, so they worked at Huffman Prairie, 13 km (8 mi.) from their home in Dayton. By January 1904, the brothers were building *Flyer II*, with a new, larger engine. Wild stories buzzed around about the Wrights' flying machines, so Wilbur and Orville invited reporters to watch *Flyer II*'s trial flights in May. The reporters gathered, but bad weather meant the flying machine flew only 9 m (30 ft.). No one was impressed.

In 1905 the Wrights built *Flyer III*. It had separate controls for the rudder and wing-warping system and in October flew an amazing 39 km (24 mi.). The flying machine could stay in the air for more than half an hour. Finally, a really practical airplane!

Wilbur and Orville decided they'd better keep their new airplane design secret. They would not fly again until they had sold it. That took longer than they hoped—almost three years. They kept busy applying for the patent for the airplane and trying to sell it.

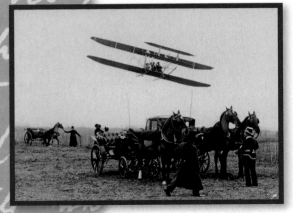

Wilbur stunned people in France, Italy, and Germany with the brothers' airplane.

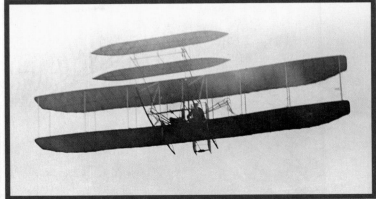

The Wrights modified *Flyer III* in 1908 and made the world's first two-passenger plane flights. It stayed in the air for a record-breaking 39 minutes.

The Wright brothers offered their machine to the U.S. government for army use, but there was no interest. However, the governments of France and England *were* interested. In 1907 Wilbur and Orville traveled to Europe and came close to a sale in France.

The brothers returned home at the end of 1907. But they soon realized they'd have to demonstrate their airplane to make the French sale. So on August 8, 1908, near Le Mans, France, Wilbur amazed the watching crowds, although he was airborne for less than two minutes. He made many more flights, some longer than an hour, because so many people wanted to see the airplane fly.

Stories of Wilbur's flights quickly got back to North America. Finally the U.S. Army became interested in the *Flyer III*. In 1908 Orville made performance trials in Fort Myer, Virginia. The early flights went well, but on September 17, a propeller broke. Orville lost control and crashed, killing his passenger, Lieutenant Thomas Selfridge. Orville broke a leg and several ribs and was in the hospital for weeks.

People rush to remove Orville from the wreckage of the crash on September 17, 1908. Selfridge is already on a stretcher just off to the right.

FLYING HIGH

When Orville recovered from the Fort Myer crash, he and his sister, Katharine, joined Wilbur in Europe in early 1909. Royalty watched and people cheered as Wilbur shattered flight records for height, time, and distance. Orville and Katharine stayed in hotels as they traveled around, but sometimes Wilbur insisted on sleeping in the hangar with the airplane to make sure nothing happened to it.

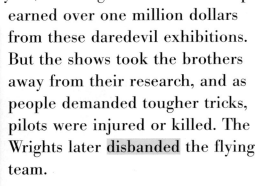

When the brothers returned to the United States, people finally seemed to understand what they had accomplished. They received a hero's welcome in New York, and their home town of Dayton held a two-day celebration.

More important to the Wright brothers was that their airplanes were selling. In July 1909, the U.S. Army bought the Military Flyer. In November Wilbur and Orville set up the Wright Company in the United States. (Three months earlier they had formed the German-Wright Company to build airplanes in Germany.) Now the brothers were running a factory, testing airplanes, and training pilots. They also had to fight lawsuits to protect the patent on their invention.

Wilbur and Orville arranged flying displays to get people interested in airplanes. One year, the Wright Exhibition Company earned over one million dollars from these daredevil exhibitions. But the shows took the brothers away from their research, and as people demanded tougher tricks, pilots were injured or killed. The Wrights later disbanded the flying team.

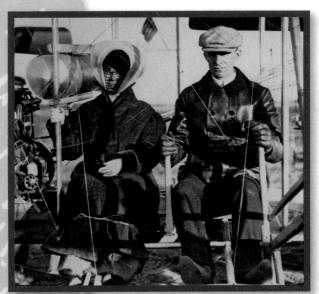

When Katharine, Orville and Wilbur's sister, flew for the first time in France in 1909, Wilbur was at the controls. Notice how Katharine's skirt is tied to keep it from blowing in the wind.

May 1910 was a month the brothers would always remember. On May 21, Wilbur flew by himself, the last time he would ever pilot an airplane in the United States. A few days later, the Wrights flew together for the first and only time, with Orville at the controls. On May 25, Orville took up their father, who was over 80. As the airplane soared upward, the old man yelled, "Higher, Orville, higher!"

The legal battles the Wright brothers fought wore down Wilbur's health. In early May 1912, he caught typhoid fever. He died on May 30, less than ten years after he and his brother had flown into history.

The brothers continued to improve their machines. To find out if they could keep an airplane straight and level in the air without the involvement of the pilot, they headed back to Kill Devil Hills in 1911 with this new glider. Orville set a world soaring record of 9 minutes and 45 seconds.

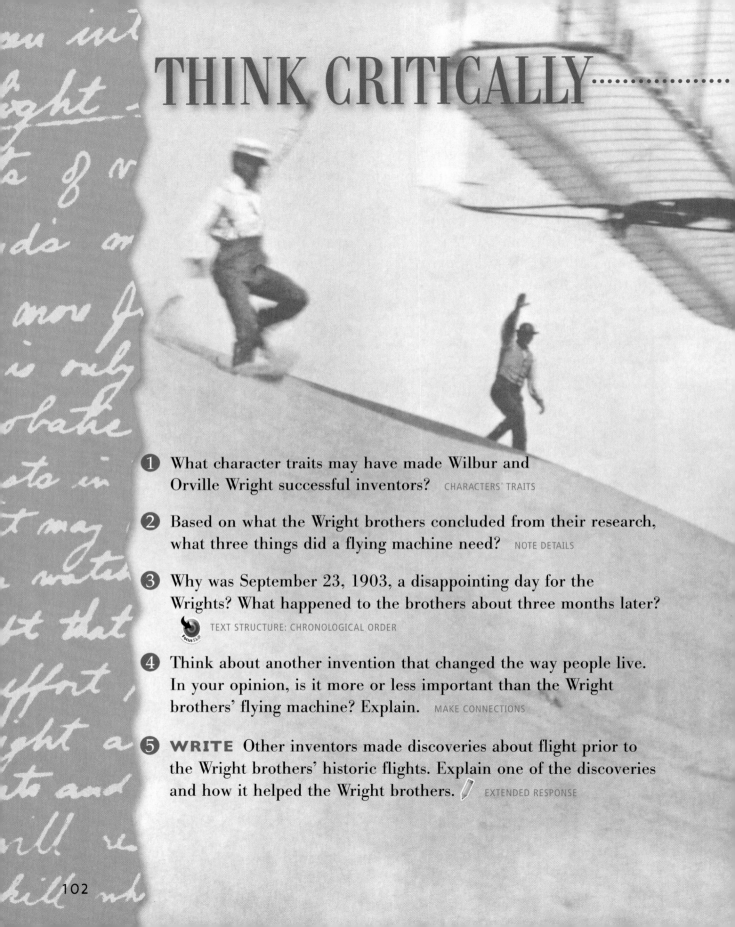

THINK CRITICALLY

1. What character traits may have made Wilbur and Orville Wright successful inventors? CHARACTERS' TRAITS

2. Based on what the Wright brothers concluded from their research, what three things did a flying machine need? NOTE DETAILS

3. Why was September 23, 1903, a disappointing day for the Wrights? What happened to the brothers about three months later? TEXT STRUCTURE: CHRONOLOGICAL ORDER

4. Think about another invention that changed the way people live. In your opinion, is it more or less important than the Wright brothers' flying machine? Explain. MAKE CONNECTIONS

5. **WRITE** Other inventors made discoveries about flight prior to the Wright brothers' historic flights. Explain one of the discoveries and how it helped the Wright brothers. EXTENDED RESPONSE

ABOUT THE AUTHOR

Elizabeth MacLeod

Elizabeth MacLeod discovered her love of writing as an adult. After studying science in college, she wrote science-related articles for newspapers and magazines. She discovered that investigating unusual topics was fun. Since that discovery, Elizabeth MacLeod has written a number of biographies of famous scientists, including Alexander Graham Bell, Albert Einstein, and Marie Curie. She enjoys writing biographies because she gets to find out little-known facts about famous people. She also likes to learn why they did what they did and what obstacles they encountered along the way. Elizabeth MacLeod lives in Toronto, Canada, with her husband and two cats.

www.harcourtschool.com/storytown

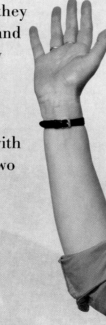

103

Magazine Article

From Inspiration to Invention

by Cate Baily

First Place

Bright Idea

She's got the right name and right stuff for inventing. Sixteen-year-old Lisa Marie Wright (no relation to the Wright brothers) created a candle that burns itself out to prevent fires.

One day, Lisa's family returned home to find that her mother had accidentally left a candle burning all day. Fortunately, there was no damage or injury that time. But this Columbus, Ohio, teen didn't want there to be a *next* time. She began to devise the Auto-Off Candle, which is now called the Wright Candle.

While Lisa spent hours on her invention—which contains crimped metal spacers and glass beads that create a new wick for each burn time—she didn't do it alone. "I learned that no matter how smart you are, or how good your invention is, you need mentors and a lot of support from other people," Lisa says. "I learned that it takes a team effort."

It may have been a team effort, but Lisa was singled out for her innovation. She was inducted into the National Gallery of America's Young Inventors.

⇦ **Lisa Marie Wright's candle allows users to control the time of the burn.**

Cool Tool

Jamila Jordan has always wanted to invent something that would save the world. At 13, she's already created a snow shovel that will save people's backs. A bent handle and wheels save the shoveler from having to bend over to heave the snow off the ground.

Jamila got the idea for this new device while clearing the walk of her Washington, D.C., home after a storm. But what inspired her to bust out the power tools and actually make what she calls the E-Z Shove? Jamila had major motivation. "For me, this was an alternative to a science fair project. So it was either do it, and turn it in, or get an F," Jamila says.

Chalk one up for homework. Jamila was named the winner for her region in the annual Craftsman/National Science Teachers Association (NSTA) Young Inventors contest. "I didn't expect it to win," she says. "I think it's important for other teens not to underestimate themselves. I didn't think I was going anywhere with my invention, but I did."

An enterprising 8th-grader, Jamila Jordan thought wheels would make it easier to shovel snow. ⇨

Connections

Comparing Texts

1. Which inventor are you more like, Wilbur or Orville Wright? Explain.

2. How are the inventors in "From Inspiration to Invention" like the Wright Brothers? How are they different?

3. Why do you think the Wright brothers are two of the best known inventors in history?

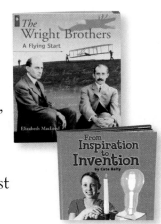

Vocabulary Review

Word Webs

Choose two Vocabulary Words, and create a word web for each one. Put the Vocabulary Word in the center of the web. In the outside ovals, write words and phrases that are related to the Vocabulary Word. Share your word webs with a partner, explaining how each word or phrase in your web is related to the Vocabulary Word.

shocking — beyond belief — **astounding** — surprising — startling

astounding

disbanded

stabilize

exerts

rigged

replica

schemes

Fluency Practice

Repeated Reading

Your reading rate is how quickly you can read a passage correctly and still understand what you read. You might read a fiction passage more quickly than a nonfiction passage that contains unfamiliar vocabulary. Work with a partner. Read aloud the section titled Early Years from "The Wright Brothers: A Flying Start." Have your partner time you with a stopwatch or wall clock. Then switch roles. Continue reading the passage and timing each other. Try to improve your reading rate with each reading.

Writing

Write a Narrative

People depend on all sorts of machines, appliances, and gadgets every day. Think of one such item that you use often. Then write a narrative that tells what happens when the item that you use often breaks or malfunctions.

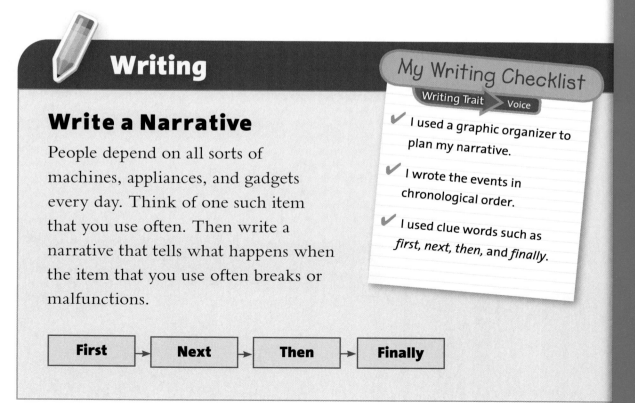

My Writing Checklist

Writing Trait → Voice

✔ I used a graphic organizer to plan my narrative.

✔ I wrote the events in chronological order.

✔ I used clue words such as *first, next, then,* and *finally.*

| First | → | Next | → | Then | → | Finally |

CONTENTS

Lesson 4

WILMA UNLIMITED
How Wilma Rudolph Became the World's Fastest Woman

KATHLEEN KRULL

ILLUSTRATED BY
DAVID DIAZ

The World's Fastest

FROM SCHOLASTIC BOOK OF WORLD RECORDS 2005

Genre: Almanac

Focus Skill

Text Structure: Chronological Order

You have learned that authors of nonfiction texts organize information in specific ways called text structures. The way an author organizes the facts depends on the subject. When a sequence of events is important, an author usually uses **chronological order**. Authors use different kinds of clue words to indicate sequence.

- Time-order words such as *first, next,* and *finally* indicate the sequence of events.
- Terms such as *meanwhile* and *simultaneously* signal that two or more events happened at the same time.
- Time indicators such as dates help readers place events in history and in relation to one another.

First
↓
Next
↓
Then
↓
Finally

Read the paragraph below, and look at the diagram that follows. It shows three important events that appear in the paragraph. The clue words that indicate the sequence of these events appear in boldface type.

Glenn Cunningham was born in Kansas in 1909. When he was six, his legs were badly burned in an explosion. Doctors said that he would never walk again. Over the next several months, Glenn proved them wrong. He pushed himself not only to walk but also to run. He became a high school track star. In 1931, he entered college, and one year later, he competed in the 1932 Olympic Games.

Glenn Cunningham was **born in 1909.**

↓

His legs were burned in an explosion **when he was six.**

↓

Over the next few months, Glenn taught himself to walk and run.

Try This!

Look back at the paragraph. What important events could you add to the diagram? What clue words help you understand where in the sequence these events belong?

www.harcourtschool.com/storytown

Vocabulary

Build Robust Vocabulary

- intense
- fumble
- luxury
- astonishment
- propel
- triumphant
- lunged
- remedies

Jackie Joyner-Kersee

Track-and-field events are **intense** physical competitions. Even after months of training, a long jumper can stumble. A relay runner can lose a race over the tiniest **fumble**. Olympic champion Jackie Joyner-Kersee owes her many wins to her fine physical condition and to her positive mental approach to competition.

Few athletes have had the **luxury** of competing in more than two Olympic Games. However, Joyner-Kersee won medals in three Olympic Games. At the 1996 games, the crowd looked on in **astonishment** as she placed third in the long jump despite a leg injury she had suffered just days earlier.

Jackie Joyner-Kersee started competing in multiple track-and-field events at the age of twelve.

This feat served to **propel** her into world history as the first athlete ever to win multi-event medals in three Olympic Games.

Following the 1998 Goodwill Games, Joyner-Kersee retired, smiling and **triumphant**. As she **lunged** across the finish line of the 800-meter race in that competition, she broke her own world record in the seven-event heptathlon.

Throughout her career, Joyner-Kersee battled asthma. Today, her work includes educating young people about asthma and the **remedies** available to them.

www.harcourtschool.com/storytown

Word Detective

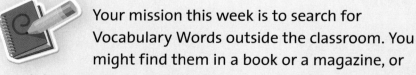

Your mission this week is to search for Vocabulary Words outside the classroom. You might find them in a book or a magazine, or you might hear them on TV or in a conversation somewhere. Each time you see or hear a Vocabulary Word, write it in your vocabulary journal. Be sure to tell where you found the word.

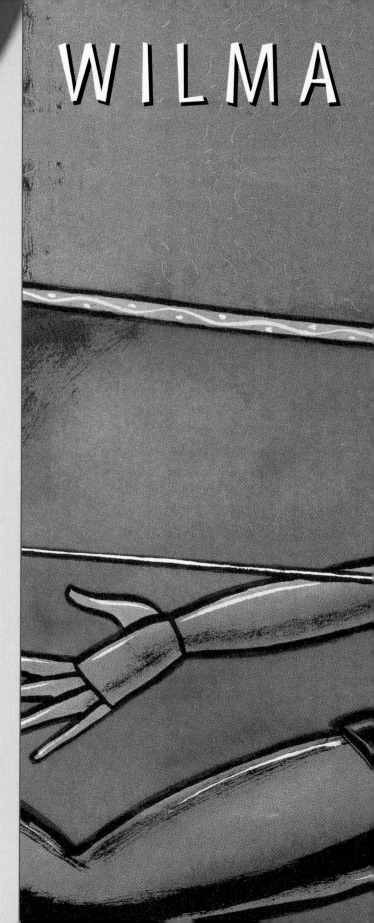

WILMA

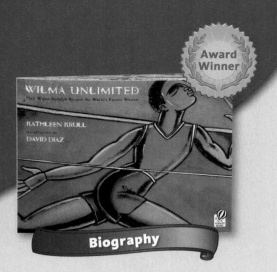

WILMA UNLIMITED
How Wilma Rudolph Became the World's Fastest Woman

KATHLEEN KRULL

ILLUSTRATED BY
DAVID DIAZ

Biography

Genre Study

A biography tells about a person's life and is written by another person. As you read, look for

- information telling why the person is important.

- events told in chronological order.

First
Next
Then
Finally

Comprehension Strategy

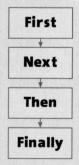

Use graphic organizers like the one shown above to keep track of the sequence of events.

UNLIMITED

How Wilma Rudolph Became
the World's Fastest Woman

by Kathleen Krull
illustrated by David Diaz

No one expected such a tiny girl to have a first birthday. In Clarksville, Tennessee, in 1940, life for a baby who weighed just over four pounds at birth was sure to be limited.

But most babies didn't have nineteen older brothers and sisters to watch over them. Most babies didn't have a mother who knew home remedies and a father who worked several jobs.

Most babies weren't Wilma Rudolph.

Wilma did celebrate her first birthday, and everyone noticed that as soon as this girl could walk, she ran or jumped instead.

She worried people, though—she was always so small and sickly. If a brother or sister had a cold, she got double pneumonia. If one of them had measles, Wilma got measles, too, plus mumps and chicken pox.

Her mother always nursed her at home. Doctors were a luxury for the Rudolph family, and anyway, only one doctor in Clarksville would treat black people.

Just before Wilma turned five, she got sicker than ever. Her sisters and brothers heaped all the family's blankets on her, trying to keep her warm.

During that sickness, Wilma's left leg twisted inward, and she couldn't move it back. Not even Wilma's mother knew what was wrong.

The doctor came to see her then. Besides scarlet fever, he said, Wilma had also been stricken with polio. In those days, most children who got polio either died or were permanently crippled. There was no cure.

The news spread around Clarksville. Wilma, that lively girl, would never walk again.

But Wilma kept moving any way she could. By hopping on one foot, she could get herself around the house, to the outhouse in the backyard, and even, on Sundays, to church.

Wilma's mother urged her on. Mrs. Rudolph had plenty to do—cooking, cleaning, sewing patterned flour sacks into clothes for her children, now twenty-two in all. Yet twice every week, she and Wilma took the bus to the nearest hospital that would treat black patients, some fifty miles away in Nashville. They rode together in the back, the only place blacks were allowed to sit.

Doctors and nurses at the hospital helped Wilma do exercises to make her paralyzed leg stronger. At home, Wilma practiced them constantly, even when it hurt.

To Wilma, what hurt most was that the local school wouldn't let her attend because she couldn't walk. Tearful and lonely, she watched her brothers and sisters run off to school each day, leaving her behind. Finally, tired of crying all the time, she decided she had to fight back—somehow.

Wilma worked so hard at her exercises that the doctors decided she was ready for a heavy steel brace. With the brace supporting her leg, she didn't have to hop anymore. School was possible at last.

But it wasn't the happy place she had imagined. Her classmates made fun of her brace. During playground games she could only sit on the sidelines, twitchy with impatience. She studied the other kids for hours—memorizing moves, watching the ball zoom through the rim of the bushel basket they used as a hoop.

Wilma fought the sadness by doing more leg exercises. Her family always cheered her on, and Wilma did everything she could to keep them from worrying about her. At times her leg really did seem to be getting stronger. Other times it just hurt.

One Sunday, on her way to church, Wilma felt especially good. She and her family had always found strength in their faith, and church was Wilma's favorite place in the world. Everyone she knew would be there—talking and laughing, praying and singing. It would be just the place to try the bravest thing she had ever done.

She hung back while people filled the old building. Standing alone, the sound of hymns coloring the air, she unbuckled her heavy brace and set it by the church's front door. Taking a deep breath, she moved one foot in front of the other, her knees trembling violently. She took her mind off her knees by concentrating on taking another breath, and then another.

Whispers rippled throughout the gathering. Wilma Rudolph was *walking.* Row by row, heads turned toward her as she walked alone down the aisle. Her large family, all her family's friends, everyone from school—each person stared wide-eyed. The singing never stopped; it seemed to burst right through the walls and into the trees. Finally, Wilma reached a seat in the front and began singing too, her smile triumphant.

Wilma practiced walking as often as she could after that, and when she was twelve years old, she was able to take off the brace for good. She and her mother realized she could get along without it, so one memorable day they wrapped the hated brace in a box and mailed it back to the hospital.

As soon as Wilma sent that box away, she knew her life was beginning all over again.

After years of sitting on the sidelines, Wilma couldn't wait to throw herself into basketball, the game she had most liked to watch. She was skinny but no longer tiny. Her long, long legs would propel her across the court and through the air, and she knew all the rules and all the moves.

In high school, she led her basketball team to one victory after another. Eventually, she took the team all the way to the Tennessee state championships. There, to everyone's astonishment, her team lost.

Wilma had become accustomed to winning. Now she slumped on the bench, all the liveliness knocked out of her.

But at the game that day was a college coach. He admired Wilma's basketball playing but was especially impressed by the way she ran. He wanted her for his track-and-field team.

With his help, Wilma won a full athletic scholarship to Tennessee State University. She was the first member of her family to go to college.

Eight years after she mailed her brace away, Wilma's long legs and years of hard work carried her thousands of miles from Clarksville, Tennessee. The summer of 1960 she arrived in Rome, Italy, to represent the United States at the Olympic Games—as a runner.

Just participating in the Olympics was a deeply personal victory for Wilma, but her chances of winning a race were limited. Simply walking in Rome's shimmering heat was a chore, and athletes from other countries had run faster races than Wilma ever had. Women weren't thought to run very well anyway; track-and-field was considered a sport for men. And the pressure from the public was intense—for the first time ever, the Olympics would be shown on television, and all the athletes knew that more than one hundred million people would be watching. Worst of all, Wilma had twisted her ankle just after she arrived in Rome. It was still swollen and painful on the day of her first race.

Yet once it was her turn to compete, Wilma forgot her ankle and everything else. She lunged forward, not thinking about her fear, her pain, or the sweat flying off her face. She ran better than she ever had before. And she ran better than anyone else.

Grabbing the attention of the whole world, Wilma Rudolph of the United States won the 100-meter dash. No one else even came close. An Olympic gold medal was hers to take home.

So when it was time for the 200-meter dash, Wilma's graceful long legs were already famous. Her ears buzzed with the sound of the crowd chanting her name. Such support helped her ignore the rain that was beginning to fall. At the crack of the starting gun, she surged into the humid air like a tornado. When she crossed the finish line, she had done it again. She finished far ahead of everyone else. She had earned her second gold medal. Wet and breathless, Wilma was exhilarated by the double triumph. The crowd went wild.

The 400-meter relay race was yet to come. Wilma's team faced the toughest competition of all. And as the fourth and final runner on her team, it was Wilma who had to cross the finish line.

Wilma's teammates ran well, passed the baton smoothly, and kept the team in first place. Wilma readied herself for the dash to the finish line as her third teammate ran toward her. She reached back for the baton—and nearly dropped it. As she tried to recover from the fumble, two other runners sped past her. Wilma and her team were suddenly in third place.

Ever since the day she had walked down the aisle at church, Wilma had known the power of concentration. Now, legs pumping, she put her mind to work. In a final, electrifying burst of speed, she pulled ahead. By a fraction of a second, she was the first to blast across the finish line. The thundering cheers matched the thundering of her own heart. She had made history. She had won for an astounding third time.

At her third ceremony that week, as the band played "The Star-Spangled Banner," Wilma stood tall and still, like a queen, the last of her three Olympic gold medals hanging around her neck.

Wilma Rudolph, once known as the sickliest child in Clarksville, had become the fastest woman in the world.

THINK CRITICALLY

1. What challenges did Wilma Rudolph face in her childhood? NOTE DETAILS

2. Why was participating in the Tennessee state basketball championship an important event in Wilma Rudolph's life, even though her team lost? SYNTHESIZE

3. In chronological order, tell the key moments of Wilma Rudolph's performance at the 1960 Olympic Games. TEXT STRUCTURE: CHRONOLOGICAL ORDER

4. Think about someone you know or have read about who overcame great challenges. Compare that person's experiences with Wilma Rudolph's. MAKE CONNECTIONS

5. **WRITE** In your opinion, why did Wilma Rudolph become a great athlete? Use specific details from the selection to support your ideas. SHORT RESPONSE

KATHLEEN KRULL

Kathleen Krull has loved reading and writing for almost as long as she can remember. In the fifth grade, she wrote a book she titled *Hairdos and People I Know*, a collection of drawings depicting her friends, family, and neighbors sporting unusual hairdos she had invented especially for them. Her quirky sense of humor has survived into adult life. She has written several biographies of famous people, including Wilma Rudolph. In her "Lives of . . ." series, she not only gives facts about famous people but also includes amusing details, such as how they dressed, what their neighbors said about them, and—yes—what kind of hairdos they had. Today, Kathleen Krull lives with her husband in San Diego, California.

DAVID DIAZ

David Diaz knew he wanted to be an artist when he was in the first grade. It was not until high school, however, that he seriously considered an art career. David Diaz has illustrated several children's books and won the Caldecott Medal in 1995. He says that when he is working on a book, he tries to imagine everything that a particular character would have experienced. Today, David Diaz lives near San Diego, California.

GO online www.harcourtschool.com/storytown

125

The World's

World's Fastest LAND MAMMAL

CHEETAH

These sleek mammals can reach a speed of 65 miles (105 km) per hour for short spurts. Their quickness enables these large African cats to easily outrun their prey. All other African cats must stalk their prey because they lack the cheetah's amazing speed. Unlike the paws of all other cats, cheetah paws do not have skin sheaths—thin protective coverings. Their claws, therefore, cannot pull back.

The World's Fastest
LAND MAMMALS

Maximum speed in miles/kilometers per hour

65 mph 105 kph	55 mph 89 kph	50 mph 80 kph	50 mph 80 kph	47 mph 76 kph
Cheetah	Pronghorn Antelope	Mongolian Gazelle	Springbok	Grant's Gazelle/ Thompson's Gazelle

Fastest

World's Fastest FLYER

PEREGRINE FALCON

When diving through the air, a peregrine falcon can reach speeds of up to 175 miles (282 km) an hour. That's about the same speed as the fastest race car in the Indianapolis 500. These powerful birds can catch prey in midair and kill it instantly with their sharp claws. Peregrine falcons range from about 13 to 19 inches (33 to 48 cm) long. The female is called a falcon, but the male is called a tercel, which means "one-third" in German. This is because the male is about one-third the size of the female.

The World's Fastest FLYERS

Top speed in miles/kilometers per hour

Peregrine Falcon	Spine-tailed Swift	Frigate Bird	Spur-winged Goose	Red-breasted Merganser
175 mph 282 kph	106 mph 171 kph	95 mph 153 kph	88 mph 142 kph	80 mph 129 kph

HAWK MOTH

The average hawk moth—which got its name from its swift and steady flight—can cruise along at speeds of up to 33 miles (53 km) per hour. That's faster than the average speed limit on most city streets. Although they are found throughout the world, most species live in tropical climates. Also known as the sphinx moth and the hummingbird moth, this large insect can have a wingspan that reaches up to 8 inches (20 cm). When alarmed, one species can produce loud squawking noises by blowing air through its tongue.

The World's Fastest FLYING INSECTS

Speed in miles/kilometers per hour

Hawk Moth	West Indian Butterfly	Deer Bot Fly	Dragonfly	Hornet
33.3 mph 53.6 kph	30.0 mph 48.2 kph	30.0 mph 48.2 kph	17.8 mph 28.6 kph	13.3 mph 21.4 kph

World's Fastest FISH

SAILFISH

Although it is difficult to measure the exact speed of fish, a sailfish once grabbed a fishing line and dragged it 300 feet (91 m) away in just 3 seconds. That means it was swimming at an average speed of 69 miles (109 km) per hour—just higher than the average speed limit on the highway! Sailfish are very large—they average 6 feet (1.8 m) long, but can grow up to 11 feet (3.4 m). Sailfish eat squid and surface-dwelling fish. Sometimes several sailfish will work together to catch their prey.

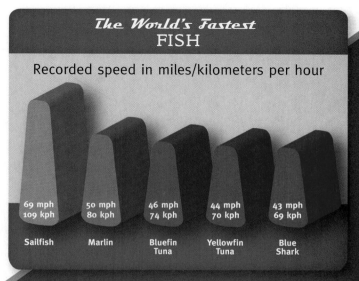

The World's Fastest FISH

Recorded speed in miles/kilometers per hour

Sailfish	Marlin	Bluefin Tuna	Yellowfin Tuna	Blue Shark
69 mph 109 kph	50 mph 80 kph	46 mph 74 kph	44 mph 70 kph	43 mph 69 kph

Connections

Comparing Texts

1. If you could meet Wilma Rudolph, what would you ask her?

2. How is "Wilma Unlimited" similar to "The World's Fastest"? How is it different?

3. What are some qualities that most great athletes share? Why are those qualities necessary?

Vocabulary Review

Nouns	Verbs	Adjectives

Word Sort

Work with a small group. Sort the Vocabulary Words into categories. You might choose language categories, such as Nouns, Verbs, and Adjectives. Or you might choose categories based on meaning or context, such as Words Sportscasters Use. Compare lists with the other members of your group. Explain why you put each word in a particular category. Then choose two Vocabulary Words in each category. Write a sentence that demonstrates why they belong in the same category.

intense

fumble

luxury

astonishment

propel

triumphant

lunged

remedies

Fluency Practice

Timed Reading

Your reading rate is the speed at which you can read a passage correctly and understand what you read. Reread page 121. Then read it aloud, using a stopwatch or clock to time yourself. Record your time on a sheet of paper. Repeat the process several times. Work to improve your reading rate each time.

Writing

Write a Sports Report

Imagine that you are a reporter for your school newspaper. Write a short article describing a game or sports event you attended or watched on television recently.

My Writing Checklist
Writing Trait ▶ Voice

✔ I organized the events in chronological order.

✔ I used vivid details to make the article interesting.

✔ The voice is consistent with things a sports reporter might say.

First → Next → Then → Finally

CONTENTS

Lesson 5

Theme Review and Vocabulary Builder

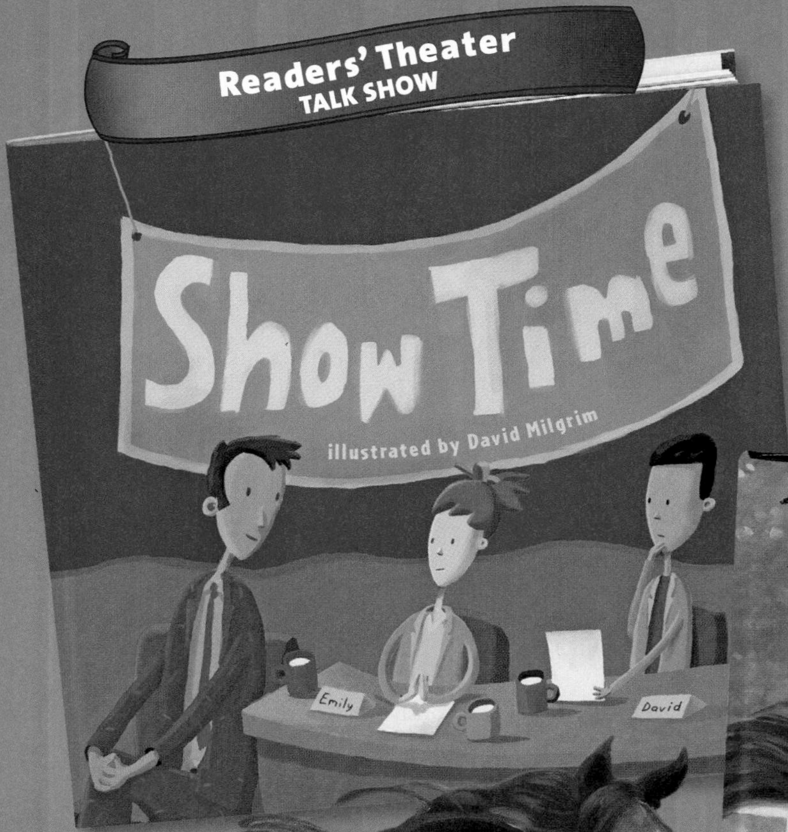

Readers' Theater
TALK SHOW
Show Time
illustrated by David Milgrim
Emily
David

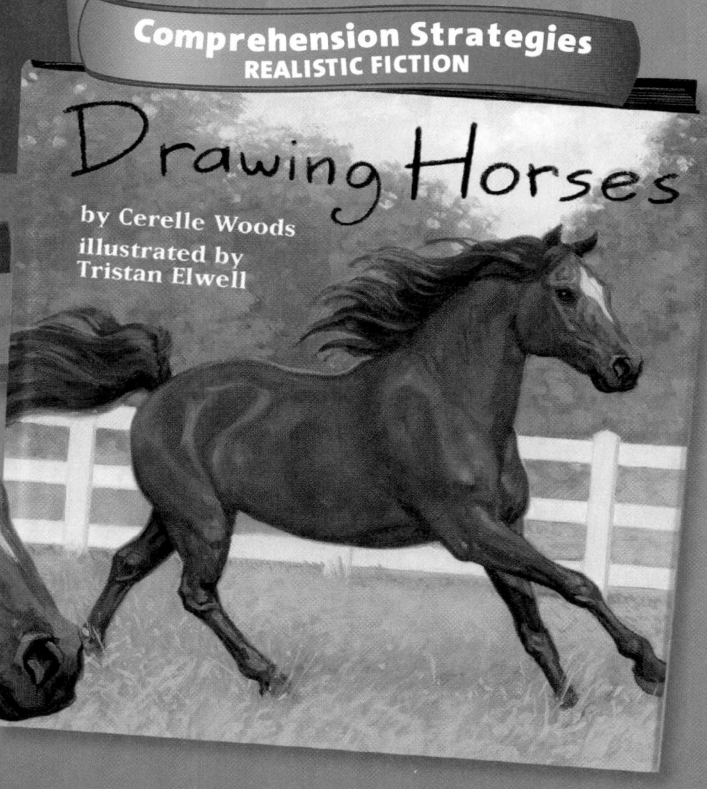

Comprehension Strategies
REALISTIC FICTION
Drawing Horses
by Cerelle Woods
illustrated by
Tristan Elwell

intimidating

calamity

invaluable

quandary

composure

hindrance

steadfast

surpassed

sage

trepidation

Reading for Fluency

When reading a script aloud,

- Read with **accuracy** so that your audience will enjoy your performance.

- Let the characters and actions determine your **reading rate**.

CHARACTERS

Narrator
Aman, student
Tisha, student
Emily, student and co-host
David, student and co-host
Mrs. Warren, drama teacher
Director
Audience
Hector Navarro, famous actor and former student

Narrator: Aman and Tisha are excited about a guest interview their drama class will be doing today. The guest is to be a real, live movie star!

Aman: Isn't it astounding that Hector Navarro is coming to be interviewed by our drama class? He's my favorite actor! I loved that scene in *Jungle of the Jaguars* where two wild jaguars were chasing him.

Show Time

illustrated by **David Milgrim**

Tisha: The special effects in that movie were awesome! I heard his next movie is a sci-fi fantasy. He's going to play a teacher who works at a school on Mars.

Aman: Wow! Do you think we could be in it? I'd be perfect for the role of a middle-school Martian!

Tisha: I'm sure you have to audition for something like that. I doubt that casting directors just take any kid who wants to be in a movie.

Aman: Maybe you're right. I just can't believe that someone famous went to our school! I want to be an actor like him someday.

Tisha: Well, maybe you'll get some tips today.

Narrator: Aman and Tisha take their seats in the audience. Emily and David, the co-hosts, fidget and flip through their cue cards, waiting for the show to start.

Emily: I'm so nervous! I can't wait to meet Hector Navarro, but I'm scared I'll say something silly or forget my interview questions.

David: I'm nervous, too. This show will be broadcast to the whole school. What if I have food stuck in my teeth?

Narrator: David shows Emily his teeth. She is inspecting them as Mrs. Warren, their drama teacher, enters.

Mrs. Warren: Are you two ready for the big interview?

Emily: We're nervous. . . .

David: . . . about meeting Mr. Navarro.

Mrs. Warren: Don't be nervous. Mr. Navarro is very down-to-earth. He isn't intimidating at all.

Emily: What about the school-wide broadcast?

Mrs. Warren: Remember, you're in your own classroom, and your classmates want you to do well. Just imagine that the camera isn't there.

David: I still feel scared. My hands are shaking.

Mrs. Warren: You two are going to be fine!

Director: Quiet on the set, everyone! We're live in 5, 4, 3, 2, 1.

Fluency Tip

Read your lines a few times to improve your **accuracy**. Make sure you know how to say all the words correctly.

137

Emily: Hello, and welcome to *Camera in the Classroom,* the show that takes you inside Littlefield Middle School. My name is Emily Carle.

David: I'm David Nastasi.

David and Emily: We're your hosts.

Emily: On today's show, we have a very special guest. He is a former Littlefield Middle School student who is now a famous actor.

David: He has appeared in many movies, including *Jungle of the Jaguars* and *Summer Camp Calamity.* He has also starred in a number of plays, including some here at Littlefield. Let's welcome Mr. Hector Navarro!

Narrator: Hector Navarro emerges from the doorway, smiles at the camera, and waves to the audience. The audience applauds and cheers.

Hector Navarro: Hello, hello! Thank you, everyone.

Emily: Also joining us is Mr. Navarro's former drama teacher, our own Mrs. Warren.

Audience: Good morning, Mrs. Warren.

Emily: Mr. Navarro, it's such an honor having you here today.

Hector Navarro: Thank you, Emily. It's lovely to be here.

David: Mr. Navarro, to begin, could you tell us a little about your time here at Littlefield Middle School?

Hector Navarro: Sure, David. I was a student here . . . oh, about a hundred years ago.

Audience: Ha, ha, ha!

Hector Navarro: I had Mrs. Warren as a teacher in this very classroom. We learned about the same things I'm sure you are now, such as makeup, set design, and, of course, performing onstage.

Emily: What was the most important thing you learned in Mrs. Warren's class?

Hector Navarro: Mrs. Warren taught me an invaluable lesson that changed my life. To tell you the truth, when I first started drama class, I was terrified to speak in front of people. If I had to make a presentation in class, I would be completely incapacitated by fear.

Audience: No way! We don't believe it!

Hector Navarro: I wanted to act in plays, but when I stood in front of an audience, my feet felt as if they were stuck in concrete. I couldn't move. Just the thought of performing tormented me! It's true! I was in a real quandary.

David: You have such composure now! How did you overcome your fear?

Hector Navarro: Mrs. Warren had a few remedies for stage fright. Right?

Mrs. Warren: Right.

Fluency Tip

Use the right **reading rate** to be sure your audience understands your lines.

Mrs. Warren: I remember that. You had such a bad case of stage fright that your arms were shaking. However, since you were a tree on a windy day, your shaking went to good use. You made a very good tree. What began as a hindrance ended up being beneficial.

Hector Navarro: That's right. After my role as an oak tree, Mrs. Warren gave me small speaking parts. Eventually, I became comfortable performing in front of people. Oh—she also gave me one secret weapon that I still use to this day.

Hector Navarro: She started by giving me small roles in school plays. My acting career began when I played the part of an oak tree. I had no lines, but I had to stand onstage in a gigantic tree costume and wave my branches around.

Audience: What is it? What's the secret?

Hector Navarro: What do you think, Mrs. Warren? Should I give away the secret?

Audience: Yes, please tell us.

Mrs. Warren: Oh, I suppose we can let them in on it.

Hector Navarro: She told me that if I start to feel afraid, I should just imagine that the people in the audience are animals. It's hard to be afraid in front of a bunch of kangaroos and turtles!

Audience: Animals? We love it!

David: Mrs. Warren, was Mr. Navarro's stage fright really as bad as he says?

Mrs. Warren: Oh yes, if not worse! He was steadfast, though. He worked very hard and eventually his bravery surpassed his fear. I am ecstatic that he has succeeded!

Emily: We're going to take a quick break, folks. When we come back, Mr. Navarro will answer questions from the audience, so stay tuned to *Camera in the Classroom.*

Narrator: The audience applauds. Emily and David think they hear a few neighs and woofs, too!

Director: Cut!

Mrs. Warren: Hector, it's truly amazing to think of all the things you've been able to accomplish since you were a student here.

Hector Navarro: I never could have done it without you, Mrs. Warren. If it weren't for your patience and sage advice, I never would have gained the courage and confidence to be an actor.

Director: Quiet on the set! We're live in 5, 4, 3, 2, 1.

Narrator: David and Emily move back behind the desk, and Mrs. Warren and Hector Navarro take their seats.

David: We're back! Today on *Camera in the Classroom*, we're speaking with actor and former Littlefield Middle School student, Hector Navarro. He is here with his former drama teacher, our own Mrs. Warren.

Narrator: Mrs. Warren and Hector Navarro smile and wave to the camera.

Emily: We've been talking with Mr. Navarro about how he overcame his stage fright and became a successful actor.

David: Now we invite the audience to ask Mr. Navarro questions. Aman, I see that you have a question.

Narrator: Aman gets up from his seat and walks over to the microphone.

Aman: Hi, Mr. Navarro. First of all, I just want to say that I'm a huge fan of yours! I thought you were hysterical in *Summer Camp Calamity*.

Hector Navarro: Thank you very much! What's your question, young man?

Aman: It sounds as if you were in quite a few plays here at Littlefield Middle School. What was your favorite role while you were a student here?

Hector Navarro: Hmm . . . let me think. I enjoyed playing the detective in *The Mystery Meat Mistake*. Still, I think my favorite role was that of the teacher in *It Came from the Principal's Office*.

Fluency Tip

A character's traits can help you choose an appropriate **reading rate**. Is your character easily excited or shy and reserved?

Audience: We just read that play!

Hector Navarro: That was my first major role. I was scared at first, but I used Mrs. Warren's trick. To my astonishment, it worked! I overcame my stage fright and actually had fun.

David: Okay. Next question.

Narrator: Aman takes his seat as Tisha stands up and walks over to the microphone.

Tisha: Mr. Navarro, you have performed both in movies and onstage. Do you prefer one to the other?

Hector Navarro: Well, each has its positive points, and I enjoy both. With live plays, I find it exciting to perform in front of an audience. On the other hand, if I'm filming a movie and I make a mistake or play a scene with spinach in my teeth, I have the luxury of trying the scene again.

Tisha: Do you ever forget your lines?

Hector Navarro: Oh, yes. Memorizing lines can be very tough. It's intimidating when I first read through a script in which I have hundreds of lines.

Tisha: How do you learn them?

Hector Navarro: The trick is to break them down scene by scene. Then I just keep going over the lines again and again until I know them cold.

Tisha: What is the toughest thing about acting in movies?

Hector Navarro: I know we've been talking about it quite a bit, but I would have to say fear. Whether it's stage fright or fear of failure, fear is a tough thing to tackle.

Tisha: Do you still get scared sometimes?

Hector Navarro: Yes, but it's nothing like the trepidation I used to feel. Now I just take a deep breath and tell myself to be confident. If I get really nervous, I imagine that the director is a big ostrich.

Audience: An ostrich! We love it!

Tisha: Are you nervous right now, being interviewed in front of us?

Hector Navarro: Not at all. Why would I be nervous talking to a bunch of penguins?

Audience: Penguins! Awk! Awk!

Narrator: Tisha takes her seat, and the camera swings back to Emily and David.

Fluency Tip

To read with **accuracy,** make sure you read all the words correctly before moving on.

David: Mr. Navarro, do you have any advice for drama students who are interested in becoming professional actors?

Hector Navarro: Yes. My best piece of advice is to stick with it. If you really want to be an actor, don't get discouraged. As with any career you choose, be prepared to face some rejection. Acting is hard work, but the effort you exert pays off in the end. If you love it, keep at it!

Emily: Great advice. Unfortunately, that's all the time we have today.

David: Do you have any last comments, Mr. Navarro?

Hector Navarro: I do have one: Above all else, believe in yourself. Never let nervousness stop you from doing what you love.

Emily and David: From Mrs. Warren's class and from *Camera in the Classroom,* good-bye to all you rabbits and zebras out there!

Director: Cut!

COMPREHENSION STRATEGIES
Review

Reading Fiction

Bridge to Reading for Meaning Realistic fiction stories describe characters, settings, and plot events that are like people, places, and events in real life. The characters face challenges and problems that could really happen. The notes on page 145 point out characteristics of realistic fiction. How can your knowledge about these characteristics help you read and understand fiction?

Review the Focus Strategies

You can also use the strategies you learned about in this theme to help you read fiction.

Use Story Structure

All stories have a similar organization, known as the story structure. Look for the conflict, or problem, near the beginning of the story. Then identify the plot events that occur as the main character tries to resolve the conflict. Last, look for the resolution, or final outcome.

Use Graphic Organizers

As you read, use graphic organizers to help you organize information. For fiction stories, you can use a story map like the one shown. A story map shows the important elements of the story structure.

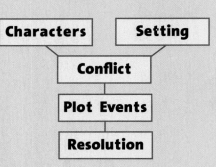

As you read "Drawing Horses" on pages 146–149, think about where and how you can use the strategies.

CONFLICT
At the beginning of the story, look for a problem that is realistic in today's world.

Drawing Horses

by Cerelle Woods
illustrated by Tristan Elwell

I'd give anything to draw horses the way Euphemia Tucker does. She draws them in the margins of spelling tests and on the back of her math homework. They're always running wild and free, their manes swirling over the paper like clouds across the sky.

Euphemia's horses look so real you can almost feel their breath on your face.

Luke Anderson, who sits next to me, says he can't decide whether my horses look more like Great Danes or kitchen tables. He also calls me Messy. I prefer Marisa, which is my real name, to Missy, which is what everyone—except Luke—calls me. If I could draw like Euphemia, I'd sign all my pictures Marisa. Nobody messes with Euphemia's name, not even Luke Anderson.

Today I sharpened my pencil and took a clean sheet of paper out of my desk. Then I closed my eyes and pictured one of Euphemia's perfect horses rearing up and pawing the air with its sharp hooves. I could see it so clearly I was sure I'd be able to draw it this time.

I started with what I do best: a big, billowing mane. Next I roughed in most of the body and drew a long tail streaming out behind. It really wasn't turning out half-bad until I got to the front-legs-pawing-the-air

part, which looked like two macaroni noodles with tiny marshmallows for hooves.

I tried again, but the hooves still didn't seem right, and rather than doing them over and over, I erased them and went on to the head. That was when I really ran into trouble.

First I drew some great donkey ears, followed by sheep ears, pig ears, kangaroo ears . . . everything except horse ears. I erased again and again until I had rubbed a hole in the paper. That was when Luke Anderson poked his nose over my shoulder.

"Hey Messy," he said. "What are you drawing? It looks like a *T. rex* with a mohawk."

I scratched a big X through my earless, macaroni-legged horse, wadded it up into a little ball, and stuffed it under the lid of my desk.

I was still upset when I got off the school bus this afternoon. I walked past the neighbors' horses standing in the field next to our house. They've been in that field for as long as I can remember. Their stringy manes never float into the sky. Their ragged old tails hang straight down to the ground, and I've never seen them run. Every few minutes they stamp their feet to knock off the fire ants, which is how I know they're alive.

ILLUSTRATIONS
Illustrations support the setting and characters described in the text.

DIALOGUE
Dialogue gives clues about what the characters are like.

Apply the Strategies Read this realistic fiction story about a girl who wants to draw as well as one of her classmates. As you read, apply comprehension strategies, such as using story structure, to help you understand the text.

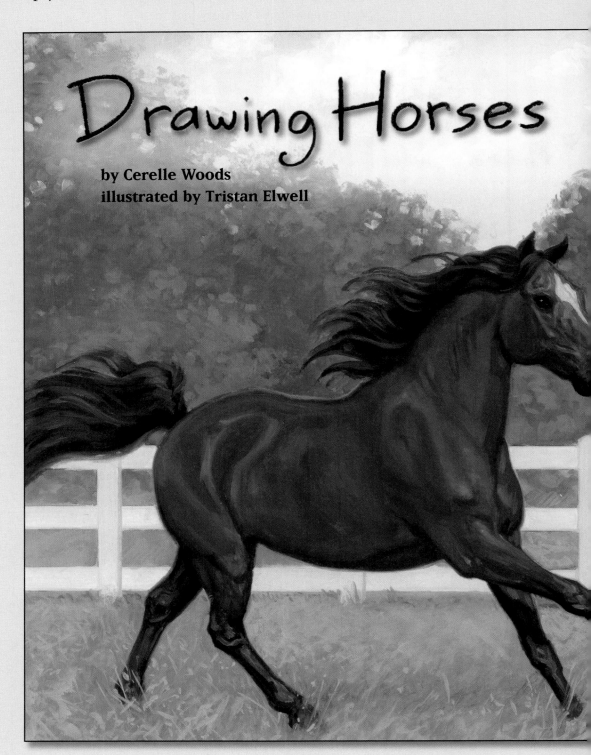

Drawing Horses

by Cerelle Woods
illustrated by Tristan Elwell

Use a story map to list the characters, setting, and conflict.

USE GRAPHIC ORGANIZERS

I'd give anything to draw horses the way Euphemia Tucker does. She draws them in the margins of spelling tests and on the back of her math homework. They're always running wild and free, their manes swirling over the paper like clouds across the sky.

Euphemia's horses look so real you can almost feel their breath on your face.

Luke Anderson, who sits next to me, says he can't decide whether my horses look more like Great Danes or kitchen tables. He also calls me Messy. I prefer Marisa, which is my real name, to Missy, which is what everyone—except Luke—calls me. If I could draw like Euphemia, I'd sign all my pictures Marisa. Nobody messes with Euphemia's name, not even Luke Anderson.

Today I sharpened my pencil and took a clean sheet of paper out of my desk. Then I closed my eyes and pictured one of Euphemia's perfect horses rearing up and pawing the air with its sharp hooves. I could see it so clearly I was sure I'd be able to draw it this time.

I started with what I do best: a big, billowing mane. Next I roughed in most of the body and drew a long tail streaming out behind. It really wasn't turning out half-bad until I got to the front-legs-pawing-the-air part, which looked like two macaroni noodles with tiny marshmallows for hooves.

I tried again, but the hooves still didn't seem right, and rather than doing them over and over, I erased them and went on to the head. That was when I really ran into trouble.

First I drew some great donkey ears, followed by sheep ears, pig ears, kangaroo ears . . . everything except horse ears. I erased again and again until I had rubbed a hole in the paper. That was when Luke Anderson poked his nose over my shoulder.

"Hey Messy," he said. "What are you drawing? It looks like a *T. rex* with a mohawk."

I scratched a big X through my earless, macaroni-legged horse, wadded it up into a little ball, and stuffed it under the lid of my desk.

I was still upset when I got off the school bus this afternoon. I walked past the neighbors' horses standing in the field next to our house. They've been in that field for as long as I can remember. Their stringy manes never float into the sky. Their ragged old tails hang straight down to the ground, and I've never seen them run. Every few minutes they stamp their feet to knock off the fire ants, which is how I know they're alive.

Euphemia probably has her own herd of wild stallions. I bet they run right past her bedroom window.

I brooded about it all through dinner. After I'd helped clear the dishes, I sat down with a stack of typing paper and a freshly sharpened pencil. Without Luke Anderson there to pester me, I hoped I'd have better luck. I practiced a few horses' heads, trying to get the ears right. Then my mother walked by, carrying a basket of laundry.

"Nice dogs, Missy," she said. "Is that one a German shepherd?"

I slammed my pencil against the table, hard. My dad looked up from his magazine.

"Was it something I said?" Mama asked.

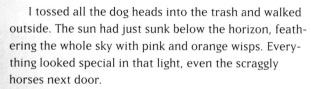

Stop and Think

Theme Review

How is the main character's problem resolved? USE STORY STRUCTURE

I tossed all the dog heads into the trash and walked outside. The sun had just sunk below the horizon, feathering the whole sky with pink and orange wisps. Everything looked special in that light, even the scraggly horses next door.

I dragged a lawn chair over to the fence and sat down to take a better look at them. They'd never be free spirits like Euphemia's horses, but they did seem patient and strong. I noticed the curves of their muscles, the shadows on their faces, the shine along their backs. Their colors reminded me of dessert—rich chocolate, deep cinnamon, creamy caramel.

I was just sitting there, feeling kind of dazzled by the unexpected beauty of it all, when I remembered the big box of pastels my grandmother had sent for my birthday.

"For Marisa," the card had said, "because she is such a bright and colorful person."

An idea began to take shape in my mind, and just then the cinnamon horse turned its head toward me and nodded three times. It was like a sign.

I hurried into the house, grabbed the pastels and some paper, and raced for the door.

"Whoa, there, Missy," my dad said. "What's the rush?"

"Gotta run," I explained. "The sun is going down!"

I choose a deep brown, pulling it across my paper in the shape of the chocolate horse. It came out right the first time, even the legs and ears! Drawing horses is easier when they're right there in front of you, and I'll say this for the ones next door—they hold their poses.

The sky is turning out just as I'd hoped, too; all the pinks and reds blending together like a strawberry parfait, and I love the way the caramel horse's mane is blowing, just barely, in the wind.

It doesn't look exactly like one of Euphemia's horses, of course. But I already know that when this drawing is finished, I'll be signing it *Marisa*.

149

READING-WRITING
CONNECTION

Lesson 6 ▶

Lesson 7 ▶

SELECTION TITLES	**Befiddled** Focus *and* Flying Solo	**S.O.R. Losers** Get in Gear with Safety
Comprehension Strategies	Monitor Comprehension: Reread	Monitor Comprehension: Reread
Focus Skills	Plot and Characters	Plot and Characters

Theme 2 Joining Forces

A Day in the Country, Anna Pugh

CONTENTS

Lesson 6

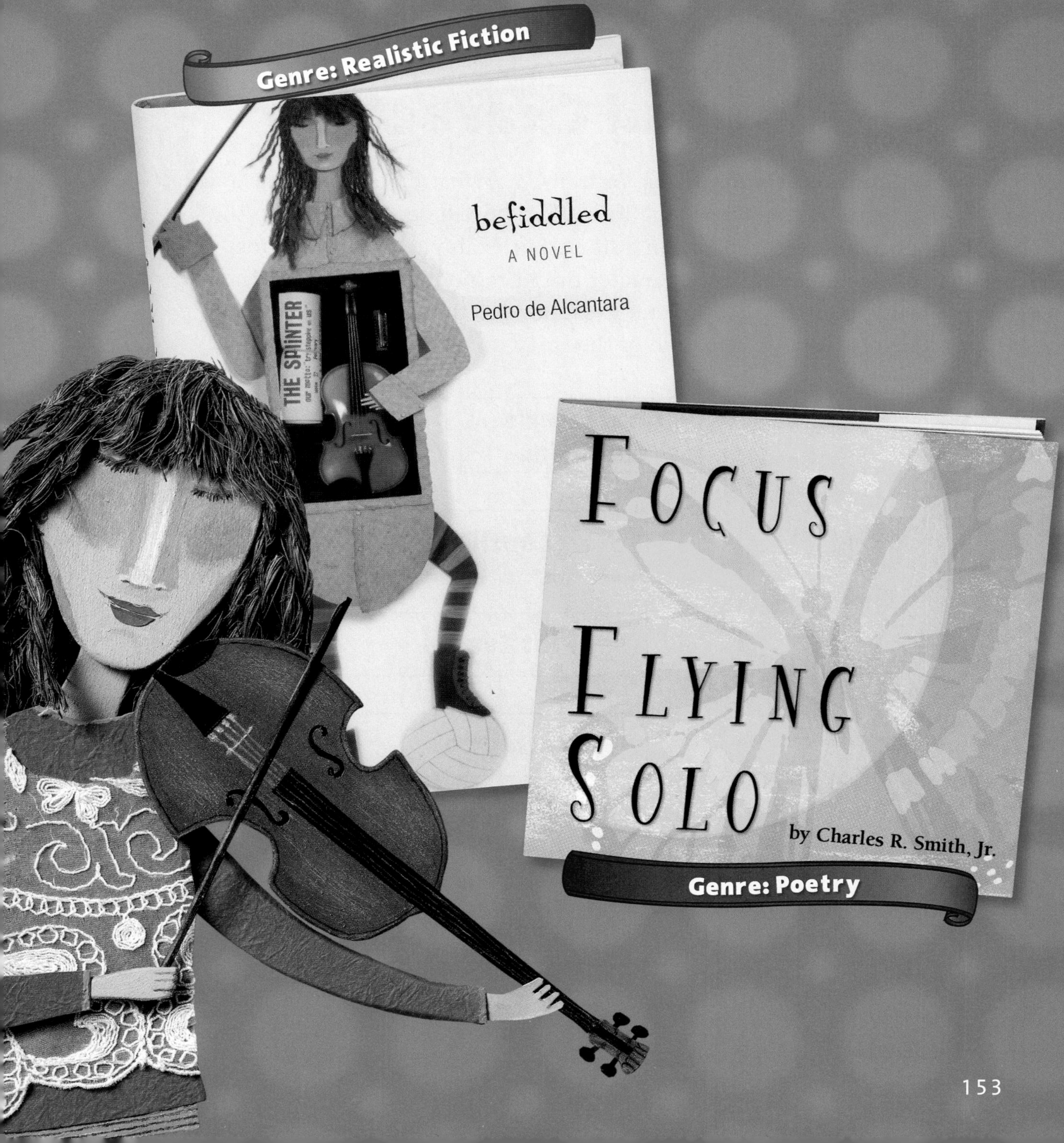
Genre: Realistic Fiction
befiddled
A NOVEL
Pedro de Alcantara
THE SPLINTER
Focus
Flying
Solo
by Charles R. Smith, Jr.
Genre: Poetry

Focus Skill

Plot and Characters

A **character's qualities**, or traits, are what he or she is like as a person. A character's qualities affect how he or she reacts to the **conflict**, or problem, in a story. For example, a hardworking character and a lazy character might respond differently to the same conflict. A character's reactions to the conflict affect the **resolution**, or outcome of the story.

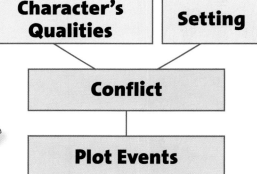

Character's Qualities	Setting

Conflict

Plot Events

Resolution

Tip

You can recognize a character's qualities through what the character thinks, does, and says.

Read the story below. Then look at the story map. It shows how Riva's traits affect the resolution of the conflict in the story.

Riva wanted more than anything to play the cello, but she was already playing violin in the school orchestra. She had faithfully practiced to develop her talent.

To help with her decision, Riva borrowed a friend's cello to try it out. She practiced playing notes and moving the large bow back and forth. She recognized the similarities and differences between playing violin and cello.

Finally, Riva made her decision. Never one to be discouraged by hard work, she decided to follow her heart and switch to the cello.

Character's Qualities

Riva is hardworking.

Setting

school

Conflict

Riva wants to switch from violin to cello but is worried about making changes.

Plot Events

1. Riva borrows a friend's cello.
2. She notices that the instruments have similarities and differences.

Resolution

Riva accepts the hard work of switching from violin to cello.

Try This!

What would the outcome be if the character's qualities were different? Imagine that Riva is not hardworking. Tell how this quality might affect the plot.

 www.harcourtschool.com/storytown

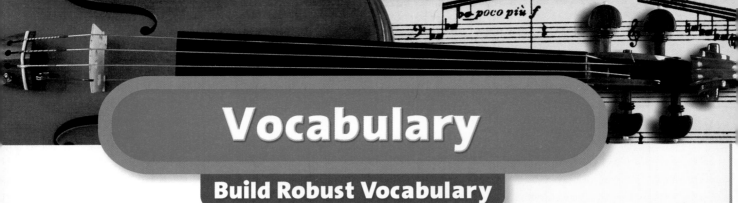

Vocabulary

Build Robust Vocabulary

- jest
- supple
- immobile
- sinuous
- intonation
- fused
- haywire

A Mixed-Up Dance

OCTOBER 16 Today our P.E. teacher announced that, starting tomorrow, modern dance will be part of P.E. class. "This will be interesting," I thought to myself in **jest**. I am not the modern dance type! Marty told me not to worry, but I did. I kept trying to picture myself leaping around like the **supple** dancers I've seen on TV. Not a chance, I concluded.

At home I stood **immobile** in front of the mirror. I did not see the **sinuous** body of a seasoned dancer. I saw average-looking, not-very-coordinated me. "How will I ever get through this?" I asked my reflection. He didn't answer.

I wondered what kind of music the teacher would play while we danced.

OCTOBER 17 Modern dance was not what I expected. The instructor asked us to form pairs and pretend we were a kitchen appliance. Marty and I chose to be a blender.

We didn't need any music at all. Marty made the high-pitched **intonation** of a blender mixing up smoothies. He became the base of the blender, **fused** to the floor. I played the blade. I spun around like a top that'd gone **haywire**. The experience was weird, but I have to admit it was fun. Modern dance might not be a total disaster after all.

Our first assignment in modern dance class was to mimic the sound and motion of a kitchen appliance.

 GO online www.harcourtschool.com/storytown

Word Champion

Your goal this week is to use the Vocabulary Words outside of your classroom. Write down the words, and tape the list to a mirror or another place at home where you will see it. Try to use each word at least once in conversation. For example, you might say to a friend, "I felt immobile before my performance!" In your vocabulary journal, write the words you use and tell how you used them.

Genre Study

Realistic fiction has characters and events that are like people and events in real life. As you read, look for

- a realistic setting.

- characters who face a problem.

Comprehension Strategy

Monitor comprehension as you read. Stop and **reread** parts of the story that you did not understand.

Befiddled

by Pedro de Alcantara
illustrated by Susan Farrington

Becky Cohen dreams of becoming a skilled violinist. She wants to enter a competition at a local performing arts school. However, her confidence is low because stage fright often spoils her performances. Then Becky meets Mr. Freeman, the new maintenance worker in her apartment building. With the approval of Becky's mother, Mr. Freeman offers to help Becky get over her fears and just enjoy the music. Becky's younger brother Benjy, a budding reporter who publishes his own newsletter, also agrees to help.

A few days after Becky met Mr. Freeman, she told her mother that he knew a lot about music and wanted to help her. At first Mrs. Cohen resisted the idea, but when Becky insisted, she relented. "At least it won't cost anything," she told Becky. "But make sure he only comes after you finish your homework."

Now it was the afternoon of their first lesson. There was a knock on the door. Benjy looked up from the newspaper he was reading and clipping, a three-week-old issue of the *Chicago Tribune* he had picked up goodness knows where. Becky put her notebook down. She had been pretending she was writing, but the pages were blank except for a treble clef doodled seventeen times.

"Come in."

Mr. Freeman entered the room. "You don't have to knock," Becky said with a smile.

"Thank you." Mr. Freeman smiled too.

Becky pointed to Benjy. "This is my little brother, boy genius of Sedgwick."

"What's your name?"

"Benjamin Samuel Cohen, sir!" Benjy trumpeted, in jest.

Mr. Freeman clicked his heels and saluted. "I'm Roy Freeman."

"Don't you have a middle name, soldier?" Benjy asked, doing his best to intimidate the newcomer.

Mr. Freeman's forehead wrinkled. He looked at Becky with eyes that said *Huh?*

Becky came to his rescue. "We'll give him a middle name, Benjy. Would you like that?"

"Yes." Benjy and Mr. Freeman spoke as one.

Becky laughed. "After my lesson," she added.

The wheels inside Benjy's reporter's brain started turning. "Can I stay and watch?" he asked.

"I don't mind," Mr. Freeman said.

Becky knew a thing or two about Benjy. "Only if you don't write anything nasty about us in the paper," she said.

"Nasty? Have I ever—"

"Have you ever!" she interrupted, smiling. "Of course you can stay."

Benjy put his newspaper away. Becky went into her bedroom and got out her violin in its case. On her way into the living room she whacked her shin against the coffee table and nearly dropped the fiddle. She ground her teeth and tightened her grip on the handle of the case. She was glad that her mother wasn't there to watch her being a klutz. At the same time, she was embarrassed that Mr. Freeman had witnessed her near disaster. "Sorry," she mumbled, addressing her remark to the coffee table.

All at once Mr. Freeman broke into a crazy dance. He swung his right leg over the back of the big armchair and shook his left arm willy-nilly near the mantelpiece, almost knocking over the vase Aunt Hannah had given Mrs. Cohen for her fortieth birthday. Then he shuffled his feet like a robot gone haywire, bunching the rug under his feet and sliding it up and down the floor in a messy bundle.

Becky's mouth dropped open, and her eyes widened to the size of a silver-dollar pancake. *The vase!* she wanted to scream. *The chair! The rug! The floor! My mother!* But not a peep would come out.

Benjy laughed and clapped. Mr. Freeman winked at him and laughed too. "Watch again." He repeated his demented jig, now in slow motion. He lifted his leg without losing his balance, as sinuous as an octopus underwater. He swung it ever so slowly over the big armchair, holding it midflight for what seemed to be a whole minute. At the same time he put his left arm way out, nearly touching Aunt Hannah's vase with his outstretched fingers, which he wiggled sleepily. He looked straight at Becky, his head and back immobile and yet supple, like a tall pine tree on a windless winter night. With his left arm suspended and motionless, Mr. Freeman put his right leg down and started shuffling his feet and bunching up the rug. His control was total.

Becky finally relaxed. She giggled and put her fiddle down on the coffee table. Mr. Freeman was a tree and a dancer and a robot and a snake charmer all fused together.

"If you aren't afraid of breaking the vase," he said, "you won't break it. But if you're stiff with fear, you might as well kiss the little fella good-bye. Here." In a flash he took the vase in his left hand and threw it to Becky. Surprised by his quick action, she raised her hands in front of her just as quickly. The vase landed in her soft palms, as safe as a baby in its mother's arms. Becky yelped.

"Please, Mr. Freeman, don't ever do that to me again," she gasped.

Benjy hollered. "Do it again, do it again!"

Mr. Freeman straightened the rug under his feet. "My friend, expect the worst from me." His eyes shone as he spoke. "Now get your fiddle out, and let's show Benjamin Samuel Cohen here what we can do."

She took her violin and tuned it, trembling half in excitement, half in fear. Mr. Freeman brought his harmonica to his mouth and played a simple C-major scale up and down once. Becky listened, gave herself time to breathe, and imitated him, her rhythm steady, her sound clear and even.

Mr. Freeman played a C-major arpeggio over two octaves, the notes rising and falling like one of Benjy's paper airplanes. Becky listened and sent up her own little glider.

"That was beautiful. But you don't need to bob your head when you play the arpeggio. It's the music that soars, not the musician." Mr. Freeman played his arpeggio again, moving up and down like a jack-in-the-box with a faulty spring.

Becky and Benjy both laughed. "All right, all right," Becky said, her cheeks flushing. "Let me try." She took another breath and played the arpeggio, doing her utmost not to move.

It was Mr. Freeman's turn to laugh. "You're trying a little too hard again. Come over here." Becky stood next to him. "Put your fist on the side of my left hip. Now lean on me as if you're trying to topple me over." Becky did as Mr. Freeman said, but he didn't move an inch. "More!" he demanded. Becky put her whole weight on him. The man was a rock. "Carry on." With Becky pressing against his body, he brought his knees in and out again and again, dancing an armless Charleston and playing his harmonica at the same time.

"You see," he said after finishing his tune, "you don't have to sway when you play, and you don't have to be rigid either. Easy and smooth like a sea lion swimming with the current, but

powerful and steady at the same time. Benjamin Samuel Cohen, drag your skinny behind here and be an anchor for your sister."

Benjy imitated the way Becky had pushed against Mr. Freeman. He stood next to her, placed his hand against her hip, and leaned on her. Becky firmed up her back and legs, then brought her violin up under her chin. Mr. Freeman played the first few notes of "The Star-Spangled Banner," and Becky joined him in midtune. As they played, Mr. Freeman marched in place, and Becky, still anchored by Benjy's pressure, bent and unbent her knees in rhythm with Mr. Freeman, without letting her fiddle sway under her chin.

"There you are," Mr. Freeman said. "You're moving without moving, neither stiff nor wobbly. Now we can make some music."

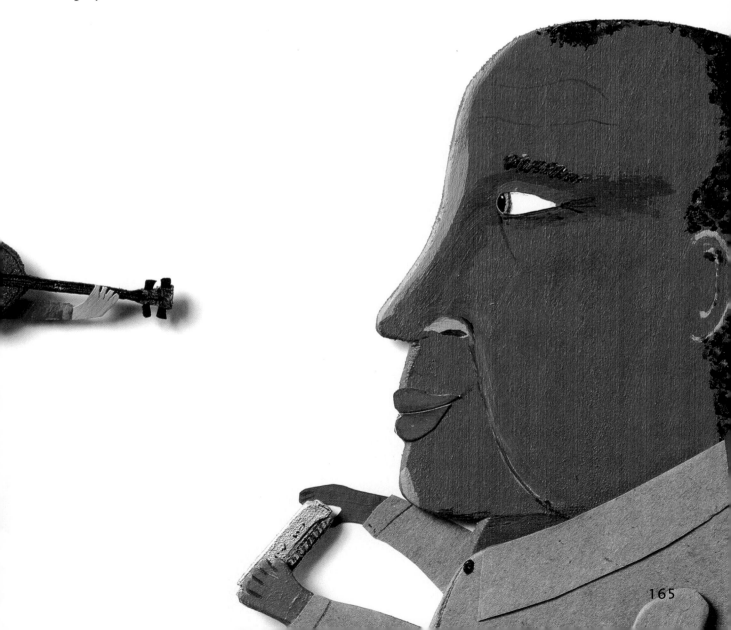

Benjy went back to his seat. Becky stayed in place as Mr. Freeman played Beethoven's "Ode to Joy." When Becky joined him, he switched over to the bass line. They finished together and Benjy clapped. "Encore! Encore!" he clamored.

"Now for something different. I'll play the first half of a tune you don't know, and you'll have to finish it on your own."

"How can you be so sure I won't know this tune of yours?" Becky asked with a haughty grin, her chin raised.

"Because I'm making it up on the spot," Mr. Freeman replied with a snap of his fingers.

"Uh-oh."

Mr. Freeman played his made-up tune. It was nothing like Beethoven or Bach or Schubert or anybody else. Becky didn't know what to make of it, and just stood there. "I can't think of anything to play."

"You're afraid of dropping the vase," Mr. Freeman said with a soft smile. "Nobody's watching. Drop it right down, and if it breaks we'll pick up the pieces together."

Becky understood. Mr. Freeman played a different made-up melody, and Becky replied with her own made-up tune on the fiddle. Her intonation swerved between too sharp and too flat, and her rhythm tottered like a man with a wooden leg. But she wasn't afraid or embarrassed anymore.

"Did the vase break?"

Becky giggled. "I guess not."

"Let's do it again, then."

And so they did, Mr. Freeman throwing his crazy tunes at Becky, Becky replying with all she had. Song after song, now elegant and witty in the style of Mozart and Haydn, now jazzy and folksy, like a yodeler from the Alps or like a preacher in a church, Mr. Freeman would sound his call and Becky would respond with hers, two nightingales in a dialogue of music and joy.

"Well done, well done," Mr. Freeman said after they had worked and played for more than an hour. He took an envelope out of his back pocket. "That competition you told me about the other day? I went over to the school and got some forms for you." He handed the envelope to Becky. "Your mother will have to sign them."

Becky did all she could to prevent herself from jumping out of her skin. "Thank you," she said, her head overflowing with the delicious noises of the afternoon and the challenge of the competition.

Think Critically

① During his visit with Becky, how does Mr. Freeman show that he is a unique person and a talented performer? NOTE DETAILS

② Describe what Becky is like before she finishes her lesson with Mr. Freeman. How does she change from the beginning of the story to the end of the story? PLOT AND CHARACTERS

③ When Mr. Freeman uses the vase with Becky, what lesson does he want her to learn? DRAW CONCLUSIONS

④ Becky plays music, and Benjy writes articles. What other kinds of creative expression can you think of? Make a list. USE PRIOR KNOWLEDGE

⑤ **WRITE** Describe two of Mr. Freeman's character traits. Explain how his traits affect the resolution of the story. Use evidence from the story to support your ideas. SHORT RESPONSE

About the Author

Pedro de Alcantara

Pedro de Alcantara's first love was the cello, but over time he has become a multitalented musician. He was born and raised in Brazil, and he now lives in Paris. He speaks Portuguese, English, and French. Pedro de Alcantara travels around the world, teaching the Alexander Technique, a special method that improves the way people move and think in everyday activities. *Befiddled* is his first children's book.

About the Illustrator

Susan Farrington

Susan Farrington has always enjoyed making things. As a professional illustrator, she loves the feeling of walking into a studio with an idea and then bringing it to life. Susan Farrington creates her eclectic and whimsical illustrations out of wood, paint, cutout letters, and other objects she finds lying around. She lives with her husband and their two children in Needham, Massachusetts.

GO online www.harcourtschool.com/storytown

FOCUS

Feet apart
arms at sides
chest puffed out
head held high

w a i t i n g

to release butterflies
inside.

Eyes focus
like
the calm
before the storm
ready to erupt
before I perform
toes tingle
feet quake
muscles twitch

hands shake
while
throat hums
hummmmmmms
hummmmmmmmmmmmmmmmmms
so that
my voice may
awake.
Focus
I must
focus
to channel my
electricity
and relax

r e l a x
r e l a x
before I set
the butterflies
free.

—CHARLES R. SMITH, JR.

FLYING SOLO

All eyes on me
I part the
sea
of harmony
setting butterflies
free
crooning
honey-drenched notes
in my
sweet
alto key.
Center stage
I engage
ears
with emotion
not found
on a page.

Heartstrings
I pluck
and tug
with conviction,
using attitude,
feeling,
presence, and
diction.
Stepping to the
front
with confidence,
talent,
and soul

flying solo
has always been
my goal.

—CHARLES R. SMITH, JR.

Connections

Comparing Texts

1. If you were a performer, would you rather perform solo or as part of a group? Why?

2. Think about the messages in the poems "Focus" and "Flying Solo." Which poem do you think Becky should read before a big performance? Explain.

3. Becky wants to enter a competition at a performing arts school. What kinds of careers might performing arts students pursue?

Vocabulary Review

Word Webs

Choose two Vocabulary Words. Create a word web for each word. In the web's outer ovals, write words and phrases that are related to the Vocabulary Word written in the center oval. Share your word webs with your partner, explaining how each word or phrase is related to the Vocabulary Word in the center.

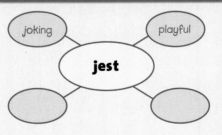

joking playful

jest

jest

supple

immobile

sinuous

intonation

fused

haywire

Fluency Practice

Repeated Reading

When you read, your voice goes up and down in pitch. This is called intonation. Intonation shows the mood of the text and the feelings of the characters. Work with a partner. Read aloud the scene from "Befiddled" starting on page 160 with *Becky pointed to Benjy* and ending with *Of course you can stay.* Have your partner give you feedback on your intonation. Then switch roles. Read the passage a second time, working to improve your intonation.

Writing

Write a Narrative

Imagine that Becky's brother Benjy decides to write a story about Mr. Freeman for his school newspaper. Write the beginning of the story Benjy might write.

Character's Qualities — **Setting**

Conflict

Plot Events

Resolution

My Writing Checklist

Writing Trait ➤ Ideas

✔ I used a story map to plan my writing.

✔ My story is focused and contains original ideas.

✔ I included dialogue and interesting descriptions.

Reading-Writing Connection

Analyze a Narrative: Response to Literature

A **response to literature** shows your understanding of a story you have read. Before you write a response to literature, ask yourself questions about the characters and events in the story. **Form opinions** about the story and its message, and think about how it **connects to your life.**

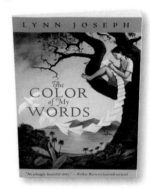

Read the passage below from "The Color of My Words." Think about the questions in the boxes.

FORM OPINIONS
What is your opinion about the way the villagers try to stop Ana Rosa from doing an important job?

Then Mami, who was usually quiet during these kinds of discussions, spoke up loud and clear. "Ana Rosa would be the best person to write a story about the sea monster."

I was shocked. This wasn't the same Mami who worshiped silence.

People began to shake their heads. "A child do something so important?" they whispered.

CONNECT TO YOUR LIFE Ana Rosa's mother gives her a chance to do an important job. How do you feel when someone encourages you to try something new or difficult?

"Yes," said Mami. "Let us give her a notebook to write in and she will write us a story about the sea monster. If we don't like it, someone else can try."

Response to Literature

A student named David wrote a response to "The Color of My Words." Read his response. Think about how you can use David's writing as a model for writing your own response to literature.

My Response to "The Color of My Words"
by David Y.

In this story, Ana Rosa learns how important it is to have someone who believes in her. Ana Rosa wants to be a writer. When a huge "sea monster" appears near her village, the people want someone to write a story about it. They don't want Ana Rosa to do it, because she is only a child. Ana Rosa's mother tells the villagers to give her daughter a chance. Ana Rosa writes a beautiful story, and all the people are amazed.

VOICE David's unique voice comes through because he states his **opinion** of Ana Rosa's mother. He also **connects** the story **to his life**.

IDEAS In this paragraph, David **analyzes the characters** in the story. The details that he includes relate to his **central message**.

In the conclusion, David **sums up** the **main ideas** in his response. He **restates** what the characters learned.

I think Ana Rosa's mother is brave to speak up. She is usually silent. When she tells the people to give Ana Rosa a chance, she is "definite and firm." I think she wants the villagers to know how smart her daughter is. My older brother spoke up for me once. When his friends wouldn't let me play basketball with them, he told them I was better than most kids my age. He persuaded them to give me a chance, and I proved him right.

In this story, Ana Rosa's older brother Guario is the opposite of Ana Rosa. He works hard and thinks about the future. Ana Rosa just dreams. She doesn't tell Guario about wanting to be a writer, because she thinks he would call her "unreasonable." But when she reads her story to the village, Guario is proud of her. He promises to buy her a new notebook every month.

Because her mother and brother believe in her, Ana Rosa gets the chance to be a writer. Ana Rosa learns that you can make your dreams come true. It helps when other people believe in you.

Now look at how David prepared his response to literature.

Summarize

First, he used a story map to help him write a **summary of events**.

Characters	Setting
Ana Rosa and her family	a village in the Dominican Republic

Plot Events

- The villagers see a "sea monster." They want someone to write a story about it.
- Ana Rosa's mother tells the villagers to let Ana Rosa write the story.
- Ana Rosa reads the story to the people.

Form Opinions and Make Connections

As David read the story, he formed opinions about the characters and events. He used note cards to write characters' exact words to support his opinions. He made notes about how the story connected to his life and what the main character learned.

What is my opinion of the characters and events?
Ana Rosa's mother is brave to speak up. She is "definite and firm."

How does this connect to my life?
My brother persuaded his friends to let me play basketball.

What did the main character learn?
Ana Rosa learns that she can achieve her dream of becoming a writer.

Organize Information

Then David made a list to organize all the parts of his response. This list shows what David planned to include in each paragraph.

1. Summarize the events.
2. State my opinions, connect to my life.
3. Compare Ana Rosa and Guario.
4. Tell what the main character learned.

CONTENTS

Lesson 7

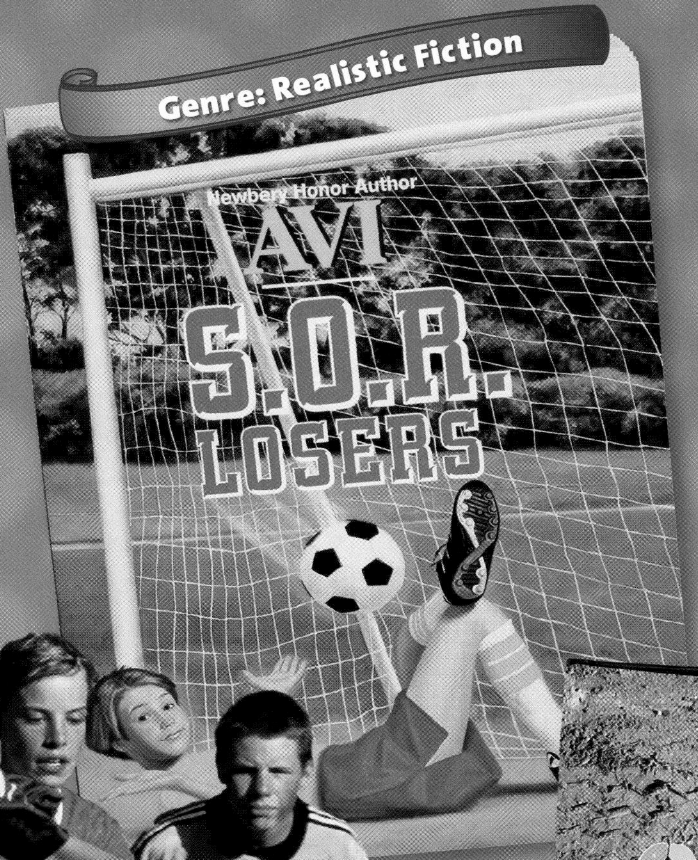

Genre: Realistic Fiction

Newbery Honor Author
AVI
S.O.R. LOSERS

GET IN GEAR WITH SAFETY

BY TRACY EARLY

Genre: Persuasive Article

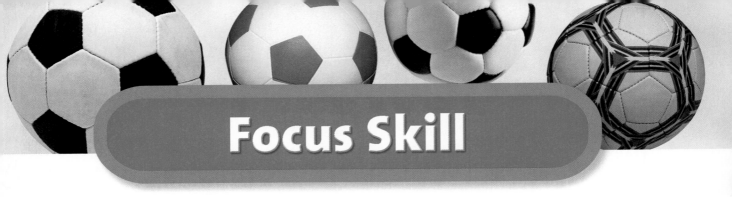

Focus Skill

 Plot and Characters

Conflict is the struggle or problem that characters face in a story. Conflict can occur

- within a character's own mind.
- between two or more characters.
- between a character and an outside force.

   Characters' qualities help determine how characters react to conflict. As you read a story, identify the characters' qualities through what they think, how they act, and what they say. Then think about how the characters' qualities affect the **resolution**, or outcome of the story.

Character's Qualities	Setting

Conflict

Plot Events

Resolution

Tip

Ask yourself how the qualities of the main character affect the way story events unfold.

Read the story below. Then look at the story map. Vince's conflict is that a camping trip and his track meet are scheduled for the same weekend. Because Vince is reliable, he decides to stay and compete in the track meet.

Vince had just qualified for the track meet on the weekend. In a bitter twist of fate, his youth group had scheduled its camping trip for the same weekend. Vince was a dedicated team member, but he didn't want to miss camping with his friends. Reluctantly, Vince decided to stay and compete— his team was counting on him. When he won his race, he was happy he had made the right choice.

Character's Qualities	**Setting**
Vince is reliable.	a track meet

Conflict

Vince's youth group plans a camping trip on the same weekend as his track meet.

Plot Events

- Vince must decide between the camping trip and the track meet.
- Vince doesn't want to let down his team, but he also wants to camp.

Resolution

Vince chooses the track meet and wins the race.

Try This!

Imagine that Vince is unreliable instead of reliable. How might this affect the plot of the story?

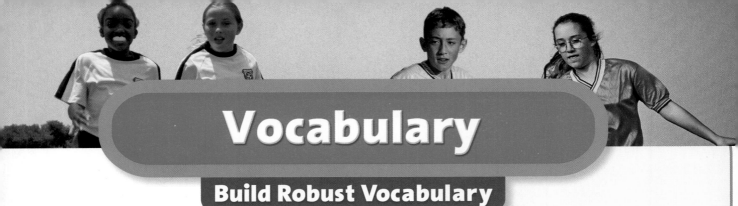

Vocabulary

Build Robust Vocabulary

ordinary

suit

treason

convince

rejected

disown

defeatist

The Society of Rollers

We were no **ordinary** sports league. We were the Society of Rollers. It didn't matter to us that we were the only *boules* (BOOLZ) league around. In fact, we were proud of our uncommon sport. We played it whenever and wherever we could.

Boules is a French game. Players toss a fist-sized metal ball so it lands as close as possible to a little wooden ball. Boules is the perfect game for us, since it requires no special athletic skill. We even changed the rules a little to **suit** ourselves.

Some may say we have committed **treason** by changing the rules, but we have fun with our own boules rules.

One day, a French exchange student named Jaqueline came to study at our school. We tried to **convince** her that she should play boules with us, but she would not hear of it. We couldn't understand why she **rejected** our offer. Wouldn't her country **disown** anyone who didn't play boules?

Jaqueline explained it this way: "*Mes amis*, my friends," she began. "I am not very . . . *athletique*. I would only help you lose." We decided to reverse her **defeatist** attitude. We'd teach her boules our way, the Rollers way! At last, Jaqueline agreed. By the end of the week, our league had gained a quickly improving new member.

Jaqueline, a French exchange student, is our league's newest member. I wonder what her parents will say when she calls to tell them what she learned in the States!

GO online www.harcourtschool.com/storytown

Word Scribe

Your challenge this week is to use the Vocabulary Words in writing. Each day, use one or two of the words in a sentence about your activities that day. For example, you might write a sentence about an invitation you rejected. Write the sentences in your vocabulary journal, and share them with your classmates.

Realistic Fiction

Genre Study

Realistic fiction has characters and events that are like people and events in real life. As you read, look for

- a plot with a beginning, middle, and end.

- characters who face a problem.

Comprehension Strategy

Monitor comprehension as you read. Stop and **reread** parts of the story that you do not understand.

184

"Everybody plays. Everybody wins." Most everyone at South Orange River School takes this motto seriously. However, Ed Sitrow and a small group of non-jocks prefer to avoid sports altogether. The school has organized a special soccer team just for them, and their first five games have been embarrassing losses. The boys' coach, Mr. Lester, and the school counselor, Mr. Tillman, try everything to motivate the team. The school has even held a pep rally to pump up the boys for their last game. Ed, the team's captain, decides it's time to call a secret meeting.

by Avi
illustrated by Aaron Jasinski

Like thieves, we met behind the school, out of sight. I looked around. I could see everybody was feeling rotten.

"I'm sick and tired of people telling me we have to win," said Root.

"I think my folks are getting ready to disown me," said Hays. "My brother and sister too."

"Why can't they just let us lose?" asked Macht.

"Yeah," said Barish, "because we're not going to win."

"We might," Lifsom offered. "Parkville is supposed to be the pits too."

"Yeah," said Radosh, "but we're beneath the pits."

"Right," agreed Porter.

For a moment it looked like everyone was going to start to cry.

"I'd just like to do my math," said Macht. "I like that."

There it was. Something clicked. "Hays," I said, "you're good at music, right."

"Yeah, well, sure—rock 'n' roll."

"Okay. And Macht, what's the lowest score you've pulled in math so far?"

"A-plus."

"Last year?"

"Same."

"Lifsom," I went on, getting excited, "how's your painting coming?"

"I just finished something real neat and . . ."

"That's it," I cut in, because that kid can go on forever about his painting. "Every one of us is good at something. Right? Maybe more than one thing. The point is, *other* things."

"Sure," said Barish.

"Except," put in Saltz, "sports."

We were quiet for a moment. Then I saw what had been coming to me: "That's *their* problem. I mean, we are good, good at *lots* of things. Why can't we just plain stink in some places? That's got to be normal."

"Let's hear it for normal," chanted Dorman.

"Doesn't bother me to lose at sports," I said. "At least, it didn't bother me until I let other people make me bothered."

"What about the school record?" asked Porter. "You know, no team ever losing for a whole season. Want to be famous for that?"

"Listen," I said, "did we want to be on this team?"

"No!" they all shouted.

"I can see some of it," I said. "You know, doing something different. But I don't like sports. I'm not good at it. I don't enjoy it. So I say, so what? I mean if Saltz here writes a stinko poem—and he does all the time—do they yell at him? When was the last time Mr. Tillman came around and said, 'Saltz, I *believe* in your being a poet!'"

"Never," said Saltz.

"Yeah," said Radosh. "How come sports is so important?"

"You know," said Dorman, "maybe a loser makes people think of things *they* lost. Like Mr. Tillman not getting into pro football. Us losing makes him remember that."

"Us winning, he forgets," cut in Eliscue.

"Right," I agreed. "He needs us to win for *him*, not for us. Maybe it's the same for others."

"Yeah, but how are you going to convince them of that?" said Barish.

"By not caring if we lose," I said.

"Only one thing," put in Saltz. "They say this Parkville team is pretty bad too. What happens if we, you know, by mistake, win?"

That set us back for a moment.

"I think," suggested Hays after a moment, "that if we just go on out there, relax, and do our best, and not worry so much, we'll lose."

There was general agreement on that point.

"Do you know what I heard?" said Eliscue.

"What?"

"I didn't want to say it before, but since the game's a home game, they're talking about letting the whole school out to cheer us on to a win."

"You're kidding."

He shook his head.

There was a long, deep silence.

"Probably think," said Saltz, "that we'd be ashamed to lose in front of everybody."

I took a quick count. "You afraid to lose?" I asked Saltz.

"No way."

"Hays?"

"No."

"Porter?"

"Nope."

And so on. I felt encouraged. It was a complete vote of no confidence.

"Well," I said, "they just might see us lose again. With Parkville so bad I'm not saying it's automatic. But I'm not going to care if we do."

"Right," said Radosh. "It's not like we're committing treason or something. People have a right to be losers."

We considered that for a moment. It was then I had my most brilliant idea. "Who has money?"

"What for?"

"I'm your tall captain, right? Trust me. And bring your soccer T-shirts to me in the morning, early."

I collected about four bucks and we split up. I held Saltz back.

"What's the money all about?" he wanted to know. "And the T-shirts."

"Come on," I told him. "Maybe we can show them we really mean it."

W hen I woke the next morning, I have to admit, I was excited. It wasn't going to be an ordinary day. I looked outside and saw the sun was shining. I thought, "Good."

For the first time I *wanted* a game to happen.

I got to breakfast a little early, actually feeling happy.

"Today's the day," Dad announced.

"Right."

"Today you'll really win," chipped in my ma.

"Could be."

My father leaned across the table and gave me a tap. "Winning the last game is what matters. Go out with your head high, Ed."

"And my backside up if I lose?" I wanted to know.

"Ed," said my ma, "don't be so hard on yourself. Your father and I are coming to watch."

"Suit yourselves," I said, and beat it to the bus.

189

As soon as I got to class Saltz and I collected the T-shirts. "What are you going to do with them?" the others kept asking.

"You picked me as captain, didn't you?"

"Mr. Lester did."

"Well, this time, trust *me*."

When we got all the shirts, Saltz and I sneaked into the home ec room and did what needed to be done. Putting them into a bag so no one would see, we went back to class.

"Just about over," I said.

"I'm almost sorry," confessed Saltz.

"Me too," I said. "And I can't figure out why."

"Maybe it's—the team that loses together, really stays together."

"Right. Not one fathead on the whole team. Do you think we should have gotten a farewell present for Mr. Lester?"

"Like what?"

"A begging cup."

It was hard getting through the day. And it's impossible to know how many people wished me luck. From all I got it was clear they considered me the unluckiest guy in the whole world. I kept wishing I could have banked it for something important.

But the day got done.

It was down in the locker room, when we got ready, that I passed out the T-shirts.

Barish held his up. It was the regular shirt with "S.O.R." on the back. But under it Saltz and I had ironed on press letters. Now they all read:

S.O.R. LOSERS

Barish's reaction was just to stare. That was my only nervous moment. Then he cracked up, laughing like crazy. And the rest, once they saw, joined in. When Mr. Lester came down he brought Mr. Tillman. We all stood up and turned our backs to them.

"Oh, my goodness," moaned Mr. Lester.

"That's sick," said Mr. Tillman. "Sick!" His happy beads shook furiously.

"It's honest," I said.

"It's defeatist," he yelled.

"Mr. Tillman," I asked, "is that true, about your trying out for pro football?"

He started to say something, then stopped, his mouth open. "Yeah. I tried to make it with the pros, but couldn't."

"So you lost too, right?"

"Yeah," chimed in Radosh, "everyone loses sometime."

"Listen here, you guys," said Mr. Tillman, "it's no fun being rejected."

"Can't it be okay to lose sometimes? You did. Lots do. You're still alive. And we don't dislike you because of that."

"Right. We got other reasons," I heard a voice say. I think it was Saltz.

Mr. Tillman started to say something, but turned and fled.

Mr. Lester tried to give us a few final pointers, like don't touch the ball with our hands, only use feet, things that we didn't always remember to do.

"Well," he said finally, "I enjoyed this."

"You did?" said Porter, surprised.

"Well, not much," he admitted. "I never coached anything before. To tell the truth, I don't know anything about soccer."

"Now you tell us," said Eliscue. But he was kidding. We sort of guessed that before.

Just as we started out onto the field, Saltz whispered to me, "What if we win?"

"With our luck, we will," I said.

And on we went.

As we ran onto the field we were met with something like a roar. Maybe the whole school wasn't there. But a lot were. And they were chanting, "Win! Win! Win!"

But when they saw the backs of our shirts, they really went wild. Crazy. And you couldn't tell if they were for us or against us. I mean scary . . .

Oh yes, the game . . .

We had been told that Parkville was a team that hadn't won a game either. They looked it. From the way they kicked the ball around—tried to kick the ball around—it was clear this was going to be a true contest between horribles.

The big difference was their faces. Stiff and tight. You could see, they *wanted* to win. Had to win. We were relaxed and fooling around. Having a grand old time.

Not them.

The ref blew his whistle and called for captains. I went out, shook hands. The Parkville guy was really tense. He kept squeezing his hands, rubbing his face. The whole bit.

The ref said he wanted the usual, a clean, hard game, and he told us which side we should defend. "May the best team win," he said. A believer!

Anyway, we started.

(I know the way this is supposed to work . . . There we are, relaxed, having a good time, not caring really what goes on, maybe by this time, not even sweating the outcome. That should make us, in television land—winners. Especially as it becomes very clear that Parkville is frantic about winning. Like crazy. They have a coach who screams himself red-faced all the time. Who knows. Maybe he's going to lose his job if they lose.)

Well . . .

A lot of things happened that game. There was the moment, just like the first game, when their side, dressed in stunning scarlet, came plunging down our way. Mighty Saltz went out to meet them like a battleship. True to form (red face and wild) he gave a mighty kick, and missed. But he added something new. Leave it to my buddy Saltz. He swung so hard he sat down, sat down on the ball. Like he was hatching an egg.

We broke up at that. So did everyone else. Except the Parkville coach. He was screaming, "Penalty! Penalty!"

So they got the ball. And, it's true, I was laughing so much they scored an easy goal. It was worth it.

"Least you could have done is hatched it," I yelled at Saltz.

"I think they allow only eleven on a team," he yelled back.

Then there was the moment when Porter, Radosh and Dorman got into a really terrific struggle to get the ball—from each other. Only when they looked up did they realize with whom they were struggling. By that time, of course, it was too late. Stolen ball.

There was the moment when Parkville knocked the ball out of bounds. Macht had to throw it in. He snatched up the ball, held it over his head, got ready to heave it, then—dropped it.

It was a close game though. The closest. By the time it was almost over they were leading by only one. We were actually in the game.

And how did the crowd react? They didn't know what to do. Sometimes they laughed. Sometimes they chanted that "Win! Win!" thing. It was like a party for them.

Then it happened . . .

Macht took the ball on a pass from Lifsom. Lifsom dribbled down the right side and flipped it toward the middle. Hays got it fairly well, and, still driving, shot a pass back to Radosh, who somehow managed to snap it easy over to Porter, who was right near the side of the goal.

Porter, not able to shoot, knocked the ball back to Hays, who charged toward the goal—only some Parkville guy managed to get in the way. Hays, screaming, ran right over him, still controlling the ball.

I stood there, astonished. "They've gotten to him," I said to myself. "He's flipped."

I mean, Hays was like a wild man. Not only had he the cleanest shot in the universe, he was desperate.

And so . . . he tripped. Fell flat on his face. Thunk!

Their goalie scooped up the ball, flung it downfield and that was the end of that.

As for Hays, he picked himself up, slowly, too slowly.

The crowd grew still.

You could see it all over Hays. Shame. The crowd waited. They were feeling sorry for him. You could feel it. And standing there in the middle of the field—everything had just stopped—everybody was watching Hays—the poor guy began to cry.

That's all you could hear. His sobs. He had failed.
Then I remembered. "SOR LOSER!" I bellowed.
At my yell, our team snapped up their heads and
looked around.
"SOR LOSER!" I bellowed again.

The team picked up the words and began to run toward Hays, yelling, cheering, screaming, "SOR LOSER! SOR LOSER! SOR LOSER!"

Hays, stunned, began to get his eyes up.

Meanwhile, the whole team, and I'm not kidding, joined hands and began to run in circles around Hays, still giving the chant.

The watching crowd, trying to figure out what was happening, finally began to understand. And they began to cheer!

"SOR LOSER
SOR LOSER
SOR LOSER!"

As for Hays, well, you should have seen his face. It was like a nature-film flower blooming. Slow, but steady. Fantastic! There grew this great grin on his face. Then he lifted his arms in victory and he too began to cheer. He had won—himself.

Right about then the horn blared. The game was over. The season was done. Losers again. Champions of the bloody bottom.

We hugged each other, screamed and hooted like teams do when they win championships. And we were a lot happier than those Parkville guys who had won.

In the locker room we started to take off our uniforms. Mr. Lester broke in.

"Wait a minute," he announced. "Team picture."

We trooped out again, lining up, arm in arm, our *backs* to the camera. We were having fun!

"English test tomorrow," said Saltz as he and I headed for home. "I haven't studied yet. I'll be up half the night."

"Don't worry," I said. "For *that*, I believe in you."

"You know what?" he said. "So do I."

And he did. Aced it. *Our* way.

THINK CRITICALLY

1 What is the biggest difference between the South Orange River team and the Parkville team? COMPARE AND CONTRAST

2 How does the narrator's resourcefulness affect the conflict and resolution of the plot? PLOT AND CHARACTERS

3 Are the characters and plot in this story believable? Explain. PERSONAL RESPONSE

4 How does the author seem to feel about people who focus strongly on winning? AUTHOR'S VIEWPOINT

5 **WRITE** Write a team slogan or motto for the S.O.R. team. Then write a brief explanation of why this motto is appropriate. SHORT RESPONSE

ABOUT THE AUTHOR

Avi

Avi says that when he was in school, writing became important to him because it was very important to his family, friends, and school. He had dysgraphia, a condition that caused him to reverse letters and misspell words, so he had to work very hard to learn to write and spell. He did work hard, certain that he would become a writer.

Now Avi is an accomplished author and the recipient of numerous awards for his books, including the Newbery Medal. When asked whether he has any advice for people who want to write, he says, "I believe reading is the key to writing. The more you read, the better your writing can be."

ABOUT THE ILLUSTRATOR

Aaron Jasinski

Aaron Jasinski is an artist and a designer. He considers himself a figurative artist, meaning that he likes to create expressive poses and interesting faces. He enjoys working in oil paints and ink and working with images on a computer. He has shown his artwork in galleries in the United States and France. Aaron Jasinski also writes electronic music. He lives in Seattle, Washington.

 www.harcourtschool.com/storytown

Get in Gear with Safety
BY TRACY EARLY

Persuasive Article

GET IN GEAR WITH SAFETY

BY TRACY EARLY

WHICH GEAR IS RIGHT?

All sports involve moving your body and using equipment in order to play. Many times they involve coming into contact with another person or object that is hard. Whether it's your feet, hands, or head that takes the pressure, there is a way to protect yourself.

GET YOUR HEAD IN GEAR

Don't lose your head! Protect it. There are many sports that require a helmet: football, baseball, and ice hockey, for example. But the following sports are also becoming required helmet sports in many states: horseback riding, bicycling, skateboarding, roller blading, skiing, and snowboarding.

FOOTBALL

Each sport has its own type of helmet. However, Randy Swart, director of the Bicycle Helmet Safety Institute in Arlington, Virginia, states that "wearing a helmet not designed for your sport is better than a bare head. It's just not ideal." If you have had a collision while wearing your helmet, you may need to replace it.

BICYCLING

The National Safety Council suggests you remember the four S's when buying a helmet:

- **SIZE:** Try on several, and buy one that is snug but not tight.
- **STRAP:** Make sure the strap fits snugly under your chin and the "V" in the straps meets under the ear.
- **STRAIGHT:** Wear the helmet low on the forehead.
- **STICKER:** Look for a sticker citing the U.S. Consumer Product Safety Commission standard, Snell certification, or the Safety Equipment Institute.

SKATEBOARDING

Other safety gear may include shin guards, padding, gloves, eye protectors, and mouthpieces. Ask your coach what you need to protect yourself while playing.

HORSEBACK RIDING

Connections

Comparing Texts

1. Did reading "S.O.R. Losers" change your attitude about the importance of sports at school? Explain.

2. Apply the ideas in "Get in Gear with Safety" to the events in "S.O.R. Losers." Are the S.O.R. team members properly protected for their sport? What additional safety gear might be helpful?

3. Ed Sitrow and his friends conclude that most people value athletic ability more than they value other kinds of talent. Does your own experience support this conclusion? Explain.

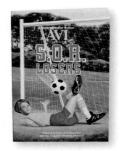

Vocabulary Review

I rejected the urge to be defeatist.

Word Pairs

Work with a partner to write the Vocabulary Words on separate index cards. Place the cards face down in two piles. Take turns picking up a card from each pile and writing a sentence that uses both words. Read your sentences aloud to your partner. If you have used both words correctly, keep the cards. If not, return them to the bottom of the piles. Continue until all the words have been used correctly. The player with more cards wins.

ordinary

suit

treason

convince

rejected

disown

defeatist

Fluency Practice

Partner Reading

You have learned that intonation is the rise and fall of your voice as you read a passage aloud. Work with a partner to reread a portion of "S.O.R. Losers" aloud. Each of you should choose four to six paragraphs. Take turns reading the passage aloud as your partner listens. Ask for feedback about your intonation. Then read the passage again, keeping your partner's comments in mind. Switch roles and repeat the process.

Writing

Write a New Ending

Imagine that the South Orange River team wins the game. Write a new ending to the story.

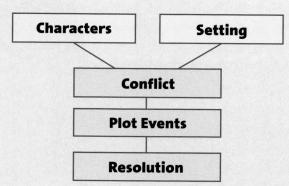

My Writing Checklist

Writing Trait ➤ Ideas

✔ I used a story map to plan my writing.

✔ My ideas support the characters' attitudes toward winning.

✔ The ending I wrote resolves the conflict of the story.

CONTENTS

Lesson 8

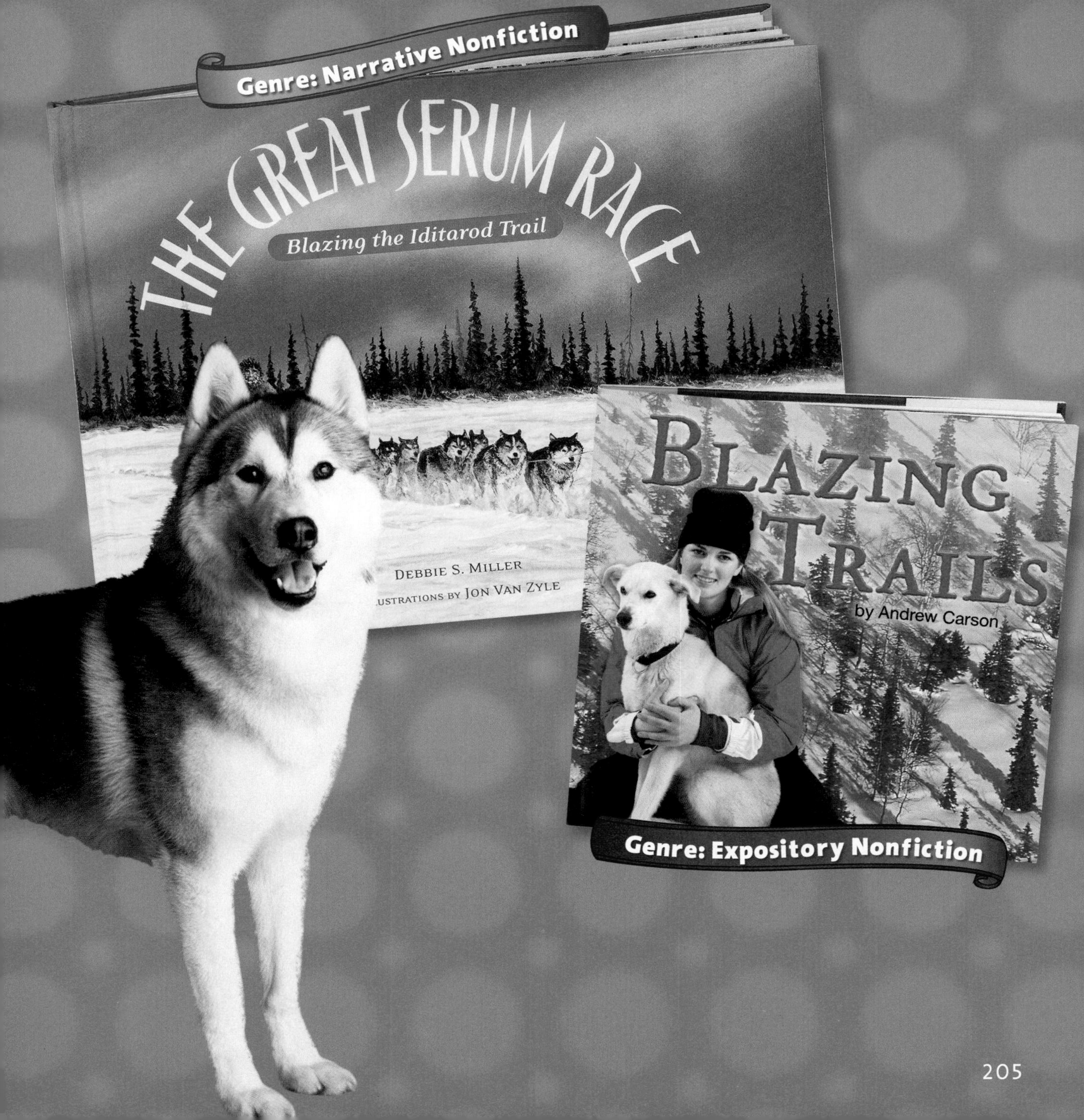
Genre: Narrative Nonfiction
THE GREAT SERUM RACE
Blazing the Iditarod Trail
DEBBIE S. MILLER
USTRATIONS BY JON VAN ZYLE
BLAZING TRAILS
by Andrew Carson
Genre: Expository Nonfiction

Main Idea and Details

The **main idea** is the most important idea in a paragraph, a passage, or a selection. **Supporting details** are facts or examples that explain or support the main idea.

- Sometimes the main idea is easy to find. It is **stated** in a topic sentence or somewhere else in a paragraph.
- Other times the main idea is **implied**, or suggested. You can identify the main idea from the details in the text.

Recognizing the main idea and the details that support it will help you better understand what you read. It will also help you make connections to ideas in other selections you have read.

Detail	Detail	Detail

Main Idea

Tip

To find the main idea, read the whole paragraph or passage. Ask yourself: What is this mostly about?

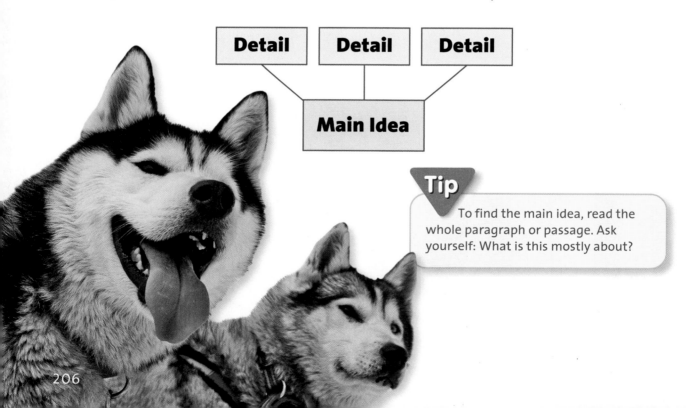

Read the paragraph. Then look at the graphic organizer below. It shows three details that support the main idea.

Dogs were the first animals to become domesticated. The relationship between dogs and their owners benefits both parties. People love and care for their dogs. In return, dogs provide affection, loyalty, and companionship. When there is danger, however, the roles can change. It may be the dog that finds a missing child, warns a family of fire, or leads a lost hiker to safety.

Detail	**Detail**	**Detail**
People love and care for their dogs.	Dogs give people affection in return.	In times of danger, dogs sometimes rescue people.

Main Idea
People and dogs benefit from each other's companionship.

Try This!

Look back at the paragraph. Find another detail that supports the main idea.

www.harcourtschool.com/storytown

Vocabulary

Build Robust Vocabulary

plea

intercept

rendezvous

seeped

diagnosed

lethal

devoured

Race to the South Pole

Roald Amundsen had hoped to be the first explorer to reach the North Pole. When he heard that another explorer had already reached it, he decided to head for the South Pole instead. At first, Amundsen kept his new plans a secret. Only when his ship was well on its way did he tell his crew of their true destination, making a **plea** for their continued support. They all agreed.

Another expedition was already headed to the South Pole. Amundsen sent a telegram that would **intercept** the expedition's leader, Robert Scott, and would courteously inform him that Amundsen was also headed there.

Explorers Roald Amundsen (left) and Robert Scott (right) did not have a **rendezvous** point at the South Pole.

Scott's crew had a head start to the South Pole, but Amundsen had a greater advantage. He had learned to use sled dogs on his visits to Alaska. The dogs enabled him to travel faster and carry more supplies than Scott could. Amundsen reached the South Pole first and returned home safely.

On the expedition led by Scott, men pulled the sleds. Bitter cold **seeped** through their clothing, causing frostbite. Apparently the men also suffered from scurvy, although that was never formally **diagnosed**. Sadly, the harsh Antarctic conditions proved **lethal**. Scott's crew made it to the South Pole but never returned from the journey.

Before the hardest part of the journey, Amundsen's sled dogs **devoured** a feast of seal meat and blubber to give them strength.

 www.harcourtschool.com/storytown

Word Champion

Your goal this week is to use all the Vocabulary Words outside your classroom. Write down the words in a list, and carry the list in your pocket. Use each word in a conversation. For example, you might tell someone that rainwater has seeped into your boots or that you have agreed on a rendezvous point with your friends later in the day. In your vocabulary journal, write the words you used and tell how you used them.

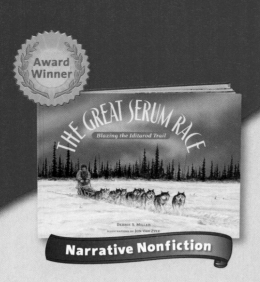

Award Winner

THE GREAT SERUM RACE
Blazing the Iditarod Trail

DEBBIE S. MILLER
ILLUSTRATIONS BY JON VAN ZYLE

Narrative Nonfiction

Genre Study

Narrative nonfiction tells about people, things, events, or places that are real. As you read, look for

- events in time order.

- factual details that support a main idea.

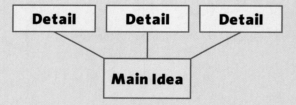

Detail	Detail	Detail

Main Idea

Comprehension Strategy

Pause now and then to **summarize** the main points of the selection in a sentence or two.

THE GREAT SERUM RACE

Blazing the Iditarod Trail

by Debbie S. Miller

illustrated by Jon Van Zyle

On a dusky January afternoon in 1925, Dr. Welch walked quickly toward the outskirts of Nome. Sled dogs howled from their yards. Outside a small cabin, a worried Inupiat Eskimo mother greeted the doctor. She led him into her home where two small children lay in bed, struggling to breathe.

"Can you open your mouth?" Dr. Welch asked the three-year-old boy.

The weak child tried to open his mouth, but it was too painful for his swollen throat. His fever was extremely high. Dr. Welch comforted the mother and children, but there was little he could do. The next day, both children died.

Soon after, another girl, Bessie Stanley, was miserable with the same symptoms. But this time, Dr. Welch could examine Bessie's throat. He immediately recognized the symptoms of diphtheria. Poor Bessie would not live through the night.

Diphtheria. Dr. Welch had not seen a case in twenty years. This fast-spreading disease could wipe out the entire community of more than 1,400 people. Dr. Welch immediately met with the city council and recommended a quarantine. The schools and other public places were closed. Community leaders told people to stay in their homes.

There was only one way to fight diphtheria. The town needed a supply of antitoxin serum. Dr. Welch sent out a desperate plea for help by radio telegraph. The message soon reached Governor Bone in Juneau and other important officials. Newspapers across the nation picked up word that the historic gold rush town needed emergency help.

The nearest supply of serum was at a hospital in Anchorage, 1,000 miles away, across a snowbound wilderness. Officials considered flying the serum to Nome, but it was too dangerous to operate open cockpit planes in extremely cold temperatures. In those days, planes were used only during the summer. Nome was an icebound port, so boats were not an option. The serum could travel partway by train, and then the only safe means of transport was by sled dog team.

On January 26, an Anchorage doctor carefully packed the glass bottles of serum for the long journey. The bottles had to be protected to keep the serum from freezing. He gave the twenty-pound bundle to the conductor at the train station. Soon, steam engine 66 began to chug its way north to Nenana, the closest railroad link to Nome. Nenana lay nearly 300 miles away, beyond the tallest mountains of North America.

On the frozen Tanana River, five-year-old Alfred John could hear the distant roar of the steam engine. His Athabaskan Indian family lived in a cabin near the train station in Nenana. Although it was late at night and nearly fifty degrees below zero, Alfred and his mother bundled up in their warmest caribou legskin boots and fur-lined parkas and walked to the station to greet the train.

As they waited by the tracks in the moonlight, Alfred watched the huge locomotive hiss steam into the frozen sky and slow to a screeching halt. He saw men unload the freight, and the conductor hand the serum package to Bill Shannon. Bill was the first of twenty mushers to carry the serum in a dog team relay to Nome. These brave men and their best dogs would travel nearly 700 miles on a snow-packed mail trail.

Bill covered the serum with a bear hide and lashed it to the sled. His strongest team of nine malamutes barked and were anxious to move. Just before midnight on January 27, Bill waved good-bye to Alfred and shouted to his dogs. *Swoosh!* Into the winter night, the dog team sped toward Tolovana, the first relay stop some fifty-two miles away.

Bill knew every turn of the trail. Like many of the mushers, his regular job was to transport mail and freight with his dog team. Traveling long distances in the extreme cold was a dangerous challenge. If the dogs ran too fast and breathed too deeply, they could frost their lungs. When the team reached bitter-cold stretches along the river, Bill slowed his dogs to protect them. He often ran behind the sled to keep himself warm.

Hundreds of miles away, Togo leaned into his harness and waited patiently for Leonhard Seppala to position Scotty and the other huskies. Togo, now twelve years old, was a proven leader for one of the strongest dog teams in the world. Leonhard, dressed in his warmest squirrel parka, sealskin pants, and reindeer mukluks, had carefully chosen twenty of his best dogs. Officials had asked the famed Norwegian musher to intercept the serum at Nulato, a village located halfway between Nome and Nenana.

Jingle, jangle—the bells on Leonhard's sled rang as the team rounded the corner. There were so many dog teams in Nome that mushers were required to carry bells to warn pedestrians. Togo led the team down Front Street while friends wished them good luck.

In Tolovana, Edgar Kalland, the twenty-year-old Athabaskan Indian mail driver, ate breakfast and waited anxiously for Bill Shannon. The Tolovana Roadhouse was a favorite rest stop for Edgar. Outside the roadhouse, Edgar's dogs pricked up their ears, and some began to howl. Bill's team drew closer.

The team looked exhausted when their frosted faces came into view. Two of the dogs would later die from frozen lungs. Following the doctor's instructions, Bill carefully removed the serum. He hurried into the roadhouse to warm the container and prevent the serum from freezing. As the two men talked about the weather, Edgar put on three pairs of socks and his boots.

Once the serum warmed, Edgar took off for Manley Hot Springs with his team of seven dogs. The thirty-one mile trip to the next relay point was brutally cold. Temperatures fell to fifty-six degrees below zero. At one point the dogs had to wade through slushy overflow, a place where the river seeped through a crack in the ice. When the team reached Manley Hot Springs, the dogs could barely lift their ice-crusted legs. Edgar's mitts were frozen stiff to the sled handle. A roadhouse worker poured a kettle of hot water over the mitts to melt the ice and free Edgar's hands.

The relay continued from musher to musher, roadhouse to roadhouse, with teams pushing west through the biting cold. At each relay point, the mushers warmed the serum over wood-fired stoves. Following the winding rivers, the teams covered an average of thirty miles each, at a speed of six or seven miles per hour. The mushers traveled around the clock, usually by moonlight or twilight. In the middle of Alaska's winter, only a few hours of sunshine fell on the teams each day.

When the twelfth dog team headed for the village of Nulato, waves of northern lights flowed across the sky. Musher Charlie Evans faced the coldest temperatures, at sixty-four degrees below zero. He wrapped the serum in a rabbit skin robe for extra protection. Charlie's nine-dog team moved slowly. Near open stretches of water on the Yukon River, a layer of eerie ice fog blanketed the valley. The ice fog, a mist of ice particles, was so dense that Charlie could barely see his wheel dogs, the ones closest to the sled. The experienced dogs followed the trail by scent rather than sight.

Nearing Nulato, two of the dogs moved stiffly and dragged their paws. The skin around their groin area was beginning to freeze. Charlie stopped the team and gently loaded the poor dogs into the sled. In their struggle to save the lives of Nome's residents, these two dogs would fall victim to the deadly weather.

When the team reached the halfway point, conditions in Nome had grown worse. Five people had died from the disease, and more than twenty cases had been diagnosed. Another thirty people were suspected of having diphtheria. Newspapers across the country reported Nome's plight and the progress of the serum run.

The relay teams pressed onward. Togo and his team worked their way east to intercept the serum. When Leonhard passed villages, he told residents about the epidemic and advised them to stay away from Nome. As the team approached the village of Shaktoolik, Togo picked up the scent of another dog team and sprinted forward. Leonhard could see a musher in the distance trying to untangle his string of dogs.

"On by!" Leonhard shouted to Togo.

Togo followed the familiar directions and steered the team away from the confusion.

"Serum—turn back!" shouted Henry Ivanoff, one of the relay mushers.

In the howling wind Leonhard barely heard the words. Luckily, he looked over his shoulder to see the musher waving frantically at him. Leonhard was surprised to see the relay team. After he set out for Nulato, twenty more mushers were chosen to travel short relays to speed up the serum run. Out in the wilderness, Leonhard had no idea that his rendezvous point was now 130 miles closer.

"Gee!" Leonhard yelled to Togo.

Togo gradually turned right and the swing dogs helped pull the sled toward the waiting team. The two men greeted each other briefly, shouting in the gale. Within minutes Leonhard had secured the serum package to his sled and instructed Togo to head home.

Togo and his teammates had traveled more than forty miles that day with the wind at their backs. Now the fierce gale blew in their faces with thirty below zero temperatures. Blowing snow plastered the team as they approached Norton Bay. Leonhard considered the risks. If they crossed the frozen bay, the sea ice might break up in the powerful gale. They could be stranded from shore on drifting ice. If they skirted the bay on land, the trip would take much longer. Leonhard thought of the children in Nome who were suffering from the disease. He decided to take the shortest route and cross the treacherous sea ice.

Leonhard believed that Togo could lead the team across twenty miles of frozen sea. As they pressed into the wind, the dogs hit slick stretches of glare ice. They slipped, fell, and struggled to move forward. But mile after mile, Togo kept his course through the wall of wind. At day's end, Togo picked up the scent of food that drifted from the Inupiat sod house at Isaac's Point. After traveling eighty-four miles, they rested for the night. The dogs devoured their rations of salmon and seal blubber.

The following morning, Leonhard discovered that the previous day's trail had vanished. The ice had broken up and drifted out to sea. Worried about the unstable conditions, Leonhard decided to hug the shoreline for safety.

Togo led the way toward Dexter's Roadhouse in Golovin, about fifty miles away. Along the coast, the wind's force became unbearable. Blowing snow blasted the dogs' faces like buckshot. Some of the dogs began to stiffen up. Leonhard stopped the sled and gently massaged the freezing muscles of Togo, Scotty, and the others. When they finally reached Golovin, the dogs collapsed and buried their ice-coated faces beneath their tails. Togo and his team had traveled farther than any other relay team.

Now it was another dog's turn to lead a fresh team of seventeen malamutes to Bluff, the final relay point. With a shout from musher Charlie Olson, lead dog Jack charged off into the blowing snow. After struggling through four hours of whiteout conditions, the experienced leader faintly heard a dog barking through the gale. It was Balto.

At Bluff, Balto and Fox waited for Gunnar Kaasen to adjust the leather harnesses and secure the serum package. Then the pair of leaders heard their musher's shout through the raging wind. Balto and Fox led the strong team of thirteen huskies into the swirling snow. Mile after mile, they trotted steadily toward Nome. During the final leg of the run, the wind assaulted them. A violent gust flipped the sled over, and the dogs went flying.

Gunnar struggled to his feet against the might of the wind. After he fought to untangle the dogs, he checked the sled to make sure the serum was securely fastened. Gunnar felt the bottom of the sled in disbelief. The serum package was gone!

In the dark, he crawled around the sled. Since he couldn't see his surroundings, he took off his mitts and felt through the snow with his bare hands. After more than 600 hard-won miles and twenty teams risking their lives, could it be that the serum was lost forever?

Panicked, Gunnar ran his numb hands across windswept bumps of snow. All he could do was hope. Suddenly, he felt something hard. It was the serum! His frostbitten fingers struggled to tie the package onto the sled. Then the wind-battered team ran off.

They struggled on through the night. With less than twenty miles remaining, two of the dogs ran stiffly and appeared to be freezing. Gunnar anchored the sled and put rabbit-skin covers on the dogs to protect their undersides from frostbite.

Through the darkness, Balto and Fox smelled familiar scents. At last the exhausted team reached Nome. They drove into town as most people slept through the blizzard. When Gunnar knocked on the door, Dr. Welch greeted him with a stunned face. How could a musher and team have fought their way through such a storm?

With stiff hands, Gunnar gave the shocked but thankful doctor the life-saving serum.

Twenty brave mushers and more than 160 strong dogs traveled hundreds of miles in the worst conditions. The incredible relay took less than six days. Four dogs perished and several others grew lame because of the lethal weather. Yet their struggle saved many lives in Nome.

One month after the epidemic first began, the quarantine was lifted. The schools reopened and children hugged their old friends. The whole town celebrated by holding a dance and watching a movie at the theater. Togo, Scotty, Balto, Fox, Jack, and all the other dogs were true heroes.

Think Critically

1. How did the author show that the sled dogs were brave and loyal? **AUTHOR'S CRAFT**

2. What is the main idea of the selection? *Focus Skill* **MAIN IDEA AND DETAILS**

3. How do you know that dogsleds were a common form of transportation in Alaska at the time the events in this story took place? **MAKE INFERENCES**

4. If you had been a resident of Nome, how would you have thanked the sled dogs and the mushers for their efforts to save your community? **PERSONAL RESPONSE**

5. **WRITE** Explain the dangers that the sled dog teams faced. Begin the paragraph with a sentence stating your main idea. Then support your main idea with details. **SHORT RESPONSE**

ABOUT THE AUTHOR
Debbie S. Miller

Debbie S. Miller lives in Alaska and writes nature books about the extraordinary wildlife that surrounds her. She says she hopes that "readers will truly experience the environment of Alaska and the lives of animals when reading."

When Debbie S. Miller was doing the research for *The Great Serum Race*, she looked for original documents and firsthand accounts of the race. She found the original telegrams sent from Nome requesting help, as well as old newspaper articles reporting on the serum race. She also listened to oral accounts of the race, taped by four of the mushers who helped deliver the serum.

ABOUT THE ILLUSTRATOR
Jon Van Zyle

Jon Van Zyle has completed the Iditarod race twice, traveling more than 1,000 miles from Anchorage to Nome by dogsled. He is the official Iditarod Artist, and in 2004, he was inducted into the Iditarod Hall of Fame. He lives in Alaska with his wife Jona and their sled dogs, and he creates between seventy and eighty paintings a year, each inspired by some aspect of Alaska. Jon Van Zyle has worked often with author Debbie S. Miller, who says this about his illustrations: "He turns simple words into captivating paintings that authentically reflect the beauty of Alaska's environment."

GO online www.harcourtschool.com/storytown

BLAZING TRAILS
by Andrew Carson

Expository Nonfiction

BLAZING

by Andrew Carson

Rachael Scdoris (sih·DOHR·ihs) cannot catch a ball. If you were to pass one to her she would see it leave your hands, disappear, and then reappear, suddenly, only a few inches from her body. This is because Rachael was born with a visual disorder that makes her near-sighted, far-sighted, and color-blind. Everything she sees is blurry and indistinct.

Rachael's visual disorder prevents her from taking part in some sports, like tennis and baseball. However, it has not stopped her from competing in other activities like running and public speaking. And sled dog racing.

Since Rachael was eleven years old, she dreamed about taking on the Iditarod Trail Sled Dog Race. This race is a grueling 1,160-mile trek across the Alaskan wilderness.

In 2005, Rachael joined the best mushers in the world for her first Iditarod race. Because she is legally blind, Rachael was allowed to have a visual interpreter race ahead of her. They communicated via two-way radio about dangers such as low-hanging branches. The first few days of the Iditarod went perfectly for Rachael. But more than halfway through the race, she became worried about the health of her dogs.

The Alaskan huskies that mushers use in the Iditarod are remarkable animals that thrive in cold climates. However, sometimes the conditions on the trail can be too much for the dogs. Rachael recognized that her dogs were ill and that she could harm them if she continued racing. She quickly dropped out of the race.

In 2006, Rachael competed in the Iditarod again. This time her dogs were in better condition, and she completed the race in 57th place out of 72 finishers, taking only 12 days, 11 hours, and 42 minutes. At 21 years old, Rachael had become the first legally blind person to compete in and complete the Iditarod.

TRAILS

- The Iditarod Trail Sled Dog Race commemorates the famous 1925 serum run from Anchorage to Nome, Alaska. The race takes place every year in March.
- Competitors take an average of 10 to 14 days to finish the course, but a few have taken longer than 30! The mushers stop at checkpoints along the trail to rest.
- The trail temperatures sometimes dip as low as −30°F.

Connections

Comparing Texts

1. Have you or your family ever helped someone in need? If so, explain what you did. If not, how might you want to help someone in the future?

2. Compare the main idea in "The Great Serum Race" with the main idea in "Blazing Trails."

3. You have probably heard or read about an emergency that inspired people to go to the aid of one community. Summarize what happened and how people helped.

Vocabulary Review

Word Sort

Sort the Vocabulary Words into three categories—noun, adjective, and verb. If you think some words belong in two categories, put them in both. Use a dictionary to confirm your placement of the words. Then choose at least one Vocabulary Word from each category, and write one sentence for each category. Compare your sentences with a partner's sentences.

Noun	Adjective	Verb

plea

intercept

rendezvous

seeped

diagnosed

lethal

devoured

Fluency Practice

Tape-Assisted Reading

Pace is the smoothness and flow of your reading. When you read aloud, use a pace that is consistent and conversational. Listen to a recording of the first three paragraphs in "The Great Serum Race." Follow along in your book. Then listen to the recording again. Read aloud with the recording, and match the pace of the reader on the recording. Repeat this procedure until your reading is smooth and consistent.

Writing

Write a Journal Entry

Imagine you were the last musher in the dog sled relay described in "The Great Serum Race." Write a journal entry that you might have written the night you returned home after safely delivering the serum to the doctor in Nome.

```
[ Detail ]   [ Detail ]   [ Detail ]
           [ Main Idea ]
```

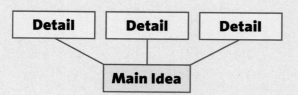

My Writing Checklist

Writing Trait ➔ Conventions

✔ I used a graphic organizer to plan my writing.

✔ I began with a main idea sentence and included supporting details about the journey.

✔ I used correct grammar, spelling, and punctuation.

CONTENTS

Lesson 9

Focus Skill

Main Idea and Details

You have learned that the **main idea** is what a text is mostly about. If the main idea is **stated**, it appears in a topic sentence or somewhere else in the text. If the main idea is **implied**, or suggested, the reader must use clues to figure it out.

Details support or explain the main idea. To help you identify the main idea, ask these questions:

- What is the text mostly about?
- What main idea do the details support?
- What is the most important thing the author is saying?
- What clues do headings provide about the main idea?

Detail	Detail	Detail

Main Idea

Tip

Details that support a main idea can be descriptions, reasons, facts, or examples. Details can also show a relationship between ideas.

Read the paragraph. Then look at the graphic organizer below. It shows three details that support the main idea.

Today, many people consider forest fires to be destructive events that should be prevented at all costs. This attitude, however, did not always exist. Long ago, some Native American groups set fire to forests to clear brush for hunting. Later, European settlers used fire to clear land for agriculture. For the past hundred years, people have worked to prevent forest fires. Ironically, this practice has made fires more dangerous; the build-up of brush makes fires burn hotter and faster.

Detail	**Detail**	**Detail**
Long ago, people burned forests to clear land.	For the past hundred years, people have worked to prevent forest fires.	The buildup of brush makes the fires of today more dangerous.

Main Idea
People's attitudes toward forest fires have changed.

Try This!

Look back at the paragraph and the graphic organizer. Is the main idea stated or implied? How can you tell? What other details support the main idea?

GO online www.harcourtschool.com/storytown

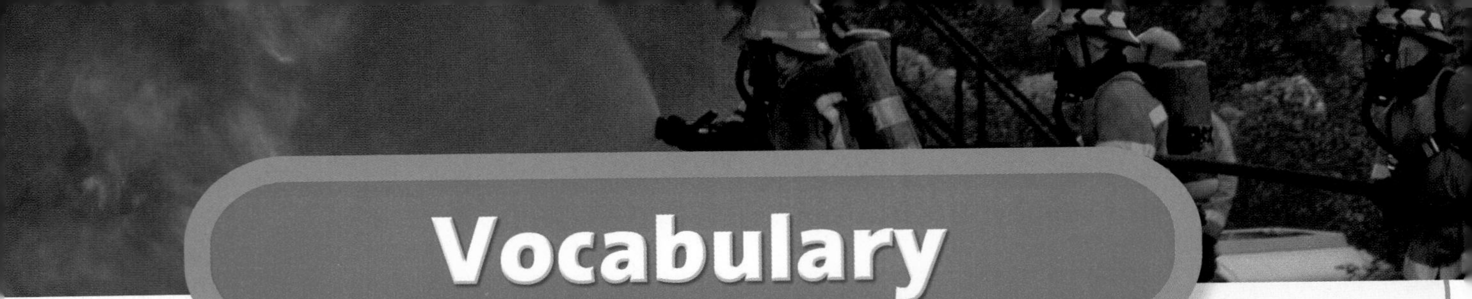

Vocabulary

Build Robust Vocabulary

- extent
- hampered
- altitude
- equipped
- reserve
- rely
- overshadowed

Wilderness Rescue

DENVER, COLORADO Yesterday, rescue workers in the Colorado wilderness located a hiker who had been missing for two days. The young man's family grew worried when he did not return from a recent hike.

The hiker, Dave Storek, was climbing at about 11,000 feet when he became dizzy and stumbled on the rocky trail, twisting his ankle. Like many hikers, he did not realize the **extent** of the effect the thinner air would have on him.

Storek's ankle injury seriously **hampered** his ability to hike, so to come down from the mountain, he looked for a trail that was shorter than the one he had taken up. In doing so, he became lost.

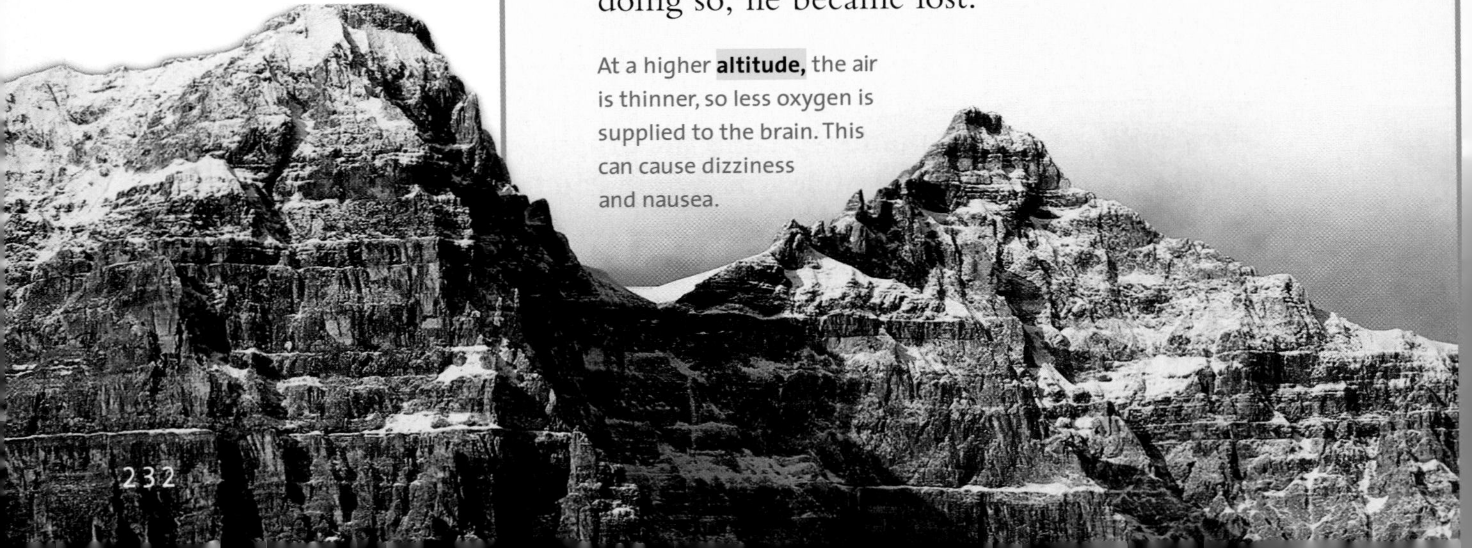

At a higher **altitude,** the air is thinner, so less oxygen is supplied to the brain. This can cause dizziness and nausea.

Storek, like most day hikers, was not **equipped** to survive in the wilderness for very long. He had not packed a **reserve** supply of trail mix, so he ran out of food on the second day. He had to **rely** on plants and berries he found that he knew were safe to eat.

Storek was happy to be reunited with his family. His successful rescue was **overshadowed**, however, by concern for three other hikers still missing in the area.

GO online www.harcourtschool.com/storytown

Word Detective

Your mission this week is to search for Vocabulary Words outside your classroom. You may read them in a book or hear them in a movie. You might also encounter a Vocabulary Word in a newspaper article. When you find a word, write it in your vocabulary journal and tell how the word was used.

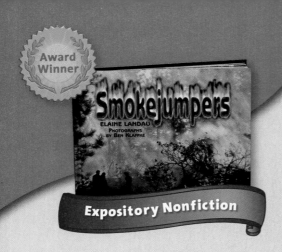

Expository Nonfiction

Genre Study

Expository nonfiction presents and explains facts about a topic. As you read, look for

- photographs and captions that support the text.

- a main idea in each section of the text.

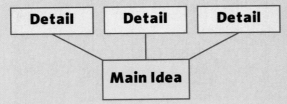

| Detail | Detail | Detail |

Main Idea

Comprehension Strategy

Pause now and then to **summarize** the main points of the selection in a sentence or two.

SMOKE

JUMPERS

BY ELAINE LANDAU

PHOTOGRAPHS BY

BEN KLAFFKE

Smokejumpers are highly skilled men and women who parachute
from the sky to fight dangerous wildfires. In the United States,
about four hundred smokejumpers are trained to protect the
remote wilderness areas that other firefighters cannot reach.

When a fire call comes into the smokejumper base, spotters plot the fire's location on a map.

FIRE CALL

A fire call comes into the dispatcher's office at a smokejumper base. A wildfire has been spotted. Seconds later the base springs into action.

A siren goes off, alerting the smokejumpers on duty. A smoke-jumper supervisor known as a spotter immediately plots the fire's location on a map. It is important to know exactly where the blaze has begun.

Meanwhile, the smokejumpers start to suit up. Their outfits and equipment have been readied for use. First the smokejumpers put on a fire-resistant bright yellow shirt and green pants. When in the field, the shirt's color helps them to be seen through the smoke and debris.

Over the shirt and pants goes a yellow jumpsuit made of fire-resistant material. The jumpsuit is worn while parachuting to the ground. It protects the wearer from sharp tree twigs, branches, and rocks. The jumpsuit is heavily padded in the shoulders, elbows, back, ribs, hips, and knees. This provides cushioning for hard landings. During the jump, smokejumpers also wear a motorcycle helmet equipped with a wire face mask for added protection.

The smokejumper's parachute harness then goes on over the jumpsuit. It contains two parachutes. The main parachute is worn over the back. An emergency reserve parachute is worn across the chest. Smokejumpers also carry a gear bag in which a hard hat, work gloves, fire shelter, compass, and other essential items have been packed. When smokejumpers exit the aircraft the combined weight of their suit and gear is about 80 pounds (36 kilograms).

As the smokejumpers dress, they can hear the roar of the aircraft starting up on the runway outside. After the smokejumpers quickly board, the plane takes off, heading for the fire zone. On arrival, the firefighters do not immediately parachute out of the plane.

Smokejumpers gear up for a fire.

237

▲ A smokejumper demonstrates the proper way to prepare to exit the aircraft while the spotter looks on.

First, the spotter along with the crew leader (also known as the crew boss) must determine the best way to attack the blaze. They develop a strategy as the plane circles the fire area, offering them an overhead view of the situation. The smokejumpers on the aircraft also look out the windows. Surveying the fire from above helps them pick up important details that may later be useful on the ground. But until they land, the smokejumpers can never be quite sure of what awaits them.

The spotter and crew leader decide how many of the smokejumpers aboard will be needed. If the fire has just begun, as few as two firefighters can handle things. In other cases, ten times as many smokejumpers are necessary. A jump spot must also be selected. This is the site where the smokejumpers will land.

Once an exact jump spot is picked, the plane slows down to circle the area. The spotter tosses weighted paper streamers out of the aircraft. This is done to learn the wind's speed and direction over the jump spot. If the streamers land on the jump spot, the parachuters probably will, too.

The aircraft continues to circle between 1,500 and 3,000 feet (457 and 914 meters) above the jump spot. On each pass around the spot, one to three smokejumpers exit the plane. If more were to go at the same time, some would miss the jump spot, and that could be dangerous.

While in the aircraft, the spotter and crew leader use their radios to remain in touch with the dispatcher. This is crucial in case additional help or supplies are needed. On the ground the smokejumpers will also use radios to keep in touch with their crew leader and one another. In an emergency, a smokejumper's radio can be a lifesaving tool.

Radios are only a small part of the equipment these firefighters rely on. Once they have landed at a jump site, they gather together all the necessary items. These are dropped to them from the aircraft after all the smokejumpers are safely on the ground.

In making the drop, the aircraft comes in low—its altitude will be only about 200 feet (60 meters) above the trees. It may seem as if the pilot is about to crash into the forest, but that does not happen. Instead, tools and supplies are dropped from the aircraft by cargo parachutes. These firepacks, as they are called, contain hand tools such as shovels, along with sleeping bags and enough food and water for two days.

Depending on the nature and extent of the fire, more supplies may be needed. Therefore chain saws, backpack pumps, tree-climbing spurs, and additional firefighting instruments can be dropped as well.

Once on the ground, the smoke-jumper crew leader determines if there are enough people and supplies to do the job. As soon as the leader is certain that they are in good shape, the aircraft leaves. The smokejumper crew can contact the dispatcher by radio, but other than that they are now on their own.

Once the firepacks have landed, their parachutes are removed and the smokejumpers unpack them.

On the ground, the crew leader briefs the smokejumpers and makes sure they all know how to get to the area that has been chosen as the safety zone.

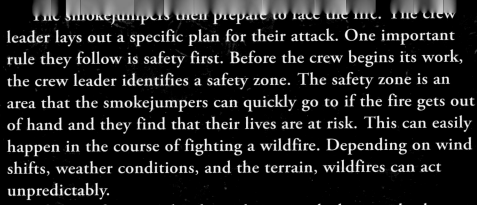

The smokejumpers then prepare to face the fire. The crew leader lays out a specific plan for their attack. One important rule they follow is safety first. Before the crew begins its work, the crew leader identifies a safety zone. The safety zone is an area that the smokejumpers can quickly go to if the fire gets out of hand and they find that their lives are at risk. This can easily happen in the course of fighting a wildfire. Depending on wind shifts, weather conditions, and the terrain, wildfires can act unpredictably.

After a safety zone has been determined, the crew leader makes sure that each smokejumper knows where it is and the various routes to it. Having more than one escape route is essential since any route can suddenly become blocked by a spreading fire. Strategically located lookouts alert the smokejumpers to changes in the fire's direction. They radio the smokejumpers when it is time to head for the safety zone.

This picture of a fireline was taken after the blaze was out.

If the smokejumpers should suddenly become trapped by the fire, they use the fire shelters packed in their gear bags. A fire shelter is a lifesaving tent made of shiny, silver fire-resistant material that a firefighter can crawl into when surrounded by flames.

The smokejumpers quickly set up their individual fire shelters in a cleared area. In the shelters, they lie on their stomachs with their feet and hands in straps at each of the structure's four corners. The shelter traps a pocket of cooler air for the person to breathe. This protects the firefighter's lungs and airways. The smokejumpers remain in the shelters until the crew leader indicates that it is safe to leave. A smokejumper is never without a fire shelter. It is hoped that these lifesaving devices will not often be necessary.

▲ A smokejumper's fire shelter looks like nothing more than a tent made from aluminum foil, but it's actually a very effective tool to use in case of emergency.

The first step in controlling a wildfire is to rob it of the forest growth it needs to continue spreading. To do this, the smokejumpers build a fireline. A fireline is a wide strip of cleared land encircling the blaze. In creating a fireline, the firefighters remove all the trees, logs, brush, and dry leaves within the strip. The size of the fireline depends on how intense the fire is. Many firelines are just 2 feet (60 centimeters) wide, while others may be 200 feet (60 meters) wide. Firelines are crucial in containing wildfires. Deprived of the fuel it needs to burn, the fire cannot advance.

Securing a fireline is not an easy task. It takes a lot of hard work. The smokejumpers must use their chain saws and crosscut saws to bring down burning trees. Fire shovels, which have a tapered blade and sharpened edges, are especially helpful in the process. They are designed for scraping and digging in forests. A special ax known as a Pulaski is used to help clear the fireline.

In some cases firefighters also need to set backfires. These are fires purposely lit along the inner edge of a fireline. Backfires are used to burn the timber in the space between the fireline and the advancing fire. The idea behind this measure is to deprive the blaze of any additional fuel in its path. Smokejumpers use drip torches to light backfires. These torches squirt small streams of fire.

Wilderness firefighting is exhausting. Fourteen- to eighteen-hour days of grueling work in burning forests are not uncommon for smokejumpers. Unfortunately, at times their efforts are hampered by the wind. Pieces of burning forest debris can easily be blown past firelines and into formerly safe areas.

In heavily wooded regions, new blazes known as spot fires can quickly begin this way. Once the fireline has been constructed, smokejumpers routinely check the area for any fires caused by windblown material. Ideally, these small spot fires will be swiftly put out before they can spread.

When dealing with large fires, however, smoke-jumpers frequently rely on help from the sky. In these cases air tankers arrive on the scene. These are aircraft used to carry and drop a water-based fire-retardant mixture that works to stop the flames.

The fire retardant coats the forest growth with a sticky substance that cools it and makes it less likely to burn. An air tanker can carry up to 3,000 gallons (11,356 liters) of fire retardant. But often that is just the first step of the air attack. After the retardant is dropped, helicopters may be used to drop water directly on the blaze and on smoldering areas known as hot spots. The water is carried in huge buckets that swing beneath the aircraft.

◄ **A helicopter drops water on a fire's hot spot.**

A smokejumper uses his backpack pump to extinguish a smoldering area.

On the ground, smokejumpers have marked this hot spot for a helicopter to drop water on.

Although the smokejumpers have done a great deal to contain the fire, the situation is still too uncertain for them to rest. Once a firm fireline has been established and things appear to be largely under control, they begin the mop-up phase of the operation.

During mop-up, the smokejumpers make certain that the fire is fully extinguished. Using their backpack pumps, they put out any remaining burning material near the fireline. Smoldering embers are extinguished with damp soil. The smokejumpers also cut down snags. These are standing dead trees or parts of dead trees.

▲ **Cold trailing is the final step in making sure a forest fire is fully extinguished.**

Only after all this is done can the smokejumper crew get a sorely needed break from firefighting. They eat the prepared food they brought with them. After that the crew members take out their sleeping bags for a few hours of rest.

When they awake they check to make sure that the fire is completely out. This is done by crawling along the forest floor to feel for any hot spots with their bare hands. Every inch of ground in the burn area is examined. This process is known as cold trailing. Once the entire fire zone is cool, the fire is considered out. The smokejumpers can then head back to the base.

BACK TO THE BASE

The smokejumper crew leader radios the dispatcher to arrange for transportation back. Sometimes a mule train can be sent in to haul out the gear and tools. But more often than not the smokejumpers pack up their own equipment and walk to the nearest path, road, or helicopter pickup point. It is not unusual for them to travel more than 5 miles (8 kilometers) on foot while carrying pack-out bags (backpacks) that weigh as much as 115 pounds (52 kilograms).

Even after the smokejumpers return to the base, they usually do not have much time to rest. During the fire season, they may likely be called again soon. Smokejumpers often travel long distances to go where they are needed. Some of their most challenging firefighting assignments last for weeks.

For most smokejumpers, however, the hard work and danger are overshadowed by the importance of their work. Smokejumpers do more than control fires. They help preserve our forests. Sometimes they save lives and homes as well. Every time they leave for a fire, they are doing an important job for us all. Their bravery and value cannot be measured.

▼ Scorched and burned hills and flatlands are the results of a wildland fire near Paskenta, in northern California. During fire season, smokejumpers will be called to many blazes in areas like this.

THINK CRITICALLY

1 How do smokejumpers prepare to fight a blaze while they are still in the aircraft? SUMMARIZE

2 How do smokejumpers ensure that a forest fire is completely out? NOTE DETAILS

3 What is the main idea of the section titled Back to the Base? MAIN IDEA AND DETAILS

4 What can people learn from smokejumpers that could help them approach other serious problems effectively? MAKE CONNECTIONS

5 **WRITE** What are the different ways in which smokejumpers implement the "safety first" rule? Use information and details from the selection to support your answer. EXTENDED RESPONSE

ABOUT THE AUTHOR
ELAINE LANDAU

Elaine Landau travels widely to research subjects for her books. When she's not traveling, she lives in Miami, Florida, where she enjoys writing by the side of her pool under a palm tree, drinking lemonade. Elaine Landau started writing when she was a child, certain that writing would be her career. She feels that writing is among the most creative and fulfilling ways to earn a living. She says, "Being a nonfiction writer is like taking an unending voyage in a sea of fascinating facts." When Elaine Landau is writing, she feels like "a pioneer with a pen."

 www.harcourtschool.com/storytown

INCREDIBLE RESCUES
by Joy Masoff

Expository Nonfiction

INCREDIBLE

by Joy Masoff

Every day the calls come in. A building collapse. A car off a bridge. A child trapped in a cave. And every day firefighters risk everything to bring people to safety. Being a firefighter involves so much more than putting out fires.

You don't just wake up one day and decide that you are going to save people. Firefighters train long and hard, learning skills that they hope they will never have to use. When a call for help does come in, they set off with hearts racing, their minds working at lightning speed. This is what they face. . .

SWIFT-WATER RESCUES

A flash flood can happen anytime and anyplace. Before you know it, a car can be swept away by a wall of water, its driver and passengers helpless to do anything to stop it. Swift-water rescues are always quick rescues. The rescue crew must move *fast* or it will be too late.

Cold water lowers body temperature, leaving a person weak. A lifeline thrown to someone who can't hold it isn't of much use. Staying afloat in rushing water takes a lot of energy and strong currents can pull you under. A firefighter has to get down and help.

RESCUES

ROPE RESCUES

Everyone has some rope lying around the house. Quite a handy little item. And in the hands of a skilled rescuer it can save a life.

Teamwork is the key to a rope rescue. Using pulleys and other specially designed hardware, even a small person can help pull up an injured victim.

249

COLLAPSE RESCUES

When earthquakes strike or fire weakens a building, walls can give way and roofs can cave in, trapping people inside. Some fire departments have highly trained Urban Search and Rescue Teams, called USARs. They depend on special equipment. Video cameras on the end of long flexible poles and trained dogs that can smell trapped victims help USARs find people who are buried under layers of rubble. And they know how to keep things from getting worse, how to lift heavy beams and concrete without having the buildings collapse even more.

CONFINED-SPACE RESCUES

Imagine being squeezed in a tiny tube. You can't move your arms or legs. You can hardly breathe. You are completely stuck. Sewers, pipelines, grain silos . . . you'd be surprised how often people get stuck in tight places.

Ropes play a big part in this type of rescue, but there are other twists. Firefighters need light and air along with extremely narrow special stretchers called SKEDS. Slithering through a tight space with an air cylinder on your back is tough. Getting a victim back out is even tougher. The sked, hooked to ropes that link up to the surface, makes it possible.

CAVE & MINE RESCUES

Deep within the earth, passageways are sometimes almost too narrow for a person to fit through. It is cold and damp, and it's easy to get lost.

Climbing skills are key here, as well as lots of special equipment—safety harnesses, ropes and pulleys, headlamps and hardwire headsets. Only one person can go down at a time, but it's not unusual for a cave rescue to take several days, so tag-teamwork is a must. When the victims are found, skeds will be brought down to help bring them to safety.

IN-WATER RESCUES

A car slides off a bridge. A skater falls through the ice. Amazingly, a person can survive under very cold water for up to 20 minutes, because the cold slows down all the body functions.

Highly trained rescue divers wear dry suits and use small inflatable boats called TENDERS. They must move slowly—they don't want to stir up the murky bottom of the lake or river—but not too slowly because time is running out! Diving through pitch-black waters, when you can't even see your hand in front of your face, is a challenge. Underwater lights help, but the most important thing is to stay calm.

Comparing Texts

1. What part of a smokejumper's job seems most challenging to you? Explain.

2. Of the jobs described in "Smokejumpers" and "Incredible Rescues," which do you think is most dangerous? Explain.

3. Firefighters work hard to protect people and property. What other workers protect people and property?

Vocabulary Review

Rate a Situation

With a partner, read aloud each sentence below. Point to a spot on the line to show how satisfied you would be in each situation. Explain your choices.

Least Satisfied ●————————————● **Most Satisfied**

- The extent of your history knowledge grew.
- Something hampered your weekend plans.
- Your reserve of snacks ran low.
- A website you rely on shut down.
- Your achievements were overshadowed.

extent

hampered

altitude

equipped

reserve

rely

overshadowed

Fluency Practice

Partner Reading

Pace is how smoothly and consistently you read a text. When you read aloud, use a pace that matches spoken conversation. Work with a partner. Choose from "Smokejumpers" a passage of several paragraphs. Read the passage aloud as your partner listens and follows along. When you finish reading, ask your partner to give you feedback about your pace. Then switch roles.

Writing

Write an Expository Paragraph

Write an expository paragraph that tells about the equipment a smokejumper uses while fighting a wildfire. Look back at the selection to recall the special tools and their uses.

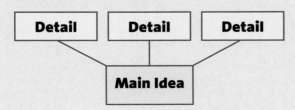

My Writing Checklist

Writing Trait ▶ Conventions

✔ I used a graphic organizer to plan my writing.

✔ All the details that I included support a main idea.

✔ I used correct grammar, spelling, and punctuation.

CONTENTS

Build Fluency
• Read with appropriate intonation.
• Use an appropriate pace while reading.

Build Vocabulary
• Read, write, and learn the meanings of new words.

Review Vocabulary
• Read theme vocabulary words in a different context.

Monitor Comprehension: Reread
• Review how to monitor comprehension by rereading parts of a text.

Summarize
• Review how to summarize the main points of a text.

Lesson 10
Theme Review and Vocabulary Builder

Readers' Theater
MYSTERY

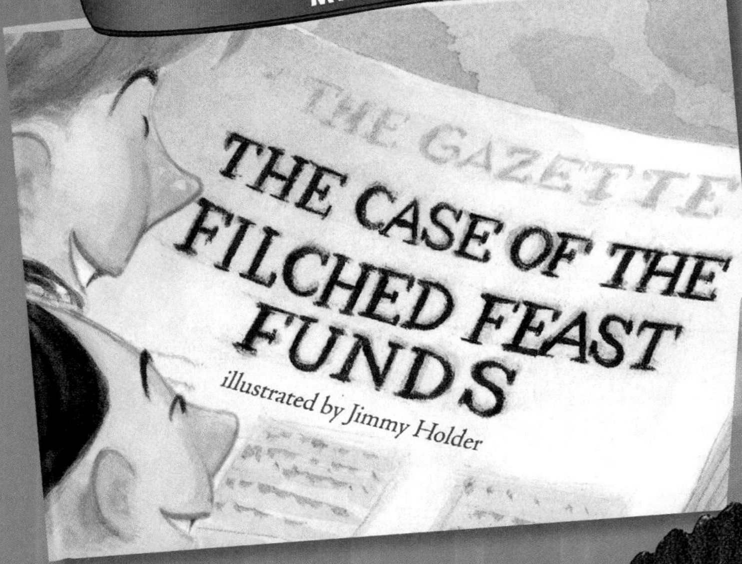
THE GAZETTE
THE CASE OF THE FILCHED FEAST FUNDS
illustrated by Jimmy Holder

Comprehension Strategies
MAGAZINE ARTICLE

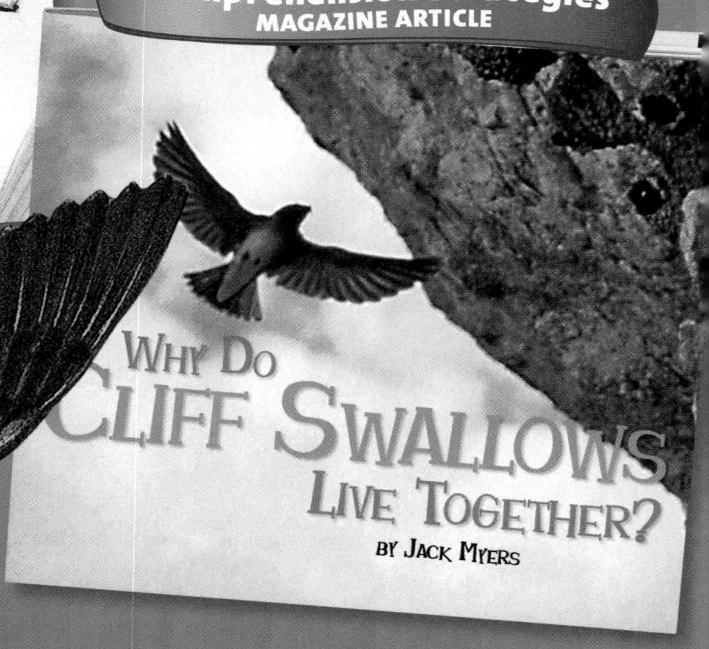
WHY DO CLIFF SWALLOWS LIVE TOGETHER?
BY JACK MYERS

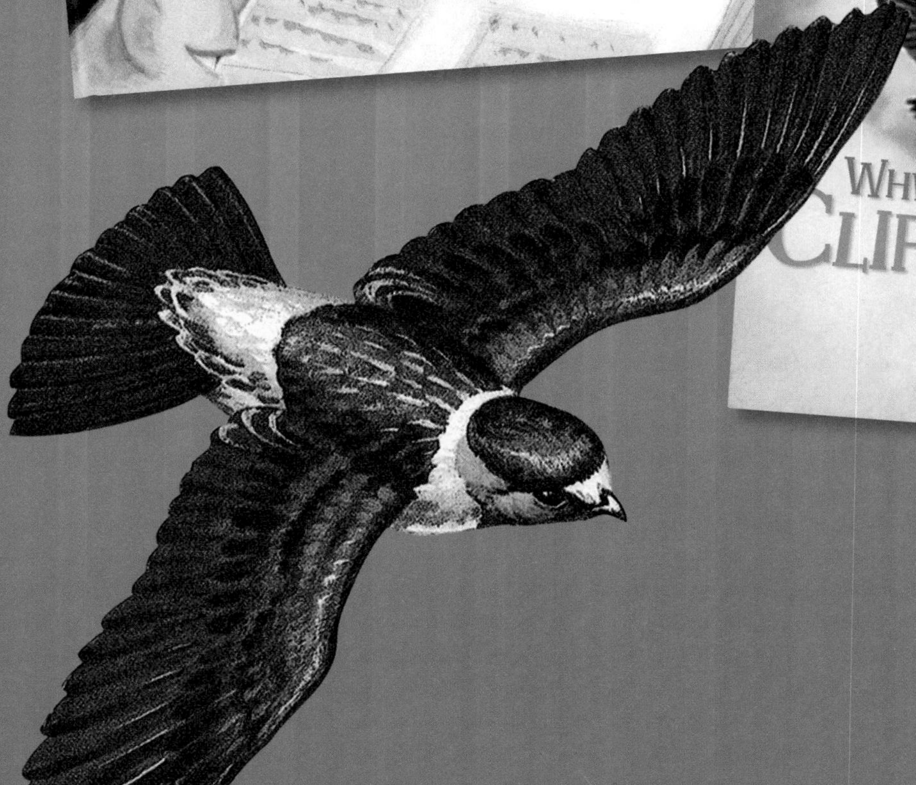

concede

confidential

justification

unearthed

alibi

culprit

confront

scandal

sheepishly

vying

Reading for Fluency

When reading a script aloud,

- Change your tone of voice, or **intonation**, to show the characters' feelings.

- Use a **pace** that is smooth and consistent.

THE GAZETTE

THE CASE OF THE FILCHED FEAST FUNDS

illustrated by Jimmy Holder

CHARACTERS

Narrator
Mrs. Holt, school newspaper advisor
Chorus
Arthur, student reporter
Mr. Ford, school custodian

Lian, student reporter
Zach, student reporter
Alisa, editor in chief of school newspaper
Sergeant Malone, school security officer
Vice-Principal Waters

Narrator: Every Monday morning before school, the newspaper staff holds its weekly meeting with their advisor, Mrs. Holt. They are discussing the content and layout of the paper's next edition.

Mrs. Holt: Good morning, students. Because of the Thanksgiving holiday, this week's edition will be released on Wednesday instead of Friday. So let's get right down to business. Who has a strong story idea for page one?

Chorus: I do! I do!

Mrs. Holt: Let me rephrase that. Does anyone have a story idea that can be completed by tomorrow?

Arthur: I do!

Mrs. Holt: OK, Arthur. Tell us what you've got.

Fluency Tip

Arthur probably sounds paranoid when he says, "No way! I don't want to be infected with copper funnel syndrome." Adjust your **intonation** by using a high pitch for this line.

Arthur: I saw a television show over the weekend that said homework can give you a disease of the wrists called copper funnel syndrome!

Mrs. Holt: Do you mean carpal tunnel syndrome, Arthur?

Arthur: That's it!

Chorus: What's carpal tunnel syndrome, Mrs. Holt?

Mrs. Holt: It's swelling and pain of the wrists, caused by too much typing or other similar movements. You'd have to *type* that story, wouldn't you, Arthur?

Arthur: No way! I don't want to be infected with copper funnel syndrome.

Narrator: Mr. Ford, the school custodian, knocks on the door and interrupts Arthur's campaign for the front-page story.

Mr. Ford: Sorry to barge in like this, Mrs. Holt, but Principal Barra has asked me to make an announcement to all the classes.

Mrs. Holt: Please go ahead, Mr. Ford.

Narrator: Mrs. Holt waits while Mr. Ford stands silently, scratching his head.

Mrs. Holt: Mr. Ford . . . the announcement?

Mr. Ford: Right! As you all know, the school has been raising money to buy supplies for a Thanksgiving feast for the local homeless shelter. Well, all the money the school had raised was sitting in a big jar in Principal Barra's office. With the money from yesterday's teacher/student basketball game—do you remember the final shot when Jerome slam-dunked the ball over Mr. Finney's head?

Mrs. Holt: What about the money?

Mr. Ford: Well, we had finally collected enough money to buy all the food for the feast, and now the money is gone!

Mrs. Holt: Gone? How could the money be gone?

Mr. Ford: I don't know. Principal Barra said the jar was here last night. But this morning, it was missing. She wanted me to spread the word in case anyone knows something about it.

Narrator: No one says anything. The students sit silently and look at each other.

Mrs. Holt: Thank you, Mr. Ford. I guess we'll all be on the lookout for that jar.

Narrator: Mr. Ford walks out of the room.

Mrs. Holt: How awful! I hope the jar is found in time for Thanksgiving . . . .

I guess we'd better get back to our next edition. Arthur, your story idea is interesting, but you need to do some research and get your facts straight. Does anyone else have an idea?

Lian: Me! I have an idea that's a real scoop.

Zach: So do I!

Mrs. Holt: Since neither of you seems willing to concede, why don't you both pitch your ideas? Convince your colleagues to give you the assignment.

Zach: I, um, can't.

Lian: I can't either.

Mrs. Holt: Why not?

Zach: It's confidential. My story idea is top secret! If I reveal it, I could compromise the whole investigation . . . er . . . the whole story.

Mrs. Holt: And you, Lian? What's your justification?

Lian: Um. What Zach said.

Mrs. Holt: Let me get this straight. You both have stories to write, but you won't tell us what they are?

Lian and Zach: Yes, ma'am.

Mrs. Holt: This makes no sense to me, but I guess we need to leave it up to the editor in chief. What do you think, Alisa? Which of these two should get the lead story?

Alisa: How about a competition? Whoever brings me the best story by tomorrow gets the front page.

Narrator: The bell rings and the students get up and leave the classroom. Zach and Lian glance at each other suspiciously as they head off to their lockers. Later that day during lunch, Lian and Zach are both lurking in the shadows in the school's boiler room. Lian sees a shape across the room and yells.

Lian: Hey! What are you doing here?

Zach: Me? I'm here for my story! What are you doing here?

Lian: I'm here to get *my* story. I'm going to solve the missing money mystery and write about it for the front page.

Zach: No way! That's what *I'm* going to do.

Lian: Fine! We'll see who solves the mystery first.

Zach: Fine!

Narrator: The reporters turn their backs on each other and begin to walk away. Then Lian stops and turns toward Zach.

Lian: Wait a minute. How will it look when we both file the same story?

Fluency Tip

Your **pace** should sound natural and conversational.

Zach: It'll look like one of us filed a better one than the other. I'll tell you what—you can proofread what I write, if you like.

Lian: No way! I'm not losing the front-page story. I guess we could write it together.

Zach: I suppose. It would be easier to collect clues if we're working together. I was just looking around down here to see what I could find. So far nothing looks out of the ordinary.

Lian: Did you check the trash can? Maybe there are clues in there.

Narrator: Both reporters peek inside the garbage can and start pulling out papers. Zach finds something that surprises him.

Zach: Look! It's a receipt for an airline ticket to the Bahamas—for Mr. Ford! And here's the label from the fund-raising jar!

Lian: Well, that finally settles it. He's guilty! Mr. Ford took the money and is running away to the Bahamas.

Zach: We've solved the mystery!

Narrator: Mr. Ford quietly approaches Lian and Zach. They do not know he is there until he speaks.

Mr. Ford: You've solved the what?

Zach and Lian: Eeek!

Narrator: Zach and Lian hurry away without answering Mr. Ford's question. They head for the main office. There they find the school's security officer, Sergeant Malone, and tell him about what they have unearthed.

Zach: . . . and that, Sergeant Malone, is how we found the clues.

Sgt. Malone: And you say you found these both in the boiler room?

Lian: Yes. No one but Mr. Ford ever goes down there. It's so far away from all the classrooms.

Sgt. Malone: You two have come up with a very convincing story.

Zach: We could never have solved the mystery individually. It took teamwork.

Lian: Do you think we have enough clues to publish the story?

Sgt. Malone: I said it's convincing, but it's not flawless. Mr. Ford left with me last night. I gave him a ride home. I also drove him to the school this morning.

Lian: So he has an alibi.

Zach: But the ticket!

Sgt. Malone: Oh, he's been talking about that vacation for months. It seeped into every conversation we had. If you look closely at the receipt, you'll probably see he bought the ticket long before the money went missing.

Lian: So we're back where we started.

Sgt. Malone: You two need to be careful about jumping to conclusions.

Zach: You're right. We'll have to do more detective work to find the culprit.

Lian: Let's go back to the boiler room. The person who left the jar's label in the trash might come back. We can intercept them when they do. Then we'll get our answers.

Sgt. Malone: Be careful, you two. You don't know the extent of this matter. Make sure your findings are accurate and based on facts you can rely on before you publish a false story and the school goes haywire.

Fluency Tip

Practice reading your lines with different tones of voice. Ask a partner to tell you which **intonation** best shows the character's feelings and personality.

Lian and Zach: Thank you for your help, sir.

Narrator: Lian and Zach walk out of the main office and pause to talk again.

Lian: It's a good thing that we came to Sergeant Malone before we wrote that story.

Zach: It sure is. If he hadn't rejected our findings, we would've been in serious trouble.

Lian: Okay, let's think about this. Who could have taken that money?

Zach: Whoever it was has access to the school and its assets. So it's probably an inside job.

Narrator: A bell rings, signaling the end of a class period. Students begin to fill the hallways.

Lian: Let's make the boiler room our rendezvous point after our next class. Maybe we'll get some answers then.

Narrator: Later that day, Lian and Zach are on the sinuous staircase leading down to the boiler room. They stop when they hear voices.

Vice-Principal Waters: So they know that the money is missing?

Mr. Ford: Yes, but no one knows that it was you.

Narrator: Lian and Zach begin whispering to each other.

Zach: Is that Vice-Principal Waters?

Lian: It is! She's with Mr. Ford! How do you think we should handle this? Should we confront them?

Zach: We have to. We've caught them red-handed. They might be gone if we go back for Sergeant Malone.

Narrator: Lian walks down the remaining stairs, with Zach following close behind. Vice-Principal Waters is speaking with Mr. Ford.

Zach: Lian, I think we've just solved the mystery of the missing Thanksgiving fund.

Lian: That's right! And we're going to write an article in the school paper about this scandal.

Zach: We have it all figured out.

Vice-Principal Waters: You do?

Lian: Oh, yes! We know that you took the charity money and are using it to . . .

Narrator: Lian and Zach look around the packed room. They slowly realize that

Vice-Principal Waters is standing among boxes full of food. Lian finishes her sentence slowly.

Lian: . . . buy the food for the shelter's dinner.

Vice-Principal Waters: Yes, I suppose you have caught me. The shelter called early this morning to say they needed the food right away to start preparations for Thursday's meal.

Narrator: Zach and Lian look sheepishly at the ground.

Vice-Principal Waters: No one else had arrived at school yet. So I took the money jar and rushed to the store to buy food. Then I came to see if Mr. Ford could help me, but I couldn't find him. I'm sorry you two don't have a juicy scandal to report on.

Lian: I think this is going to make a much more upbeat story, ma'am.

Narrator: On Tuesday, the newsroom staff meets again in Mrs. Holt's classroom.

Mrs. Holt: Welcome back, everybody. It's time to discuss the layout for tomorrow's paper. Do we have something for the front page?

Arthur: My story on copper funnel— I mean, carpal tunnel—syndrome is finished. I just need someone to type it.

Alisa: Ahem . . . we're running a story on the missing charity money and the Thanksgiving feast at the shelter.

Mrs. Holt: Zach and Lian were both vying for the front-page story. I'm curious—how did you decide who got it?

Alisa: The honor goes to the reporter who wrote the best story!

Chorus: But you both wrote the story.

Lian and Zach: Precisely!

COMPREHENSION STRATEGIES
Review

Reading Nonfiction

Bridge to Reading for Information Magazine articles are a kind of nonfiction writing. They present facts and information about a topic. The author uses evidence to support ideas in the text. The notes on page 267 point out characteristics of magazine articles. How can features such as these help you find information in magazine articles?

Review the Focus Strategies

You can also use the comprehension strategies you learned about in this theme to help you read magazine articles.

 Monitor Comprehension: Reread

It is important to monitor your own comprehension as you read. If you come to part of the text that you don't understand, stop and identify the part that is unclear. Then reread the word, sentence, or paragraph.

 Summarize

When you summarize, you tell the most important ideas in your own words. Using this strategy will help you make sure that you understand what you read. It will also help you remember information. Pause several times while you read to summarize the ideas in one or two sentences.

As you read "Why Do Cliff Swallows Live Together?" on pages 268–271, think about where and how you can use the strategies.

HEADINGS
Headings give clues about what you will read in each section.

WHY DO CLIFF SWALLOWS LIVE TOGETHER?

BY JACK MYERS

CLIFF-SWALLOW NESTS

Most of the birds we see build their nests in lonely, hard-to-find places. Most birdsongs are really bird language that says: "Stay away. This place is mine." So there's a surprise in thinking about cliff swallows because they nest close together.

Cliff swallows get part of their name from a habit of attaching their mud nests to the faces of rock cliffs. They have found that many man-made sites are even better than rock cliffs—wooden barns, stucco houses, and (best of all) highway bridges. Even with all the room at those nesting sites, they choose to build their nests so close together that they form bird cities, or *colonies*. Some of these colonies have thousands of nests.

CLIFF-SWALLOW EXPERTS

Dr. Charles Brown and his wife, Mary, have found cliff swallows so interesting that they have been studying them for more than 22 years. They and their students have a great study site in southern Nebraska, with more than 150 colonies that vary in size from 2 nests to 6,000 nests. The research has centered on a question that Dr. Brown puts very simply: "Why do cliff swallows live in colonies?"

Answering that question has taken a lot of work that is still going on. The scientists use ladders to get up close to the nests. Then they look inside, using flashlights and little mirrors like the ones dentists use to look at your teeth. They put leg bands on the adult birds for identification, and they use marker pens to keep track of nestlings. So they have learned a bookful of information about the private lives of cliff swallows through the stages of mating, nest building, egg laying, and bringing up nestlings.

A key to why these birds live in colonies has to do with their food. Cliff swallows make their living by catching flying insects, especially tiny insects like mosquitoes that often fly close together in swarms. So an important part of hunting for food is to find an insect swarm. Some swarms can be as far as a mile from the nest.

CLIFF SWALLOWS BUILD THEIR CLAY NESTS CLOSE TOGETHER ON THE FACE OF A CLIFF.

FACTS
Details about the topic support the main idea of the text.

CAPTIONS
Captions explain the photographs and provide additional information about the topic.

Apply the Strategies Read this magazine article about the interesting habits of cliff swallows. As you read, use different comprehension strategies, such as summarizing, to help you understand.

WHY DO CLIFF

BY JACK MYERS

CLIFF-SWALLOW NESTS

Most of the birds we see build their nests in lonely, hard-to-find places. Most birdsongs are really bird language that says: "Stay away. This place is mine." So there's a surprise in thinking about cliff swallows because they nest close together.

Cliff swallows get part of their name from a habit of attaching their mud nests to the faces of rock cliffs. They have found that many man-made sites are even better than rock cliffs—wooden barns, stucco houses, and (best of all) highway bridges. Even with all the room at those nesting sites, they choose to build their nests so close together that they form bird cities, or *colonies*. Some of these colonies have thousands of nests.

Stop and Think

How are cliff swallows different from other birds? MONITOR
COMPREHENSION: REREAD

SWALLOWS
LIVE TOGETHER?

CLIFF-SWALLOW EXPERTS

Dr. Charles Brown and his wife, Mary, have found cliff swallows so interesting that they have been studying them for more than 22 years. They and their students have a great study site in southern Nebraska, with more than 150 colonies that vary in size from 2 nests to 6,000 nests. The research has centered on a question that Dr. Brown puts very simply: "Why do cliff swallows live in colonies?"

Answering that question has taken a lot of work that is still going on. The scientists use ladders to get up close to the nests. Then they look inside, using flashlights and little mirrors like the ones dentists use to look at your teeth. They put leg bands on the adult birds for identification, and they use marker pens to keep track of nestlings. So they have learned a bookful of information about the private lives of cliff swallows through the stages of mating, nest building, egg laying, and bringing up nestlings.

A key to why these birds live in colonies has to do with their food. Cliff swallows make their living by catching flying insects, especially tiny insects like mosquitoes that often fly close together in swarms. So an important part of hunting for food is to find an insect swarm. Some swarms can be as far as a mile from the nest.

CLIFF SWALLOWS BUILD THEIR CLAY NESTS CLOSE TOGETHER ON THE FACE OF A CLIFF.

Stop and Think

Summarize the advantages and disadvantages of colony living for cliff swallows. SUMMARIZE

Once eggs have hatched in late spring, bringing food for the usual three or four nestlings is almost more than a full-time job for the parents. By watching individual birds, scientists found that most parents were making a hunting trip and food delivery about once every four minutes most of the day.

A parent may have a hard time finding that much food. To do it, birds watch their neighbors. The scientists noticed that a bird that came home from a hunting trip without finding food seemed to know what to do. It watched neighbors to see who had been successful. Then it followed the lucky neighbor on its next flight. In larger colonies it is even easier because there is usually a steady stream of birds watching others and finding their way to the best hunting site. Thinking of the big advantage the swallows get by living close together, Dr. Brown called the colony an *information center* because it allows birds to pool information to help everyone.

BLOOD-SUCKING BUGS

The Browns also found some disadvantages of colony living. Cliff swallows have a problem with a blood-sucking parasite called a *swallow bug*. It has no wings, but travels by clinging to the feet of adult swallows. It has long needle-like mouth parts and uses them to take blood from tender nestlings.

Scientists studied the effect of the swallow bugs by counting them—sometimes as many as 2,000 in a nest. Then they weighed the nestlings. Nests with the most bugs had the smallest nestlings. Some of the babies were so puny they would not survive their loss of blood to the parasites.

One other important result came out when the scientists checked their records. Close-packed colonies with the most nests also had the most bugs per nest. So the effects of parasites give a disadvantage to colony living but not enough to outweigh the advantages.

By showing these (and other) advantages and disadvantages of nesting close together, the Browns make it understandable why cliff swallows choose colonies of different sizes for their nests. Each time a bird picks a nest site, it must choose between a big colony (with lots of information but lots of swallow bugs) or a small colony (with fewer bugs but less information). Not all birds make the same choice.

It even looks as if a bird's choice of where to live is inherited from its parents. Each bird prefers to nest in a colony that's about the same size as its birth colony.

Most importantly, Dr. Brown has shown that most cliff swallows nest close together because of the big advantage of the colony as an information center that helps everyone.

LIVING CLOSE TOGETHER HAS GOOD POINTS AND BAD POINTS. THE BIRDS SHARE INFORMATION AND HARMFUL PARASITES.

271

READING-WRITING
CONNECTION

Lesson 11 >   **Lesson 12** >

Theme ③ A Changing Planet

Apple Tree with Red Fruit, Paul Ranson

CONTENTS

Lesson 11

Genre: Expository Nonfiction

LIFE UNDER ICE

PHOTOGRAPHY BY BILL CU...

cool science

Life the Edge

Cherie Winner

Genre: Expository Nonfiction

Focus Skill

Figurative Language

Words or phrases that mean something other than their literal definitions are called **figurative language**. Authors use figurative language to describe ordinary things in interesting ways. Figurative language also creates an image in the reader's mind.

- A **simile** compares two unlike things by using the word *like* or *as*.
- A **metaphor** compares two unlike things and does not use the word *like* or *as*.
- **Personification** is a comparison in which something nonhuman is given human characteristics.

Look at the examples of figurative language in the chart below.

Figurative Language	Literal Meaning
Simile: I felt like a fish out of water.	I felt uncomfortable in a new situation.
Metaphor: The wind was a fierce lion roaring through the night.	The wind was loud and threatening.
Personification: The sun smiled in the sky.	The sun was bright and made people feel cheerful.

Tip

To distinguish a simile from a metaphor, look for the words *like* and *as*. A simile uses one of them, but a metaphor does not.

Read the paragraph below, and try to picture the place that is being described. Then look at the chart. It shows two examples of figurative language from the paragraph and the literal meaning of each one.

Ice and snow cover most of Antarctica. Icebergs loom like guards near the frozen coast. The inland ice may appear solid, but it is a predator ready to swallow a careless hiker in an instant. Powdery snow camouflages cracks in the ice some hundreds of feet deep. Darkness wraps its arms around the continent for months at a time, so hikers must be extremely careful.

Figurative Language	Literal Meaning
Simile: Icebergs loom like guards near the frozen coast.	Very tall icebergs can be seen near the coast.
Metaphor: The inland ice is a predator ready to swallow a careless hiker in an instant.	Hikers can fall into cracks in the ice and disappear.

Try This!

Find an example of personification in the paragraph. What nonliving thing has been given human qualities? What does the figurative language help you picture?

www.harcourtschool.com/storytown

Vocabulary

Build Robust Vocabulary

bearable

illuminates

refuge

phenomenon

abundant

thrive

Emperors of the South

Emperor penguins are the largest penguin species. They live in Antarctica all their lives.

Built for the Cold Emperor penguins are well equipped for the freezing Antarctic weather. Four layers of feathers help them retain their body heat in temperatures as low as minus 60°C. Special oil on the penguins' feathers makes the icy water **bearable** by keeping it away from their skin.

Light shining through a hole in the ice **illuminates** these emperor penguins as they hunt for the fish, crustaceans, and squid that are their main food.

Winter Nursery Unlike most birds, emperors breed in the winter. Throughout the winter, each male emperor cares for a single egg. During this period, all the males huddle together in a large mass. Those at the center find temporary **refuge** from the extreme cold. To share the burden of keeping the group warm, the penguins take turns standing on the outside. The penguins' cooperation is a remarkable **phenomenon** to observe.

Survival Strategies Some scientists think emperors breed in the winter for a good reason. When the chicks are old enough to live on their own, spring is near and food in the sea is **abundant**. This timing gives the young penguins the best chance to grow and **thrive**.

Emperor penguins can dive several hundred feet below the surface, deeper than any other diving bird.

GO online www.harcourtschool.com/storytown

Word Detective

Your goal this week is to find the Vocabulary Words outside your classroom. You might read them in a wildlife magazine or in a book about wild animals, or you might hear them in a nature show on television. Each time you see or hear a Vocabulary Word, write it in your vocabulary journal. Don't forget to tell where you found the word.

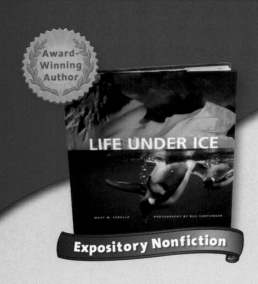

Expository Nonfiction

Genre Study

Expository nonfiction tells about real people, things, places, or events. As you read, look for

- photographs and captions.

- facts and information about someone's experiences.

K	W	L
What I Know	What I Want to Know	What I Learned

Comprehension Strategy

Monitor comprehension while you read by **adjusting your reading rate.** Slow down when you come to difficult sections of text.

LIFE UNDER ICE

by **MARY M. CERULLO**
PHOTOGRAPHY BY
BILL CURTSINGER

AN EMPEROR PENGUIN
WATCHES NEW ARRIVALS.

THE WEDDELL SEAL

THE FUR SEAL AND THE
WEDDELL SEAL ARE TWO
OF ANTARCTICA'S MARINE
MAMMALS.

THE FUR SEAL

Since Antarctica was discovered in 1820, scientists and researchers have braved gale-force winds, mountainous waves, thick fog, and giant icebergs to study one of the few wild places left in our world. Antarctica is a land of extremes—the coldest, driest, windiest, and highest continent. Its name—Antarctica—means the opposite of the Arctic. Ninety percent of the world's ice and 70 percent of the world's fresh water is frozen in antarctic glaciers up to two miles thick. (If they were broken up, there would be enough to supply every person on earth with an ice cube as large as the Great Pyramid!) In the winter, this continent at the bottom of the earth doubles in size as sea ice spreads out from the coast for thousands of miles.

On the surface, Antarctica is a frozen desert. But beneath the sea ice lies a strange oasis, home to an amazing variety of animals and plants that thrive in sub-freezing water, sheltered by the ice that covers their home like a glass roof.

Nature photographer Bill Curtsinger has traveled to this frozen continent many times to dive in its chilly waters and learn about creatures that are able to live in water that is as cold as it can get before you have to walk on it. His dives beneath the ice are adventures in science and survival.

On this trip, Bill and a research team board a helicopter at McMurdo Station, the main center for scientists in Antarctica. The helicopter will drop them off 50 miles away near the edge of the frozen McMurdo Sound. Bill, Paul Dayton from the Scripps Institution of Oceanography, and two other dive partners are planning to study and photograph the animals that live on the bottom of the Southern Ocean—the benthic life.

WHY DOESN'T THE
OCEAN FREEZE?

The water temperature around Antarctica ranges from 28°F (–1.9°C) to 35.4°F (1.9°C). Fresh water freezes at 32°F (0°C). Salt water freezes at a lower temperature because the dissolved salt blocks the water molecules from linking to form ice crystals. Sea water eventually freezes around 28°F (–1.9°C). (It also melts at a lower temperature, which is why road crews salt icy roads in winter.)

In the ocean, the salt is left in the water during the freezing process. This makes antarctic water saltier than most of the world's oceans.

When you dive in Antarctica, you don't just tumble off the side of a boat—or you might end up with a concussion. First you must drill through 5 to 10 feet of sea ice. In the past, underwater explorers used chain saws and dynamite to create diving holes. Today divers use machine-powered augers to drill neat, round tunnels.

Bill and his team land near a breathing hole left by a Weddell seal. The seal had found a crack in the ice, and with its sharp, protruding teeth it chiseled a hole to reach the surface to breathe. This makes the divers' first task easier—all they have to do is enlarge on the Weddell seal's work.

To prepare for his dive, Bill wriggles into his dry suit, a well-insulated dive suit that doesn't allow water to get next to his skin like a regular wet suit does. The dry suit covers all of his body except his face and hands. He pulls on insulated gloves that look like giant mittens. Then he slips on his flippers and mask and lifts his dive tank. He gives his dive companions a thumbs-up to show that he is ready to go.

As Bill drops down through the crack in the ice he feels a little like Alice in Wonderland falling down the rabbit's hole. He can't help gasping at the cold water. His lips and cheeks—the only exposed parts of his body—go numb, and within a few seconds his head starts to ache from the cold. Even in summer, water temperatures average 29°F (–1.5°C) to 35.4°F (1.9°C).

WINTER OR SUMMER?

When it's winter in the Northern Hemisphere, it is summer in Antarctica. Summer temperatures around the coast average a balmy 32°F (0°C). Winter air temperatures hover around –60°F (–51°C). It's so cold that ice cream stored outside has to be microwaved before it can be eaten!

They are making this dive in October—which is early spring in Antarctica. The water is still as clear as a tropical sea, but by New Year's, when the sun is overhead twenty-four hours a day, billions of tiny floating plants called phytoplankton will be in full bloom. They form a thick sea soup, and Bill would barely be able to see his hand in front of his face. But now, after six months

of darkness (May through August), there isn't enough plankton to block Bill's view, and he can clearly see the diving hole from several hundred feet away.

The sun illuminates the open water of the hole like a spotlight. Bill and his dive partners turn back frequently to make sure the hole is still in sight—it's their only link to the world above. Should Bill lose track of the hole, he will retrace his route until his escape hatch is once more in view. Bill shivers—not just from the cold, but as he imagines being trapped beneath a solid ceiling of ice.

Almost immediately a Weddell seal spies Bill. Like an eager puppy, it dashes over to size him up. The curious seal moves in for a closer look until it is nose to nose with Bill's face mask. It circles the divers for a few minutes before swooping past them to poke its head through the dive hole for a quick breath. Then it plunges into deeper water.

The divers also descend, but much more slowly than the seal. Within seconds, the seal returns from the depths to check them out again.

Weddell seals can dive deep and then surface quickly because they don't get the bends like humans do. The bends—also called decompression sickness—are caused by nitrogen gas that becomes trapped in the blood. If a human diver returns to the surface too quickly, the change in pressure may release gas bubbles into the bloodstream that may burst and cause dizziness, paralysis, collapse, and even death. But as a Weddell seal dives, its rib cage partially collapses, squeezing air out of its lungs until it equalizes the pressure of the water above, keeping the dangerous gas bubbles from forming in its blood. Like whales, these seals store oxygen efficiently, and their blood is pumped away from their flippers to their heart, lungs, and brain where it is needed most.

Scientists have outfitted Weddell seals with instruments that record how deep they dive. They usually dive to 650–1,300 feet (200–400 meters), but can descend to almost 2,000 feet (600 meters) in search of fish, squid, and bottom animals. They can hold their breath for over an hour!

Bill stops a few feet above the ocean floor. It's a beautiful and haunting place, carpeted with sea anemones, sponges, sea stars, brittle stars, sea urchins, sea spiders, worms, and soft corals. It's as colorful as diving on a coral reef in the tropics, and Bill almost forgets how cold he is. As they swim along, Bill and his diving team are careful not to cause damage with their long flippers.

Out of the corner of his eye, Bill sees a chunk of ocean floor drifting slowly upward toward the surface. Unfolding before him is the answer to a mystery that used

 A DIVER WATCHES AS ANCHOR ICE FLOATS TOWARD THE SURFACE.

STARFISH

to puzzle scientists. Every so often someone would find a starfish or a sponge sitting on the surface of the sea ice. Since these bottom-dwellers can't swim, how did they get up there?

Scientists love to find the answer to a mystery! By careful observation they discovered that every spring, fresh water from melting ice pours off the land and the surface ice and sinks to the bottom of the ocean. Slightly colder than the surrounding salty water, this "anchor ice" freezes as soon as it touches a rock, mud, or an unlucky animal lying on the ocean bottom.

As the bits of anchor ice gradually merge, it becomes more buoyant and floats up, carrying sea stars, sponges, and an occasional slow-moving fish up through the water until they bump into the surface ice and freeze onto the underside of the ice. Gradually the ice above melts away, exposing the sea stars and other creatures that would normally be living on the ocean floor.

Bill's diving team follows a slope down to a depth of about 120 feet (37 meters)—it's like taking a slow elevator down a twelve-story building. Paul is a benthic ecologist who is diving today to learn more about sponge growth in antarctic waters. He finds a giant sponge larger than himself, and while he measures it, Bill swims around him capturing shots of his work. Paul is careful not to push too hard on the sponge for fear of damaging its delicate structure.

After about a half hour, Bill's hands and feet have grown numb. His fingers are so stiff he can no longer adjust the focus on his camera, so he signals his partners that it's time to go up. They rise up to a depth of 30 feet (9 meters), where they stop and allow their bodies to decompress for several minutes. Returning to their dive hole in the ice takes longer than they expect because distances in crystal-clear water seem much closer than they really are.

 COLORFUL SEA ANEMONES COVER THE OCEAN FLOOR.

 STARFISH

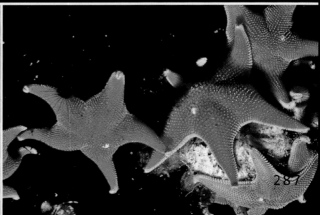

287

Diving in cold water uses much more energy than diving in warmer seas, and the divers rise to the surface completely exhausted. Bill and the others crawl into a tent and crank up a kerosene stove to get warm. They are going to spend three nights in the tent so they can make several more dives before returning to the science station. Each member of the team devours a stack of steaks, then settles into his or her thick, down sleeping bag.

Before turning off his headlamp, Bill writes down his thoughts and makes some quick sketches of the strange animals he has seen. He has a lot of questions to ask the scientists back at the science station and is looking forward to hearing their explanations and ideas.

Bill falls asleep soon, but he tosses and turns all night, and never really warms up. His dreams are jumbled with images of ice and snow. He wakes up before 6 A.M. The sun is still as bright as it was when they went to bed, but it's freezing cold in the tent. The condensation from their breath has formed a coating of rime ice inside the tent. Their toothpaste is frozen solid. The bravest one climbs out of his sleeping bag to start the stove. Soon the temperature inside the tent is bearable and coffee is made. Getting ready for another dive, Bill reminds himself that the water under the ice will be warmer than the air above.

Bill and the dive team spend four days out on the sea ice before the helicopter comes to take them back to McMurdo Station. After a long, hot shower and a huge meal at headquarters, Bill pulls out his journal and peppers the scientists sitting around the table with his questions. A geologist, a marine biologist, a meteorologist, a physical oceanographer, an astronomer, and even a veterinarian are all working on various projects at the science station.

Bill has dived in all the seas of the world, but diving in Antarctica still amazes him. Nowhere else do marine animals face the challenges they have to contend with under the ice.

Here, they have to swim in water cold enough to freeze their blood. It is dark for six months of the year, and without sunlight to fuel plankton growth, plant-eaters have no food. Bottom animals risk becoming trapped in anchor ice. Air-breathing seals have to find holes just to breathe. Penguins sometimes commute hundreds of miles between their nesting sites and the sea to find food for their chicks.

Bill asks the scientists around the table, "Why do the animals put up with the cold and ice?" The researchers, digging into a plate of freshly baked cookies, respond in a chorus, "FOOD!"

The Southern Ocean is like a giant food factory, they explain to Bill between bites. Strong currents act like a spoon in a pot, stirring up a thick soup of nutrients. Minerals from melting glaciers mix with decaying plants and animals from the ocean floor, and when you add abundant sunlight, you have ideal conditions for an underwater greenhouse. Tiny plants called ice algae grow in pockets on the underside of sea ice, and phytoplankton—microscopic floating plants—bloom in the water near the surface. These are eaten by shrimp-like creatures called krill. Each krill is only the size of a human thumb, but when there are thousands of them together, they can turn the ocean pink.

KRILL ARE SHRIMP-LIKE ANIMALS EATEN BY MOST OF THE OTHER ANIMALS IN ANTARCTICA'S MARINE FOOD WEB.

There isn't much variety to eat in Antarctica—the food web is simple—so krill are very important. Penguins, squid, fish, seals, seabirds, and even enormous whales all eat a steady diet of krill.

Bill has spotted several kinds of whales swimming in the open water surrounding the antarctic continent. Well insulated from the cold by thick layers of blubber, killer whales, minkes, humpbacks, finbacks, and even the giant blue whales feast on the krill. In fact, the word "krill" is the Norwegian term for "whale food."

Bill doodles a picture of a krill on his napkin, which prompts him to recall the sketch he made in his notebook of an animal on the ocean floor that he couldn't identify. He turns to Paul Dayton sitting at the far end of the table and asks, "What was that huge, prehistoric-looking 'bug'? It seemed familiar, but I've never seen one so big—it looked like something you'd see in an Age of Dinosaurs diorama in a natural history museum."

Paul laughs and replies that what Bill saw was a giant isopod, an animal related to a shrimp. Bill is amazed. He's seen thousands of isopods wriggling around in rocky tidepools, but each was only the size of a fingernail. "This isopod had to be five inches long!"

Paul explains that it's a phenomenon called "gigantism" found in extremely cold seas. Here in Antarctica you can find sea spiders as large as dinner plates, jellyfish the size of umbrellas, sponges big enough to stand inside, and sea stars almost two feet across!

"Maybe it's because the animals have found a habitat that no one else wanted, so there's no competition for food or space," suggests another scientist. "With less pressure from competitors and predators, they don't have to rush growing up so they grow large, if slowly." Paul explains that the cold water slows their body functions and leads to a longer lifespan. One starfish was known to have lived thirty-nine years!

"Cold-blooded animals also move slower in frigid water," points out Allan Child, a scientist from the Smithsonian Institution who is studying sea spiders. Even ice fish and giant isopods move so slowly they have been caught in anchor ice. Bill remembers watching sea spiders (called pycnogonids) creep slowly across the ocean floor on their spindly legs. "They're the original slow motion animals," agrees Allan. "You just want to get behind them and push!"

GIANT SEA
SPIDER

A MEMBER OF THE
DIVE TEAM EYES A
SEA SPONGE BIG
ENOUGH TO SLEEP
INSIDE.

Although there are more than 20,000 species of fish in the world, only 120 kinds can live in cold antarctic waters. Bill knows that most fish are cold-blooded and take on the temperature of the surrounding water. So how do these fish keep from freezing in sub-freezing water? He learns that one fish in particular is well suited for life in antarctic waters.

The antarctic ice fish has a natural antifreeze that runs through its veins instead of red blood. (Red blood cells don't carry oxygen well in low temperatures.) It also has a large heart and wide blood vessels to help pump its thin, clear blood through its body. Its colorless blood gives the ice fish a pale, ghostly appearance. Bill has heard that antarctic whalers used to call it the white crocodile fish because of its large mouth with many long teeth.

Antarctica's ice is important to creatures living below it and on top of it. Like a lid covering the ocean, it keeps heat in so the water is always warmer than the air. The underside of the ice supports a marine meadow of microscopic plants that feed krill and the rest of the antarctic food web. The top side provides a relatively safe refuge for penguins from leopard seals—a place where the birds can rest, nest, and raise their young. When there are changes in the sea ice—either from natural cycles or brought on by human activities—the effects are felt in Antarctica and far away.

THE ICE FISH HAS ANTIFREEZE IN ITS VEINS.

THINK CRITICALLY

1. Why is Antarctica known as a land of extremes? NOTE DETAILS

2. The author says that a Weddell seal dashed over to diver Bill Curtsinger "like an eager puppy." What kind of figurative language is this phrase? What does it help you understand? FIGURATIVE LANGUAGE

3. What happens if divers return to the surface of the water too quickly? How does this affect the divers? SUMMARIZE

4. Why do you think that the penguins and seals of Antarctica show curiosity toward humans, but no fear? SPECULATE

5. **WRITE** Why is Antarctica a challenging place for divers to study? Use information and details from the selection to explain. EXTENDED RESPONSE

ABOUT THE ››
AUTHOR

MARY M. CERULLO's passion for the world's oceans began early in her life. In high school and college, she planned to be an oceanographer, and her first job was at the New England Aquarium. Mary Cerullo wrote her first book to tell the truth about what sharks are like. Since then, she has written several more children's books about ocean life. She has explored a range of topics, from tiny zooplankton to coral reefs, dolphins, and sea turtles. In addition to writing, Mary Cerullo helps run an organization dedicated to preserving the health of Casco Bay, along the coast of Maine, where she lives.

ABOUT THE ››
PHOTOGRAPHER

BILL CURTSINGER, also a resident of Maine, first visited Antarctica as a young sailor in the U.S. Navy. His job at the time was to photograph the work of science researchers. While in the navy, Bill Curtsinger became an accomplished diver. After his naval service was completed, he began a career as a freelance photographer. *Life Under Ice* is the third children's book he and Mary Cerullo have worked together to create.

GO online www.harcourtschool.com/storytown

Expository
Nonfiction

LIFE ON THE EDGE

BY CHERIE WINNER

What do scientists mean when they talk about an "extreme environment"? How bad can it be?

Think of a setting that makes you miserable—searing summer heat, icy winter wind, the stench from an industrial plant, or a pile of rotting garbage. Then picture something much, much worse. Imagine living in a pool of boiling hot water, clinging to a snow-covered rock in Antarctica. Or think about being stuck in a pile of toxic sludge that could burn a hole in concrete.

All extreme organisms, or extremophiles (eks-TREEM-oh-files), have one thing in common. They've figured out how to survive in conditions that would kill almost every other creature on the planet. They don't avoid the bad stuff, like birds that fly south when the weather gets cold. Extreme organisms live in their hostile habitat full-time.

If extreme environments are so bad, why does anything bother to live in them? Wouldn't it be easier to stay in a coral reef, grass meadow, or lush jungle?

Yes, in some ways it would be easier. But life on the edge has a few advantages. "Normal" places are crowded. A meadow or jungle is home to millions of animals and plants, and billions of microbes. Living there means competing with all those neighbors for food, water, space, and light, and putting up with predators that try to eat you. On the other hand, if you live in an extreme environment, you have the place almost all to yourself.

Besides, what seems extreme to us is normal to these creatures. The nasty conditions that keep other organisms out offer extremophiles just what they need. In fact, most extreme organisms die if they're brought to a "normal" environment. To them, the world *we* live in is extreme—and deadly.

BRINE SHRIMP THRIVE IN THE WATERS OF A SALT LAKE. THEY CAN SURVIVE IN VERY SALTY WATER THAT IS DEADLY TO OTHER ORGANISMS.

Connections

Comparing Texts

1. The creatures of Antarctica have adapted to life in a cold region. Describe a time when you have adapted to a particular environment.

2. Which creature from "Life Under Ice" do you think is the most interesting extremophile? Explain.

3. What do you think is the value of studying the animals that thrive in Antarctica?

Vocabulary Review

Word Webs

Choose two Vocabulary Words. Create a word web for each word. Write the Vocabulary Word in the center of your web. Then write words and phrases that are related to the Vocabulary Word. Share your webs with a classmate, explaining how each Vocabulary Word is related to the words around it.

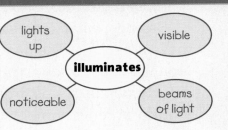

lights up — illuminates — visible

noticeable — beams of light

bearable

illuminates

refuge

phenomenon

abundant

thrive

Fluency Practice

Partner Reading

When reading a passage aloud, good readers group words in a sentence into "chunks," or meaningful units. This is known as phrasing. Pausing when you see commas, dashes, periods, and other punctuation marks makes your reading sound natural. Read aloud the first two paragraphs in "Life Under Ice" as your partner follows along. Have your partner identify sentences in which you can improve your phrasing, and read the sentences again. Then switch roles.

Writing

Write a Description

Imagine that you are a scientist who is trying to describe something in nature, such as a sunset or an unusual animal, to someone who has never seen it. Think of ways to describe it by using figurative language. Then write a descriptive paragraph.

My Writing Checklist

Writing Trait ▶ Sentence Fluency

✔ I used a graphic organizer to plan my writing.

✔ I used figurative language to write interesting descriptions.

✔ I used a variety of sentence types.

Figurative Language	Literal Meaning

Reading-Writing Connection

Analyze Writer's Craft: Expository Nonfiction

Expository nonfiction gives information about a topic. It may **explain** how or why something happens. When you write expository nonfiction, you can use the works of writers such as Mary M. Cerullo as writing models. Read the paragraph below from "Life Under Ice," and notice how the author used **sentence fluency** and **conventions**.

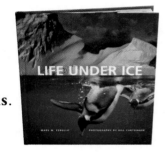

LIFE UNDER ICE

Writing Trait

SENTENCE FLUENCY
The paragraph begins with a short **simple sentence** describing the opening in the ice. Long, **complex sentences** describe the dangers below the ice.

Writing Trait

CONVENTIONS The way sentences are punctuated creates the *rhythm* in a piece of writing. Notice how the author uses **dashes** to signal partial stops. This gives the passage a jittery, nervous rhythm.

The sun illuminates the open water of the hole like a spotlight. Bill and his dive partners turn back frequently to make sure the hole is still in sight—it's their only link to the world above. Should Bill lose track of the hole, he will retrace his route until his escape hatch is once more in view. Bill shivers—not just from the cold, but as he imagines being trapped beneath a solid ceiling of ice.

Expository Composition

In **expository compositions,** a writer tells what he or she knows about a topic. An expository composition may explain how or why something happens. A student named Maricela wrote the composition below. In it, she explains how penguins survive in Antarctica. Notice the different types of **sentences** she uses as she describes her topic.

Student Writing Model

Emperor Penguin: Ultimate Survivor
by Maricela H.

Is there any animal more amazing than the emperor penguin? I learned a lot about these creatures by watching documentary films and nature shows. They live in Antarctica, the harshest environment on earth, but they still manage to survive. Emperor penguins feed in the summer, migrate in the fall, and raise chicks in the winter.

Writing Trait

SENTENCE FLUENCY Here, Maricela uses an **interrogative sentence** to draw the reader into the composition.

Maricela introduces the **topic** with three **supporting ideas** in her **introduction.**

Summer

In summer, emperor penguins swim and dive for fish. Penguins have flipper-like wings that are useless for flying but perfect for swimming. They also have waterproof feathers that keep their skin dry. These adaptations allow them to eat well all summer and build up a layer of fat, which they need in order to keep warm in the colder fall and winter.

Fall

When fall comes, the penguins hop out of the water and waddle overland on the Antarctic ice. They slowly walk and slide on their bellies for miles and miles. Each year, they travel to the same place to find mates and begin families.

Winter

In winter, female penguins lay their eggs and then leave in search of food. The male holds the egg on top of his feet, keeping it off the cold ice. He can't leave to eat until the female comes back—at the end of winter! Two months later, a baby penguin hatches. It stays on its father's feet for another month so it won't freeze.

Emperor penguins are amazing creatures that repeat the cycle of feeding, migrating, and reproducing year after year. To me, they are the most heroic survivors on our planet.

Maricela uses a **heading** to introduce each section of information.

Maricela writes about one **supporting idea** in each paragraph and sums them up in a **concluding paragraph**.

Writing Trait

CONVENTIONS
Maricela proofread her final piece for correct grammar, spelling, and punctuation.

Now look at what Maricela did to prepare to write her composition.

Organizing Ideas

After Maricela chose her topic, she organized her ideas for her composition. She decided to explain how penguins survive by describing what they do during each season.

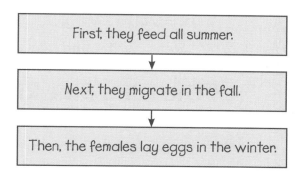

First, they feed all summer.

↓

Next, they migrate in the fall.

↓

Then, the females lay eggs in the winter.

Outlining

Then Maricela created an outline to organize the paragraphs and the supporting ideas for her composition.

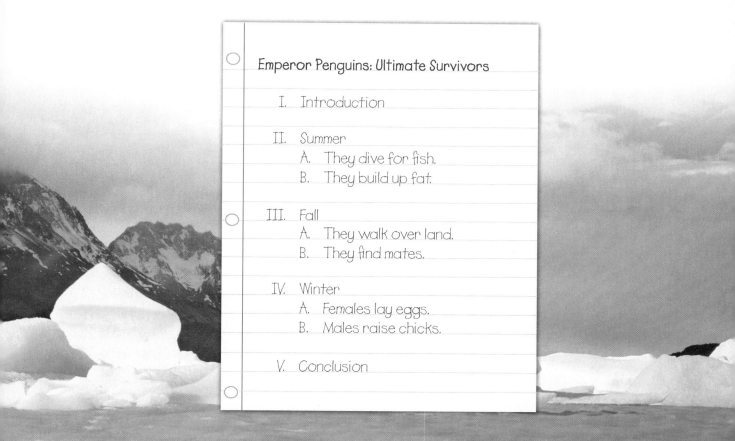

Emperor Penguins: Ultimate Survivors

I. Introduction

II. Summer
    A. They dive for fish.
    B. They build up fat.

III. Fall
    A. They walk over land.
    B. They find mates.

IV. Winter
    A. Females lay eggs.
    B. Males raise chicks.

V. Conclusion

CONTENTS

Lesson 12

Genre: Short Story

THE LONG BIKE RIDE

by Mélina Brown
illustrated by Alex Bostic

EMBROIDERY

WASHED AWAY: A DOUBLE HAIKU

by Jane Yolen

Genre: Poetry

Focus Skill

Figurative Language

When authors describe something by comparing it with something else, they are using **figurative language**. Figurative language shows the author's unique way of looking at the world and creates interesting images in the reader's mind.

The opposite of figurative language is literal language, or words that mean exactly what they say. Figurative language means more than what the individual words say. The most common types of figurative language are listed below.

- A **simile** compares two unlike things by using the word *like* or *as*.
- A **metaphor** compares two unlike things and does not use the word *like* or *as*.
- **Personification** is a comparison in which something nonhuman is given human characteristics.

Figurative Language	Literal Meaning
Simile: The team worked like a well-oiled machine.	The people on the team worked well together.
Metaphor: He was a cannon ready to explode.	He had a bad temper.
Personification: The boulder wouldn't budge.	The boulder was too heavy to move.

Read the paragraph below. As you read, make a mental picture of what the author describes. Then look at the chart. It shows three examples of figurative language from the paragraph and the literal meaning of each one.

Saturday, May 12, was a spectacular day for a bicycle ride. A heavy rain just before dawn had scoured the grime from the world. The highway wound like a silver ribbon through the hills. To the south, Flathead Lake was a big blue oval bowl sparkling in the sun. A brisk wind invited me to pedal faster.

Figurative Language	Literal Meaning
Simile: The highway wound like a silver ribbon through the hills.	The highway twisted and turned through the hills.
Metaphor: Flathead Lake was a big blue oval bowl sparkling in the sun.	The water in the large oval lake was blue and reflected the sunlight.
Personification: A brisk wind invited me to pedal faster.	The wind made pedaling easier.

Try This!

Reread the metaphor in the chart above. Rewrite the sentence as a simile without changing its original meaning. What words did you add or delete?

GO online www.harcourtschool.com/storytown

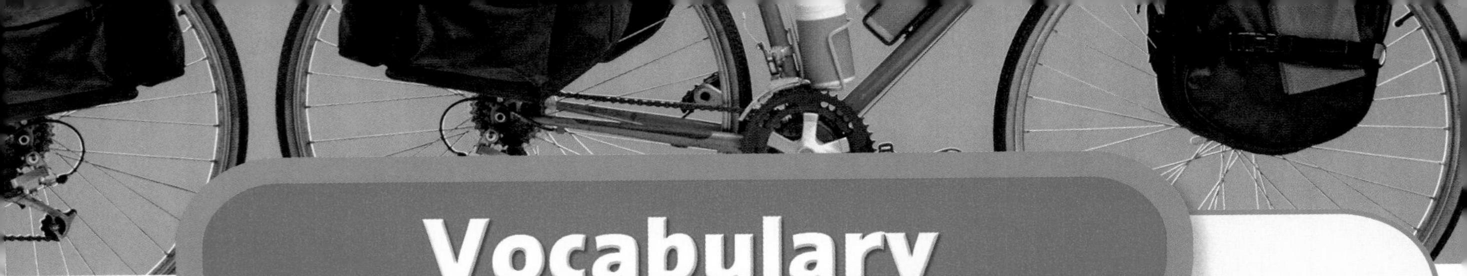

Vocabulary

Build Robust Vocabulary

wedged

ideal

perched

pelting

stranded

blurted

slunk

Bird's Eye View

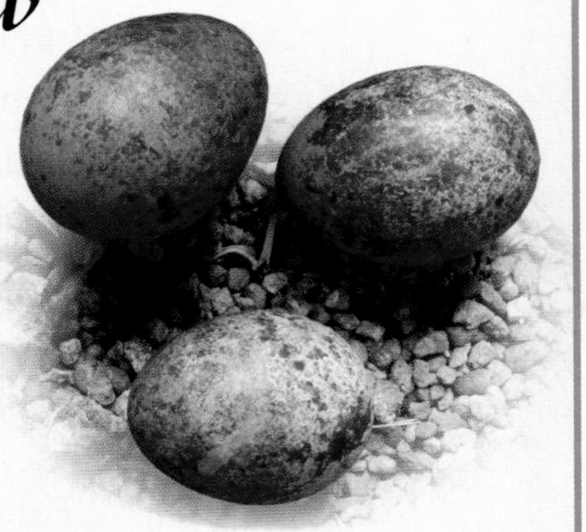

March 3 Tori and I went mountain climbing in Vermont today. High on a cliff, I spotted a nest. I **wedged** myself between two rocks to get a closer look. Three brown speckled eggs lay in a shallow bowl in the dirt. I guessed that they were peregrine falcon eggs. It was an **ideal** falcon nesting spot.

March 11 I was right! When I returned to the cliff, I saw one parent falcon **perched** on the ledge guarding the nest. The other parent was hunting for prey.

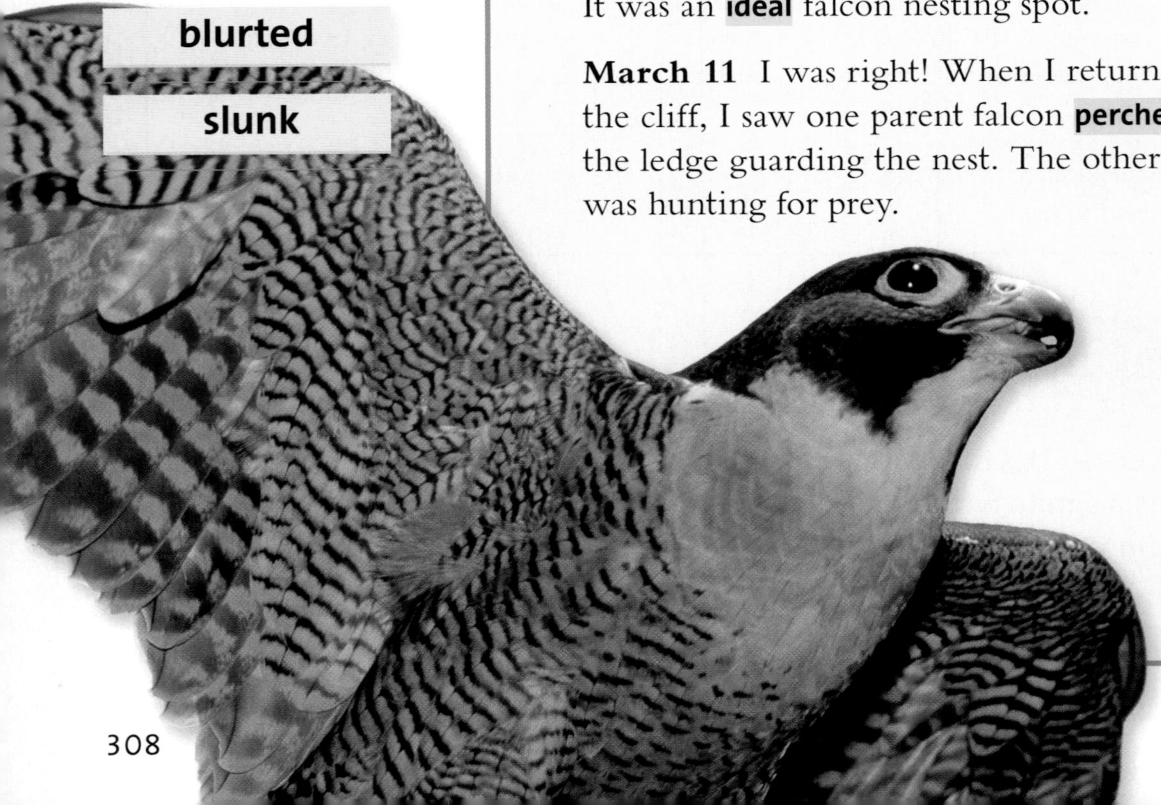

April 15 I went to check on the nest. Raindrops were **pelting** my face as I climbed, but it was worth it. The eggs had hatched. Three fluffy chicks peered out from the ledge!

April 30 The chicks are trying to fly now, but it takes practice! Today, one chick got **stranded** on a ledge about 10 feet below the nest. As I watched, a raccoon emerged from a bush and went straight for the chick. I **blurted** out a warning and then yelled at the intruder until it **slunk** away. Soon, the parents returned and coaxed the chick back up to the nest.

 www.harcourtschool.com/storytown

Word Scribe

This week your task is to use the Vocabulary Words in your writing. In your vocabulary journal, write sentences to show the meanings of the words. For example, you could write about an ideal place to visit. Write sentences about as many of the Vocabulary Words as you can. Share your writing with your classmates.

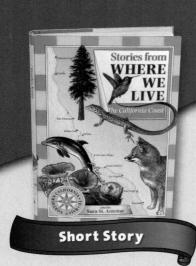

Genre Study

A short story is a fictional narrative that is not part of a novel. As you read, look for.

- a main character who faces a challenge.

- a plot with a conflict and a resolution.

Comprehension Strategy

Monitor comprehension while you read by adjusting your **reading rate**. Slow down when you come to difficult sections.

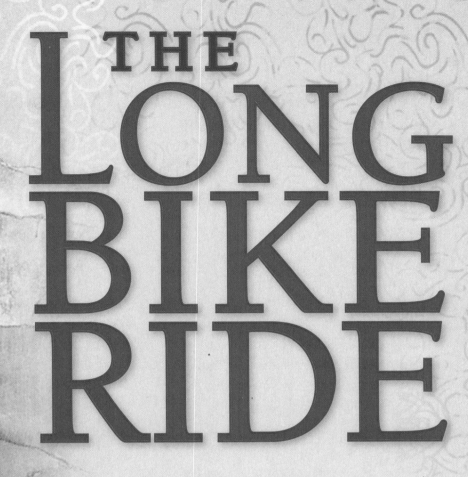

THE LONG BIKE RIDE

BY MÉLINA BROWN

ILLUSTRATED BY ALEX BOSTIC

California's rocky shores are an ideal place to watch the surf crash, to clamber over rocks, and to go exploring. And sometimes that's just the beginning of the day's adventure.

"Look out for the rock!" Jake yelled at me. I turned away from Michael to look straight ahead, but I didn't see any rock.

"Made you look," laughed Jake, speeding up to pass me.

Jake Hernandez and Michael Choi were my two best friends. I biked with them whenever I could because Mama didn't like me biking on my own, and I sure wasn't about to go with my little sister, Keyana. Keyana had to stay in her after-school program anyway.

Dad had said I was supposed to stay away from certain areas of the old army base, Fort Ord. Unexploded grenades had been buried there, and lead bullets still littered the dunes near old target ranges. He hadn't told me to stay away from the other side of Highway 1, though, probably because he never thought I'd go there. He knows I don't like the water. It's freezing, even in summer.

I had learned about that the hard way. When Michael and Jake first brought me to the beach, I had taken off my T-shirt and run right into the water with nothing on but my swimming trunks. Cold shocked through my body like lightning and I jumped right out. When I ran back, shivering and shouting, both Jake and Michael were doubled over in laughter. "Antoine, man! I can't believe you did that!" laughed Jake as he zipped up a black rubber outfit.

"Hey, Antoine, we forgot to tell you. You need a wet suit around here," Michael had added with concern, before breaking out in laughter again. Since then, I'd begged Mama and Dad for one, but Dad said I was lucky I got a mountain bike for my fourteenth birthday. I'd have to get a job and start saving for anything else I wanted.

I tightened my helmet as we bounced over sandy bumps and jumped over mounded cypress tree roots. Cypress trees are so different from the evergreens I saw near the army base in Georgia, where Dad was stationed before being transferred out here. Their branches spread out with flat bunches of needles, like they're trying to reach the water.

We rode down a trail, past the dunes, avoiding the thorny shrubs and tufts of needlegrass. In science, we'd learned how to identify these and other beach plants that grow in the dunes. We also learned that we had to be careful and ride on the packed, wet sand so we didn't contribute to beach erosion.

We followed the wet part of the beach as it curved around in wavy arcs. The sky had been steel gray all day, but I didn't care. It felt good to be riding next to the ocean, with wind whipping my face and cold sprinkles of water splashing up from the waves washing ashore. Even though I had just turned fourteen, I felt like a man. I didn't have to worry about all my parents' rules out here. I was free.

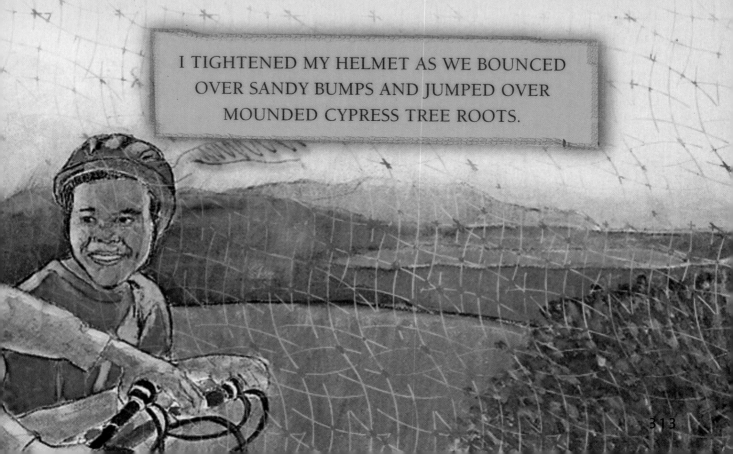

I TIGHTENED MY HELMET AS WE BOUNCED OVER SANDY BUMPS AND JUMPED OVER MOUNDED CYPRESS TREE ROOTS.

We pedaled for a long time, racing and then coasting, until the beach became rocky. Waves crashed against rocky little ridges, sending showers of water into the air.

"Hey, guys, we're almost at the Aquarium." Jake pointed straight ahead. "I think we've gone at least six miles."

"Yeah, and I think it's time for a break," Michael said, jumping off his bike and landing in the sand. Jake joined him, but I rode a little farther toward the rocks.

"What's the matter? You guys can't go the distance, hmmm?" I said, teasing them. I threw my arms in the air over my head as if I'd just won a race. "Antoine Graves wins his *third* triathlon! Antoine, how *do* you do it?" I said in a loud sports announcer's voice. Maybe Michael and Jake were good swimmers, but no one could outdistance me on a bike.

Michael shook his head at me, then lay down on the sand. Jake said, "Show-off. We'll see how far you ride when you wreck your new bike!" Then he lay down too.

I pedaled until the sand ended. The black cluster of rocks stopped me, blocking my way like a small mountain. I got off my bike and just stood there,

a few feet from the waves. I still didn't like the water, but I sure didn't mind being near it. From a distance, the water looked as dark as the steel gray sky. But at my feet, it was so clear I could see the red and peach-colored starfish stretching on the rocks like sunbathers. They looked soft and furry, like velvet. I almost expected them to stand up and start swaying with the waves, dancing to the music of the ocean.

The mist sprinkled and cooled me down from the ride. But when it really started to chill me, I turned around to head back. Then I heard a loud cry. It could not have come from the black cormorants flapping above me. A chill ran down my spine. What was it?

A CHILL RAN DOWN
MY SPINE.
WHAT WAS IT?

I inched my bike closer to the rocks and closer to the harsh, hoarse cry. If I had been younger and still believed in monsters, I would have guessed it was an evil sea creature. But the more I listened to it, the more it actually sounded like a moaning, yelping cry for help. It sounded like something being tortured. I had to see what it was.

I climbed up onto the slippery rock, using my hands the way I'd seen rock climbers do. The water gurgled and chugged as it splashed into the narrow passages between each rock. I climbed over a few more rocks, peeking down into each cranny. Then I saw the sea creature down in a crevice in the rocks. It wasn't an evil one, though. It stared at me with big, sad, filmy eyes. It was a sea lion pup and it was stuck.

I leaned on the closest rock, trying to avoid the slimy seaweed and curly barnacles coating the sides of it. I reached over and stuck my hand out to pet the sea lion. Luckily, I was still out of reach because the sea lion flashed its sharp teeth and tried to bite me! But only its long, stiff whiskers scraped my hand. They looked like porcupine quills and felt like them too. I looked at the whisker marks on my hand, wondering what would have happened if its teeth had made contact instead.

I backed away and watched as the sea lion's nostrils flared up and then closed to let out another wail. Its mouth was like a pink cavern, letting out so much sound I thought people back in Seaside would be able to hear it. But the waves crashed harder against the rocks, drowning out even those scared moans.

I looked more closely at the sea lion, trying to see if it was cut or hurt. Its coat looked dark and oily, the same color as the rocks. Its front flippers perched on a rock, but I couldn't see its hind flippers. They must have been wedged in between the rocks. How would it ever get out?

"Hey, Antoine!" came Michael's voice from behind me. "We couldn't see you anymore. We thought you'd fallen in or something. What are you doing?"

Before I could answer, Jake's voice jumped in. "Wow! It's a seal. You trying to talk to it or something?" he laughed.

"It's a sea lion," I answered, pointing to its tiny ears, which stuck out like little flaps. I'd learned that seals didn't have them. "It's stuck." The sea lion opened its mouth again to holler, and Jake and Michael laughed at the sound.

"Let's try to free it," said Michael, reaching toward the sea lion.

"No!" I yelled as he extended his arm. "It'll try to bite you!" The sea lion lunged at Michael's hand before I had even finished my sentence. Michael pulled back his hand quicker than I had. He didn't even get nicked by the sea lion's whiskers.

"Whoa!" Jake laughed from a safe distance. "That little guy is fierce!"

Michael jumped off the rock and immediately started scanning the nearby sand. He stooped to pick up a long branch, then ran back. "We'll use this," he said with a smile.

He inched closer to the sea lion again, and I couldn't help feeling annoyed. The sea lion was my discovery, and now Michael was going to poke it with a stick.

"Leave it alone, Michael," I ordered. "It didn't do anything to you."

"Just relax, Antoine. I'm trying to help free it. Maybe I can just push it out with this branch."

"Stop!" I yelled as Michael moved to poke the sea lion. "That's not going to help it. Just put the branch down." The sea lion yelped even more when a loud clap of thunder burst nearby.

"We should get out of here, guys," Jake said, inching himself off the rocks. "Look at the sky!" He pointed to the black clouds hovering over us.

Michael threw the branch into the water and shook his head. "That thing won't budge. It's really stuck. Man, and now it's going to storm on us!" He ran to his bike as if he'd completely forgotten about the stranded sea lion.

I stared at the pup again, then at the sky. It would take us awhile to get back and I'd be in serious trouble if I were caught this far away from home. But I didn't want to leave the sea lion alone. What would happen to it?

"Come on, Antoine!" Jake yelled back at me. They were already pedaling away. Fat raindrops started pelting me. I had to go. I took one last look at the sea lion, then got on my bike and rode away.

317

"You're in *big* trouble, Antoine! Dad said you should've been back by five o'clock." Keyana looked up at me with wide, worried eyes.

I brushed past her and glanced at the kitchen clock. Six-thirty. Mama worked at the hospital until eight o'clock on Thursdays. I'd have to face Dad alone. What would I tell him? Would he understand if I told him about the sea lion? He called me before I had a chance to decide. I grabbed a kitchen towel to dry myself, but I was soaking wet.

"Look at the time, Antoine. What have you been doing?" Dad tapped his watch so hard he could have broken it. He had changed out of his uniform, but he still wore his serious face.

"Just biking? All this time? I don't want to hear any more excuses right now. Go eat the stir-fry I saved for you before your mother gets back. If you hurry, you should have time to do the dishes and your homework by then, too. We'll have to see how she feels about grounding you."

I slunk back into the kitchen, knowing better than to argue anymore with Dad. I scowled at Keyana from her peeking spot on the upstairs landing. It wasn't fair—getting in trouble for trying to save a sea lion. Why couldn't Dad understand? I hadn't done anything wrong. Who would save the sea lion now? And what if Jake or Michael went back before me?

All night I thought about how I could get back to that spot. Mom and Dad still hadn't listened to my story and had grounded me from using the phone, but not from using my bike. They knew it was the quickest way for me to get to school. And that's how I'd get back to the beach. I'd bike back the next day, alone.

"Dad, I didn't mean to be late. I was just biking around and we lost track of time—and—"

"Who's 'we'?"

"Jake and Michael and me. I didn't realize it had gotten so late because we were—"

"The same guys who let you jump into freezing water? What were you guys up to?" Dad's eyes were on fire.

"We were just biking and stuff and—"

When Dad's heavy knock on my door woke me up the next morning, all I could think about was how much I wanted to keep sleeping. Then I remembered the sea lion and my plan to save it. I sprang out of bed and quickly got ready for school. When I got to the kitchen, Mama's face reminded me that I was still in trouble. She looked at me with disappointment in her eyes as she went to do Keyana's hair. That's when I slowed down. What had I been thinking? I didn't want them mad at me anymore. The plan I'd thought up was crazy. I couldn't risk getting in trouble again like I had the day before. But why hadn't they let me explain?

I started feeling angry and scraped the chair loudly as I pulled it away from the table. Dad stared at me over his newspaper with his 'don't-start-with-me' look. I tried not to look his way as I sat down to eat my cereal, but a headline caught my attention.

"What's wrong now?" Dad confronted me as I stared his way.

I tilted my head to read the article from Dad's lowered paper.

A sea lion pup caught in a crevice swam away shortly after Aquarium workers arrived. They'd received numerous phone calls from beachcombers about the young sea lion, which had been spotted as early as Tuesday. When workers arrived, however, the sea lion just swam away. "It had probably lost weight, being stuck there for a few days," commented one of the Aquarium outreach employees. . . .

"That's the sea lion I found yesterday!" I blurted out.

Dad squinted at me, waiting for an explanation. Before I could stop myself, words flowed out of me like rain from the night before. "I found the stranded sea lion and I wanted to free him and then it looked like a storm was coming and—"

"When did all this happen?" Dad looked at me hard.

"When we were biking," I said, moving my eyes back down to the article.

Dad looked at me as if he were putting together a puzzle. After several minutes, he said quietly, "Well, I'm glad to know you don't hate being near the water anymore." He shook his head in disbelief. "My son, Antoine Graves, rescuer of sea lions," he chuckled.

"But I didn't save it. I wanted to. I wish I had been the one to do it." Then I wondered what would have happened if I had been able to touch it, feed it, or move it. Would I have helped?

I looked back at the article, relieved that the sea lion had escaped and that I didn't have to execute my plan. When I looked up, I caught Dad smiling at me, the way he does when he's with his friends. I don't think he saw a know-nothing little boy anymore. He looked the way I'd always wanted him to be: proud.

THINK CRITICALLY

1. Why doesn't Antoine know what to do when he finds the stranded sea lion? CHARACTER'S EMOTIONS

2. Antoine says that starfish were "stretching on the rocks like sunbathers." Identify the kinds of figurative language used in this phrase, and explain their effect. FIGURATIVE LANGUAGE

3. What happens when Antoine sees the newspaper headline about the sea lion? CAUSE AND EFFECT

4. How would you feel if you saw a wild animal that was in danger? What would you do? MAKE CONNECTIONS

5. **WRITE** How can you tell that Antoine always wants to do the right thing? Use details from the selection to support your answer. SHORT RESPONSE

ABOUT THE AUTHOR

Mélina Brown

Mélina Brown was born in France and raised in Wisconsin, Michigan, and Minnesota. She works as a librarian and media specialist at an elementary school in Minneapolis. As ideas for her writing, she uses experiences from her travels, memories from her childhood, and what she learns from her students. Mélina Brown is the author of several biographies and novels for young people. She has also written for magazines and radio.

ABOUT THE ILLUSTRATOR

Alex Bostic

Alex Bostic was influenced by his sixth-grade art teacher, who encouraged him to attend art school on Saturdays. That teacher is still his mentor. During his career, Alex Bostic has illustrated greeting cards, designed art for movie sets, and taught art in colleges and universities. He lives in Glen Allen, Virginia.

GO online www.harcourtschool.com/storytown

Jane Yolen
Water Music
PHOTOGRAPHS
Jason Stemple

Poetry

EMBROIDERY BY JANE YOLEN

On this green loom,
In this wet place,
The ocean makes
Fine water lace.

Each patterned wave
Lays down a thread
Upon the ground
Of ocean bed.

Enduring
It shall never be,
This water lace
Embroidery.

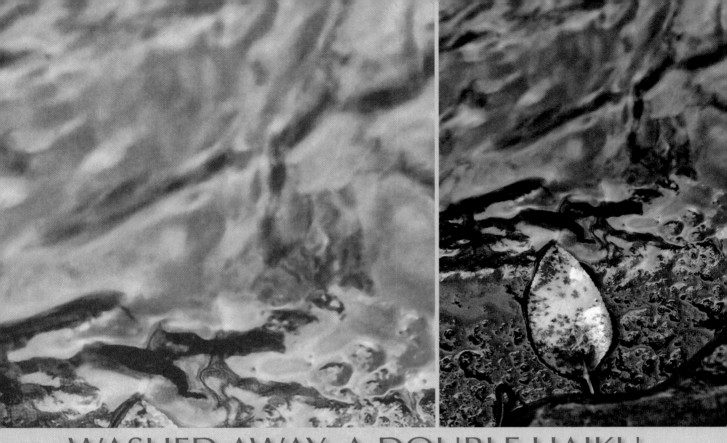

WASHED AWAY: A DOUBLE HAIKU

BY JANE YOLEN

Leaf upon the land,
The wild and raging water
Washes you away.

I am such a leaf:
Too many furious words
Rip me from my shore.

Connections

Comparing Texts

1. Antoine feels free when he is riding his bike at the beach. What activity gives you the same kind of feeling?

2. Compare the descriptions of water in the poem "Embroidery" and on page 314 of "The Long Bike Ride."

3. The newspaper article Antoine's father reads tells about several people who reported the stranded sea lion pup. Do you think most people would report this? Explain.

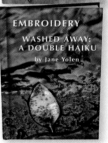

Vocabulary Review

Rate a Situation

Copy the word line below on a separate sheet of paper. Then read the sentences. Think about how each situation might make you feel, and write the Vocabulary Word in each item at an appropriate place on the word line. Discuss your choices with a partner.

Upset •————————————————• Excited

- Your lucky penny is wedged under a car tire.
- You're about to visit your ideal vacation spot.
- Giant hailstones are pelting the roof.
- Your brother blurted out the secret about the surprise.

wedged

ideal

perched

pelting

stranded

blurted

slunk

Fluency Practice

Repeated Reading

When you read with appropriate phrasing, you read several words together before pausing. Paying attention to punctuation marks will help you know when to pause. Read aloud the last paragraph of "The Long Bike Ride." Pause when you see periods, commas, and the colon in the last sentence. Practice rereading the paragraph until your phrasing sounds smooth and natural.

Writing

Write a Narrative

Imagine that you are Antoine in "The Long Bike Ride." Write a personal narrative that tells what you would have done if you had seen the stranded sea lion pup.

Characters		Setting

Conflict

Plot Events

Resolution

My Writing Checklist

Writing Trait ➤ Sentence Fluency

✓ I used a story map to plan my writing.

✓ I included dialogue and figurative language to make my story come alive for readers.

✓ I used different kinds of sentences.

CONTENTS

Lesson 13

Genre: Realistic Fiction

ESCAPING the Giant Wave

PEG KEHRET

Genre: Expository Nonfiction

A WORLD IN MOTION

FROM SCHOLASTIC ATLAS OF OCEANS

Focus Skill

Theme

The **theme** of a story is the author's main message. Often, a story's theme gives a message or moral about real life. An author rarely states a story's theme directly. Instead, the author expects readers to use clues from the story to figure out the theme. Ask yourself these questions as you read:

- Why are the qualities of the characters important?
- What do the characters learn as a result of their actions?
- How is the setting important to the story?

Character's Qualities	Character's Actions	Setting

Theme

Tip

Usually a story's theme can be expressed in a short statement, such as "Everyone has positive traits."

Read the paragraph below. Then look at the graphic organizer. It shows how the character's qualities, his actions, and the setting are all clues to the theme of the paragraph.

Last winter, Bernie insisted that his family create an emergency survival kit. The kit they put together included a flashlight, water, canned food, blankets, a radio, and extra batteries. In February, a strong storm blew down the power lines. Everyone in the area was without power for two days. Bernie's family used the kit and thanked him for his careful planning.

Character's Qualities	**Character's Actions**	**Setting**
organized and thoughtful	gets his family to create a survival kit	Bernie's neighborhood during a strong storm

Theme
Preparation pays off.

Try This!

How does the time of year in which this story takes place contribute to the theme?

www.harcourtschool.com/storytown

Vocabulary

Build Robust Vocabulary

- premonition
- disoriented
- imperative
- haphazardly
- remorse
- receded
- optimistic

A Survivor Remembers

I was just seven years old during the 1906 earthquake in San Francisco. I had a **premonition** the day before that something awful was going to happen. For that reason, the earthquake did not come as a complete surprise.

I remember how **disoriented** I felt after the quake. The buildings around my home had crumbled to the ground. The city was nothing like what it had been the day before.

More than 28,000 buildings were destroyed during the San Francisco earthquake and fire in 1906.

Over the next few days, fires engulfed the city. We were told it was **imperative** that we pack quickly and leave until the fires were out. Mother packed **haphazardly**. She was so rushed that she packed four hats but no cooking pan. My father was filled with **remorse** because he had been away from home when the quake struck.

Firefighters battled the flames as best they could. When the fires **receded,** only rubble remained in their path. One week later, we returned. Our house was still standing! I felt **optimistic** for the first time. The city was soon rebuilt, but the memory of the earthquake will always be with me.

Fires burned throughout the city for several days after the earthquake.

GO online www.harcourtschool.com/storytown

Word Champion

Your goal this week is to use Vocabulary Words outside your classroom. Put the list of words on your refrigerator or in another place in your home where you will see it. Use each word in conversations with your family. For example, you might tell your parents that you feel optimistic about how your team will perform in an upcoming game. Write the words you used in your vocabulary journal, and tell how you used them.

Realistic Fiction

Genre Study

Realistic fiction has characters
and events that are like people
and events in real life. As you
read, look for

- characters with feelings that
  real people might have.

- a setting based on a real place.

Comprehension Strategy

Answer questions you have
about a story by looking in the
text and thinking about what
you already know.

Thirteen-year-old Kyle and his family are vacationing in Fisher Beach, Oregon. Kyle thinks his greatest challenge on vacation will be seeing Daren, a bully from school back in Kansas. One evening, Kyle is left in charge of his younger sister, BeeBee, while his parents are on a dinner cruise on the *Elegant Empress*. Then the unthinkable happens— an earthquake triggers a fire. Kyle knows a tsunami could be next. Kyle and BeeBee quickly head uphill and inland. They join a friendly couple, Norm and Josie, and their dog Pansy. The group survives one giant wave together. Fearing another wave might come, Kyle and his sister continue inland. Then they find Pansy alone.

ESCAPING THE GIANT WAVE

BY PEG KEHRET ILLUSTRATED BY JOHN SANDFORD

I felt bad for Norm and Josie, knowing they would be worried about Pansy. They'd been so kind to us; I wished I had a way to let them know that Pansy had found us, and that we would take care of her and bring her back when the danger was over. That is, we'd bring her back *if* we survived.

We went deeper into the trees. I felt as if I were having a nightmare—the kind where I know I'm in danger and it's imperative to run away, but I can't seem to make my legs work.

I wished I had paid more attention to the maps of the Oregon coast that Dad had shown us when we were planning this trip. In particular, I wondered what lay straight east of Fisher Beach. If we were running away from the ocean—and I hoped we were still going in that direction, although I knew it was possible that by now we were disoriented and going around in circles—I wished I knew what was ahead of us. Would we eventually come to a road? A town? Farms? Or did these lonely woods go on for miles?

Pansy stopped.

"Come, Pansy," BeeBee said. "This way."

The terrier, who moments before had willingly trotted alongside us, now stood stiff-legged, refusing to budge.

"Is she hurt?" I asked. "Is her paw caught in a bramble?"

I shined the light on Pansy. The dog was shaking with fear. "It's okay, Pansy," I said.

"Woof!"

The sharp bark made me jump— and sent a shiver of premonition up my back. Did Pansy sense something that I couldn't yet know?

"Woof! Woof! Woof!" It was the same bark Pansy had given just before the tsunami hit.

"Another wave is coming," BeeBee said.

I swung the flashlight in a circle, looking for a safe place to wait. We were near a large tree, a giant old-growth cedar. I ran to the tree and put both arms straight out sideways; the tree trunk went from the fingertips of one hand to the fingertips of the other.

"Come here," I said. "We're going to stand on the far side of this big tree. If another wave comes, the tree will protect us."

It was a sturdy shield, but would it really be strong enough to protect us from a tsunami?

BeeBee followed me to the back side of the tree.

"Stand as close to it as you can," I said. "Press up against the bark."

BeeBee stepped up on a large root that angled away from the bottom of the tree and leaned her forehead against the trunk.

I turned off the light and put it in my pocket, then gathered the terrified dog in my arms and stood directly behind BeeBee. I felt BeeBee's shoulders shake and knew she was crying.

"Turn around," I said. "Put your back against the tree, and face me. We're going to make a dog sandwich."

BeeBee turned, wiping her nose on the back of one hand. "Dog sandwich?"

"You and I are the bread, and Pansy's the filling in the middle," I said.

BeeBee put her arms around Pansy. "Good dog," she whispered. "You're a good, good dog."

Pansy's tail swished against me as she licked the tears from BeeBee's cheeks.

I wondered how I could make up a silly joke about a dog sandwich when I feared we were going to die any minute. Still, my words had helped. BeeBee wasn't crying any more, and now that we were holding her close, Pansy had stopped shaking.

If disaster strikes, I thought, *I've spent my last few minutes on Earth hugging a dog and calming my sister's fear.* Those are good things—but I didn't want these to be my last minutes on Earth. I didn't want to die making a dog sandwich or running through the woods or any other way. I wanted to live! I wanted to survive the tsunami and find Mom and Dad and go back home to Kansas. I wanted to play baseball and hang out with my friends and read some good books and ride my scooter and . . .

I heard what Pansy must have heard a few minutes earlier.

"Here it comes," BeeBee said.

We huddled behind the tree and listened to the second giant wave roar toward us. I could tell from the sound that it was higher than the first one had been and coming farther inland.

Pansy began to tremble again.

"It's coming over the top of the hill!" BeeBee shouted.

I tightened my hold on Pansy and pushed even closer to BeeBee.

I heard trees crash to the ground, and for one awful moment I feared I had made a terrible mistake by staying behind the big cedar tree. What if the force of the water pushed the tree over on top of us, trapping us beneath it?

Well, it was too late to change my mind. The fastest runner in the world wouldn't be able to escape the wave when it was this close.

The water thundered forward. I ducked my head down, shielding BeeBee, and braced my legs to keep my balance.

"It's going to hit us!" BeeBee screamed.

Small stones, propelled forward by the water, hit our tree, then bounced to the ground like hailstones.

I closed my eyes.

Pansy whimpered.

BeeBee pulled me even closer.

The wave splashed to Earth just before it reached us. It must have crested over the treetops, because now I heard water smashing down on the woods we had run through minutes before.

The ground shook as the water poured down. I heard crashes and loud thuds. Something more than trees was being dropped by the wave. Rocks? Pieces of driftwood? Charred timbers from the hotels? It was too dark to see what the wave carried; all I could do was hope that none of it landed on us.

Water rose around our ankles, then quickly receded. Once the wave hit, it reversed course and hurried back to where it had begun.

As the wave rushed away from us, we stayed where we were, fearing a third wave would follow.

"That was close," I said.

"Too close," BeeBee said.

I shifted Pansy to a different position. For such a small dog, she sure got heavy in a hurry.

"How many giant waves will there be?" BeeBee asked.

I wished BeeBee would quit asking questions as if I were somehow an authority. I wasn't the expert. I was just a kid who no longer wanted to be responsible for his sister.

"I don't know," I said. "If the worst is yet to come, we should keep running." I stepped out from behind the tree.

BeeBee did too. "Thank you, tree," she said.

"Thank you, Pansy," I said. If she hadn't alerted us that another wave was coming, we wouldn't have made it behind the tree in time.

I tried to put Pansy down but she whimpered so pathetically that I continued to hold her even though my arms ached. I turned on the flashlight and moved it slowly back and forth.

"Everything's changed," BeeBee said.

The woods we had walked through now looked as if loggers had chopped down trees at random and left them leaning haphazardly against each other.

Much of the low undergrowth had washed away; what was left wore a thick layer of sand. A twisted piece of metal the size of a car's bumper glinted in my light; I couldn't tell what the metal had been, but I knew if it had come down on a person, it would have inflicted serious injury.

The ground was littered with beach chairs, broken bicycles, and other odd pieces of man-made items that had been lifted by the water and transplanted here.

I stopped my light on a large rectangular piece of wood that stuck out of the ground at an angle, one corner of it jammed into the dirt.

"It's a sign," BeeBee said as she walked closer to it. "It's the big sign from the front of the Totem Pole Inn!"

The foot-high carved letters and the life-size totem faces were black from the fire. The sign had been mounted on two tall logs the size of telephone poles near the front door of our hotel. I thought of the power necessary to rip that heavy sign free and carry it over the top of the hill.

"I wonder if Norm and Josie are okay," BeeBee said.

I was afraid they weren't, since the wave had landed right where they had been, but I didn't say that. I didn't even want to think it.

I couldn't hold Pansy any longer. I set her down. The dog sniffed the sign, then rolled in the wet sand. Her fur was a mess, but it didn't matter. She was alive. That's all that mattered for Pansy, and for BeeBee and me. We were alive.

I cupped my hands around my mouth and shouted, "Norm! Josie! Can you hear me?"

My words floated away like soap bubbles.

"We'd better keep going," I said.

"No. I can't run any more. I'm worn out."

"There might be another wave, even bigger than the last one."

"I don't care," BeeBee said. "I'm too tired to run anymore; I need to rest." Her face was pale, her arms were scratched from running through the woods, and I knew she wouldn't make it much farther no matter how desperate our situation.

My burned hand throbbed, my head ached, and my legs felt like rubber. BeeBee was right; we both needed to rest.

"I don't have the energy to keep running either," I said. "If another wave comes this far, we'll stand behind our big tree again and hope for the best."

"Good. I'm going to sit right here and wait for Mom and Dad to find us." She plopped down on the trunk of a downed tree.

I sat beside her. I doubted that anyone would find us, but if no more waves came, we could wait here until daylight. By then surely it would be safe to return to Fisher Beach.

I wondered what was left of Fisher Beach and the town of Fisher. Had the small village survived? Was anyone there to broadcast an all-clear signal when it was safe to return?

Where were Mom and Dad? Was the *Elegant Empress* unharmed somewhere out at sea—or had the tsunami waves destroyed it?

What had happened to Norm and Josie?

My mind overflowed with questions, but I didn't know how to find any of the answers.

Each minute seemed like an hour.

We sat on the fallen tree, listening for another giant wave. I kept the flashlight off, saving the batteries in case we needed to see.

My mind was as weary as my body. The fire, the fear of a tsunami, and my worry about Mom and Dad had drained me of energy as much as climbing the hill and running through the woods had.

Tired as I was, I worried that we shouldn't stay where we were; we ought to keep going. When we first got to the top of the hill, we should have kept running rather than sitting on the bench. That decision had probably been fatal for Norm and Josie. Now we were sitting again instead of running farther inland. Was I making the same mistake twice?

With so many trees down, the next wave would have less resistance. It might travel faster and farther. I fretted and stewed over the possibility, but I didn't move. BeeBee and I were exhausted. If a bigger wave came now we wouldn't be able to outrun it anyway.

I had done my best to save us. Now I sat in the dark, and waited.

The only sound was Pansy's gentle snoring.

BeeBee's head kept drooping down, then jerking back up, the way it does when she falls asleep in the car.

"Let's sit on the ground," I said, "and lean back against the tree."

We sat in the damp sand.

"My clothes are getting dirty," BeeBee said, "and my shoes are all wet. Mom won't like that."

"It's okay. Mom will be so glad to see us, she won't care how dirty we are."

"I wonder if Daren drowned," BeeBee said.

"He should have come with us."

"I'm glad he didn't."

The anger in her voice surprised me.

"I didn't tell Mom and Dad the truth about Daren," BeeBee went on.

"What do you mean?"

"He hits me. At school he sneaks up behind me during recess and pushes me. Sometimes he pokes me with a pencil, and if I cry, he calls me a baby."

Outrage exploded inside me. I was far more furious at Daren for bullying BeeBee than I had ever been over getting hit myself. I wondered if Daren had picked on BeeBee because she was my sister. That possibility made me feel sick.

"I never told on him because I was scared he'd do something worse to get even."

Remorse settled on me like a quilt; I felt its weight on my shoulders.

"I know this is a terrible thing to say," BeeBee continued, "but if Daren doesn't come back, I won't miss him."

I wouldn't miss him either, but I hoped he was alive. If I never saw Daren again I would always regret letting him get away with hassling me for so long. I should have taken a stand with Daren years ago. If I hadn't wanted to confront him myself, I should have talked to a teacher or my parents about the problem.

I had always been afraid to tell him off, for the same reason BeeBee hadn't told a teacher. I feared Daren would get angry and beat up on me. Now I saw that there are worse things in this life than getting thrashed, and one of them is feeling shame for not having the courage to do what's right.

343

I'm not a coward, I thought. *I saved us from the fire, and so far we've survived the tsunami because of me. Daren's the one who panicked on the hotel stairs, not me.*

Why did I ever let him bully me? If I had stopped him years ago when his bullying first began, he might never have picked on BeeBee at all.

"If Daren escapes from the tsunami," I vowed, "I'll see that he never bothers you again."

"I thought you were scared of him too."

"I used to be, but I'm not anymore."

BeeBee thought about that for a minute. Then she said, "If Mom and Dad don't come back, what will happen to us?"

I'd already thought about that, and I knew the answer. "We'll live with Grandma and Grandpa," I said. "They'd move to a bigger house so they could take us."

"Good." BeeBee laid her head in my lap and promptly fell asleep.

Pansy draped her muzzle across my ankle and resumed snoring.

I was more tired than I'd ever been in my life, but I couldn't sleep. I was too anxious. I sat in the dark thinking about everything that had happened and wondering what tomorrow would bring. Would there be a joyous reunion with Mom and Dad? Or would BeeBee and I learn that we were orphans? I loved Grandma and Grandpa, but I wanted Mom and Dad back.

The night dragged on. No more waves came.

Eventually I must have dozed off because when I opened my eyes, I saw the first hint of daylight. BeeBee had shifted away from me and lay on her side, curled around Pansy. Pansy's ears pricked up when I stirred. Her tail thumped the sand.

I moved my head from side to side, working the stiffness out of my neck. Then I looked at my burned right palm. It was blistered and red, but it didn't hurt as much as it had the night before.

The sun rose, bringing light and warmth and hope.

As soon as I stood up, BeeBee awoke. "Is it safe to go back?" she asked. "Did you hear the all-clear signal?"

"I didn't hear a signal, but I'm sure the tsunami is over."

"Good. I'm starving."

We walked through the sand, stepping over downed trees and going around an astonishing amount of debris. What had been a woods last night now looked more like a movie set for a film about the end of the world.

A woman's straw hat lay upside down, pink ribbons trailing across the sand. A portable barbecue was wedged into the ground. An inflatable raft with a crab pot still attached to a cord nested six feet up in a tree.

Pansy ran a short way ahead, then returned. It was clear that she wanted to stay close to us.

"Is that a refrigerator?" BeeBee asked.

I looked where she was pointing. A full-size white refrigerator had been plucked from a seaside cottage or a home in Fisher and deposited on top of the hill.

"Maybe there's something in it that we can eat," I said.

"Like cold Snickers bars."

We hurried to the refrigerator and opened the door. It was no colder inside the appliance than it was outside, but the shelves contained a package of sliced ham, a carton of eggs, a half loaf of bread, a quart of milk, and a jar of dill pickles.

Curious, I opened the egg carton. Not a single egg was broken.

"No Snickers," BeeBee said, "but we can make ham sandwiches."

"We can't eat the ham," I said. "The fridge has been off too long; we might get food poisoning. We can't drink the milk either, but we can eat the bread and the pickles."

We each wrapped a slice of bread around a dill pickle. I gave Pansy a piece of bread too, which she gobbled without chewing. I gave her a second piece.

"This bread is stale," BeeBee said. Then she smiled. "Maybe we should complain and ask for our money back."

"It could be worse," I said. "The fridge might have been full of cauliflower and spinach."

"I'm thirsty," BeeBee said. "Too bad whoever owns this refrigerator didn't keep bottled water or soft drinks on hand."

Unsure when we'd get a chance to eat again, I took the rest of the bread with us.

"Do you want me to carry the jar of pickles?" BeeBee asked.

"No. They're too salty. They'll make us even thirstier."

Pansy walked as if she were glued to my pant leg, whining and poking her nose at the bread bag, until I let her eat a third slice. BeeBee and I each ate another piece too. Stale bread was better than hunger pangs.

"Are you sure we're going the right way?" BeeBee asked. "This doesn't look anything like it did last night."

I looked in every direction. The sun was higher now, and the sunlight still came from behind us. That meant we were walking westward, toward the ocean. "This is right," I said. "We need to keep the sun at our backs."

A short while after we found the refrigerator, I spotted something green half-buried in the sand. Kicking at it with my foot, I uncovered a six-pack of 7-Up.

"How about a warm 7-Up for breakfast?" I asked.

"Yum, yum," said BeeBee. "Stale bread and warm 7-Up."

I still had the hotel towel, so I used it to wipe the sand off the tops of two cans. We each popped one open. The 7-Up fizzed over the top and ran down the side. It wasn't cold, but it tasted fantastic.

I wondered if it was okay for a dog to drink soda pop. Since Pansy must be every bit as thirsty as we were, I decided to let her have some.

I cupped my left hand and poured some of my pop into It. Then I held my hand in front of Pansy, who lapped up some 7-Up, stopped in surprise, stuck her tongue in and out a couple of times, and then drank the rest, licking my hand to be sure she got it all.

Refreshed by the food and drink, we continued walking. Maybe Norm and Josie did survive, I thought. Daren too. It's easier to be optimistic when you're not hungry.

When we came to a clump of tall trees, Pansy stood at the base of the trees and yipped, a high excited bark. She ran behind the trees and came back with a piece of white fabric in her mouth which she dropped at BeeBee's feet.

"She found Josie's handkerchief!" BeeBee said. "Josie let me use it last night, and I noticed the roses on it."

Pansy stood on her hind legs, put her front paws on the trunk of the largest tree, and yipped again.

BeeBee and I looked up into the branches. I half expected Norm and Josie to be perched on one of the limbs like two big birds, though I knew that was silly. Even if they had climbed a tree to escape the tsunami, they'd have come down by now.

"Norm and Josie must have been here," BeeBee said.

"Maybe they stood behind these trees, the way we stood behind that big cedar. Maybe the trees protected them."

"I bet that's what happened," BeeBee said. She put the handkerchief in her pants pocket. "I'll give this to Josie when I see her."

I hope you will, I thought. *Oh, I hope you will.*

We hurried on, expecting to come out of the last of the trees and see the wide area of low shrubs that had stretched from the park bench to the beginning of the woods. The woods ended, but now, instead of the open area, there was a sharp drop-off. The wave had washed away the whole west side of the hill.

347

"The road is gone," BeeBee said. "So is the bench."

We walked to within ten feet of the edge. "Don't go any closer," I said. "It might crumble."

As we looked at the destruction, Pansy ran off to one side, sniffing the sand. "What has Pansy found?" I asked, and went to find out.

"It's footprints!" I called. "Someone else has been here this morning!"

We squatted beside the footprints and saw that they were two different sizes. "Two people," BeeBee said.

I watched Pansy closely. If Norm and Josie had made those footprints, I thought Pansy would get all excited. She didn't. She smelled the footprints while we looked at them, but when we walked on, she came with us.

We could see the remains of the two hotels now, and we saw the beach, although the wooden steps that had led from the hotels to the beach were no longer there.

Gentle waves lapped the shore just as they had before the tsunami. It was as if the ocean had forgotten all about yesterday's violence and returned to business as usual.

"I see people!" BeeBee said.

Sure enough. People were walking on the beach.

"They're probably looking for souvenirs of the tsunami," she said.

"Or they're looking for survivors. Maybe Mom and Dad are down there!"

That possibility gave both of us a spurt of energy, and we looked for a way to get off the hill. With the road washed away, it took us awhile. Most of the way, we simply sat down and slid in the sand, letting Pansy get down as best she could. When we reached the bottom, we headed toward the remains of the Totem Pole Inn.

Anticipation and dread wrestled within me. Would we see Mom and Dad soon— or would we learn that the *Elegant Empress* had disappeared? I didn't know whether to rush forward or hang back.

BeeBee made the decision for me by taking off at a trot, with Pansy loping beside her. I had to run to catch up to them.

Two women saw us approaching and hurried toward us. "Were you up on the hill all night?" one of them asked. When I said yes, she held out a snapshot of a young man and said, "I'm looking for my nephew. Did you see him?"

"No. There was an older couple up there for awhile but we got separated from them. We never saw your nephew. I'm sorry."

"He worked at the Frontier Lodge," the woman said, "in the kitchen."

I wondered if he had made our pizza and the two milkshakes.

"Do you know anything about the *Elegant Empress*?" I asked.

"Who?"

"It's a ship. Our parents were on it when the earthquake hit, and we don't know what happened to them."

"I haven't heard anything about a ship," the woman said.

"Nor have I," said her companion.

"Good luck," the woman said.

"I hope you find your nephew," BeeBee said.

We had similar conversations with other people. One was hunting for his son, who was a bellhop at the Totem Pole Inn. Another said her teenage daughter had been at a birthday party on the beach the night before. The third asked if we had seen any of the firefighters.

We disappointed each person with our answers—and they disappointed us with theirs.

"The power is still out in most of the county," the last man told us. "Phone lines are out too, and the cell phone tower washed away. I haven't heard a news broadcast since I came out here about two this morning, when a Portland station broadcast an all-clear."

349

We asked everyone we saw, but nobody knew what had happened to the *Elegant Empress*.

BeeBee and I walked slowly around the remains of the Totem Pole Inn. "If Mom and Dad are okay," I said, "I know they'll come here."

Helicopters droned overhead, following the coastline.

A woman wearing an armband approached. "Do you need help?"she asked. "I'm with the emergency management service, and we're here to help survivors."

"We're looking for our parents."

"We're also looking for Pansy's owners," BeeBee said.

I told the woman what had happened to us.

"We have a temporary headquarters set up in a tent, only half a mile up the beach," she said. "Go there, and they'll give you something to eat and help you search the information we have, to see if your parents and your friends have been found."

"Thanks," I said.

We headed toward the tent.

"What if Mom and Dad haven't been found?" BeeBee asked.

"Then we'll keep looking for them. The emergency people probably have a computer network where names can be entered. We'll put our names in, so if Mom and Dad are searching for us somewhere else, they'll know we're okay." I sounded confident, but it was all an act.

"There's still no power," BeeBee said. "They could use laptops running on batteries to collect data, but without telephone lines they can't send that information elsewhere. How would the modem work?"

"Did Norm and Josie ever say their last name?" I asked.

"I don't think so. If they did, I don't remember it."

A long line of people stretched out of the tent. "Before we get in line," I said, "let's walk past everyone who's waiting, in case Mom and Dad are here."

We walked beside the line of people. My eyes skimmed each face as I hoped desperately that the next one would be familiar.

None were.

When we reached the point where the line of people went inside the tent, there was a table where workers were serving sandwiches and juice.

"I'll look for Mom and Dad inside," BeeBee said. "You get us some food."

I took three sandwiches and two cans of juice. Soon BeeBee came back. "There are twelve people waiting inside," she reported, "plus the twenty-five in line outside, but I don't know any of them."

We took our place at the end of the line and started to eat. BeeBee was so glad to get decent food that she didn't even bother to pick the lettuce out of her sandwich.

I broke the third sandwich into pieces and gave them to Pansy.

"This is a *real* dog sandwich," BeeBee said, "Not like the one we made during the tsunami last night."

Last night. Less than half a day. I could hardly believe that so little time had passed since BeeBee and I had held Pansy between us while we hid behind the cedar tree. The night had seemed endless.

Yesterday morning at about this time, I had been walking on the beach with Mom and Dad. We had read the warning sign and I had made my sea picture. It seemed like ten years ago, like a happy memory from when I was only three or four years old.

A fist jabbed me right between the shoulder blades. "Well, well," said a familiar voice. "The scaredy-cat made it through the big bad wave."

Last night I had hoped Daren would survive. Now that he was here, I had mixed feelings.

"I'm glad I went uphill," I said. "It saved my life."

"You were scared stiff," Daren said. "While you were running away, I walked down to the beach and waded in the water."

"What happened when the big waves came?" BeeBee asked.

"The first one picked me up and dropped me on top of the Totem Pole Inn's elevator tower. I clung to the edge of the roof when the wave receded."

"We saw the two people on the tower roof," I said, "but we couldn't tell who they were."

"It was me and a cook from the hotel. We found a trap door in the roof that went inside the tower to the elevator equipment. We stayed in there all night and climbed down this morning. We heard the second wave, but the concrete tower held."

"You were lucky," I said.

"Not lucky, just brave. I wasn't scared for one second."

Liar, I thought. *We were all scared.*

"You're the one who was afraid," Daren went on.

"Anyone with sense would be afraid of a tsunami," I said.

"Are you saying I don't have any sense?"

"I'm saying you were just as frightened as I was."

Daren raised his hand as if to punch me.

I pushed his hand away and looked him in the eye.

"You're alive because of me," I said. "You should be grateful."

He glared at me, but he didn't deny what I said. I knew we'd never be friends and I knew my problems with Daren probably weren't over permanently, but I had taken a giant step on the road to solving them.

"Have you heard from your parents?" I asked. "Do you know what happened to the *Elegant Empress*?"

"No. I was on my way to the tent to ask about the ship when I saw you."

"This is the line for information," I said. "You can wait with us."

BeeBee gave me a surprised look. I was surprised too. I never thought I'd invite Daren to spend two seconds with me, but now that I had finally confronted him, he had lost his power over me. He was just another kid looking for his parents, the same as we were.

"Where did you get the sandwich?" Daren asked.

I told him, and he left to get some food.

We had waited in the line half an hour when Pansy gave an excited "Yip!" and took off down the beach. She ran in circles around the man walking toward us, leaping in the air with joy.

"It's Norm!" BeeBee said.

"Norm!" I called, waving my hands over my head.

BeeBee ran to him and threw her arms around him. Together they returned to where I waited in line.

"I'm so glad to see you," Norm said, wiping tears from his wrinkled cheeks. "And Pansy!" He picked the wriggling dog up and hugged her. "We let her go last night, figuring she'd follow you kids. We wanted her to be safe even if we didn't make it."

"Where's Josie?" BeeBee asked.

"She's gone," Norm said, his voice breaking. "When we heard that second big wave coming, I climbed up a tree and pulled Josie up after me. When the wave hit us, I was able to hang on but Josie couldn't. The force of the water was too much for her. She lost her grip and was swept away."

Norm stroked the dog, unable to talk for a moment. "I thought of going with her," he said. "We were together forty-seven years, and it would have been easy to release my hold on the tree and let the water take me too. But then I thought about our son and our grandkids. I'd like to see those grandkids grow up. I worried about Pansy too. She needs me to look after her."

"I'm sorry about Josie," I said. "I liked her a lot."

"I *loved* her," BeeBee said. "I have her handkerchief. Pansy found it this morning." BeeBee held the handkerchief toward Norm.

"You keep that, honey," Norm said. "Think of my Josie whenever you use it."

"Thank you." BeeBee folded the handkerchief carefully and tucked it in her pocket.

"You kids saved Pansy's life," Norm said.

"And she saved ours," I replied. "She barked to let us know when the second wave was coming, and we hid behind a big tree."

Norm stood with us while we waited in line. He told us that his house had been destroyed by the tsunami. "One of the firefighters helped me get down the hill," he said. "He managed to stay afloat on a beam from the hotel during the first wave, then swam ashore and ran up the hill before the second wave hit. He found me as soon as it got light, and we came down together."

"We saw footprints," BeeBee said. "We knew someone else had been in the woods."

The line moved slowly. We had not yet reached the entrance to the tent when a man with a megaphone came out and shouted an announcement: "If any of you are here to inquire about passengers on the *Elegant Empress*, please follow me."

BeeBee, Daren, and I hurried toward the man. So did several other people who had been waiting in the line. When we were all grouped around the man with the megaphone, he said, "I have good news for you. The *Elegant Empress* was far enough away from shore that it was able to ride the tsunami waves without capsizing. All passengers and crew are safe."

"Wasn't the ship damaged?" someone asked.

"No. The captain waited until the all-clear signal was radioed to him and then . . ."

The man kept talking, but I found it hard to concentrate on his words. They were safe! Mom and Dad were alive!

THINK CRITICALLY

1 What thoughts and emotions does Kyle experience as he stands behind the tree, before the second wave strikes? CHARACTER'S EMOTIONS

2 What theme about nature do the setting and the characters' actions suggest? THEME

3 Do the characters and the events in this story seem believable to you? Explain. MAKE JUDGMENTS

4 How should hikers, boaters, and others who enjoy the outdoors prepare for unexpected events, such as the earthquake and the tsunami in this story? MAKE CONNECTIONS

5 **WRITE** Compare how Kyle acts around Daren before and after the tsunami. Why do you think Kyle's actions change? Use details from the selection to support your answer. SHORT RESPONSE

ABOUT THE AUTHOR

PEG KEHRET

When Peg Kehret was nine, she created her own newspaper, called *Dog Newspaper*. Each week, she interviewed neighbors about the latest news regarding their dogs. When she was twelve, Peg Kehret was diagnosed with polio. She was paralyzed for several months. Although she recovered, she clearly remembers what it was like. Because of the experience, she says that she finds it easy to write from a child's perspective. Peg Kehret likes to write about ordinary young people who use their wits to solve extraordinary problems.

ABOUT THE ILLUSTRATOR

JOHN SANDFORD

John Sandford was born in Hannibal, Missouri, and grew up in a family of five children and several irritable cats. Everyone in his family drew. John Sandford has illustrated more than sixty children's books. He now lives in Chicago, Illinois.

GO online www.harcourtschool.com/storytown

SCHOLASTIC ATLAS OF
OCEANS

Expository Nonfiction

A WORLD

Earth's crust looks like a gigantic puzzle. It is cut into about a dozen pieces, called tectonic plates. The plates float on a thick layer of magma, soft and burning-hot rock found in the center of the planet. As the magma shifts, the plates slide, meet up, and rub together. Plates crashing together may set off gigantic earthquakes. In the ocean, these events can trigger tsunamis—killer tidal waves that are dozens of feet high. Over a very long period of time, the movement of plates is powerful enough to change the features of the continents and the ocean floor, carving out deep trenches and building towering chains of undersea mountains.

Continental Drift About 250 million years ago, Earth had only one continent, Pangaea, and only one ocean covered the rest of the planet. Movement in Earth's plates caused Pangaea to break up, and the separate pieces, or continents, began to drift apart. They're still moving today: the Atlantic Ocean is slowly widening, and Europe is drifting away from America, moving 1 in. (2.5 cm) farther each year.

VOLCANIC MOUNTAINS

The movement of plates causes magma to escape from deep inside Earth. The magma cools and hardens when it comes into contact with the water or air. As it collects and builds up, the magma forms different kinds of volcanic mountains.

 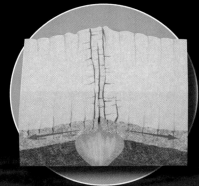 

Volcanic Chain

When two plates collide at the edge of a continent, the pressure becomes so great that magma starts to escape, forming a chain of volcanic mountains over time.

Oceanic Ridge

When two plates move apart under the ocean, a long crack appears between them. Escaping magma builds up on both sides of the crack and forms an oceanic ridge.

Island Arc

When two plates collide under the ocean, the pressure causes magma to escape. The magma forms volcanoes that grow up to the surface and become island arcs.

Connections

Comparing Texts

1. In "Escaping the Giant Wave," Kyle looks out for his little sister. Describe a time you were responsible for taking care of someone or something else.

2. Explain what caused the tsunami in "Escaping the Giant Wave." Use details from "A World in Motion" to describe what happened underground before the tsunami hit.

3. Imagine that the fictional disaster described in "Escaping the Giant Wave" really happened. Describe how people around the world would find out about the tsunami.

Vocabulary Review

Word Sort

Work in a small group. Sort the Vocabulary Words into categories, such as Words That Describe People or Actions and Words That Describe Nature. You may find that some words fit into more than one category. Take turns explaining why each word belongs in the category where you placed it.

Words That Describe People or Actions	Words That Describe Nature

premonition

disoriented

imperative

haphazardly

remorse

receded

optimistic

Fluency Practice

Partner Reading

When you read aloud with expression, you use your voice to reflect the feelings of the characters and the mood of the story. Select a passage from "Escaping the Giant Wave" to read aloud to a partner. Change your voice to match the emotions of the characters you are portraying. Ask your partner to give you feedback on your expression. Then switch roles.

Writing

Write a New Scene

Imagine that the author of "Escaping the Giant Wave" has asked you to write a scene in which Kyle and BeeBee are reunited with their parents. Write a short narrative for that scene.

My Writing Checklist

Writing Trait ▶ Organization

- ✔ I used a graphic organizer to plan my writing.
- ✔ I included a theme and clues to make the message clear to readers.
- ✔ I used sensory details to develop the plot and characters.

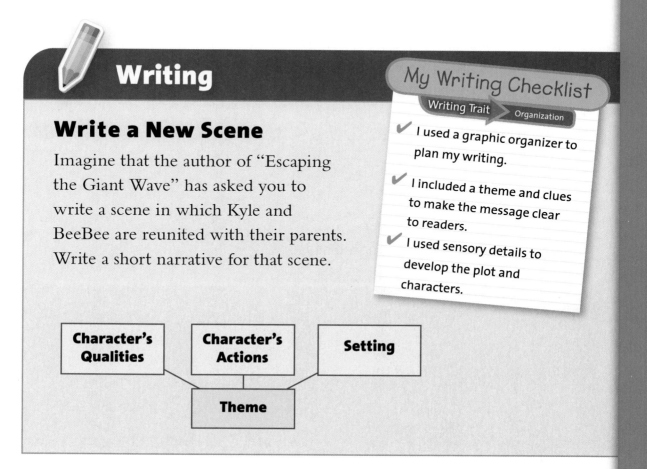

Character's Qualities	Character's Actions	Setting

Theme

CONTENTS

Lesson 14

BRIAN'S WINTER

GARY PAULSEN

Author of the award-winning novel *Hatchet*

FIND YOUR WAY
ANYWHERE
using only the Sun and your
WRISTWATCH

BY MERRY VAUGHAN

Theme

You have learned that a story's **theme** is the main message its author wants to convey to readers. The theme of a realistic fiction story is not directly stated. To determine the theme, you must think about everything you have learned from the story:

- the qualities of the characters
- the characters' actions and what they learn
- the setting of the story

Many story themes are universal—they appeal to people across cultures and from different time periods. As you read, connect the experiences of the characters to your own life experiences. This can sometimes help you identify the theme.

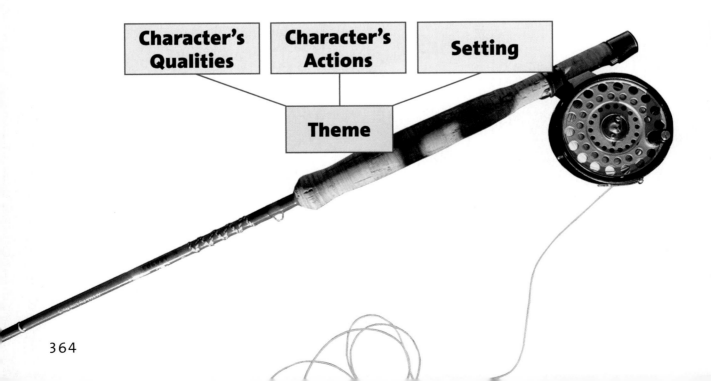

Character's Qualities	Character's Actions	Setting

Theme

Read the paragraph below. The graphic organizer shows how thinking about the main character's qualities and actions as well as the story's setting can help you determine the theme.

It was a beautiful day, but the fish were not biting. After two restless hours, Zoe's brothers went home. Zoe was determined to catch dinner. She sat quietly by the river and concentrated. Then she moved upstream a bit. Another hour passed. Suddenly, Zoe felt a strong tug. She fought the fish for several minutes and then reeled in the line and grinned. She had caught a large trout!

Character's Qualities	**Character's Qualities**	**Setting**
Zoe is patient and determined.	Zoe stays to fish after her brothers leave.	the shore of a river

Theme
Rewards come to those who are patient.

Try This!

Sometimes, a story can be interpreted in more than one way. What is another theme of the story about Zoe?

www.harcourtschool.com/storytown

Vocabulary

Build Robust Vocabulary

acquaintance

rank

gingerly

winced

cocky

stymied

terminal

retrieve

Strange Pets

Ferret, anyone? Dogs and cats may be fine pets for most people, but some animal lovers prefer more exotic pets, such as ferrets. If you or an **acquaintance** might like to have a pet ferret, there are some things you should know. A baby ferret is a called a kit. A kit is easier to train than an adult ferret. Ferrets are entertaining and playful, but they have a **rank** odor that many people dislike. Some states do not allow people to keep ferrets as pets.

You should handle a pet ferret **gingerly** so as not to startle it.

A pig, perhaps? You may want to consider a potbellied pig as a pet. However, be aware that a cute little piglet may become a 300-pound pig. If you have ever **winced** at the cost of food, imagine what a 300-pound pig will do to your family's grocery bill! Pigs are very clever. An untrained potbellied pig can be **cocky** and full of mischief.

A fine fennec fox? If you are still **stymied** about what kind of pet to get, consider a fennec fox. With proper training, this North African fox can be social and friendly. If you are a **terminal** dog lover but really want an exotic pet, the fennec fox may be right for you!

A trained fennec fox can **retrieve** a ball just as a dog can.

 GO online www.harcourtschool.com/storytown

Word Detective

Your mission this week is to search for the Vocabulary Words outside your classroom. You may see them in a newspaper or hear them on a TV news report. Each time you see or hear a Vocabulary Word, write it in your vocabulary journal. Tell where you encountered the word and how it was used.

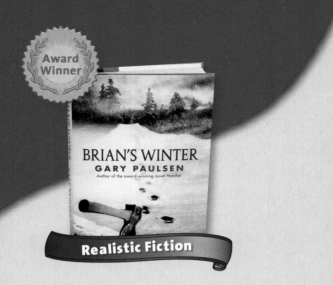

Realistic Fiction

Genre Study

Realistic fiction has characters and events that are like people and events in real life. As you read, look for

- a main character who overcomes a challenge.

- details that help readers picture the setting.

Comprehension Strategy

Answer questions you have about a story by looking in the text and thinking about what you already know.

BRIAN'S WINTER

by Gary Paulsen
illustrated by Raúl Colón

Thirteen-year-old Brian Robeson is alone in the
Canadian wilderness. Several months before, he had
been in a plane crash after the pilot suffered a heart
attack at the controls. Brian had retrieved from the
plane a survival pack that helped him get through
summer and fall. But now he faces a harsh winter
and spends all day making preparations. He has
weatherproofed his small shelter near a lake and busies
himself with making a bow and arrows and practicing
his aim. Despite Brian's many hardships, he considers
himself lucky to find a deer carcass. In his shelter, he
stores the deer meat left behind by wolves.

By dark this day all nine arrows were finished. Brian had used
the hunting knife as a scraper to shape the limbs of the bow more
equally and to put in notches for the string to get it ready to string
the next day for the first shooting trials. He was just leaning back,
half cocky about how well things were going, when he smelled the
skunk.

He had run into skunks before, of course, saw them all the
time, but had only had the one really bad experience when he got
sprayed directly. He knew they moved at night, hunting, and didn't
seem very afraid of anything. He looked out of the shelter opening
carefully.

The skunk wasn't four feet away, looking in at him at the shelter
and the fire and as he watched, it whipped up its rear end and
tipped its tail over and aimed directly at his face.

I'm dead, he thought, and froze. For a long time they stayed
that way, Brian holding his breath waiting to be nailed, and the
skunk aiming at him. But the skunk didn't spray, just aimed and
held it.

He's hungry, Brian thought. That's all. He's hunting and he's hungry. Slowly Brian reached to his right, where the meat was stored back in the corner, and took a piece of the venison. With a smooth, slow movement he tossed the meat out to the right of the skunk. For a split second he thought it was over. The skunk's tail jerked when the meat hit the ground but then its nose twitched as it smelled it and it lowered its tail, turned and started eating the meat.

Brian carefully reached out to the side and pulled the door back over the opening and left the skunk outside eating.

Great, he thought, crawling back into his bag to sleep. If I quit feeding him he'll spray me. Just great. His eyes closed and he sighed. Maybe he'll be gone in the morning.

In the morning he pushed the door to the side gingerly, looking both ways. He didn't see the skunk and he pushed the door all the way open and went outside. Still no skunk. Before heading back for the trench he had dug for a toilet he pulled the door back over the opening—no sense taking chances—and then trotted off into the woods.

When he came back he looked all around the area and still couldn't see the skunk and he shrugged. It must have moved on.

He kindled an outside fire using coals from the shelter fire and soon had a small cooking fire going. The cold lasted longer now into the morning and the ice had moved farther out into the lake, almost forty feet from the shore all around. The rabbit-skin vest and the fire felt especially good.

He took the last of the jellied meat in the pot, added a piece of red venison, and put it on the side of the fire to cook while he took stock of his situation. The shelter was done, or as done as he could get it, and almost airtight and warm when he had a fire going inside. He had nine arrows finished, which seemed like a lot. How many times would he have to defend himself? Besides, even if he used all the arrows he could get more tips from the arrow stone, and the wood shafts would be there in the winter as well.

Winter.

The word stopped him. He knew nothing about it. At home in upstate New York, there was snow, sometimes a lot of it, and cold at times, cold enough to make his ears sting, but he could get inside, and he had good warm clothes. Here, he suspected, the winter would be a lot worse, but he didn't know how much worse or how to prepare for it.

Just then the meat was done and at exactly that moment, as he pulled the pot off the fire, the skunk came waddling around the end of the rock, stopped four feet away and raised its tail.

"What . . ." Brian winced, waiting, but the skunk did not spray and Brian took a piece of meat from the pot and threw it on the ground next to it. The skunk lowered its tail, smelled the meat, and when it proved too hot to eat, it backed away and raised its tail again.

"Listen, you little robber—I'm sorry it's too hot. You'll just have to wait until it cools . . ."

The skunk kept its tail up, but lowered it a bit and seemed to understand, and in a moment when the meat cooled it picked up the chunk and disappeared with it around the corner of the large rock that was the back wall of Brian's shelter.

"Where are you going?"

Brian stood up and followed at a distance, moving slowly, and when he came around the rock the skunk was gone, disappeared completely.

"But . . ."

Brian walked all around the end, back again, and was on his second loop when he saw some grass wiggling at the edge where the rock met the ground. The grass here was thick and about a foot tall and hid the dirt from view. Brian moved closer and saw some fresh earth and a hole beneath the rock and as he watched he saw black-and-white fur moving down inside the hole.

"You're living here?" Brian shook his head. "You've moved in on me?"

The skunk stopped moving inside for a moment, then started again, and while Brian watched, little spurts of dirt came out of the entrance as the skunk dug back in under the rock.

Brian turned away. "Wonderful— I've got a roommate with a terminal hygiene problem . . ."

Inside of four days a routine was established. The skunk came to the entrance in the morning, flicked its tail in the air and waited to be fed. Brian fed it and it went back to its burrow until the next morning.

It wasn't exactly friendship, but soon Brian smiled when he saw the skunk. He named it Betty after deciding that it was a female and that it looked like his aunt, who was low and round and waddled the same way. He looked forward to seeing it.

After developing the acquaintance with the skunk Brian had gone back to work on the heavy bow. The arrows were done but he had yet to string the bow and was stymied on where to get a string long enough until he saw the cord at the end of the sleeping bag. It was braided nylon, one eighth of an inch thick and close to six feet long—enough to go around the bag twice when it was rolled up.

The cord was sewn into the end of the bag but he sharpened the knife on his sharpening rock and used the point to open the stitching enough to free the cord.

It proved to be difficult to string the bow. In spite of his scraping and shaping, the limbs were still very stout and the bow bent only with heavy pressure. He tied the string to one end, then put the tied end in a depression in a rock on the ground and used his weight to pull down the top end while he tied the cord in place.

It hummed when he plucked it and the strength of the wood seemed to sing in the cord. He took four of the arrows and moved to a dirt hummock near the lakeshore.

He put an arrow in the bow and fitted it to the string, raised the bow and looked down the shaft at the target and drew the arrow back.

Or tried to. When it was halfway to his chin the bow seemed to double in strength and he was shaking with the exertion by the time he got the feathers all the way back and the cord seemed to be cutting through his fingers. He released quickly, before he had time to aim properly, and saw the arrow crease the top of the hummock, skip onto the lake ice, jump off the ice and fly across the open water in the middle and land skittering across the ice on the far side of the lake—a good two hundred yards.

At the same time the string slapped his arm so hard it seemed to tear the skin off and the rough front end of the feathers cut the top of his hand as they passed over it.

"Wow . . ."

He could not see the arrow but he knew where it had gone and would walk around the lake later and retrieve it. Now he had to practice. He changed the angle he was shooting at so that the arrows wouldn't go across the lake if he missed—*when* he missed, he thought, smiling—and moved closer to the hummock.

It was hard to judge the strength of the pull of the bow. He guessed fifty, sixty pounds of pull were required to get the string back to his chin, and every shot hurt his arm and fingers and hand. But it was worth it. The arrows left the bow so fast that he couldn't see them fly and they hit so hard that two of them drove on through the hummock and kept going for fifteen or twenty yards and broke the stone tips.

He made new tips that night and it was while he was making them that he knew he would be hunting bigger game. It was strange how the thought came, or how it just seemed to be there. He had made the bow for protection, had thought only in terms of protection all the while he was making arrows, but somewhere along the way the knowledge that he would use it to hunt was just there.

Maybe it was eating the meat from the doe that had done it. There was so much of it, and it tasted so good and was easier to deal with than the smaller animals. Whatever the reason, when he aimed at the hummock to practice he saw the chest of a deer.

He shot all that day, until his shoulders were sore and he had broken an arrow and two more tips by hitting small rocks along the ground. Then at dark he built a fire, cooked some meat, fed Betty, who arrived just as the meat was done, and retired to the shelter to fix arrows.

He would hunt big tomorrow, he thought. He would try to get a deer.

He didn't know the time but somewhere in the middle of the night he awakened suddenly. He had come to rely on his senses and he knew something had changed to snap him awake that way and he lay with his eyes wide in the dark, listening, smelling, trying to see.

He did not have long to wait.

There was a soft rustle, then a whoofing sound and the whole wall of the shelter peeled away from the rock as if caught in an earthquake, away and down and Brian—still in his bag—was looking up in the dark at the enormous form of a bear leaning over him.

There was no time to react, to move, to do anything.

Meat, Brian had time to think—he's smelled the venison and come for it. He's come for the mea—

And it was true. The bear had come for the meat but the problem was that Brian lay between the bear and the meat, and the bear cuffed him to the side. As it was it wasn't much of a cuff—nowhere near what the bear could have done, which would have broken Brian's legs—but the bag was zipped and Brian became tangled in it and couldn't move fast enough to stay out of the way so the bear hit him again.

This time hard. The blow took Brian in the upper thigh and even through the bag it was solid enough to nearly dislocate his hip.

He cried out. "Ahhhh . . ."

The bear stopped dead in the darkness. Brian could see the head turn to look back and down at him, a slow turning, huge and full of threat, and the bear's breath washed over him and he thought I am going to die now. All this that I have done and I'm going to die because a bear wants to eat and I am in the way. He could see the bear's teeth as it showed them and he couldn't, simply couldn't do anything; couldn't move, couldn't react. It was over.

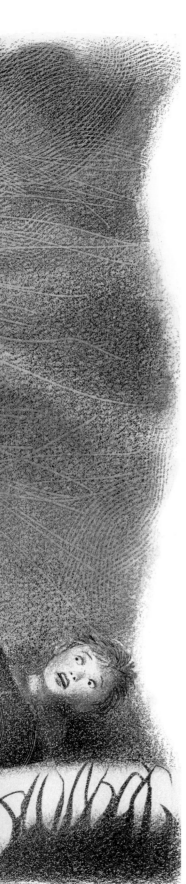

The bear started to move down toward Brian and then hesitated, stopped and raised its head again and turned to look back over its shoulder to the left.

Half a beat and Brian lay still, staring up at the bear. But now a new smell, over the smell of the bear; a rank, foul, sulfurous and gagging smell as the bear turned and took a full shot of skunk spray directly in the eyes.

Betty had arrived. Whether she'd just been out hunting and had come back or had been awakened and surprised or simply didn't like bears very much—whatever the reason she had dumped a full load in the bear's face.

The effect was immediate and devastating.

"Rowwrrrmph!"

The bear seemed to turn inside itself, knocking Brian farther to the side, and rolled backward out of the shelter area, slamming its head back and forth on the ground, trying to clear its eyes, hacking and throwing up as it vanished in the night.

Brian looked to the source of all this. Betty stood near the end of the shelter, still with her tail raised, only now aimed at Brian. She twitched it once, then again, and Brian shook his head.

"I'm sorry. I just didn't think you'd be thinking of food . . ." He took a piece of meat from the pile—a big one—and tossed it to her and she lowered her tail, picked up the meat and waddled off into the dark in the direction of her burrow.

Brian lay back in his bag. His shelter was a mess, the wall tipped over, and his hip hurt, but it wasn't raining and the bag was warm. He could fix things up in the morning.

The stink of skunk was everywhere—much of what Betty had shot at the bear had gone around it and hit the wall—but Brian didn't mind. In fact, he thought, I've grown kind of fond of it. I'll have to make sure to give her extra food. It was like having a pet nuclear device.

He went to sleep smiling.

THINK CRITICALLY

1. Why was Brian nervous about the coming of winter? PLOT EVENTS

2. If Betty hadn't come to Brian's rescue during the bear's visit, what might have happened? SPECULATE

3. Based on what you know about the outdoors, do the events in this story seem believable? Explain. MAKE JUDGMENTS

4. What theme does the relationship between Brian and Betty suggest? THEME

5. **WRITE** Write a paragraph that describes what Brian's actions in the wilderness reveal about his character. Use details from the story to support your answer. SHORT RESPONSE

ABOUT THE AUTHOR

Gary Paulsen

Gary Paulsen often writes about characters who face challenging situations in the wilderness. His own adventurous life has inspired many of these stories. He has worked for a carnival, on farms and ranches, and as a truck driver, a sailor, a teacher, and an engineer. He has even participated in an Alaskan dogsled race. Gary Paulsen has written more than 150 books for children and young adults.

 www.harcourtschool.com/storytown

ABOUT THE ILLUSTRATOR

Raúl Colón

Raúl Colón grew up in Puerto Rico, and now he lives in New City, New York, with his sons and his wife. His illustrations have appeared in many children's books, magazines for adults, theater posters, and advertisements. Raúl Colón says that he enjoys playing guitar by moonlight and still hopes that one of his childhood dreams— traveling to the moon—will come true.

381

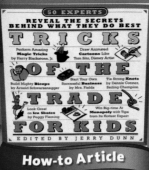

50 EXPERTS
REVEAL THE SECRETS
BEHIND WHAT THEY DO BEST
TRICKS

Perform Amazing
Magic Tricks
by Harry Blackstone, Jr.

Draw Animated
Cartoons Like
Tom Sito, Disney Artist

OF THE

Build Mighty **Biceps**
by Arnold Schwarzenegger

Start Your Own
Successful **Business**
by Mrs. Fields

Tie Strong **Knots**
by Dennis Conner,
Sailing Champion

TRADE

Look Great
on **Ice Skates**
by Peggy Fleming

Win Big-time At
Monopoly with Tips
from Its Hottest Expert!

FOR KIDS
EDITED BY JERRY DUNN

How-to Article

FIND YOUR WAY ANYWHERE
using only the sun and your
wristwatch BY MERRY VAUGHAN

Let's say you don't know where you are. (This describes me most of the time!) You're on a hike, or even a walk across town, and you've gotten turned around. You feel lost. If you can reckon which direction is south, you're saved, because then you can also figure out north, east, and west.

All you need is a watch and a thin, straight twig (or a pencil, a tightly rolled dollar bill, or anything you can think of). Lay your watch faceup on the ground. Be sure it's in the sunshine. Hold the twig so it's straight up and down, and position it above the pointed end of the hour hand. The twig casts a shadow on the watch. Now rotate the watch until the shadow falls across the center point of the watch face (the place where the hands are attached). Here's the rule to figure out which direction is south: It lies exactly halfway between the hour hand and twelve o'clock.

STEP 1

For example, let's say the time is four o'clock in the afternoon. Position the twig at the end of the hour hand, and rotate the watch until the twig's shadow falls across the center point.

South would be halfway between twelve o'clock and four o'clock—that is, at two o'clock. North is in exactly the opposite direction (at eight o'clock). Now that you know south and north, you can also figure out which ways are east and west.

With this system, you'll always know where you're going.

Connections

Comparing Texts

1. Brian must rely on his own resources in order to survive the winter. Describe a time when you needed to rely on your own common sense, creativity, or problem-solving skills.

2. How might a how-to article like "Find Your Way Anywhere" be useful to Brian? What topic would be most useful to him?

3. What is Brian learning that might help him when he returns home from the wilderness?

Vocabulary Review

Word Pairs

Work with a partner to write each Vocabulary Word on a separate index card. Place the cards face down in two piles. Take turns picking up a card from each pile and writing a sentence that uses both words. Read the sentences aloud to each other. Continue until all the words have been correctly used.

retrieve

stymied

I was stymied when I asked my dog to retrieve a stick and he came back with a stranger's sock.

acquaintance

rank

gingerly

winced

cocky

stymied

terminal

retrieve

Fluency Practice

Repeated Reading

You have learned that to read aloud with expression means to use your voice to match the action of the story and the feelings of the characters. Locate the passage that begins on page 376 about Brian's encounter with the bear. Read the first paragraph aloud. Then listen as your partner reads the second paragraph. Continue reading alternate paragraphs until the two of you reach the end of the story. Give each other feedback on expression. Then switch roles and read the passage again.

Writing

Write About Changing Seasons

Imagine that a new season is approaching. How are you feeling? What are you doing to prepare? Create a piece of writing that expresses your concerns or excitement about the change in season.

Feelings	Actions	Setting

My Writing Checklist

Writing Trait ▸ Organization

✓ I used a graphic organizer to plan my writing.

✓ I chose the form of writing that best suits my purpose.

✓ I included clues that express a theme.

CONTENTS

Readers' Theater
LEGEND

On Turtle Backs

illustrated by Amanda Hall

A Native American Legend

Comprehension Strategies
SCIENCE TEXTBOOK

YOUR
Science
TEXTBOOK

communal

dissatisfied

demands

apparent

indebted

bliss

stationary

arduous

prudent

entwined

Reading for Fluency

When reading a script aloud,

- Focus on **expression** by making your voice reflect the feelings of the characters.

- Pay attention to **phrasing**. Group words together, pausing between groups.

Turtle Backs
A Native American Legend

illustrated by Amanda Hall

CHARACTERS
Narrator
Village Storyteller
The People (several students)
Dolphin
Eldest Turtle
Eagle
Turtle Brothers (two students)
Turtle Sisters (three students)

Narrator: One evening, long ago, along the coast of Southern California, a group of Native Americans gathered at the center of their village. As families settled around the communal fire pit, an elderly man emerged from his hut. On his head, he wore a special headdress used only for storytelling. When the man reached the edge of the fire, all eyes turned his way. In a soft but clear voice, he declared that once again it was time to tell the tale of how the land of California came to be.

Storyteller: Long ago, the world was a huge ball of water. There was no land. There were no mountains, no valleys, no rivers, no lakes, no plants, and no trees. The endless ocean stretched as far as the eye could see, and even farther.

Narrator: The storyteller paused to let the image sink into the minds of the youngest members of the community. Many of them had not heard this tale before. Then, with the firelight gleaming in his eyes, he continued.

Storyteller: High above the endless water, the People lived in a world among the clouds. It was a fine place to live. At first, the People were quite happy to float along from day to day. But after a while, they began to grow restless.

The People: We're getting tired of these clouds. Everything's the same, day after day after day.

Narrator: The storyteller paused again and slowly scanned the audience. The youngest children had settled into their parents' laps. But not one eye had turned from the storyteller's face.

Storyteller: The People became dissatisfied in their gray and white world.

The People: The clouds are empty. There's no color—just whites and grays. Why is there no land? Why are there no plants or animals?

Storyteller: The People began to search for something better. But below them was only water and above them only sky. The bravest among the People explored parts of the cloud world they had never before visited. Although they had always walked gingerly among the clouds so as not to slip through any thin spots, they now began to stomp about in anger.

The People: We feel stranded on these clouds. We want to get off . . . NOW!

Storyteller: As if answering their demands, the clouds grew thin and weak. And the People, at first one by one and then in large numbers, dropped from the clouds straight into the waters below.

The People: Help! Help! How will we ever return to the clouds? What should we do? Help!

Storyteller: The creatures of the sea heard the People's cries. The first to arrive on the scene was the wise Dolphin.

Dolphin: Dear People, do not worry. You will find a way to return to the clouds. Until then, my sisters and brothers and I will keep you afloat when you grow weary of swimming.

Storyteller: Sure enough, Dolphin's kin arrived to help the People. Together, they swam about, searching for a way back to the clouds, but none was apparent. Just then, a large mound rose up from the depths and slowly began to move toward the People. They were frightened, and they scattered in all directions.

391

To read Eldest Turtle's words with appropriate **expression**, use a slow, booming voice, which the storyteller says the turtle had.

Narrator: Here, the storyteller looked up at the night sky. All the children in the audience stared at him, wide-eyed with worry.

Storyteller: The mound was the shell of Eldest Turtle, the oldest creature in those parts. As he got closer, he raised his wrinkled head and spoke in a slow, booming voice that made the water shake and the People tremble.

Eldest Turtle: What's going on here?

Dolphin: Oh Eldest Turtle, the People have fallen from the clouds. They need our help to return to the sky.

Eldest Turtle: Those who are tired may rest on my back.

The People: Thank you! Thank you!

Storyteller: Many of the weary People crawled up onto Eldest Turtle's shell and rested.

Dolphin: That gives me an idea.

Storyteller: Dolphin had thought of a plan to save the People. She swam over and whispered into Eldest Turtle's ear. Dolphin knew that the turtle had two younger brothers and three younger sisters. What if he could get them together to make a place for the People to stay? Eldest Turtle wasn't sure he could persuade his brothers and sisters to join him, but he was willing to give it a try.

Narrator: By now, as the moon rose high in the night sky, a few of the very youngest children at the fire had drifted to sleep. The storyteller sat down on a log near the edge of the fire. He reached down to the ground and grabbed a fistful of dirt, which he held before him in the firelight.

Storyteller: It took several days for Eldest Turtle to gather his brothers and sisters. Some did not come willingly at first, but eventually they all arrived. Dolphin explained her plan to them.

Dolphin: First, you must all link head to tail to form a long chain. Then you must rise up so that your shells stand above the ocean surface. When you do, the water will recede from your backs. Once you have done this, you must remain motionless. Your shells will form a surface on which we can create a place for the People to live.

Storyteller: The turtles grumbled a bit about the plan, but after some encouragement from their elder brother, they did as Dolphin told them. Then other sea animals dove to the ocean floor and brought up dirt to put on the turtles' shells. Dolphin directed the work.

Dolphin: Make some mounds over there. We can fill some of those crevices with water to make lakes. Now, form some channels there, there, and there. We can use those for rivers.

Storyteller: The shells proved to be an ideal surface on which to build. After much work, the turtles formed a landscape that stretched from north to south. All the sea creatures worked together to create a beautiful land with mountains, valleys, lakes, and rivers.

Narrator: The storyteller let the dirt pour from his hand to form a mound on the ground. Then, with a few swift movements, he patted and shaped it to create a small mountain. He leaned back to admire his work.

Storyteller: Soon birds came to visit the land. With them, they carried seeds from faraway gardens. Not long after that, plants took root in the rich soil. Trees began to grow. The abundant plant life attracted animals. Soon the land was full of life. For the first time, the People were optimistic. Perhaps Dolphin's plan would be a success!

393

The People: Now we have a beautiful place to live. Thank you, Turtles. Thank you, Dolphin. Thank you, creatures of the sea. Thank you, birds and plants and land animals. We are indebted to you for all you have done for us.

Storyteller: Just then, a huge shadow passed over the land, darkening the sky. It was Eagle, swooping in from the clouds. After a few rapid turns, he flew down and perched on a nearby tree.

Eagle: Oh People of the clouds, my brothers and I have just heard about your fall from the sky. We can take you back to the clouds, to your home.

Storyteller: The People looked at each other. Then they looked around at the new world they had yet to explore.

The People: No, Eagle, we want to stay here.

Storyteller: So the People remained on the earth. The plants, the animals, and the People were happy and thrived. But their bliss did not last. The turtles were getting tired of being stationary. They began to argue. Eldest Turtle had to work hard to keep the peace.

394

Turtle Brothers: We're tired of sitting around with nothing to do. We need some exercise.

Eldest Turtle: But we must remain together to keep the People happy and safe.

Turtle Sisters: Our brothers are so cocky. They think they can hold up the land all by themselves. We say, let them handle the arduous task themselves. They don't give us any credit.

Eldest Turtle: It would be prudent to stay together—for the People's sake!

Storyteller: For a time, Eldest Turtle was able to keep the family together. But the fighting continued, and one day the brothers and sisters could stand it no longer.

Fluency Tip

To read the turtles' lines in this scene with proper **expression**, use what you know about how people sound when they are upset.

Turtle Brothers and Sisters: That's it! We've had enough! This is unbearable.

Turtle Brothers: We're heading west.

Turtle Sisters: We're heading east.

Storyteller: And the turtles did just that. As they moved in opposite directions, the ground began to rumble and shake. And the People ran in fear that their beautiful land would be ripped apart beneath them.

The People: The earth is quaking. What will we do?

Storyteller: As luck would have it, the huge amount of dirt on the turtles' backs did not pull apart so easily. The weight of the land was immense. Roots from tall trees had grown deep into the soil and entwined the rocks. After a while, the turtles tired of the effort and stopped moving.

Turtle Brothers: We haven't gotten very far. We're exhausted.

Turtle Sisters: This dirt is too heavy.

Eldest Turtle: My sisters and brothers! Can't we try to keep the family together? Please!

Storyteller: Eldest Turtle was a forceful speaker. Besides, his brothers and sisters were tired of fighting. So, for a long time, the turtle family lived together in peace. The People thrived once again as they explored and settled on the land. But every once in a long while, the brothers and sisters still get annoyed with each other. Or a muscle becomes cramped from being in one position for so long. It is then that the earth begins to quake. At such times, we must hope

that Eldest Turtle can make peace among his brothers and sisters and get them back together again.

Narrator: The storyteller had finished his tale. As he turned his gaze from the last glow of the fire, he looked up at the people still gathered around it. By now, most of the youngsters were sleeping in their parents' arms. For those little ones, the moon and sun will rise and set without pause until the time has come to tell the story once again. And we hope that between now and then, the turtles will remain at peace with each other.

397

COMPREHENSION STRATEGIES
Review

Reading a Science Textbook

Bridge to Content-Area Reading A textbook is an example of expository nonfiction. Expository nonfiction presents and explains facts and information about a topic. The notes on page 399 point out textbook features. How can these features help you find and remember important information in a science textbook?

Review the Focus Strategies

You can also use the strategies you learned about in this theme to help you read your science textbook.

Monitor Comprehension: Adjust Reading Rate

When you monitor your comprehension, you identify parts of a text that you don't understand and use strategies to resolve the problem. One of these strategies is adjusting your reading rate. Slow down or speed up to fit the difficulty of the text. Then check your understanding.

Answer Questions

Answering questions can be easier if you know where to find the answers. Some answers are stated right there in the text. Sometimes you will need to combine information from different parts of the text to answer a question. Some answers are not in the text at all, but you can use your prior knowledge and experiences to help you.

As you read the pages from a science textbook on pages 400–403, think about where and how you can use the strategies.

HEADINGS
Headings give the topic of each section of text.

HIGHLIGHTED WORDS
Important vocabulary words are highlighted.

Reading in Science

VOCABULARY
intertidal zone p. 354
near-shore zone p. 356
open-ocean zone p. 356

SCIENCE CONCEPTS
▶ what kinds of ecosystems can be found in the ocean
▶ what environmental conditions help define each ocean ecosystem

READING FOCUS SKILL
COMPARE AND CONTRAST
Look for the ways different ocean ecosystems are alike and different.

alike — different

Intertidal Zones

Earth's oceans contain the world's largest animals as well as countless microscopic organisms. With all of this biological diversity, it should be no surprise that the oceans have many different types of ecosystems. Recall that an *ecosystem* is a community of organisms and their nonliving environment. Each of the ecosystems in the ocean exists in a major ocean zone. Each ocean zone is a layer of the ocean that has unique types of plant and animal communities.

Ocean zones are determined by the depth of the water. As depth increases, there is less light. The shallowest and brightest ocean zone is the intertidal zone. The **intertidal zone** is the area of the ocean between the levels of high tide and low tide. The environment of the intertidal zone is always changing. At low tide, organisms in this zone may have to find shelter from the hot sun. As the tide comes in, they must survive the

▼ **Intertidal Zone**

Math in Science
Interpret Data

The amount of sunlight determines which organisms can live at which depth in the ocean. Do you think more organisms live closer to the surface or closer to the bottom of the ocean? Explain.

Sunlight Zone	Twilight Zone	Midnight Zone	Abyssal Zone	Hadal Zone
0 to 200 m	200 m to 1,000 m	1,000 m to 4,000 m	4,000 m to 6,000 m	6,000 m to 11,000 m

Dolphins and other marine mammals must live close to the ocean's surface so they can come up for air to breathe.

This squid lives deep beneath the surface of the ocean.

▲ The intertidal zone is an important feeding ground for birds and other animals.

When the tide goes out, tide pools still hold water. Tide pools are home to many different organisms.

rough water of incoming waves. They may spend hours in an undersea world until the tide goes out again.

Intertidal organisms handle the changes in their surroundings in different ways. Many of them bury themselves in the mud during low tide. This keeps them moist and protected. Crabs hide under rocks and in other sheltered, moist spots when the tide goes out.

Mussels and barnacles close their shells tightly during low tide, trapping water inside. During high tide, they open up to feed on *plankton* (PLANK•tuhn) and other organic matter. Plankton are microscopic organisms that live near the ocean's surface. A single gallon of seawater

may contain more than a million plankton! Many plankton use sunlight to produce food by photosynthesis. Because many marine organisms feed on plankton, they are the base of most marine food chains. This means that most marine organisms, just like land organisms, acquire their energy directly or indirectly from sunlight.

COMPARE AND CONTRAST How does the environment of the intertidal zone differ during high tide and low tide?

GRAPHIC AIDS
Charts and graphs support ideas in the text or provide additional information.

QUESTIONS
Questions help you check your understanding of the text.

Apply the Strategies Read these pages about ecosystems in the ocean from a science textbook. As you read, use different comprehension strategies, such as adjusting your reading rate, to help you understand.

Reading in Science

VOCABULARY
intertidal zone p. 354
near-shore zone p. 356
open-ocean zone p. 356

SCIENCE CONCEPTS
▶ what kinds of ecosystems can be found in the ocean
▶ what environmental conditions help define each ocean ecosystem

 READING FOCUS SKILL
COMPARE AND CONTRAST
Look for the ways different ocean ecosystems are alike and different.

alike ———— different

Intertidal Zones

Earth's oceans contain the world's largest animals as well as countless microscopic organisms. With all of this biological diversity, it should be no surprise that the oceans have many different types of ecosystems. Recall that an *ecosystem* is a community of organisms and their nonliving environment. Each of the ecosystems in the ocean exists in a major ocean zone. Each ocean zone is a layer of the ocean that has unique types of plant and animal communities.

Ocean zones are determined by the depth of the water. As depth increases, there is less light. The shallowest and brightest ocean zone is the intertidal zone. The **intertidal zone** is the area of the ocean between the levels of high tide and low tide. The environment of the intertidal zone is always changing. At low tide, organisms in this zone may have to find shelter from the hot sun. As the tide comes in, they must survive the

▼ Intertidal Zone

Math in Science
Interpret Data

The amount of sunlight determines which organisms can live at which depth in the ocean. Do you think more organisms live closer to the surface or closer to the bottom of the ocean? Explain.

Sunlight Zone	Twilight Zone	Midnight Zone	Abyssal Zone	Hadal Zone
0 m to 200 m	200 m to 1,000 m	1,000 m to 4,000 m	4,000 m to 6,000 m	6,000 m to 11,000 m

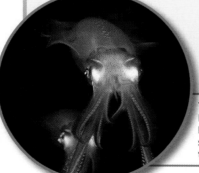

This squid lives deep beneath the surface of the ocean.

Dolphins and other marine mammals must live close to the ocean's surface so they can come up for air to breathe.

Stop and Think

Look back through the text to see if the answer to the question at the end of the page is right there. ANSWER QUESTIONS

▲ The intertidal zone is an important feeding ground for birds and other animals.

When the tide goes out, tide pools still hold water. Tide pools are home to many different organisms.

rough water of incoming waves. They may spend hours in an undersea world until the tide goes out again.

Intertidal organisms handle the changes in their surroundings in different ways. Many of them bury themselves in the mud during low tide. This keeps them moist and protected. Crabs hide under rocks and in other sheltered, moist spots when the tide goes out.

Mussels and barnacles close their shells tightly during low tide, trapping water inside. During high tide, they open up to feed on *plankton* (PLANK•tuhn) and other organic matter. Plankton are microscopic organisms that live near the ocean's surface. A single gallon of seawater

may contain more than a million plankton! Many plankton use sunlight to produce food by photosynthesis. Because many marine organisms feed on plankton, they are the base of most marine food chains. This means that most marine organisms, just like land organisms, acquire their energy directly or indirectly from sunlight.

 COMPARE AND CONTRAST How does the environment of the intertidal zone differ during high tide and low tide?

Stop and Think

Slow down and think about the meanings of difficult words to help you understand what you are reading. MONITOR COMPREHENSION: ADJUST READING RATE

Near-Shore and Open-Ocean Zones

Moving seaward from the intertidal zone, you enter the near-shore zone. The **near-shore zone** includes most of the ocean over the continental shelf where the water gets no deeper than about 200 m (650 ft). The near-shore zone is relatively shallow and receives a great deal of sunlight. It is a much more stable ecosystem than the intertidal zone. This is why it is teeming with life. Many different kinds of marine organisms inhabit the near-shore zone. These include fish, jellyfish, krill (a small shrimp-like animal), seaweed, shrimp, and plankton. The plentiful supply of fish attracts sea birds. It also attracts larger marine animals. Dolphins, porpoises, sharks, and whales often feed on fish and krill in the near-shore zone.

Some types of whales, even the huge baleen whales, feed almost entirely on krill, small fish, other small crustaceans, and plankton! Baleen whales eat by sucking seawater in through their mouths. Comb-like structures in their mouths capture the food.

Farther out to sea, past the continental shelf, you enter the open-ocean zone. The **open-ocean zone** includes most of the water over the continental slope and abyssal plain. Most of the animals in the open-ocean zone live near the surface. Dolphins, krill, seals, swordfish, tuna, whales, and plankton live in the open-ocean zone.

Because of the depth of the open-ocean zone, food is limited to water near the surface. In this zone, many organisms are active swimmers. They must be able to swim long distances to obtain food.

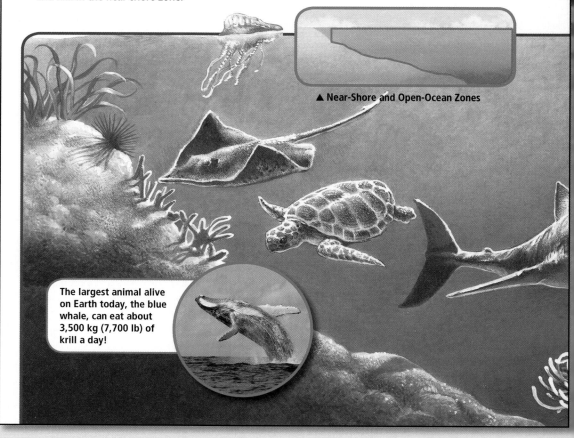

▲ **Near-Shore and Open-Ocean Zones**

The largest animal alive on Earth today, the blue whale, can eat about 3,500 kg (7,700 lb) of krill a day!

Food becomes even scarcer as the ocean becomes deeper. At about 1,000 m (3,200 ft) below the surface of the ocean, there is little or no light. The extreme darkness means that no producer organisms that rely on sunlight can live there. Those that can be found have sunk down from the surface. Life is also difficult at these depths because of enormous pressure from the water above. At this depth, most organisms with lungs would be crushed! However, sperm whales can dive to 3,000 m (9,600 ft) where they feed on giant squid. This deep region of the ocean, which makes up about 90 percent of all the oceans, is like the barest of deserts on land. Much of this zone is cold, deep, and dark.

 COMPARE AND CONTRAST What are some differences between the near-shore zone and the open-ocean zone?

Insta-Lab

Jellyfish Movement

Many jellyfish are unable to propel themselves effectively from place to place. How do jellyfish move around? Set an aluminum baking pan on a table that is protected with newspaper. Fill the pan half-full with water. Sprinkle a handful of confetti over the water to represent a group of jellyfish. Gently move the pan to make small waves. Observe how the confetti moves. What can you hypothesize about how jellyfish move around?

Squid live in both the near-shore zone and the open-ocean zone. They eat fish, shrimp, and other squid.

The organisms found in a particular ocean zone depend on the depth and on the amount of light the zone receives.

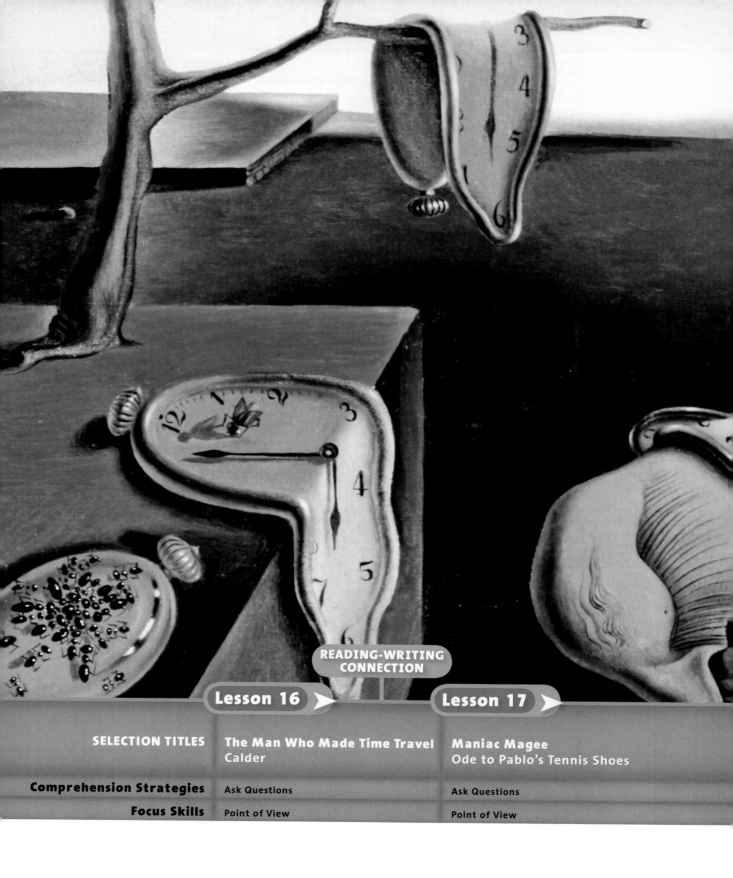

Perspectives

▶ *The Persistence of Memory,* Salvador Dalí

405

CONTENTS

Lesson 16

Genre: Biography

THE MAN WHO MADE TIME TRAVEL

Genre: Magazine Article

CALDER
by Doug Stewart

Focus Skill

 ## Point of View

Point of view is the standpoint from which a text is written.

- In **first-person point of view**, the narrator is part of the story. The narrator uses pronouns such as *I*, *me*, and *we*.
- In **third-person point of view**, the narrator is an outside observer who tells the story. The narrator uses pronouns such as *he*, *she*, and *they* to tell about the characters.
- **Autobiographies** are written in the first-person point of view. The narrator is telling about his or her own life.
- **Biographies** are written in the third-person point of view. The narrator is telling about someone else's life.

Genre	Characteristics
autobiography	• told in first-person point of view • uses pronouns such as *I*, *me*, and *we* to tell about events the author experienced
biography	• told in third-person point of view • uses pronouns such as *he*, *she*, and *they* to tell about events someone else experienced

Read the paragraph. Then look at the chart below. It shows clues from the text that suggest the writing is an autobiography told from the first-person point of view. The author uses the pronouns *I* and *me* to talk about herself. She also tells how certain events made her feel.

Reading about famous inventors in history inspired me at an early age to develop creative ideas for solving everyday problems. One of my biggest problems was getting to school on time. My ordinary alarm clock didn't wake me up, so I created a device that tickled the bottoms of my feet instead of making noise. It was foolproof, and I always woke up smiling! I was thrilled when my invention was featured on the local news. That was the first of my many successes as Kathleen Bloom, Inventor.

Genre	Characteristics
autobiography	story by Kathleen Bloom, written about her own experiences
	told in first-person point of view, using the pronouns *I*, *me*, and *my* to tell about events she experienced

Try This!

Rewrite the paragraph as a biography. How did you change the text? What is different about the point of view?

www.harcourtschool.com/storytown

Vocabulary

Build Robust Vocabulary

precise

regulates

compensate

perfectionist

meticulously

counteracted

trial

petition

Clocks

Mechanical clocks were not invented in Europe until the late 1200s. The first clocks had no hands and no face. They announced the time by ringing a bell. These clocks were not very **precise**, and they often broke down.

In the 1600s, timekeeping improved dramatically. Clockmakers began to use a swinging pendulum, which **regulates** the clock's speed. The pendulum was powered by springs or weights. These had to be reset at regular intervals.

Little by little, more improvements were made. Clockmakers experimented with different metals to **compensate** for the expansion and contraction of clock parts due to weather changes. Being a clockmaker required mechanical knowledge and the care of a **perfectionist**.

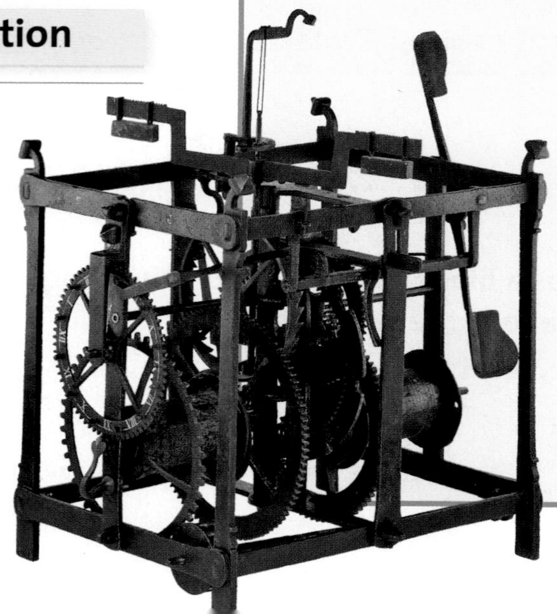

Early clocks were **meticulously** built by hand.

In the 1700s, nautical clocks were built for use at sea. These clocks required special parts that **counteracted** the motion of the waves. Several **trial** journeys at sea were required to test the accuracy of each new model.

Today, atomic clocks keep perfect time for centuries. This is not good news for those who like to blame faulty clocks when they are late. Perhaps they will **petition** to require clocks to be less accurate!

Nautical clocks helped early explorers navigate the world's oceans.

 www.harcourtschool.com/storytown

Word Scribe

 This week, your job is to use the Vocabulary Words in writing. In your vocabulary journal, write sentences that use the Vocabulary Words. For example, you could note the precise time at which a TV show begins. Write sentences about as many Vocabulary Words as you can. Share your sentences with your classmates.

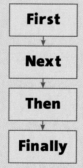

Biography

Genre Study

A biography tells about a person's life and is written by another person. As you read, look for

- information telling how the person made a difference.

- events told in chronological order.

First
Next
Then
Finally

Comprehension Strategy

Ask questions as you read to check your own understanding of the text.

THE MAN WHO MADE TIME TRAVEL

BY KATHRYN LASKY

ILLUSTRATED BY
KEVIN HAWKES

EIGHTEENTH-CENTURY SAILORS FACED MANY CHALLENGES BECAUSE THERE WAS NO ACCURATE WAY TO MEASURE LONGITUDE, OR EAST–WEST POSITION, AT SEA. THEY OFTEN GOT LOST AND FOUND THEMSELVES IN DANGEROUS CONDITIONS.

IN 1714, BRITAIN OFFERED A PRIZE TO THE PERSON WHO COULD SOLVE THIS PROBLEM. MANY SCIENTISTS KNEW THAT WITH AN ACCURATE CLOCK AT SEA, A SHIP'S LONGITUDE COULD BE CALCULATED. HOWEVER, NO CLOCK AT THE TIME WAS ACCURATE ENOUGH TO BE RELIABLE, SO SCIENTISTS TRIED SOME OFTEN RIDICULOUS WAYS TO CALCULATE LONGITUDE. THEN NEWCOMER JOHN HARRISON DEVELOPED IDEAS THAT NO ONE HAD TRIED BEFORE.

A Curious Boy

John Harrison was twenty-one years old when the Longitude Prize was announced. He knew full well the dangers of the sea. The village where he lived was near the bustling port of Hull.

As a boy he was one of the bell ringers in the village church of Barrow. His sense of hearing was so good that he was asked to tune the church bells. Soon he was tuning the bells of a neighboring church as well.

But bells were only John Harrison's hobby. His real work, like his father's, was carpentry. He knew wood and he knew simple mathematics. He knew these things from experience, not from a formal education.

John was curious about how things worked. When a visitor lent him a book of lectures on mathematics and Isaac Newton's laws of motion, John copied out every single word. But he also liked to figure things out for himself. So he tested Newton's basic principles of motion.

Would a heavy ball roll down a hill faster than a light ball? Does the ball gain speed as it rolls down the hill? Would the clapper in a bell swing faster if it was shorter or if it weighed more?

John Harrison proved each and every principle for himself.

From Bells to Clocks

John Harrison began to realize that bells and pendulum clocks were similar: the swinging action of the bell marked the passage of time just as the pendulum regulates the motion of a clock. He decided to build a clock. Perhaps clock building interested him because it was a way of combining his hobby, bells, with his real work, carpentry. Some people, however, snickered at the very idea of a carpenter's son making a clock.

Clocks were rare and made of valuable materials such as brass. John could not afford much brass, so he used mostly wood. The larger clock wheels he cut from oak, and the smallest gears, spindles, and axles from boxwood. He completed his first clock by the time he was twenty. Within the next four years he had built two more pendulum clocks. As his reputation grew, he was hired to build a clock in the tower of a new stable on a wealthy landowner's estate. He made a remarkable timepiece that showed the precise time from its airy perch, its wheels and gears hidden in the rafters, sharing space with roosting pigeons.

With each new clock John Harrison made improvements.

He began to use a very hard wood, lignum vitae, which had its own natural oils, so that his clocks never needed to be lubricated.

Temperature changes were the enemies of precision timekeeping. In very hot weather clocks slowed down, and in cold weather they speeded up. Harrison designed a pendulum composed of brass and steel rods that expanded in heat and contracted in cold by different amounts to compensate for each other. Because of the gridlike arrangement of the brass and steel rods, his pendulum is known as the gridiron pendulum.

Friction, the rubbing between surfaces, is another enemy of precision timekeeping. To prevent friction, Harrison invented a new type of escapement. The beating heart of every clock, the escapement provides the impulse to keep the pendulum swinging. Unlike other designs, Harrison's, instead of sliding, hopped like a grasshopper and thus avoided friction.

John Harrison's intricate mechanical forest of turning wheels never missed more than a single second over an entire month of testing.

A Shipshape Clock

Like others of his generation, John Harrison puzzled over the longitude problem. He became convinced that the solution was a clock that could measure time at sea, a clock in which time could travel—travel and never lose a second because of dampness, salt air, changing temperatures, or stormy seas—a clock accurate enough to calculate longitude. Instead of using a pendulum, which wouldn't work on a rolling sea, he created seesaw balances linked—like dancing couples—by squiggly threads of steel he called worm springs. Free of gravity, they would swing evenly, no matter how rough the ocean.

Harrison dreamed of gears and spirals. He dreamed and he worked for several years on his plans. In 1730 he went to London to present his drawings and diagrams to the Board of Longitude, the group in charge of awarding the prize. He hoped it would give him enough money to build his clock.

When he arrived in London, however, the Board seemed to have vanished. Still determined, he sought out Sir Edmund Halley, the Astronomer Royal at the Greenwich Observatory. Halley was impressed by his drawings and sent him to see George Graham, London's most famous clockmaker. Graham, too, was impressed and found enough money for him to build his sea clock. John Harrison went back to Barrow to begin work.

Five years later, after hundreds of drawings and thousands of hours of delicate cutting of wooden wheels and tooling of metal parts, John Harrison completed his first sea clock, the clock now referred to as **H1**.

But in 1735 when he presented it to the learned men of the Royal Society, they squinted and whispered among themselves. For **H1** was like no other clock. Just over two feet tall and weighing 75 pounds, it stood bright and bristling with brass rods and strange spirals, knobs, balls, and odd little springs. The twin balances with their worm springs teeter-tottered back and forth in a rhythm not unlike that of a rolling ship. Some said the clock even looked like a ship. There were no sails and no rudder, yet it seemed ready to sail, sail on any sea.

H1
- ❖ 25 INCHES TALL, WEIGHS 75 POUNDS
- ❖ WHEELS MADE OF WOOD
- ❖ INTRODUCES SEESAW BALANCES WITH WORM SPRINGS
- ❖ COMPLETED IN 1735—HARRISON AGE 42

A year later the Board arranged a trial voyage to Lisbon, Portugal, for John Harrison and his clock. Throughout the entire trip the clock lost barely a second. Harrison, however, lost his breakfast, lunch, and dinner. He spent his days hanging over the ship's rail, throwing up. He must have envied his sea clock and wished that he could have devised such seaworthy balances for his own insides.

SIMPLY TOO SIMPLE

The sea clock had proven itself. The Board of Longitude, which had not met in over twenty years, called a meeting. The members wanted to question John Harrison and see his timepiece.

But Harrison was a perfectionist. When he met with the Board, he spoke only of the improvements that he wished to make, and requested more money for designing a new clock. The Board agreed to provide funds so he could keep working, but the members must have wondered if a man-made object, a mechanical ticking thing in a box, could really tell a captain where his ship was on the vast ocean. It seemed too simple, especially when compared to measuring by the stars.

ANOTHER CLOCK

John Harrison moved to London, where he spent another two years building a second sea clock. H2 was narrower and taller, so it didn't take up as much space as H1, but it was heavier, its wheels made of brass instead of wood. Bar balances counteracted the rocking motion of a ship. And the clock worked better in varying temperatures. H2 also had a new device called a remontoire that allowed it to self-wind every few minutes. This increased its precision.

Every imaginable test was performed on H2. It was heated up, cooled down, jiggled, and shaken. And still H2 kept perfect time. Yet this second sea clock was never tried at sea. Perhaps Harrison noticed a slight flaw in the bar balance. Or maybe he observed some other tiny error anyone else would have ignored. For Harrison, only perfection was good enough. So he decided to make a third sea clock.

H2
- ❖ 26 INCHES TALL, WEIGHS 86 POUNDS
- ❖ WHEELS MADE OF BRASS
- ❖ INTRODUCES A NEW KIND OF REMONTOIRE (A DEVICE TO KEEP THE CLOCK RUNNING DURING REWINDING)
- ❖ COMPLETED IN 1739—HARRISON AGE 46

A Third Clock

For almost twenty years John Harrison worked, tinkered, and fiddled with **H3**, his third sea clock. He invented a new kind of thermostat called the bimetallic strip that allowed the clock to adjust to temperature changes. He replaced the seesaw balances with balance wheels. In every way, **H3** was his most complicated clock. It had 753 different parts. But it was his smallest and lightest clock so far.

As the clockmaker meticulously fine-tuned **H3**, he himself was also changing. The hair beneath his wig grew thinner, his face more drawn and wrinkled. His son, William, only a baby when he had first started **H1** and most likely a nuisance in Harrison's workshop, had grown into a young man in his twenties who now helped his father on this clock, **H3**.

Although **H3** was sleek and beautiful, like **H2** it was never tested at sea. It also did not keep time as accurately as John Harrison had hoped. In fact, he was so disappointed that even after all his years of work, he felt that he must invent a completely *new* timepiece.

H3

- ❖ 23 inches tall, weighs 60 pounds, 753 separate parts (takes up less than a third the space of H1)
- ❖ Replaces balance bars with circular balances linked by metal ribbons
- ❖ Introduces the bimetallic strip and the caged roller bearing (forerunner of today's ball bearing)
- ❖ Completed in 1757—Harrison age 64

H4

- ❖ 5 INCHES ACROSS, WEIGHS 3 POUNDS
- ❖ LOOKS LIKE A LARGE, BEAUTIFULLY DECORATED POCKET WATCH
- ❖ USES JEWELS AS BEARINGS TO REDUCE FRICTION
- ❖ COMPLETED IN 1759—HARRISON AGE 66

RUNNING OUT OF TIME

For John Harrison himself time was becoming a problem—it was running out. At sixty, he was tired from his work on H3 but not too tired to design a new pocket watch for himself. Not having the skills of a watchmaker, he asked a fellow clockmaker, John Jeffreys, to build it for him.

It was a perfect little watch, and he admired it greatly. And then he had an idea. Could a pocket watch be made accurate enough for use on a ship? The more John Harrison considered this possibility, the more sense it made.

He began working on his new timepiece in 1755. When he finished, H4 measured five inches across—only slightly larger than a typical pocket watch—and weighed only three pounds. Its calm white face was encased in two dazzling silver shells decorated with fruits and leaves. Beneath this face was a miniature world of spinning wheels and tiny cut jewels, diamonds and rubies, that made all the parts turn smoothly.

In 1760 John Harrison asked the Board of Longitude for a sea trial for H4. They agreed. Soon John's son, William, was on a ship bound for Jamaica. On the return trip the weather was so stormy that he had to wrap up H4 in blankets and hold it like a newborn to protect it from the raging seas. But still it ticked on. After 147 days at sea, H4's error was only one minute and 54 seconds, a remarkable achievement for any clock in an era when even a timepiece on solid land might have errors of several minutes.

AN ENEMY OF CLOCKS

It had been nearly fifty years since the Longitude Act had been passed and the prize offered. H4 should have won the moment William returned to England. Every requirement had been met, but suddenly H4's reliability was questioned. Was the trial a fluke? Could its performance be repeated? New tests were ordered for H4. One member of the Board of Longitude was chiefly responsible for these tests. His name was Nevil Maskelyne.

Nevil Maskelyne believed absolutely in the Lunar Distance Method. As Astronomer Royal, he insisted it was the only practical solution to the longitude problem. He thought ticking things in boxes were untrustworthy and pocket watches that solved mathematical and astronomical problems unbelievable. Even though H4 had passed the new tests with flying colors, Maskelyne called John Harrison a "mere mechanic." He would move H4 and Harrison's other timepieces to the Royal Observatory at Greenwich. There he would test them himself.

It must have been painful for John Harrison to watch Nevil Maskelyne cart away the clocks that had ticked quietly in his workshop for thirty years. He returned to his private room, only to suddenly hear a terrible crash. H1 lay shattered! One of Maskelyne's workers had dropped it.

Under Maskelyne's critical eyes, H4, which had gone through two sea voyages while losing less than two minutes, failed its tests miserably. But the testing conditions were far from ideal. Not only was H4 housed in direct sunlight, where it endured stifling heat, it was monitored by elderly retired seamen who were so feeble they could barely climb the hill to the Royal Observatory. Maskelyne announced to the world that "the watch could not be trusted." So the Board ordered John Harrison to make yet another timepiece.

THE CLOCKMAKER AND THE KING

H5 was very plain. There were no leaves or flowers on its dial as there had been with H4. Nearing his seventy-ninth birthday, perhaps John Harrison felt he did not have the time for such decorations. His eyesight was failing. He was bothered by gout.

The clock met every single requirement of the Longitude Act, but still the Board would not give him the prize. How much time did such an old man have left? There was only one thing to do: petition the King.

H5
❖ SIMILAR TO H4, BUT WITHOUT DECORATIONS
❖ COMPLETED IN 1772—HARRISON AGE 79

So he did. In January 1772, his son William presented their case to King George III. "These people have been cruelly treated," the King reportedly whispered after William finished recounting their history. Then he is said to have exclaimed, "Harrison, I will see you righted!"

A trial was arranged for H5 in the King's quarters. At first the watch behaved strangely. Then it was discovered that in a nearby closet there were magnetic rocks, called lodestones, that affected the metallic parts of the clock. As soon as the lodestones were removed, H5 performed perfectly.

Finally, on June 21, 1773, an Act of Parliament awarded John Harrison the remaining prize money he deserved. Even so, the Board of Longitude *still* refused to name him as the official prizewinner. In fact, the long-sought-after Longitude Prize was never officially awarded to anyone.

THINK CRITICALLY

1. How did John Harrison's interest in bells lead him to clock-building? CAUSE AND EFFECT

2. What personal qualities or traits did John Harrison possess? CHARACTER'S TRAITS

3. From what point of view is "The Man Who Made Time Travel" told? How can you tell? POINT OF VIEW

4. John Harrison was never named as the winner of the Longitude Prize. Do you think that people who lived after John Harrison should appreciate his work? Explain. PERSONAL RESPONSE

5. **WRITE** Explain the improvements that John Harrison made over the years to his clocks. EXTENDED RESPONSE

ABOUT THE AUTHOR
KATHRYN LASKY

Kathryn Lasky says that all her best ideas for books come from experiences with her family and from being a careful observer. She got the idea for *The Man Who Made Time Travel* when she and her husband sailed across the Atlantic Ocean from Boston, Massachusetts, to England. There she saw John Harrison's clocks on display in the National Maritime Museum. Kathryn Lasky set aside the idea for nearly thirty years before traveling back to England to visit the timepieces again and research the book. She lives with her husband in Cambridge, Massachusetts.

ABOUT THE ILLUSTRATOR
KEVIN HAWKES

Kevin Hawkes studied illustration in college. Then he worked in a bookstore in Boston, where he spent his lunch breaks looking carefully at the illustrations in children's books. A few years later, he illustrated his first of more than thirty children's books. He lives with his family in Gorham, Maine.

While creating the illustrations for *The Man Who Made Time Travel*, Kevin Hawkes enjoyed researching eighteenth-century England. He was inspired by John Harrison's craftsmanship and determination.

 www.harcourtschool.com/storytown

muse

FROM THE PUBLISHERS OF CRICKET
AND SMITHSONIAN MAGAZINE

Exploding Trousers
page 16

Reverse
Evolution
page 8

Pac-
Manhattan
page 34

Magazine Article

CALDER

by Doug Stewart

THE MAN WHO MADE ART OUT OF THE ORDINARY

When Alexander Calder was a young man living with his parents in the 1920s (several years before he became famous for inventing the mobile), he never knew what time it was—his tiny bedroom had a window but no clock. So, using heavy wire and a set of pliers he carried everywhere, Calder made his own sundial. He shaped the timepiece like a crowing rooster and perched the fowl on his windowsill. Problem solved.

For 70 years Sandy Calder made art out of everything he touched, although he didn't always call it art. While he designed gigantic public sculptures that weighed as much as 42 tons, in private he scavenged old cans, boxes, scrap lumber, and wire to make artful gadgets and decorations for himself. Some of the homemade contraptions he devised for the Connecticut farmhouse he shared with his wife, Louisa, were as delightfully ingenious as the giant mobiles that made his reputation.

Calder enjoyed inventing chairs. As a young man, he made this miniature elephant chair with its own attached reading light.

As a boy, Sandy was nicknamed "the scavenger" by his father. For this beautiful and ingenious bell, he used shards of broken glass he'd scrounged as clappers (placed, with his typical originality, on the outside instead of the inside).

429

Calder, a stocky, rumpled man who almost always wore baggy khaki pants and flannel shirts, was a do-it-yourselfer. Painting outdoors, he might nail his canvas to a tree instead of putting it on an easel someone else had made. Not that he was interested in simplicity—far from it. As a young artist in Paris in the late 1920s, he ran a string from his bed through a series of pulleys to the kitchen stove so he could get his morning coffee going without getting up. When the gizmo didn't work, he'd reluctantly climb out of bed to tinker with it, then get under the covers and try again. Walking over to the stove would have been a lot easier, but what fun would that be?

Why buy a fork when you can make your own? Calder's deft fingers were constantly shaping metal, such as these fanciful silver serving forks. No two were alike.

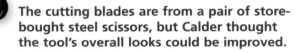

The cutting blades are from a pair of store-bought steel scissors, but Calder thought the tool's overall looks could be improved.

The "scales" on this hanging fish are actually shards of broken crockery or translucent colored glass.

Louisa, whom Sandy married in 1931, took a more no-nonsense approach to cooking, and her well-fed husband insisted on making kitchen utensils for her—one-of-a-kind ladles, serving spoons, flour scoops, roasting pans, bacon forks, and the like. She may not have needed 20 different wire strainers, but she understood her husband's mania for metalworking. "He wasn't happy unless he was fiddling with wire," she said a few years after he died.

Like his well-known sculptures, Calder's kooky housewares are the creatures of a playful and utterly original mind. He was a serious modern artist with a young child's imagination. After a one-man show in New York City, he remarked, "My fan mail is enormous—everyone is under six."

The Calders drank coffee from traditional Chinese teacups they'd collected. Unfortunately, the handleless cups could burn a person's fingers, and they tipped easily. Sandy "improved" them by adding brass-wire handles and tip-proof bases.

Connections

Comparing Texts

1. What lesson about hard work and determination did you learn from John Harrison's life experiences?

2. As young men, John Harrison and Alexander Calder worked with clocks. What problem did each man hope to solve? How did their solutions differ?

3. How have clocks changed since John Harrison invented his sea clock?

Vocabulary Review

Word Pairs

Work with a partner. Write the Vocabulary Words on index cards. Place the cards in two piles, face down. Take turns flipping over two cards and writing a sentence that correctly uses both words. Read your sentence aloud to your partner. Each time you use a word correctly, you get one point. After all of the words have been used once, the player with the most points wins.

> Julie is a perfectionist and organizes her closet meticulously.

precise

regulates

compensate

perfectionist

meticulously

counteracted

trial

petition

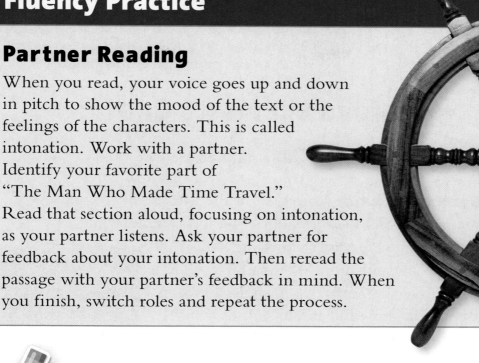

Partner Reading

When you read, your voice goes up and down in pitch to show the mood of the text or the feelings of the characters. This is called intonation. Work with a partner. Identify your favorite part of "The Man Who Made Time Travel." Read that section aloud, focusing on intonation, as your partner listens. Ask your partner for feedback about your intonation. Then reread the passage with your partner's feedback in mind. When you finish, switch roles and repeat the process.

Writing

Write a Biography

Write a brief biography about someone you admire. The subject may be someone you know or someone you've read about.

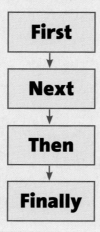

First
Next
Then
Finally

My Writing Checklist

Writing Trait ▸ Voice

✔ I organized the events in chronological order.

✔ I used appropriate pronouns for third-person point of view.

✔ I used interesting words and ideas to show my personal voice.

Reading-Writing Connection

Analyze Writer's Craft: Biography

Biographies are true stories about the lives of real people. Some biographies focus on a brief period of time, while others describe a person's entire life. The paragraph below is from the biography "The Man Who Made Time Travel" by Kathryn Lasky. Notice how the author's **voice** reveals her admiration for her subject, John Harrison.

Writing Trait

ORGANIZATION
Biographies are usually organized in **chronological order**. Time-order phrases, such as *For almost twenty years*, help the reader follow the sequence of events.

Writing Trait

VOICE Each writer has a personal **voice** that conveys his or her feelings. Here the writer shows her admiration for John Harrison's relentless hard work.

For almost twenty years John Harrison worked, tinkered, and fiddled with H3, his third sea clock. He invented a new kind of thermostat called the bimetallic strip that allowed the clock to adjust to temperature changes. He replaced the seesaw balances with balance wheels. In every way, H3 was his most complicated clock. It had 753 different parts. But it was his smallest and lightest clock so far.

Autobiographical Narrative

An **autobiographical narrative** tells a true story about something that happened to the author. It includes the writer's personal thoughts and feelings. Read this autobiographical narrative by a student named Andrea. Notice how she organizes the events in chronological order.

The Great Marshmallow Challenge
by Andrea L.

ORGANIZATION In the opening paragraph, Andrea introduces the **setting** and **characters**. She also describes a **conflict**: she will have to compete against her best friend.

VOICE Andrea uses **pronouns** such as *I*, *me*, and *my* to write from a first-person **point of view**.

It was the first day after spring break when my science teacher, Mr. Vogel, said, "Who wants to enter a marshmallow catapult contest?" I love science contests. I've been hooked on them for years, ever since I entered my first egg drop challenge. My best friend, Mina, won that contest, but I was proud of the container I made. My egg survived some pretty high drops.

Mina would be the toughest competition this time, too. My brain kicked into action. How could I design a machine that could fling marshmallows as far as possible? I thought about levers, fulcrums, plastic spoons, rubber bands, and all sorts of other things. My mind was racing.

After school, I met up with Mina. "Did you hear about the catapult contest?" she asked.

That's when the marshmallow challenge started to get . . . well *sticky*! How could I tell her about my ideas? What if she wanted to use them for her own catapult?

"Uh . . . , I haven't really thought about it yet," I said lamely. Mina just shrugged.

"I've got a few ideas," she said. "I'm going home to work on them."

For the next few days, Mina and I did not talk about the contest. It was like a huge stone wall between us. In our case, though, the wall was made of marshmallows!

The night before the competition, I knew I was in trouble. My catapult had a design flaw. The mousetrap part was working fine, but the plastic spoon and rubber bands weren't.

Just then the phone rang. "I need some help on my design." Mina said.

So I helped Mina, and she helped me. Our catapults flung those marshmallows clear across Mr. Vogel's classroom. Neither of us ended up winning the contest, but we sure had a *sweet* time trying!

Writing Trait

VOICE Andrea uses creative expressions, such as *the wall was made of marshmallows,* that reveal her clever personality.

Writing Trait

ORGANIZATION Andrea **uses time-order phrases,** such as *for the next few days* and *the night before,* to describe the **sequence of events**.

Now look at what Andrea did to prepare to write her autobiographical narrative.

Making a Web

Andrea wanted to write about a challenge she had faced. She made an idea web and wrote different story ideas in it. Then she chose the idea that she thought would make the best story.

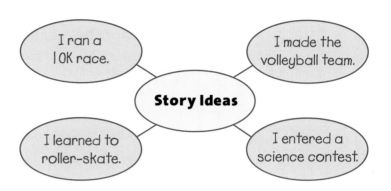

Organizing Ideas

Andrea used a sequence chart to organize her narrative. She listed the events she wanted to include at the beginning, middle, and end of her story. She also described her feelings about the events.

BEGINNING
Events: I found out about the catapult contest.
Feelings: I was excited. I love science and contests.

↓

MIDDLE
Events: I planned my catapult, met up with Mina, and worked on my catapult.
Feelings: Things got awkward with Mina. We didn't talk about the contest.

↓

END
Events: We helped each other with designs. Neither of us won the contest.
Feelings: I was happy to be talking to Mina again.

CONTENTS

Lesson 17

JERRY SPINELLI
THE NEWBERY AWARD–WINNING AUTHOR

Maniac Magee

Ode
to
Pablo's
Tennis
Shoes
by
Gary Soto

Genre: Poetry

439

Focus Skill

 ## Point of View

You have learned that every piece of writing is told from a particular **point of view**. A story that is narrated by a character is in the **first-person** point of view. A story narrated by an outside observer is in the **third-person** point of view.

- A third-person narrator may tell what only one person in the story knows and thinks. This kind of narration is **third-person limited**.
- A third-person narrator may tell what *all* the characters know and think. This kind of narration is **third-person omniscient**. *Omniscient* means "all knowing."

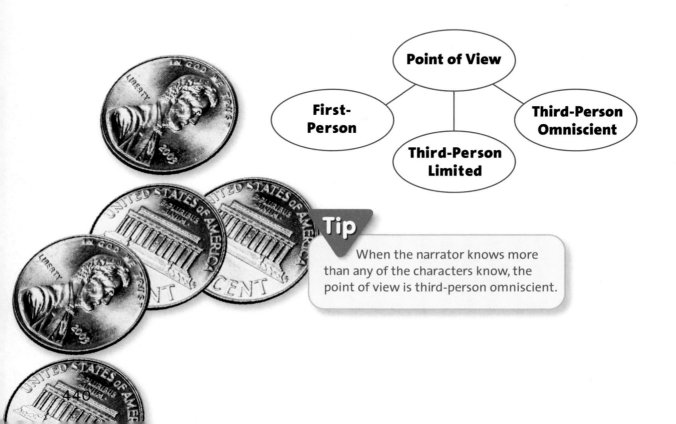

Point of View

First-Person

Third-Person Limited

Third-Person Omniscient

Tip

When the narrator knows more than any of the characters know, the point of view is third-person omniscient.

Read the paragraph below. Then look at the web. It shows clues indicating that the point of view in the paragraph is third-person omniscient.

How many pennies were in the jar? Everyone in the room was strategizing a method for estimating that number. Jake planned to count the pennies packed into 1 cubic inch and then multiply by 1,000. Marta was calculating the jar's volume. Edith planned to make a wild guess and hope for luck. Every mind in the room agreed on this: the prize for the best guess, a year's supply of bagels, was worth the effort.

Third-Person Omniscient

- narrator, an outside observer
- tells what all the characters know and think
- does not use the pronoun *I*

Try This!

Choose one character mentioned in the paragraph. Imagine that the story is told from that person's point of view. How would the passage be different?

GO online www.harcourtschool.com/storytown

Vocabulary

Build Robust Vocabulary

- foresight
- publicize
- distraction
- testimony
- contortions
- faint
- grimy

Treasure or Trash?

With an unusual lack of **foresight**, Gerry hadn't brought a camera to document the day. In every other way, however, he was prepared for the treasure hunt. He and Cole were about to investigate a mystery on the land next to Cole's house. Ever since Cole had found a purple plastic tassel sticking out of the ground, they suspected that buried treasure lay there.

All week, Gerry had kept the operation a secret. "Why **publicize** a buried treasure?" he reasoned. "In fact, we should create a **distraction** to keep others from getting suspicious."

On the day of the dig, Gerry brought a space rocket jigsaw puzzle to keep Cole's younger brother occupied inside the house. Gerry's idea was **testimony** to his careful planning.

At last, Gerry and Cole started to dig. Immediately, they struck something and determined that it was large. They worked hard to unearth the strange object. Finally, they pulled it from the ground and brushed off the dirt. It was a rusty tricycle bent into odd **contortions**. They could see a **faint** hint of purple paint under the **grimy** rust.

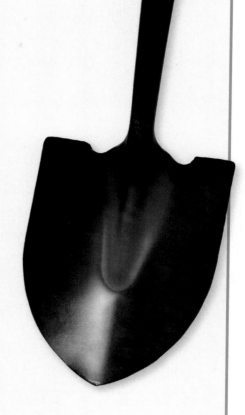

GO online www.harcourtschool.com/storytown

Word Detective

Your mission this week is to search for Vocabulary Words outside your classroom. You may read them in a book or in a newspaper. Listen for them in television shows and movies. When you find a Vocabulary Word, write in your vocabulary journal where you found it. Then explain how it was used.

Realistic Fiction

Genre Study

Realistic fiction has characters and events that are like people and events in real life. As you read, look for

- a plot with a beginning, middle, and end.

- a main character who faces a problem.

Characters		Setting
	Conflict	
	Plot Events	
	Resolution	

Comprehension Strategy

Ask questions as you read to check your own understanding of the text.

IAC MAGEE

BY JERRY SPINELLI
ILLUSTRATED BY DAVID GORDON

Everyone in Two Mills is talking about the new kid in town. Jeffrey Lionel Magee looks like a normal boy. However, some things about Jeffrey make him stand out.

- *He can outrun anyone around.*

- *He's allergic to pizza.*

- *He's an expert at untying tricky knots.*

The people of Two Mills are slow to accept Jeffrey, and they have given him an unusual nickname—Maniac Magee. One day, Maniac's friend Amanda gets an idea that she hopes will change the town's opinion of him. She tells Maniac about Cobble's Knot.

If the Wonders of the World hadn't stopped at seven, Cobble's Knot would have been number eight.

Nobody knew how it got there. As the story goes, the original Mr. Cobble wasn't doing too well with the original Cobble's Corner Grocery at the corner of Hector and Birch. In his first two weeks, all he sold was some Quaker Oats and penny candy.

Then one morning, as he unlocked the front door for business, he saw the Knot. It was dangling from the flagpole that hung over the big picture window, the one that said FROSTED FOODS in icy blue-and-white letters. He got out a pair of scissors and was about to snip it off, when he noticed what an unusual and incredible knot it was.

And then he got an idea. He could offer a prize to anyone who untangled the Knot. Publicize it. Call the newspaper. Winner's picture on the front page, Cobble's Corner in the background. Business would boom.

Well, he went ahead and did it, and if business didn't exactly boom, it must have at least peeped a little, because eons later, when Maniac Magee came to town, Cobble's Corner was still there. Only now it sold pizza instead of groceries. And the prize was different. It had started out being sixty seconds alone with the candy counter; now it was one large pizza per week for a whole year.

447

Which, in time, made the Knot practically priceless. Which is why, after leaving it outside for a year, Mr. Cobble took it down and kept it in a secret place inside the store and brought it out only to meet a challenger.

If you look at old pictures in the *Two Mills Times*, you see that the Knot was about the size and shape of a lopsided volleyball. It was made of string, but it had more contortions, ins and outs, twists and turns and dips and doodles than the brain of Albert Einstein himself. It had defeated all comers for years, including J.J. Thorndike, who grew up to be a magician, and Fingers Halloway, who grew up to be a pickpocket.

Hardly a week went by without somebody taking a shot at the Knot, and losing. And each loser added to the glory that awaited someone who could untie it.

"So you see," said Amanda, "if you go up there and untie Cobble's Knot—which I *know* you can—you'll get your picture in the paper and you'll be the biggest hero ever around here and *nooo*-body'll mess with you then."

Maniac listened and thought about it and finally gave a little grin. "Maybe you're just after the pizza, since you know I can't eat it."

Amanda screeched. "Jeff-*freee*! The pizza's not the point." She started to hit him. He laughed and grabbed her wrists. And he said okay, he'd give it a try.

They brought out the Knot and hung it from the flagpole. They brought out the official square wooden table for the challenger to stand on, and from the moment Maniac climbed up, you could tell the Knot was in big trouble.

To the ordinary person, Cobble's Knot was about as friendly as a nest of yellowjackets. Besides the tangle itself, there was the weathering of that first year, when the Knot hung outside and became hard as a rock. You could barely make out the individual strands. It was grimy, moldy, crusted over. Here and there a loop stuck out, maybe big enough to stick your pinky finger through, pitiful testimony to the challengers who had tried and failed.

And there stood Maniac, turning the Knot, checking it out. Some say there was a faint grin on his face, kind of playful, as though the Knot wasn't his enemy at all, but an old pal just playing a little trick on him. Others say his mouth was more grim than grin, that his eyes lit up like flashbulbs, because he knew he was finally facing a knot that would stand up and fight, a worthy opponent.

He lifted it in his hands to feel the weight of it. He touched it here and touched it there, gently, daintily. He scraped a patch of crust off with his fingernail. He laid his fingertips on it, as though feeling for a pulse.

Only a few people were watching at first, and half of them were Heck's Angels, a roving tricycle gang of four- and five-year-olds. Most of them had had sneaker-lace or yo-yo knots untied by Maniac, and they expected this would only take a couple of seconds longer. When the seconds became minutes, they started to get antsy, and before ten minutes had passed, they were zooming off in search of somebody to terrorize.

The rest of the spectators watched Maniac poke and tug and pick at the knot. Never a big pull or yank, just his fingertips touching and grazing and peck-pecking away, like some little bird.

"What's he doin'?" somebody said.

"What's taking so long?"

"He gonna do it or not?"

After an hour, except for a few more finger-size loops, all Maniac had to show for his trouble were the flakes of knot crust that covered the table.

"He ain't even found the end of the string yet," somebody grumbled, and almost everybody but Amanda took off.

Maniac never noticed. He just went on working.

By lunchtime they were all back, and more kept coming. Not only kids, but grownups, too, black and white, because Cobble's Corner was on Hector, and word was racing through the neighborhoods on both the east and west sides of the street.

What people saw they didn't believe.

The knot had grown, swelled, exploded. It was a frizzy globe—the newspaper the next day described it as a "gigantic hairball." Now, except for a packed-in clump at the center, it was practically all loops. You could look through it and see Maniac calmly working on the other side.

"He found the end!" somebody gasped, and the corner burst into applause.

Meanwhile, inside, Cobble's was selling pizza left and right, not to mention zeps (a Two Mills type of hoagie), steak sandwiches, strombolis, and gallons of soda. Mr. Cobble himself came out to offer Maniac some pizza, which Maniac of course politely turned down. He did accept an orange soda, though, and then a little kid, whose sneaker laces Maniac had untied many a time, handed up to him a three-pack of Tastykake butterscotch Krimpets.

After polishing off the Krimpets, Maniac did the last thing anybody expected: he lay down and took a nap right there on the table, the knot hanging above him like a small hairy planet, the mob buzzing all around him. Maniac knew what the rest of them didn't: the hardest part was yet to come. He had to find the right routes to untangle the mess, or it would just close up again like a rock and probably stay that way forever. He would need the touch of a surgeon, the alertness of an owl, the cunning of three foxes, and the foresight of a grand master in chess. To accomplish that, he needed to clear his head, to flush away all distraction, especially the memory of the butterscotch Krimpets, which had already hooked him.

In exactly fifteen minutes, he woke up and started back in.

Like some fairytale tailor, he threaded the end through the maze, dipping and doodling through openings the way he squiggled a football through a defense. As the long August afternoon boiled along, the exploded knot-hairball would cave in here, cave in there. It got lumpy, out of shape, saggy. The *Times* photographer made starbursts with his camera. The people munched on Cobble's pizza and spilled across Hector from sidewalk to sidewalk and said "Ouuuu!" and "Ahhhh!"

And then, around dinnertime, a huge roar went up, a volcano of cheers. Cobble's Knot was dead. Undone. Gone. It was nothing but string.

Bugles, cap guns, sirens, firecrackers, war whoops . . . Cobble's Corner was a madhouse.

Traffic had to beep and inch through the mob. Kids cried for autographs. Scraps of paper fluttered down in a shower of homemade confetti.

A beaming Mr. Cobble handed up a certificate to Maniac for the year's worth of large pizzas. Maniac accepted it and said his thanks. The undone knot lay in a coiled heap at Maniac's feet. Mr. Cobble grabbed it. Already people were guessing how long it was.*

* It turned out to be four and a half blocks long. Someone tied it to a stop sign and started walking, and that's how far he got before it gave out.

THINK CRITICALLY

1 What was Mr. Cobble's motivation for offering a prize to the person who untangled Cobble's Knot? CHARACTER'S MOTIVATIONS

2 Why did Amanda want Maniac Magee to try to untangle Cobble's Knot? CAUSE AND EFFECT

3 Is this selection written from the third-person limited or the third-person omniscient point of view? How can you tell? POINT OF VIEW

4 Maniac Magee's approach to untangling Cobble's Knot was to be patient and take his time. How might this approach help you solve a difficult problem? MAKE CONNECTIONS

5 **WRITE** Explain the factors that made Cobble's Knot into a legend before Maniac Magee ever touched it. SHORT RESPONSE

ABOUT THE AUTHOR

Jerry Spinelli

When Jerry Spinelli was growing up, he dreamed of becoming a star athlete, not a star author. But after the local newspaper published a poem he had written about his high school football team, his career as an author was set in motion. Jerry Spinelli has a talent for blending his memories and observations into characters. He was awarded the Newbery Medal for *Maniac Magee*.

ABOUT THE ILLUSTRATOR

David Gordon

David Gordon is the author and illustrator of three adaptations of traditional stories—*Hansel and Diesel*, *The Three Little Rigs*, and *The Ugly Truckling*. He has also done work in television and movies, designing concepts and characters for several well-known animated shows. David Gordon grew up in Colorado and now lives in New York City, where he continues to work on stories and illustrations for children's books.

GO online

457

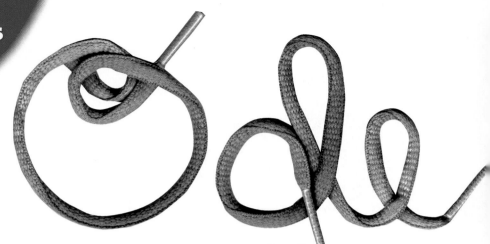

Ode
to Pablo's Tennis Shoes

by Gary Soto

They wait under Pablo's bed,
Rain-beaten, sun-beaten,
A scuff of green
At their tips
From when he fell
In the school yard.
He fell leaping for a football
That sailed his way.
But Pablo fell and got up,
Green on his shoes,
With the football
Out of reach.

Now it's night.
Pablo is in bed listening
To his mother laughing
To the Mexican *novelas* on TV.

His shoes, twin pets
That snuggle his toes,
Are under the bed.
He should have bathed,
But he didn't.
(Dirt rolls from his palm,
Blades of grass
Tumble from his hair.)
He wants to be
Like his shoes,
A little dirty
From the road,
A little worn
From racing to the drinking fountain
A hundred times in one day.
It takes water
To make him go,
And his shoes to get him
There. He loves his shoes,
Cloth like a sail,
Rubber like
A lifeboat on rough sea.
Pablo is tired,
Sinking into the mattress.
His eyes sting from
Grass and long words in books.
He needs eight hours
Of sleep
To cool his shoes,
The tongues hanging
Out, exhausted.

An ode celebrates a person, animal, or object; it is often written without the constraints of formal structure or rhyme.

459

Connections

Comparing Texts

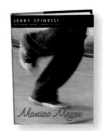

1. Maniac Magee has his own methods for untying knots. What is one activity or procedure that you do in your own particular way?

2. Compare "Maniac Magee" with "Ode to Pablo's Tennis Shoes." What do Maniac Magee and Pablo have in common?

3. According to "Maniac Magee," Cobble's Knot ranks among the Wonders of the World. What other human-made objects or places would you consider "wonders"?

Vocabulary Review

Word Webs

Work with a partner. Choose two Vocabulary Words. Create a word web for each word. Put a Vocabulary Word in the center of each web. In the outside ovals, write words and phrases that are related to the Vocabulary Word. Share your word webs with your partner, explaining how each word or phrase is related to each Vocabulary Word.

broadcast — advertise

publicize

foresight

publicize

distraction

testimony

contortions

faint

grimy

Fluency Practice

Repeated Reading

You have learned that intonation is the raising and lowering of pitch as you read a text aloud. Repeated reading can help you improve your intonation. Read aloud the last five paragraphs of "Maniac Magee" to a partner. Think about how you might improve your intonation to fit the tone of the story. Then read the passage again. Switch roles. Listen to your partner's intonation for ways to improve your own reading.

Writing

Write a Tall Tale

Think of an impossible task or challenge, such as digging a canyon by hand. Then write a tall tale about a character who succeeds at the task.

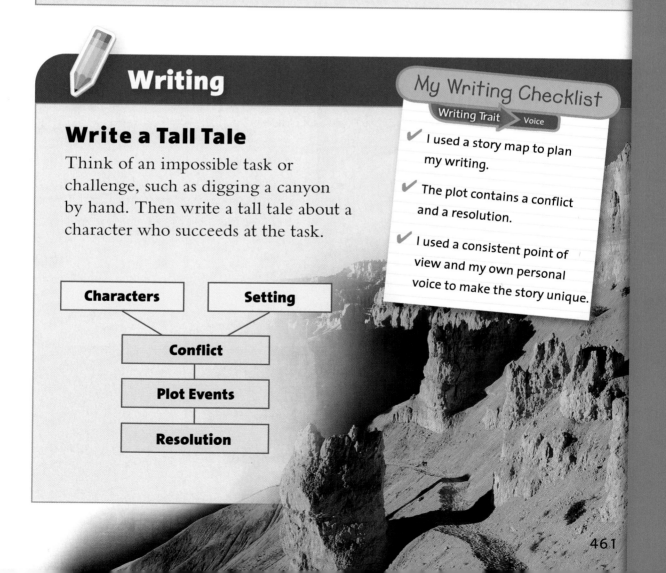

```
┌──────────────┐    ┌──────────────┐
│  Characters  │    │   Setting    │
└──────────────┘    └──────────────┘
        │                  │
        └────────┬─────────┘
          ┌──────────────┐
          │   Conflict   │
          └──────────────┘
                 │
          ┌──────────────┐
          │ Plot Events  │
          └──────────────┘
                 │
          ┌──────────────┐
          │  Resolution  │
          └──────────────┘
```

My Writing Checklist

Writing Trait ▶ Voice

✔ I used a story map to plan my writing.

✔ The plot contains a conflict and a resolution.

✔ I used a consistent point of view and my own personal voice to make the story unique.

CONTENTS

Lesson 18

The KiD WHo Named PlUto

and the
Stories of Other
Extraordinary
Young People in
Science

HOW ATHENS WAS NAMED

A PLAY BASED ON A GREEK MYTH

retold by
Pat Betteley
illustratred by
David Scott Meier

Make Judgments

Careful readers of nonfiction evaluate what they read and **make judgments** about information in the text. A judgment is an **assertion**—a statement or a claim. Assertions are valid, or reasonable, if the reader can support them with **evidence** from the text. When you make an assertion, evaluate the evidence to see how well it supports your claim.

Evidence	Evidence	Evidence

Judgment/Assertion

Tip
Evidence includes facts, examples, or quotations from the text.

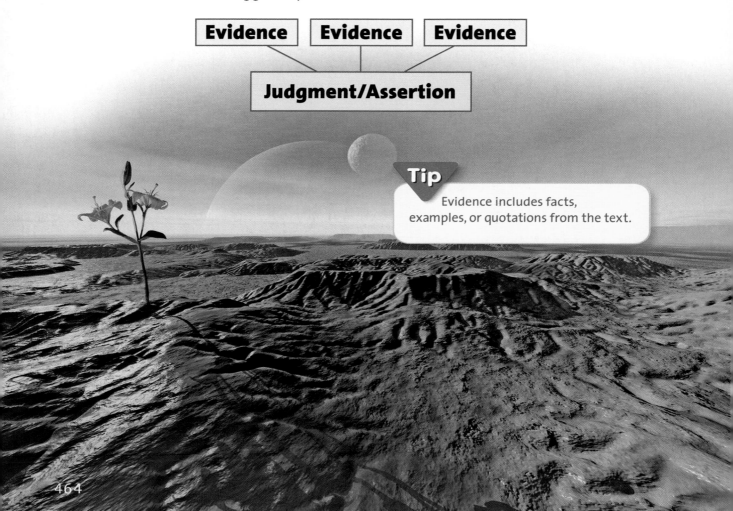

Read the paragraph below. Then look at the graphic organizer. It shows one assertion that someone might make after reading the paragraph and the evidence that supports it.

Is there life on Mars? Researchers disagree on the answer. Some argue that there is strong evidence for life on Mars because of the presence of methane gas. (On Earth, most methane gas is produced by bacteria, living organisms.) However, methane is also produced when olivine, a mineral present on Mars, comes into contact with water containing carbon dioxide. Some scientists believe that this fact argues against the possibility of life on Mars.

Evidence	**Evidence**	**Evidence**
There is methane gas on Mars.	On Earth, bacteria produce most methane.	Bacteria are living organisms.

Judgment/Assertion

There is strong evidence for life on Mars.

Try This!

Read the paragraph again. What evidence supports the assertion that there is no proof for life on Mars?

Vocabulary

Build Robust Vocabulary

- beacon
- marvel
- enthralled
- persisted
- objections
- disturbances
- clamor
- coincidentally

Our Solar System

It's not hard to spot Venus low on the horizon or see Mars shine like a pale red **beacon** in the night. Many people **marvel** at the fact that Earth is merely one planet in the solar system. People have long been **enthralled** by the night sky.

For many centuries, people had to rely only on what their own eyes could tell them. They **persisted** in believing that Earth was the center of the universe. Many people raised **objections** when Copernicus said that Earth and the other planets revolved around the sun. Then Galileo invented the telescope and began a new era in astronomy.

Earth is the third planet from the sun.

Today, scientists study our solar system in various ways. They observe how objects move and how much light they give off. They also look for **disturbances** around objects.

In 2003, great **clamor** and excitement were created when scientists thought they had discovered a new planet. In 2005, another potential planet was discovered. **Coincidentally**, the space object discovered in 2005 lies close to the place where the earlier planet was thought to be. Are these space objects really planets? Further study and debate are needed to answer this question.

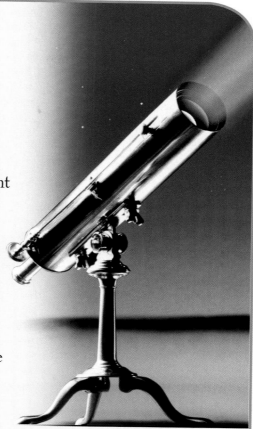

 www.harcourtschool.com/storytown

Word Scribe

This week your task is to use the Vocabulary Words in your writing. In your vocabulary journal, write sentences that show the meanings of the words. For example, you could describe a story that enthralled you. Use as many of the Vocabulary Words as you can. Share your writing with your classmates.

Award Winner

Expository Nonfiction

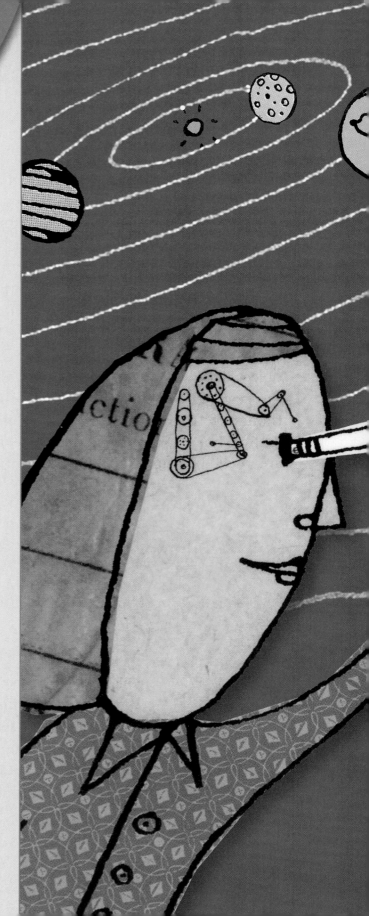

Genre Study

Expository nonfiction presents and explains facts about a topic. As you read, look for

- information about real people and events.

- events told in chronological order.

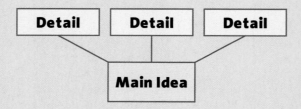

Detail	Detail	Detail

Main Idea

Comprehension Strategy

Monitor comprehension as you read. Stop and **self-correct** mistakes that change the meaning of the text.

The Kid Who Named Pluto

by Marc McCutcheon
illustrated by Jon Cannell

At the Lowell Observatory in Flagstaff, Arizona, on February 18, 1929, an astronomer named Clyde Tombaugh couldn't believe what he was seeing. Through an eyepiece on a machine called a Blink-Comparator, Tombaugh examined two photos of the Gemini constellation. Each showed the same glimmering stars, but the pictures were not identical. The second photograph was taken a week after the first, and during that time something had changed. The astronomer saw that a tiny beacon of light—a mere pinprick—was in a different place in the second photograph than it had been in the first.

An unknown object was traveling across the solar system!

Tombaugh was certain it wasn't a comet or an asteroid—the light was too big. Nor could it be a star—stars were too far away to detect movement of this kind. The object could only be one thing: Planet X!

For years, scientists had hunted for Planet X, the ninth planet in the solar system. Odd disturbances in the orbits of the planets Neptune and Uranus showed that a source of gravitational pull was nearby, and astronomers believed that this mysterious source *must* be a planet, but year after year, they were unable to spot it. Now Tombaugh had a photograph of it.

With Tombaugh's discovery, the Lowell Observatory faced a question: What should they name the new planet? One idea was to name it after the great astronomer Percival Lowell, who had spent much of his lifetime searching for Planet X. Lowell had died before Tombaugh made his discovery, but Planet X turned out to be very close to where Lowell had predicted it might be. On the other hand, many scientists felt that the planet should be named after a character in Greek or Roman mythology, to follow tradition. Mars is named after the Roman god of war, Mercury after the messenger god, Venus after the goddess of love and beauty. *Percival* or *Lowell* just didn't seem to fit.

On March 13, 1930, which coincidentally was Percival Lowell's birthday, the Lowell Observatory announced the great discovery. The public was enthralled. How big was the new planet? How far away was it? Could it be seen without a telescope? Although many questions could not be answered right away, the question of what to name the new planet created an immediate clamor. Suggestions poured in from astronomers and citizens around the world.

471

Which Name Would You Choose for a Planet?

These are just a few of the suggestions people made:

Apollo

Artemis

Atlas

Bacchus

Cronus

Diana

Erebus

Idana

Minerva

Osiris

Pax

Perseus

Tantalus

Tombaugh

Vulcan

One person wrote in to suggest the name *Zymal* because that was the last word in the dictionary and this was the last word on planets in the solar system. Another wrote, "Why have only one lady in our planetary system?" and suggested *Idana* to accompany Venus.

Nearly 100 different names were suggested in all, but the final decision was left up to the members of the Lowell Observatory. At first they favored *Cronus*. In mythology, Cronus was the son of Uranus and the father of Neptune—perfect, right? But Cronus had already been used to name a falsely identified planet years earlier. So to avoid confusion, the observatory decided against it.

The debate persisted for weeks. In coffeehouses and observatories all over the world, people discussed the possibilities and their favorite choices.

As luck would have it, 11-year-old Venetia Burney of Oxford, England, had just learned in school about the eight planets and the mythological characters they were named after. The planets and their names fascinated Venetia for many reasons, but especially because, 40 years before she was born, her great-uncle, Henry George Madan, had named the moons of Mars: Deimos and Phobos. The naming brought a great honor to her family. Hearing about the discovery of the new planet, she began flipping through her books on mythology. Could she be as clever as her uncle and name a celestial body? Would anyone in Arizona listen to an 11-year-old girl halfway around the world?

After much study and thought, Venetia went to her father and told him she had found the perfect name for the new planet. He thought her idea was brilliant and offered to telegram her suggestion to the observatory in America. Nearly everyone who read the telegram agreed that Venetia's suggestion was a winner. Her name? *Pluto*.

Pluto was the Greek god of the dark and distant underworld, and as the farthest planet from the sun, Planet X was certainly dark and distant. Furthermore, the god Pluto could make himself invisible, and Planet X had been frustratingly hidden for years. In mythology, Pluto was the brother of Jupiter and Neptune. And Pluto began with the letters PL, which would be a thoughtful tribute to Percival Lowell.

At the age of 11, Venetia was hardly a world-class astronomer or scientist, but that didn't matter—her choice was perfect. The observatory officially proposed the name on May 1, 1930, and it caught on almost instantly. A few mild objections were heard, but *Pluto* stuck and most astronomers agreed that it was well chosen.

{ Pluto }

Venetia Burney, 1930

Fascinating Fact!

Friends and family affectionately started calling Venetia "Plutonia" after she named the planet.

Today, scientists marvel that Pluto was ever found. Decades later, when space probes were visiting the planets, they discovered that the disturbances that scientists thought they had seen in the orbits of Uranus and Neptune, the same ones that had caused astronomers like Percival Lowell to conclude there was a ninth planet to be found, never really existed. It had been a coincidence that Lowell followed his Planet X prediction, and sheer luck that Tombaugh stumbled upon it.

Pluto is less than half the size of the moon and 3.5 billion miles from the sun (Earth is 91 million miles from the sun). No space probe has ever visited this tiny frozen sphere, but scientists at NASA say that someday one will.

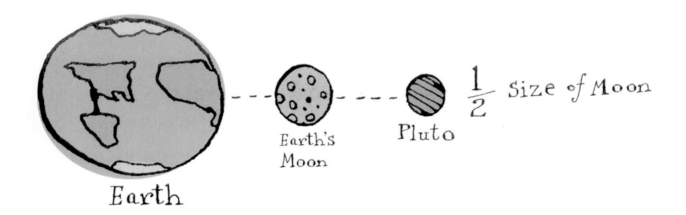

Earth

Earth's Moon

Pluto

$\frac{1}{2}$ Size of Moon

Pluto was thought to be the last planet in Earth's solar system, but not the last planet to be found in all of space. Scientists have recently found more than 100 others. Astronomers say that billions and perhaps trillions more are waiting to be discovered.

And who will name all those new planets? Although the planet's discoverer and the International Astronomical Union (an organization of astronomers) usually name new celestial bodies, anyone can make a suggestion—just like Venetia Burney.

Prepare to Name a Planet

Here are some steps to follow if you want to name a planet yourself:

- Visit the International Astronomical Union's website (www.iau.org) for its rules on naming new celestial bodies.

- Read science and astronomy magazines to learn about newly discovered planets. Visit astronomy websites to see what scientists are saying about new planets.

- Read Greek and Roman mythology and compile a list of the names you like, with reasons why they would make good celestial names.

- Read science fiction stories and classic works, such as those by Shakespeare, for other interesting names.

- Research which names have already been used to name new planets.

Note: So-called star registry companies will let you pay to register a name by computer, but this naming carries absolutely no legal weight. It is neither official nor internationally recognized by scientists or governments.

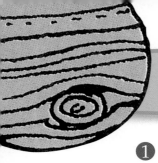

Think Critically

1 What clues led Clyde Tombaugh to find Planet X? NOTE DETAILS

2 Why did many scientists believe that Planet X should be named after a character in Greek or Roman mythology instead of after Percival Lowell? DRAW CONCLUSIONS

3 Is Pluto an appropriate name for the planet that was discovered in 1929? Explain. MAKE JUDGMENTS

4 Many discoveries, inventions, and products get their names in surprising ways. What do you think is the best way to name an invention or product? Explain. MAKE CONNECTIONS

5 **WRITE** Write a paragraph that explains the steps a person should follow to suggest a name for a planet. Use evidence from the selection to support your answer. SHORT RESPONSE

About the Author
Marc McCutcheon

About the Illustrator
Jon Cannell

Author, journalist, and amateur scientist Marc McCutcheon taught himself everything he needed to know about writing. Today, he is a best-selling author and the owner of a bookstore. He enjoys writing nonfiction books and encourages others to do so, too. He calls his work "the ultimate dream job." He lives with his wife and two children in South Portland, Maine.

Illustrator Jon Cannell runs his own design business, Jon Cannell Design. In addition to illustrating books for young readers, he does graphic design work for many major American corporations. He lives in North Bend, Washington, with his wife and three children.

GO online **www.harcourtschool.com/storytown**

Myth

HOW ATHENS

A PLAY BASED ON A GREEK MYTH

retold by Pat Betteley
illustrated by
David Scott Meier

Characters: *Narrator, City Leader, Citizen 1, Citizen 2, Citizen 3, Poseidon, Athena*

Narrator: A group of people stood on the Acropolis in Greece trying to choose a name for their new city.

City Leader: Thank you all for joining me here today. From this shelf of rocks, we have a great view of the place that will shape our futures. I hope it will inspire us all.

Citizen 1: Let's name it Rockview.

Citizen 2: No. How about Hilltop-opolis?

Citizen 3: I've got it—Hilltopolis?

Narrator: The democratic leader looked up to the sky in frustration.

City Leader: Those are all very . . . er, creative . . . suggestions, but since this is such an important decision, let's call upon the gods to help.

Narrator: Poseidon, god of the sea, and Athena, goddess of wisdom, immediately appeared before them.

City Leader: Thank you for coming, immortal ones. Please help us choose a name for our fair city.

Poseidon: That is easy. Name it after me. Now I need to be getting back to the sea.

WAS NAMED

A *trident* is a *three-pronged spear.*

Athena: Not so fast, Poseidon. Explain to the good people why they should name their city for you.

Poseidon: Well, er . . . because . . . because of THIS . . .

Narrator: The god of the sea hurled his three-pronged trident across the rock ledge. Water gushed out in a stream from the place where it had landed. Poseidon made a sweeping gesture with his hand.

Poseidon: Behold, this stream will give you access to the sea, which will carry trade ships and make you all rich and powerful. I like the sound of Poseidonapolis, I think.

Narrator: The people turned to each other with eyes sparkling, smiling happily at their good fortune.

Athena: Very impressive, Poseidon. But the water is as salty as the sea that you rule. Let the people hear my proposal. Perhaps they will want to name their city after me.

Poseidon: Choose the gift of a mere goddess over that of an all-powerful god such as me? Ha, that is rich! But of course, Athena, you are right. You must present your little gift. Go ahead, we are all waiting breathlessly.

Narrator: Poseidon stood back, smirking, and Athena continued calmly.

Athena: It is my great honor to present my gift to the people.

Narrator: She tapped the rock with her toe, took a deep breath, and blew gently on the ground. A tiny seedling with silvery leaves appeared.

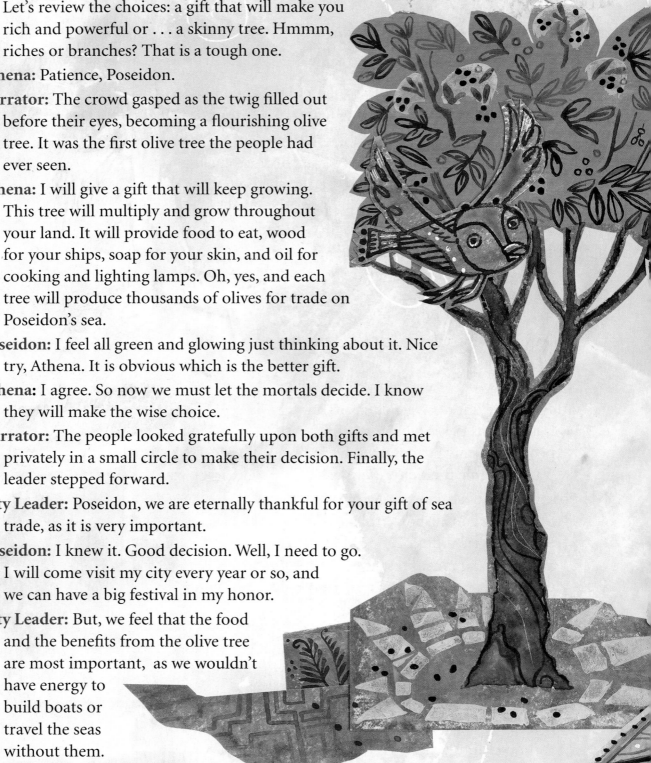

Poseidon: Ha! A scrawny little twig. What a difficult decision! Let's review the choices: a gift that will make you rich and powerful or . . . a skinny tree. Hmmm, riches or branches? That is a tough one.

Athena: Patience, Poseidon.

Narrator: The crowd gasped as the twig filled out before their eyes, becoming a flourishing olive tree. It was the first olive tree the people had ever seen.

Athena: I will give a gift that will keep growing. This tree will multiply and grow throughout your land. It will provide food to eat, wood for your ships, soap for your skin, and oil for cooking and lighting lamps. Oh, yes, and each tree will produce thousands of olives for trade on Poseidon's sea.

Poseidon: I feel all green and glowing just thinking about it. Nice try, Athena. It is obvious which is the better gift.

Athena: I agree. So now we must let the mortals decide. I know they will make the wise choice.

Narrator: The people looked gratefully upon both gifts and met privately in a small circle to make their decision. Finally, the leader stepped forward.

City Leader: Poseidon, we are eternally thankful for your gift of sea trade, as it is very important.

Poseidon: I knew it. Good decision. Well, I need to go. I will come visit my city every year or so, and we can have a big festival in my honor.

City Leader: But, we feel that the food and the benefits from the olive tree are most important, as we wouldn't have energy to build boats or travel the seas without them.

480

So, we have decided to name our city in honor of Athena.

Narrator: Poseidon muttered under his breath, dug his trident into the rock, and disappeared. The City Leader turned to the goddess of wisdom.

City Leader: To show our sincere appreciation for your gift of the olive tree, Parthenos, we will build a temple to you on this very spot.

Citizen 1: Let's call it the Athena-Dome.

Citizen 2: No, how about the Athen-iseum.

Citizen 3: I've got it. We'll call it the Parthenon.

Athena: Perfect.

Narrator: Athena whistled for her wise and trusted owl to come perch on her shoulder.

Athena: Thank you all. From this beautiful spot, I shall proudly keep watch over my city, Athens.

Narrator: And she did.

Parthenos is a Greek word meaning "maiden." The Greeks used it as a title for Athena. The crowning jewel of Athens is the Parthenon, the temple to the goddess Athena. Near the Parthenon is the famous olive tree that continues to live as long as Athens is free.

Connections

Comparing Texts

1. Describe a planet or another astronomical object you have observed in the night sky.

2. How are the purposes of "The Kid Who Named Pluto" and "How Athens Was Named" similar? How are they different?

3. How might reading about Venetia Burney inspire other young people to tackle a challenge?

Vocabulary Review

Rate a Situation

Copy the line below onto a piece of paper. Then, for each sentence, think about how upset or excited the situation would make you feel. Write the Vocabulary Word in the appropriate place on the line. Explain to a partner why you ranked the sentences in the order that you did.

Upset •————————————————• Excited

- You are lost at night and see a beacon ahead.
- People are enthralled by the story you are telling.
- A mosquito persisted in buzzing around you.
- People clamor for the cookies you baked.

beacon

marvel

enthralled

persisted

objections

disturbances

clamor

coincidentally

Fluency Practice

Partner Reading

Remember that pace refers to the smoothness and consistency of oral reading. When you read aloud, keep a smooth, even pace. Work with a partner. Read aloud your favorite passage from "The Kid Who Named Pluto" as your partner follows along. Ask your partner for feedback on your pace. Read the passage again. Then switch roles.

Writing

Write a Proposal

Venetia Burney became famous for naming a planet. Think of a natural feature or a structure that you would like to rename. Then write a proposal in which you tell why the name you have chosen would be better.

My Writing Checklist

Writing Trait ▶ Sentence Fluency

✔ I used a graphic organizer to plan my writing.

✔ I used an organization that makes sense.

✔ I used a variety of sentence types.

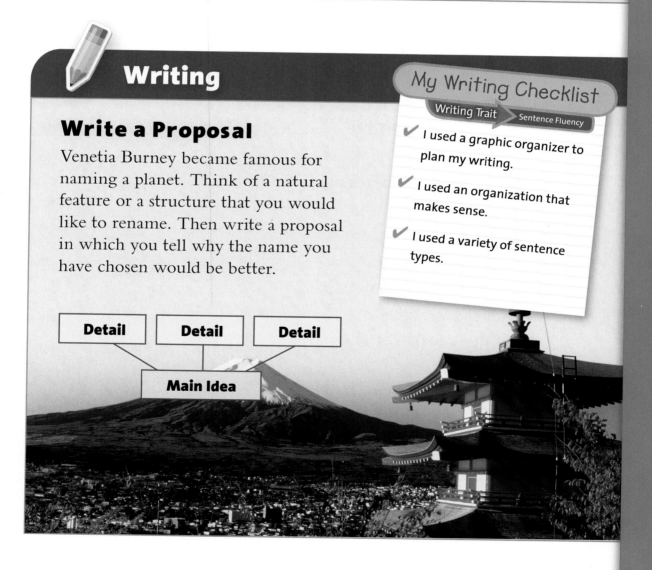

| Detail | Detail | Detail |

Main Idea

CONTENTS

Genre: Expository Nonfiction

Buildings in Disguise

Architecture That Looks Like Animals, Food, and Other Things

by
Joan Marie Arbogast

STATUE OF LIBERTY

by J. Patrick Lewis

Genre: Poetry

Focus Skill

Make Judgments

Remember that careful readers of nonfiction **make judgments**, or **assertions**, about information in the text. Assertions are valid if they can be supported by text **evidence**. Facts, examples, and quotations are kinds of evidence that can be used to support an assertion. Reliable evidence makes your assertions convincing. As you read, use the steps below to evaluate the text.

- Think about the evidence the author presents.
- Think about how reliable the evidence is.
- Make an assertion based on the evidence.

Evidence	Evidence	Evidence

Judgment/Assertion

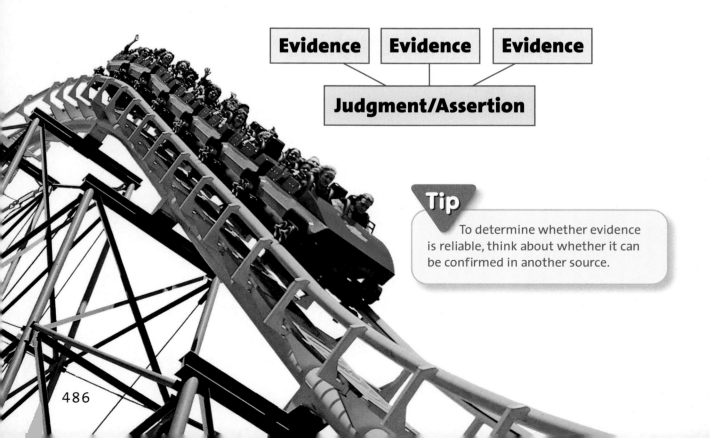

Tip

To determine whether evidence is reliable, think about whether it can be confirmed in another source.

Read the paragraph below. Then look at the graphic organizer. It shows an assertion based on information in the paragraph and the evidence that supports it.

People disagree about the safety of amusement parks. According to the amusement park industry, visiting these parks is safer than many other leisure activities. Every year, more than 300 million people visit amusement parks and attractions in the United States. Only about 6,500 visitors suffer injuries. Far more people get hurt each year while bicycling or playing basketball.

Evidence
Visiting an amusement park is safer than many other leisure activities.

Evidence
Only 6,500 out of 300 million visitors are injured at amusement parks.

Evidence
More people get hurt while bicycling or playing basketball.

Judgment/Assertion
People shouldn't worry about amusement park safety any more than they worry about safety in other leisure activities.

Try This!

What kind of information could be added to support the evidence that more people are hurt each year while bicycling or playing basketball? In your opinion, would the evidence become more or less reliable?

www.harcourtschool.com/storytown

Vocabulary

Build Robust Vocabulary

eager

beloved

humongous

abandoned

neglected

demolished

severe

Puppy Love

On Valentine's Day 2005, **eager** spectators gathered to witness the return of a **beloved** community symbol. The Doggie Diner head, a **humongous** sculpture of a smiling dachshund wearing a white chef's hat, was proudly displayed in its new home near Ocean Beach in San Francisco, California.

The 700-pound dachshund head was one of many such sculptures that once drew customers to the Doggie Diner restaurant chain. When the restaurant chain went out of business in 1986, its diner near the beach was **abandoned**.

After the Doggie Diner near Ocean Beach closed, the **neglected** dachshund head became chipped and faded. Its nose was damaged in a storm.

In the year 2000, residents learned that the old diner might be **demolished**. Community leaders planned to rescue the Doggie Diner head and move it to a new home. Unfortunately, in April 2001, **severe** winds toppled the sculpture. It smashed onto a phone booth as it fell, and its nose was badly damaged.

Luckily, the giant dachshund head was saved. City workers repaired it, and today it has a new permanent home near the San Francisco Zoo.

Dozens of people turned out to see the unveiling of the repaired Doggie Diner head.

 GO online www.harcourtschool.com/storytown

Word Champion

Your challenge this week is to use the Vocabulary Words outside the classroom. Post the words where you will see them often. Use as many of the words as you can when you talk with family members or friends. For example, you might tell a friend about a humongous insect you saw. At the end of each day, write in your vocabulary journal the words you used. Tell how you used them.

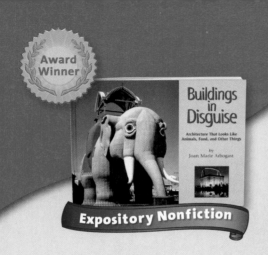

Buildings in Disguise
Architecture That Looks Like Animals, Food, and Other Things
by
Joan Marie Arbogast

Expository Nonfiction

Genre Study

Expository nonfiction presents and explains facts about a topic. As you read, look for

- headings that tell the topic of each section.

- main ideas supported by details.

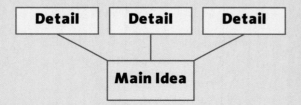

| Detail | Detail | Detail |

Main Idea

Comprehension Strategy

Monitor comprehension as you read. Stop and **self-correct** mistakes that change the meaning of the text.

Build

ings in Disguise

by Joan Marie Arbogast

Some buildings don't look like buildings. They look like oversize elephants, beagles, or ducks. These buildings are meant to grab your attention, and they usually do. Architects call these structures mimetic because they mimic other objects.

Lucy, the Margate Elephant

As engineer and land-developer James V. Lafferty, Jr., admired his very unusual building, he knew people would come to see it. But that was only part of his plan. The other was to convince people to purchase parcels of his land along the Atlantic coast.

That was back in 1881—and his idea worked! His plan, after all, had been simple. Make it big. Make it fun. Make it in disguise. And that's exactly what he did. With the help of an architect and a crew of burly builders, Mr. Lafferty constructed a one-of-a-kind, sixty-five-foot-tall elephant-shaped building near the growing seaside resort of Atlantic City, New Jersey. People came from miles around to see his extraordinary building.

To prevent others from copying his idea, Mr. Lafferty applied for and received a patent on his building in 1882.

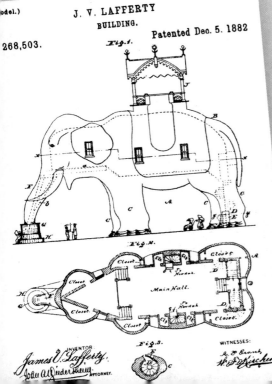

Statistics: Lucy, the Margate Elephant

Location: Margate, New Jersey

Built: 1881

Materials used: Nearly 1 million pieces of wood, 200 kegs of nails, 4 tons of bolts and beams, 12,000 square feet of tin

Main room: 18' by 18', a little smaller than a two-car garage

Height: 65' tall, which means if Lucy were hiding in the woods, her *howdah* could be seen above most of the trees

Ears: 17' long, 10' wide, roughly the size of a full-size car

Glass eyes: 18" diameter, the size of a beach ball

Number of windows: 17

Curious customers climbed the spiral staircases to the *howdah*, or canopied carrier, on the elephant's back. There they viewed the lots for sale. Some eager land-buyers even sealed their deals inside the elephant's belly.

Two years later, Lafferty built Elephantine Colossus in Coney Island, New York—*the* amusement park of its time. This spectacular building towered 122', nearly twice the height of Lucy. Visitors paid to view its innards of seven floors and thirty-one rooms. But in 1896, a fire leveled the mammoth pachyderm.

A third elephant, Light of Asia, was constructed in 1884 by a gentleman who purchased the building rights from Lafferty. It stood in Cape May, New Jersey—one of the most popular seaside resorts of the mid-1800s. It was shorter than Lucy by twenty-five feet, and it never attracted the attention that Lafferty's elephants did. In 1900, the neglected elephant was torn down.

In 1887, Mr. Lafferty sold his original elephant to Anton Gertzen, who'd helped construct the unusual building. The Gertzen family owned and operated the elephant as a tourist attraction for nearly eighty years. It was his daughter-in-law, Sophia Gertzen, who named the elephant Lucy, though no one seems to know why.

During the early 1900s, tourists paid ten cents to enter the awesome structure. People traveled the states and sailed the sea to examine this remarkable building. You can see for yourself by examining the guest list below. Notice how many different states are represented. How many countries? Do you recognize any of the names?

Though Lucy survived severe storms along the Atlantic coast for eighty years, the terrible storm of 1962 left her tattered and torn. Years of saltwater mists had already weakened her wooden "bones." Years of sandy winds had worn her tin "skin" thin. No longer safe for curious tourists, Lucy's doors were locked to the public.

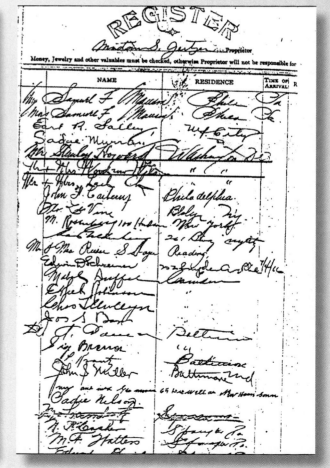

A National Historic Landmark is a building, structure, or object that has been recognized as having played a significant role in American history.

LUCY, THE MARGATE ELEPHANT
has been designated a

NATIONAL
HISTORIC
LANDMARK

This site possesses national significance
in commemorating the history of the
United States of America

Afraid that their unusual landmark would be toppled to make room for condominiums, concerned citizens formed the Save Lucy Committee, which sprang into action in 1969. Even children pitched in to protect the aging elephant. The group raised enough money to move their beloved pachyderm to a safe spot in a city park farther from the water's edge.

Though Lucy moved only two short blocks, it took nearly seven hours to inch her down the road. Once secured in her new location, lengthy repairs and restorations began. Then, in 1976, Lucy was honored as a National Historic Landmark.

Today Lucy welcomes guests through her doors as she did when she was young. People still climb to the howdah on Lucy's back, where they can view the seascape and the city of Margate, New Jersey, that Lucy helped to create.

Lucy is our nation's oldest functioning example of mimetic architecture. She's also our oldest zoomorphic (animal-shaped) structure. Both are designed to grab your attention. And Lucy has for more than 120 years!

Statistics: The Big Duck

Location: Flanders, Long Island, New York

Built: 1931

Height: 20', equal to three minivans stacked on top of each other

Width: 15', equal to two minivans parked side by side

Length: 30', equal to two minivans parked end to end

Materials used: Wood, wire mesh, concrete

Original eyes: Taillights from a Model T Ford

Patented in 1932

Listed on National Register of Historic Places

Ducks are structures where the building is the advertisement or sign; often these buildings are shaped like the products they sell.

The Big Duck

While vacationing in California, duck farmers Martin and Jeule Maurer visited a coffee shop shaped like a super-sized coffeepot. That's when they decided to construct a head-turner of their own.

That was back in 1931, when three-fourths of the nation's duck business was located on New York's Long Island, where the Maurers lived. When the couple returned from vacation, they hired a carpenter and two brothers to construct a "duck" to increase the sales of their ducks and eggs.

First, the men studied one of the Maurers' Peking ducks. Then they constructed a wooden skeleton, added wire mesh, and applied tons of concrete. Finally, they painted the bird and placed taillights from an old Model T Ford into its head for its eyes. Even on the darkest of nights, the red glowing eyes could be seen from down the road. The duck gained so much attention that it was featured in the November issue of *Popular Mechanics* in 1932.

Later, in 1972, the duck became more famous when architects Robert Venturi, Denise Scott Brown, and Steven Izenour wrote about it in their book, *Learning from Las Vegas*. Suddenly buildings shaped like the products they sold were nicknamed "ducks."

But fame alone can't save buildings from destruction. Much like Lucy the Elephant, the duck's future was doomed when the land on which it perched was sold.

Without the aid of the local community, this famous Long Island landmark would have been demolished in 1987. But the community sprang into action and raised enough money to move the giant Peking duck to the entrance of the Sears Bellows County Park, a few miles away. Today "The Big Duck" doubles as a visitors' center and gift shop, operated by Friends for Long Island's Heritage.

Entertainment Complexes

Castles and palaces have stood for centuries, but not in the United States. So when the people of Mitchell, South Dakota, decided to construct a palace-like building back in 1892, it caused quite a stir. And that's exactly what they wanted to do.

When Lewis and Clark traveled through the southern Dakota plains in 1804 and again in 1806, they noted in their journal that sections of the plains were "naked" and "void of Timber" though other sections were lush with life. Afraid that outsiders might view the area as uninviting, the people of Mitchell constructed a very unusual building to attract people into town. This building, they decided, would showcase their abundant crops and hopefully attract settlers, too. Much like Lucy the Elephant in Margate, New Jersey, Mitchell's "palace" drew people from miles away.

Not only were goods displayed inside the building, they were also displayed on its walls. The palace attracted so many people that a larger one was built in 1905 and another in 1921, which still stands today.

Every summer the designs and murals are replaced with new ones. The process takes nearly all summer to complete. It also takes 3,000 bushels of grasses and grains plus more than 275,000 ears of corn. Each ear of corn is cut in half lengthwise, then nailed to the building's wooden panels.

Today's Corn Palace continues to attract folks to Mitchell, South Dakota, where they can enjoy sporting events, stage performances, and concerts inside this one-of-a-kind mimetic structure.

Statistics: Corn Palace

Location: Mitchell, South Dakota

Built: 1892 - the original wooden structure was built, known as The Corn Belt Exposition

1905 - a larger wooden Corn Palace was built

1921 - the current structure was built, minus the turrets and domes

1937 - 2 turrets and 5 domes were added Designed by the same architects who designed Radio City Music Hall in New York City, Rapp and Rapp from Chicago

Materials used: steel, brick, wood-paneled walls to hold decorations
Wall decorations include black, blue, red, brown, calico, white, and yellow corn, plus oats, rye, sour dock (a grass) and milo (a grain used for cattle feed)

Size: Width equal to ½ city block
Depth equal to 1 city block

This structure mimics a medieval castle. It is found in the Enchanted Forest in Turner, Oregon. Guests enter Storybook Lane by way of this "castle."

By the early 1950s, storybook parks opened from east to west. Complete with buildings and characters borrowed from childhood stories, these parks brought nursery rhymes and fairy tales to life. Fairy tale–type castles that welcomed guests to their parks years ago still welcome guests today.

At Story Land in Glen, New Hampshire, Cinderella greets guests outside the Cinderella castle. Guests can even arrive at the castle by way of a pumpkin carriage!

Story Land has several mimetic structures throughout its park. As young visitors climb in and out of a walk-in shoe house, it's easy to see how mimetic structures bring nursery rhymes to life.

> There was an old woman
> who lived in a shoe,
> She had so many children
> she didn't know what to do.

DUTCH WONDERLAND®

Young guests who visit DUTCH WONDERLAND® Family Amusement Park in Lancaster, Pennsylvania, can attend story hour inside this mimetic castle. That humongous black spider appears in the fall as the park prepares for spooktacular fun. This forty-foot-tall building has been around since 1963.

Long before storybook parks opened, amusement parks used mimetic buildings to attract guests. This oversize shoe once stood in Luna Park in Cleveland, Ohio, during the early 1900s. Notice the chutes (slides) on either side of the shoe.

INGERSOLL'S LUNA PARK, CLEVELAND, OHIO.

Believe it or not, this giant-size shoe holds three bedrooms, two bathrooms, a kitchen, and a living room! Built by millionaire "Colonel" Mahlon N. Haines in 1948, the odd-shaped building provided roadside advertisement for his shoe-selling business.

Though this "shoe" once served as a guest house, it is now a museum, with an ice-cream parlor tucked into its heel. The Haines Shoe House sits on a hill overlooking US 30 (Lincoln Highway) in York County, Pennsylvania.

501

Some mimetic buildings were originally built as museums. This monstrous muskie looks like a sculpture. But it's really one of the buildings that house The National Fresh Water Fishing Hall of Fame in Hayward, Wisconsin. Though other fish pose in the Hall of Fame's Sea of Fishes, this is the only one you can enter.

Inspired by his childhood memories of Lucy the Elephant, Claude Bell constructed this 140-foot Apatosaurus in Cabazon, California. Creating it in his spare time, it took him nearly a dozen years to complete. Though it was designed to hold a dinosaur museum, it now holds a gift shop in its belly. Curious customers enter through the door in its tail. The Tyrannosaurus Rex in the background was built by Bell, too. But it's not open to the public.

Yesterday's Tomorrows

Though Lucy the Elephant is our oldest example of mimetic architecture, these structures have been around for centuries. They date back to ancient times with the Trojan Horse. But it wasn't until the invention of the affordable automobile that this form of architecture took off by leaps and bounds. During the 1920s and 1930s, roadside businesses mushroomed. But when faster-paced superhighways bypassed smaller towns, many of these roadside businesses saw fewer and fewer guests.

Eventually, many of these buildings were abandoned and have since toppled to the ground. Fortunately, during the 1970s preservation groups spread across the country. They've worked tirelessly to save historic buildings and landmarks, including a number of mimetic buildings.

Today concerned citizens continue to work to save buildings that serve as symbols of our country's past, like this coffeepot located along the Lincoln Highway in Bedford, Pennsylvania.

The Coffee Pot was saved from the wrecker's ball in December of 2003 when it was moved a short distance down the road to the Bedford County Fairgrounds, where it will be restored to its original beauty.

Think Critically

1. What are mimetic buildings? MAIN IDEA

2. Why was the Save Lucy Committee formed? Was it successful?
Explain. DRAW CONCLUSIONS

3. Are mimetic buildings worthy of restoration? Use evidence from the
selection to support your answer. MAKE JUDGMENTS

4. If you were to design a mimetic building, what object would your
building mimic? MAKE CONNECTIONS

5. WRITE Compare the ways two mimetic buildings mentioned in the
selection are used. SHORT RESPONSE

About the Author

Joan Marie Arbogast

When Joan Marie Arbogast was growing up, she liked to ride bicycles, climb trees, and roast marshmallows over a campfire. She also did some things that most young people don't do. Because her father was an architect, she looked at many building plans and models, and she regularly visited construction sites. As a result, she developed an interest in architecture at a very young age. Today, she writes articles and books from her home in Stow, Ohio.

GO online www.harcourtschool.com/storytown

STATUE OF LIBERTY

by J. Patrick Lewis

DATE: Arrived from France on July 4, 1884
LOCATION: New York, New York
ARCHITECT: Frédéric Auguste Bartholdi
PHYSICAL FACT: The foundation alone required 24,000
tons of concrete. It took six months to
mount the statue to her base.

My nose is four and a half feet long,
My mouth is three feet wide,
My head's ten feet from ear to ear . . .
I'm a gal you can step inside.

My hand is over sixteen feet.
I'm the first stop on the tour.
My index finger's eight feet long.
I'm America's signature.

My waist is thirty-five feet thick.
In tons, I'm two twenty-five—
I'm the biggest lady ever known
To keep freedom alive.

◀ One hundred years after America's War of Independence, which the French
did so much to help win, France presented the U.S. with a lasting monument
to commemorate the two countries' abiding friendship and love of freedom.

Connections

Comparing Texts

1. What mimetic buildings from "Buildings in Disguise" or other landmarks would you like to visit?

2. The selection "Buildings in Disguise" and the poem both describe architectural landmarks. Compare their treatments of a similar subject.

3. Give some examples of buildings that people treasure, such as government buildings, historic homes, schools, and sports stadiums. What do these buildings represent?

Vocabulary Review

Positive	Negative

Word Sort

Sort the Vocabulary Words into two categories, Positive and Negative. If you think some words belong in both categories, put them in both. After you finish, work in a small group. Compare the contents of your categories with those of the rest of your group. Take turns explaining why you categorized each word as you did. Then choose two Vocabulary Words from each category. Write a sentence for each word, showing it as positive or negative.

eager

beloved

humongous

abandoned

neglected

demolished

severe

Tape-Assisted Reading

You have learned that pace refers to the consistency of speed with which you read. Listen to the beginning of "Buildings in Disguise" on *Audiotext 4*. Follow along in your book, tracking the print as you read along, matching the pace of the reader in the recording. Repeat this procedure until you have a good sense of the pace.

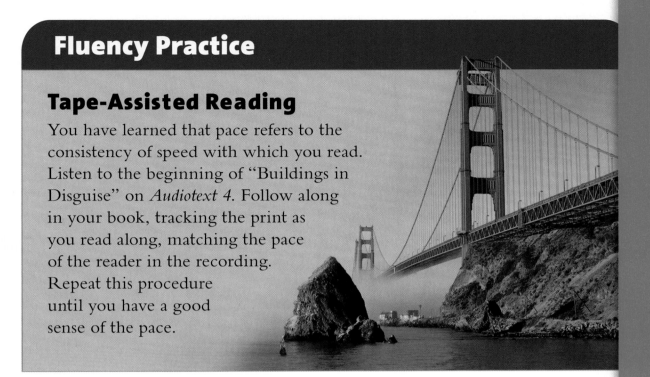

Writing

Write a Letter to the Editor

Identify a building or another landmark in your area that has historic or cultural importance. Then write a letter to the editor of your local paper that explains why your community should protect that building or landmark.

My Writing Checklist

Writing Trait ➔ Sentence Fluency

✔ I used a graphic organizer to plan my writing.

✔ I used convincing evidence to support my assertions.

✔ I used different kinds of sentences.

Evidence	Evidence	Evidence

Judgment/Assertion

CONTENTS

Lesson 20
Theme Review and Vocabulary Builder

Readers' Theater
NEWS REPORT

Let's Fly a Kite

illustrated by Rafael Lopez

Comprehension Strategies
LETTERS

Letters to Young Poets
from *Seeing the Blue Between*

by Kalli Dakos
and Naomi Shihab Nye

To all my Dearest
writing
friends,

aficionados

brainchild

astute

conventional

utilitarian

wage

commemorate

traction

unison

avid

Reading for Fluency

When reading a script aloud,

- Change your **intonation** to show the different feelings of your character.

- Adjust your **pace** to match the action.

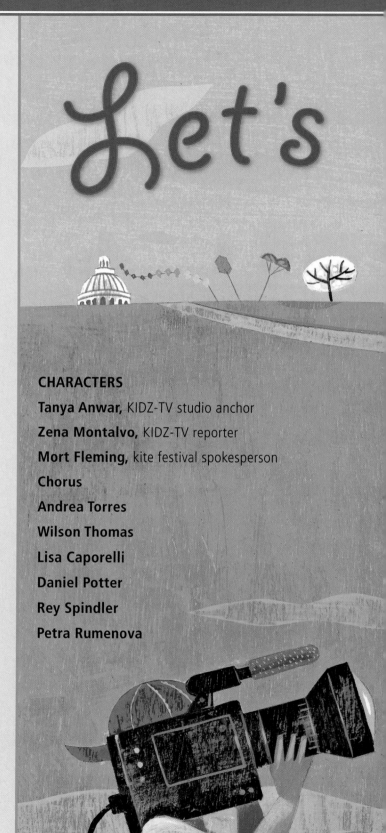

Let's

CHARACTERS

Tanya Anwar, KIDZ-TV studio anchor

Zena Montalvo, KIDZ-TV reporter

Mort Fleming, kite festival spokesperson

Chorus

Andrea Torres

Wilson Thomas

Lisa Caporelli

Daniel Potter

Rey Spindler

Petra Rumenova

Fly a Kite

illustrated by Rafael Lopez

Tanya Anwar: I'm Tanya Anwar and this is KIDZ-TV's *Youth News Report*. Our first story takes us to the nation's capital, where thousands of kite aficionados have gathered for an important celebration. Zena Montalvo has our report.

Zena Montalvo: Spring on the National Mall. It brings up images of cherry trees in full bloom. But cherry blossoms aren't the only things blowing in the breeze on this first weekend in April. It's time, once again, for the annual Smithsonian Kite Festival. I'm here with Mort Fleming, the festival spokesperson. Mr. Fleming, what can you tell us about this weekend's gathering?

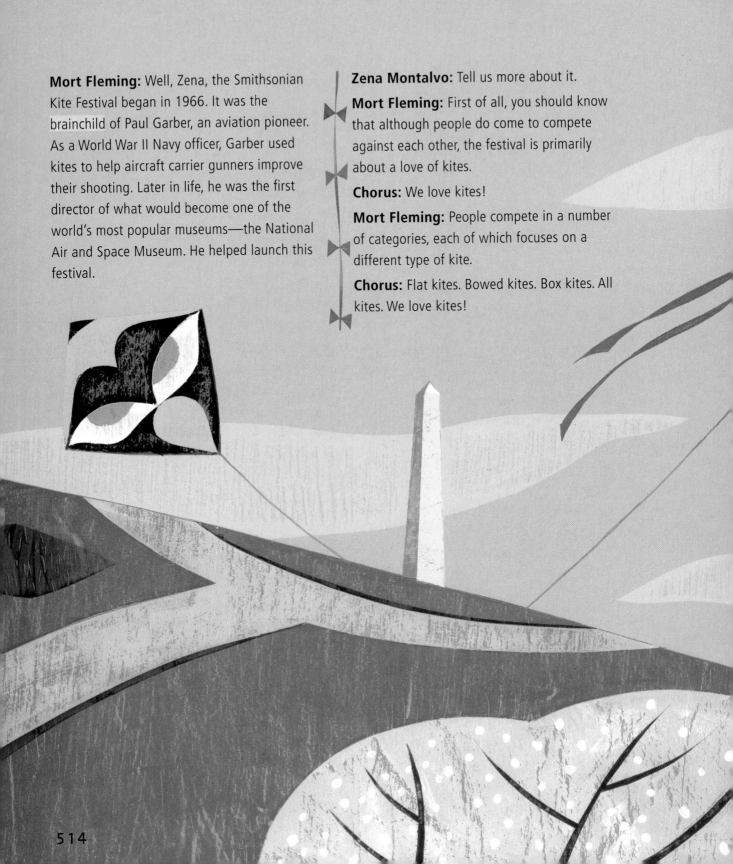

Mort Fleming: Well, Zena, the Smithsonian Kite Festival began in 1966. It was the brainchild of Paul Garber, an aviation pioneer. As a World War II Navy officer, Garber used kites to help aircraft carrier gunners improve their shooting. Later in life, he was the first director of what would become one of the world's most popular museums—the National Air and Space Museum. He helped launch this festival.

Zena Montalvo: Tell us more about it.

Mort Fleming: First of all, you should know that although people do come to compete against each other, the festival is primarily about a love of kites.

Chorus: We love kites!

Mort Fleming: People compete in a number of categories, each of which focuses on a different type of kite.

Chorus: Flat kites. Bowed kites. Box kites. All kites. We love kites!

Fluency Tip

Read at a **pace** appropriate for your character. A news reporter would speak at a steady, even pace so that listeners can easily understand.

Mort Fleming: Kids compete against kids, and adults against adults. There are also competitions for master kite makers, with categories such as train kites and fighting kites.

Zena Montalvo: Fighting kites? What are those?

Mort Fleming: Fighting kites are kites that are very maneuverable. They have special flying lines designed to cut the lines of opposing kites. Astute flyers battle in the sky to see who can cut the opponent's string and bring the other kite down.

Chorus: Fighting kites! Fighting kites! Let the battles begin!

Zena Montalvo: And I thought kite flying was relaxing. Thanks, Mr. Fleming. I think it's time to go and have a firsthand look at what's flying. Here's a young girl flying a butterfly-shaped kite. Excuse me, I'm Zena Montalvo, KIDZ-TV. I was wondering if I could ask you a few questions.

Andrea Torres: Sure.

Zena Montalvo: Tell us who you are and why you're here.

Andrea Torres: I'm Andrea Torres from Reno, Nevada. This is my third year at the kite festival. With this kite, I'm hoping to win the Beauty in the Air award.

Zena Montalvo: Well, that certainly is a beautiful kite.

Andrea Torres: Thanks. It's modeled on a Tiger Swallowtail butterfly.

Chorus: Butterfly, flutter by. Watch it fly in the sky.

Zena Montalvo: Here's a conventional diamond-shaped kite. Excuse me, young man. Do you mind answering a few questions?

Wilson Thomas: No problem.

Zena Montalvo: Can you tell us your name and what brought you here?

Wilson Thomas: Okay. My name is Wilson Thomas. I'm originally from Nigeria, but I've been living in the D.C. area for the past five years. I used to fly kites in my homeland, so when I heard about the festival I just couldn't resist.

Zena Montalvo: Your kite looks like a classic.

Wilson Thomas: Thanks. But, you know, no one really knows what the first kites were like or exactly when they were first made.

Zena Montalvo: Really?

Wilson Thomas: Yes. I've done quite a bit of reading about the history of kites. While their precise origins remain a mystery, people think they go back at least 2,000 years, maybe more. Some say that kites were invented coincidentally around the same time in both China and Malaysia.

Zena Montalvo: No kidding?

Wilson Thomas: The earliest written evidence suggests that kites were being flown widely in China around 200 B.C., where, among other things, they were used to figure out distances in battle.

Chorus: Long ago, kites were tools, not toys!

Wilson Thomas: Some people think that kites were brought from China to Japan and then traveled to Europe with explorers and traders. In 1295, the famous Italian explorer Marco Polo accurately described how to build and fly kites he'd seen while exploring.

Zena Montalvo: Wilson, that's fascinating.

Wilson Thomas: Yes. And by the mid-eighteenth century, Europeans began using kites for scientific experiments. One example was the Scottish meteorologist Alexander Wilson, who used kites to measure how temperature changed at different altitudes.

Chorus: Kites in battle. Kites in science. What about kites and fun?

Fluency Tip

Practice reading your lines with different tones of voice. Using the proper **intonation** will help you express the character's feelings.

516

Wilson Thomas: Don't get me wrong. There is plenty of evidence that Europeans used kites for play, but they were also utilitarian.

Zena Montalvo: Clearly. Thanks so much, Wilson. Good luck with your kite.

Wilson: Thanks.

Zena Montalvo: We've seen all kinds of kites here at the festival. But perhaps the most remarkable is Lisa Caporelli's giant dragon kite. It's more than 50 feet long! Lisa came all the way from New Orleans, Louisiana, to fly her monster kite at the festival. Lisa, can you tell us about your kite?

Lisa Caporelli: Sure. Dragos—that's what I call my kite—is 53 feet from nose to tail. She took me almost a year to make. I can fly her by myself in a 3 mile-per-hour wind, but if the wind is any stronger than that, I have to tie her down to something really heavy . . . like a pickup truck!

Zena Montalvo: Wow! That's a kite to be envied!

Chorus: Look out for Dragos, the giant dragon kite!

Zena Montalvo: We now turn our attention from humongous kites to those that fight. Rokkaku kites wage fierce battles overhead, trying to make their opponents crash. Here's one of the competitors, Daniel Potter. Hello, Daniel. I see you have a Rokkaku kite. Could you tell us about it?

Daniel Potter: Okay. Rokkaku kites are one of several types of traditional Japanese fighting kites. Rokkaku kites are hexagonal, or six-sided. Legend has it that fighting kites were used in Japan to settle quarrels between neighboring villages. Teams of kites would battle until all of the kites of one side were demolished.

Zena Montalvo: Fights in the sky to settle quarrels on land. Hmm, that's an interesting concept.

Daniel Potter: Yes, but mostly I think these kites are beautiful, and they are so much fun to fly.

Chorus: Fighting kites are fun to fly, but you'd better watch out!

Zena Montalvo: I can see that. Thanks for taking the time to speak with us, Daniel. Say, what's that over there? There's a big crowd gathered around one kite flyer. Hey, he looks a little bit like. . . . Is that guy dressed like Benjamin Franklin? Let me see if I can get close enough to find out what is going on. Excuse me, sir, would you mind telling our audience what you've been up to?

Rey Spindler: Oh, hi. My name is Rey Spindler. I'm from Boston, Massachusetts. You know, Ben Franklin's hometown. I thought it'd be great to come out here today to commemorate the scientific work of that great American.

Zena Montalvo: Most people know something about kites and Franklin, but could you tell us the story?

Rey Spindler: That's why I'm here. Ben Franklin was a person of tremendous curiosity. In 1752, he had the idea that lightning was electricity. In order to prove it, he flew a kite with a wire attached to it during a severe thunderstorm. The kite was hit by lightning, and an electrical charge traveled down the string to a key attached further down. This caused a spark, proving Franklin's theory.

Zena Montalvo: Don't try that at home!

Chorus: Don't fly kites in a thunderstorm!

Rey Spindler: You're absolutely right. Franklin was lucky he wasn't electrocuted, but he learned from the experience and eventually devised the lightning rod that helped protect people and their property.

Zena Montalvo: What a clever fellow!

Rey Spindler: Yes. He was inventing things from the time he was a child. In fact, when Franklin was just a youngster, he figured out that he could use a kite to pull himself across a pond while floating on his back. He eventually used a similar technique to pull himself along while ice skating.

Zena Montalvo: Hey, that sounds a bit like the traction kites I saw out here earlier today. Folks were sitting on buggies getting pulled along by huge triangular-shaped kites.

Rey Spindler: I've heard that people have gone as fast as 50 miles per hour with one of those buggy contraptions.

Zena Montalvo: Human inventiveness never ceases to amaze me.

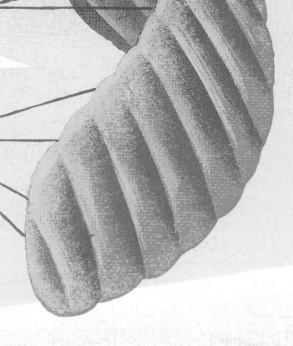

519

Rey Spindler: Franklin isn't the only one who made kite history as a kid. A boy named Homan Walsh was only ten years old when he flew a kite across Niagara Falls. The line from his kite helped engineers get a cable across the falls. That cable became an important part of a suspension bridge they built there.

Chorus: Good work, Homan Walsh!

Zena Montalvo: Many awards have been given out today to some absolutely marvelous kites. One that seems to have both the judges and the crowd enthralled is a train kite designed by Petra Rumenova. Ms. Rumenova, can you tell us a little bit about your kite?

Petra Rumenova: Well, actually, this is only half of my 24-kite rainbow train. It's got twelve identical four-foot kites in a rainbow of colors. They're all attached together, and they fly in unison. Their long tails can trace looping designs across the sky.

Chorus: They soar. They swoop. They dive. They twist.

Zena Montalvo: Some kites can do really amazing stunts. And they seem to travel so fast.

Petra Rumenova: Yes, you want to be careful when you're around stunt kites in flight. Don't get distracted and walk underneath them. Stunt kites can reach speeds in excess of 60 miles per hour, so you don't want to be where one could hit you!

Zena Montalvo: That's good advice. Beyond the speed and the stunts, we've seen some kites out here today that are works of art. And there have been others that are truly ingenious—like kites in the shape of superheroes.

Petra Rumenova: Did you see the flying ostrich or the flying penguin?

Chorus: Ostriches and penguins can't fly.

Zena Montalvo: They can if they're kites! Oh, look, there's Mr. Fleming. Let's check in with him again. Mr. Fleming, how is the festival going?

Fluency Tip

Your **intonation** should reflect a character's change in emotion. For example, adjust your tone if your character changes from being serious to being excited.

Mort Fleming: Once again, the festival has been a huge success. There were more competitors than ever before in every category. And it looks like we've had a record turnout of spectators as well.

Zena Montalvo: Anything else you'd like to add?

Mort Fleming: Well, for those who want to learn even more about kites, I want to publicize a new exhibit about the role of kites in human flight.

Zena Montalvo: Tell us more.

Mort Fleming: Your audience probably knows that the Wright brothers were the first to successfully fly a motor-powered flying machine. But what they might not know is that Orville and Wilbur were avid kite flyers. Some important aspects of the design of that first plane came from their experiences with kites.

Zena Montalvo: So kites are part of the history of aviation. You know, when I first got to the festival, I was thinking mostly about old-fashioned kites—you know, the diamond-shaped ones with the cloth tails. But now that I've had a chance to see all that kiting has to offer, I've opened my eyes to a whole new world.

Mort Fleming: We'd love to have you back next year, maybe as a competitor!

Zena Montalvo: We'll have to see about that. Well, that's all from the Smithsonian Kite Festival. This is Zena Montalvo, KIDZ-TV.

COMPREHENSION STRATEGIES
Review

Reading Nonfiction

Bridge to Reading for Meaning Letters are a type of nonfiction writing with a message for the reader. There are three different kinds of letters—personal letters, business letters, and persuasive letters. The notes on page 523 point out some features of a letter. How can knowing these features help you identify the kind of letter you are reading?

Review the Focus Strategies

You can also use the strategies you learned about in this theme to help you read.

Ask Questions

To check your understanding of what the author is saying, ask yourself questions as you read. Use questions like these:

- What does the author mean here?
- What is the main idea?
- Are there any words that I don't understand?

Monitor Comprehension: Self-Correct

When you read, you may come across a word you don't know at first, or you may mispronounce a word. Self-correcting mistakes is one way to monitor comprehension as you read. When you feel you've made a mistake and something isn't clear to you, stop and think about the mistake. Then try to read the text correctly.

As you read "Letters to Young Poets" on pages 524–527, think about where and how you can use the strategies.

TONE
The author's writing is friendly and conversational. This means the letter is a personal letter.

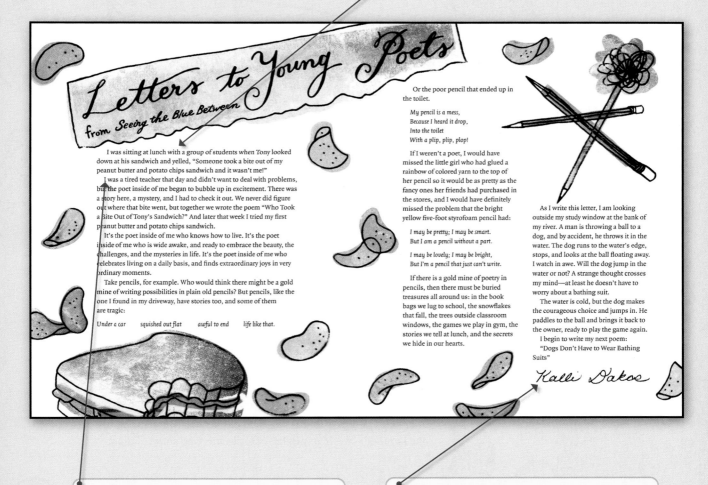

Letters to Young Poets
from *Seeing the Blue Between*

I was sitting at lunch with a group of students when Tony looked down at his sandwich and yelled, "Someone took a bite out of my peanut butter and potato chips sandwich and it wasn't me!"

I was a tired teacher that day and didn't want to deal with problems, but the poet inside of me began to bubble up in excitement. There was a story here, a mystery, and I had to check it out. We never did figure out where that bite went, but together we wrote the poem "Who Took a Bite Out of Tony's Sandwich?" And later that week I tried my first peanut butter and potato chips sandwich.

It's the poet inside of me who knows how to live. It's the poet inside of me who is wide awake, and ready to embrace the beauty, the challenges, and the mysteries in life. It's the poet inside of me who celebrates living on a daily basis, and finds extraordinary joys in very ordinary moments.

Take pencils, for example. Who would think there might be a gold mine of writing possibilities in plain old pencils? But pencils, like the one I found in my driveway, have stories too, and some of them are tragic:

Under a car   squished out flat   awful to end   life like that.

Or the poor pencil that ended up in the toilet.

My pencil is a mess,
Because I heard it drop,
Into the toilet
With a plip, plip, plop!

If I weren't a poet, I would have missed the little girl who had glued a rainbow of colored yarn to the top of her pencil so it would be as pretty as the fancy ones her friends had purchased in the stores, and I would have definitely missed the problem that the bright yellow five-foot styrofoam pencil had:

I may be pretty; I may be smart.
But I am a pencil without a part.

I may be lovely; I may be bright,
But I'm a pencil that just can't write.

If there is a gold mine of poetry in pencils, then there must be buried treasures all around us: in the book bags we lug to school, the snowflakes that fall, the trees outside classroom windows, the games we play in gym, the stories we tell at lunch, and the secrets we hide in our hearts.

As I write this letter, I am looking outside my study window at the bank of my river. A man is throwing a ball to a dog, and by accident, he throws it in the water. The dog runs to the water's edge, stops, and looks at the ball floating away. I watch in awe. Will the dog jump in the water or not? A strange thought crosses my mind—at least he doesn't have to worry about a bathing suit.

The water is cold, but the dog makes the courageous choice and jumps in. He paddles to the ball and brings it back to the owner, ready to play the game again.

I begin to write my next poem:
"Dogs Don't Have to Wear Bathing Suits"

Kalli Dakos

FIRST-PERSON
The author uses the pronouns *me* and *I* to describe her own experiences and feelings.

SIGNATURE
The author signs her name at the end of the letter.

Apply the Strategies Read the following letters from experienced poets to young poets like you. As you read, use different strategies, such as asking questions, to help you understand.

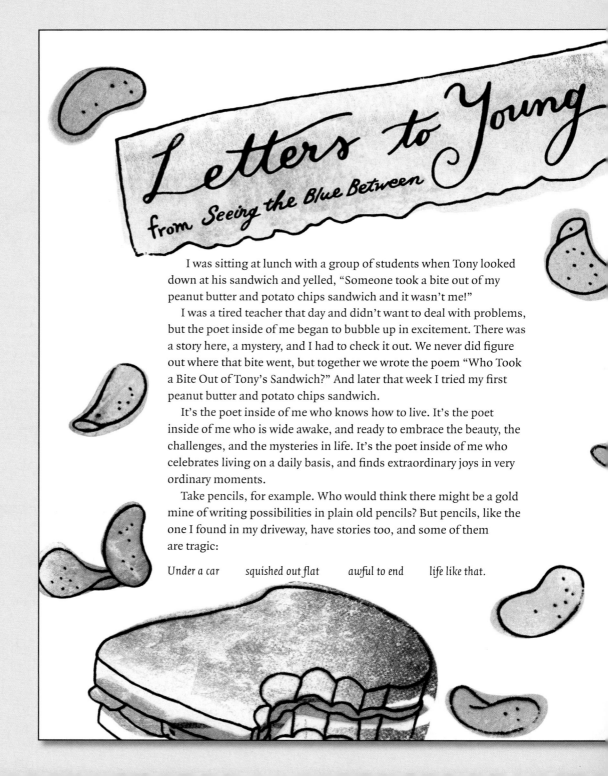

Letters to Young
from Seeing the Blue Between

I was sitting at lunch with a group of students when Tony looked down at his sandwich and yelled, "Someone took a bite out of my peanut butter and potato chips sandwich and it wasn't me!"

I was a tired teacher that day and didn't want to deal with problems, but the poet inside of me began to bubble up in excitement. There was a story here, a mystery, and I had to check it out. We never did figure out where that bite went, but together we wrote the poem "Who Took a Bite Out of Tony's Sandwich?" And later that week I tried my first peanut butter and potato chips sandwich.

It's the poet inside of me who knows how to live. It's the poet inside of me who is wide awake, and ready to embrace the beauty, the challenges, and the mysteries in life. It's the poet inside of me who celebrates living on a daily basis, and finds extraordinary joys in very ordinary moments.

Take pencils, for example. Who would think there might be a gold mine of writing possibilities in plain old pencils? But pencils, like the one I found in my driveway, have stories too, and some of them are tragic:

Under a car   squished out flat   awful to end   life like that.

Stop and Think

Words like *part, mine,* and *bank* have multiple meanings. You may need to try more than one meaning. MONITOR COMPREHENSION: SELF-CORRECT

Poets

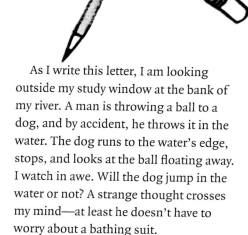

Or the poor pencil that ended up in the toilet.

My pencil is a mess,
Because I heard it drop,
Into the toilet
With a plip, plip, plop!

If I weren't a poet, I would have missed the little girl who had glued a rainbow of colored yarn to the top of her pencil so it would be as pretty as the fancy ones her friends had purchased in the stores, and I would have definitely missed the problem that the bright yellow five-foot styrofoam pencil had:

I may be pretty; I may be smart.
But I am a pencil without a part.

I may be lovely; I may be bright,
But I'm a pencil that just can't write.

If there is a gold mine of poetry in pencils, then there must be buried treasures all around us: in the book bags we lug to school, the snowflakes that fall, the trees outside classroom windows, the games we play in gym, the stories we tell at lunch, and the secrets we hide in our hearts.

As I write this letter, I am looking outside my study window at the bank of my river. A man is throwing a ball to a dog, and by accident, he throws it in the water. The dog runs to the water's edge, stops, and looks at the ball floating away. I watch in awe. Will the dog jump in the water or not? A strange thought crosses my mind—at least he doesn't have to worry about a bathing suit.

The water is cold, but the dog makes the courageous choice and jumps in. He paddles to the ball and brings it back to the owner, ready to play the game again.

I begin to write my next poem:

"Dogs Don't Have to Wear Bathing Suits"

Kalli Dakos

Stop and Think

Ask questions to help you understand. For example, *Why does the author like revision?* ASK QUESTIONS

To My Dear Writing Friends,

I know *revision* may sound like an ugly word to you. I didn't love it when I was in school. If a teacher told me to *revise*, I thought that meant my writing was a broken-down car that needed to go to the repair shop. I felt insulted. I didn't realize the teacher was saying, "Make it shine. It's worth it."

Now I see *revision* as a beautiful word of hope. It's a new vision of something. It means you don't have to be perfect the first time. What a relief!

In first drafts, you may write phrases and fragments, then connect and develop them later into something larger like a poem. Or you may overwrite first— lavishly, loosely—and pare it down later. Most of us work both ways, depending on moods and the moment.

The possibilities of revision take away pressure, which helps the whole process. Who needs stress?

Many students say they don't like to revise because they don't want to tamper with their first pure, honest expression. But why should your second (or fourth) consideration of something be less genuine than your first? You're still you! Now that you've had time to think a bit more, you may find it very helpful to rearrange words or specify or animate a thought or detail.

Revision may be as small as a single, crucial word change. I replaced the word "nowhere" with "everywhere" in the last stanza of a poem and that one difference changed everything.

Or a revision may be dramatic. Once an editor suggested I cut the first thirty lines of a poem. "Then you'll really have something," he said. But the poem only had thirty-six lines! At first I thought he was ridiculous. But the more I ruminated, the more I could see he was right. The first thirty lines were a preface to the real poem.

I love the little arrows that invite more words into a line. And what a pleasure it is, striking extra or weaker ones out! *Adios, you unnecessary "very"! Farewell, cluttery "the"!*

A line or phrase grows lean and strong before our eyes. Penciled *x*'s! Punched delete buttons! (Make sure you keep copies of drafts. Save, save, save.)

It's a good idea to leave time (an hour, a day, a week, whatever) between writing a first draft and revising it. That space and distance help you see your work with a fresher eye. Also, I STRONGLY advise that you read your work out loud to yourself as you revise it. No need to feel foolish. The best writers do this, and it will help you more than anything else.

Now and then, something you write comes out wonderfully well in a first draft. Changes aren't necessary. The more you write, the more this may happen. But the delicious gift of revision is that *it doesn't have to happen all the time.*

Love,

Naomi Shihab Nye

READING-WRITING
CONNECTION

Lesson 21 >   Lesson 22 >

SELECTION TITLES	Ancient Greece A Time to Dance	The Emperor's Silent Army A Hidden City in the Andes
Comprehension Strategies	Use Graphic Organizers	Use Graphic Organizers
Focus Skills	Compare and Contrast	Text Structure: Compare and Contrast

Theme 5 Ancient Wisdom

▶ *Excavation of the Great Temple of Rameses II at Abu Simbel,*
Louis Linant de Bellefonds

529

CONTENTS

Lesson 21

Genre: Expository Nonfiction

EARLY CIVILIZATIONS

Ancient Greece

BY KIM COVERT

A Time to Dance

retold and illustrated by Helen Ward

Genre: Fable

Focus Skill

Compare and Contrast

Nonfiction texts often contain information about related topics and ideas. Readers should compare and contrast in order to understand the relationships between these topics and ideas.

To **compare** is to tell how two or more things are similar. To **contrast** is to tell how they are different. The topics and ideas that you compare and contrast may appear within one paragraph or in different paragraphs. Use words and phrases like the ones below to help you explain similarities and differences.

- **Compare:** *similar, like, both, also, too, as well as*
- **Contrast:** *different, but, on the other hand, however, although, unlike, yet*

Both

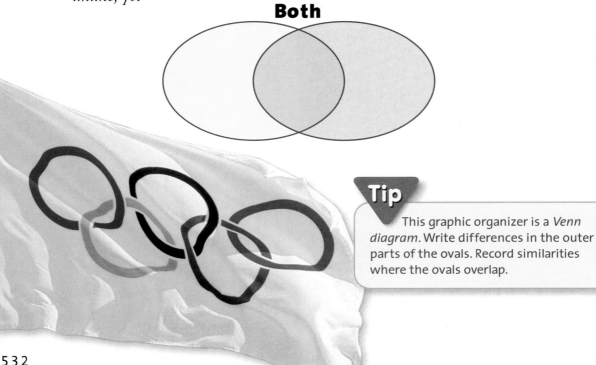

Tip

This graphic organizer is a *Venn diagram*. Write differences in the outer parts of the ovals. Record similarities where the ovals overlap.

Read the paragraph below. The graphic organizer under it shows that both the ancient and modern Olympics have attracted great athletes. However, the ancient Olympics had only a few events, while the modern Olympics have more than 400 events.

Like the Olympics of ancient Greece, the modern Olympic Games attract great athletes and spectators from around the world. The ancient Olympics included only a few events. Today's Olympic Games include more than 400 events—including original events such as footraces and wrestling. In ancient Greece, only men could compete. Today, both men and women participate.

Ancient Olympics	Both	Modern Olympics
a few events	attract great athletes	more than 400 events

Try This!

Reread the paragraph. Find another way the ancient Olympics and the modern Olympics are similar and another way they are different. Tell where you would add these details in the graphic organizer. Then use the word lists on page 532 to write sentences that explain the similarities and differences.

www.harcourtschool.com/storytown

Vocabulary

Build Robust Vocabulary

- logic
- promote
- pursuit
- ethics
- banned
- influenced
- modern
- urges

Athena and Arachne

The people of ancient Greece did not use **logic** to answer all their questions about the world. Instead, they used stories about gods and goddesses to explain why things happen. The goddess Athena is one well-known character in Greek mythology.

Athena was the goddess of arts and crafts, of wisdom, and of warfare. She was believed to **promote** peaceful activities, such as weaving.

The Parthenon is on a hill known as the Acropolis. Some parts of the Parthenon's original structure still survive today.

In one Greek myth, a mortal woman named Arachne was in **pursuit** of fame. She bragged about her weaving skills and challenged Athena to a contest. According to the **ethics** of the gods, it was wrong for mortals to brag. To punish the woman, Athena **banned** her from human society by turning her into a spider and forcing her to spin threads forever.

The characters Athena and Arachne have **influenced** the **modern** age. The Greeks named the city of Athens after the goddess Athena, and the Parthenon is a temple built to honor her. Arachne's name is the origin of the scientific term *arachnid*. The term names members of the class of organisms that includes spiders.

 GO online www.harcourtschool.com/storytown

Many statues of Athena show her wearing body armor and a helmet. With these symbols, Athena **urges** mortals to be fearless.

Word Champion

Your challenge this week is to use Vocabulary Words outside your classroom. Keep the list of words in a place at home where you can see it. Use as many of the words as you can when you speak to family members and friends. For example, you might ask your family who or what has influenced their daily lives. At the end of each day, write the sentences you spoke that contained the words in your vocabulary journal.

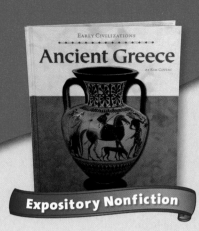

EARLY CIVILIZATIONS

Ancient Greece
BY KIM COVERT

Expository Nonfiction

Genre Study

Expository nonfiction presents and explains facts about a topic. As you read, look for

- sections organized by headings.

- facts about the past and about modern times.

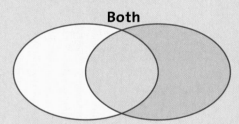

Both

Comprehension Strategy

Use graphic organizers like the one shown above to compare and contrast.

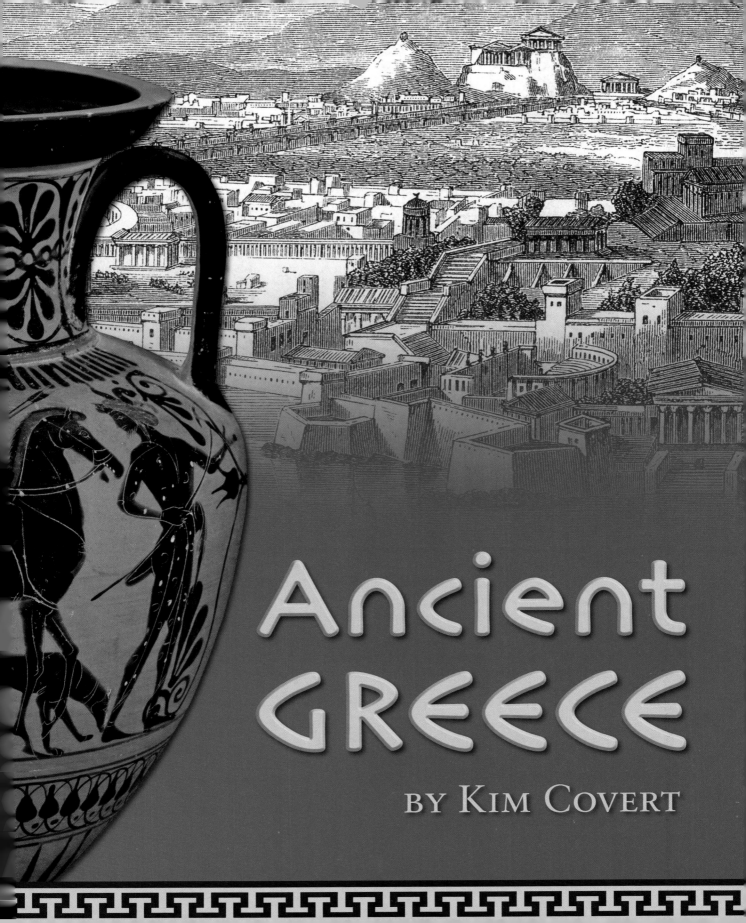

Ancient GREECE

BY KIM COVERT

The Ancient Olympics

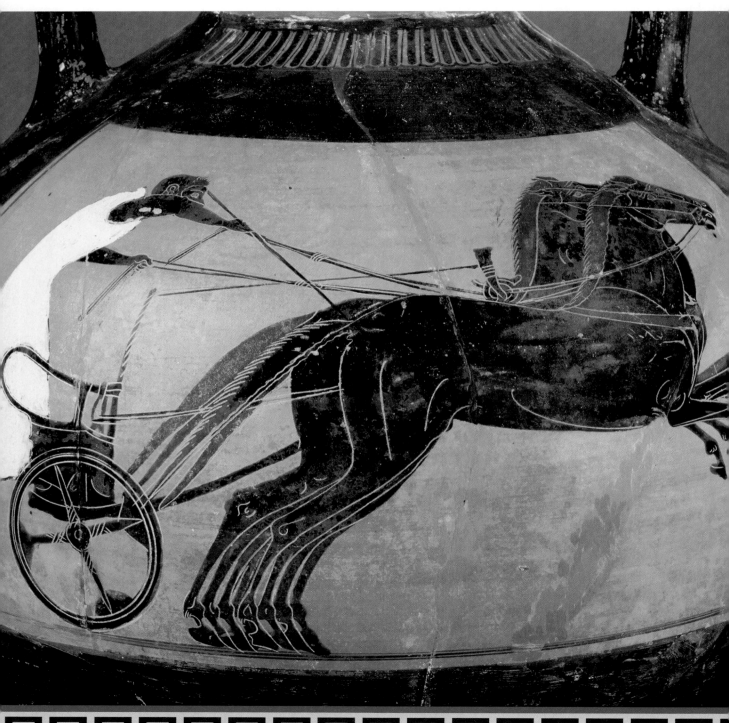

Twenty runners get into position on the starting line. A trumpeter sounds the start of the race. Sand flies up as the runners race down the 210-yard (192-meter) track. The crowd cheers as the runners cross the finish line. The judges place a wreath of olive leaves on the winner's head.

Later, horse-drawn chariots line up on an oval track. At the sound of the trumpet, each driver urges his horses forward. In the first turn, a driver cuts in front of another chariot. The two chariots run into each other and tip over. The horses and drivers crash to the ground. Several more chariots fall in the pileup. Many horses and drivers are hurt. The drivers who missed the wreck bolt to the finish line. The owner of the winning chariot receives a wreath of olive leaves.

Footraces and chariot races were part of the Olympic Games of ancient Greece. Wrestling, boxing, and the pentathlon were other events. The pentathlon included javelin, discus, long jump, running, and wrestling.

The first recorded Olympics were held in 776 B.C. The games took place in Olympia, a town in western Greece. They honored the Greek god Zeus. In Greek mythology, Zeus was the ruler of all the Olympian gods.

For 1,000 years, the Olympic Games were held every four years. Before each Olympics, the Greeks stopped all warfare. No wars could be fought just before, during, or just after the games. Wars were stopped so athletes and people coming to watch could travel to and from the games safely.

The modern Olympics are one of many traditions developed in Greece. Ancient Greece is often called the cradle of western civilization. It was the birthplace of many modern ideas. Greek ideas are found in today's governments, art, architecture, and literature. They are also seen in science, drama, and athletics.

◄ *The scene on this vase from the 500s B.C. shows a chariot race, one of the ancient Olympic events.*

Architecture & Art

The Greeks built many structures that still stand today. Temples are the most famous of their buildings. Most of the temples have a similar design. The buildings are rectangular with columns holding up the sloping roof. Modern architects base many of their designs on Greek styles.

The most famous example of Greek architecture is the Parthenon. Completed in 432 B.C., this temple honored the goddess Athena. She was the goddess of war and wisdom.

The Greeks created their own forms of sculpture, pottery, and painting. They were the first to sculpt human statues in a natural style. Greek statues usually showed perfect bodies. Earlier statues had looked stiff and unnatural. Athenians made the most valued pottery of the ancient Western world. They painted their pots with pictures of gods, heroes, and ordinary people. Greek artists decorated buildings with beautiful paintings called frescoes. These wall paintings on plaster showed scenes from Greek myths.

The Parthenon stands on the Acropolis in Athens. ▼

Sculptures of women support the roof on this porch of the Erechtheum, a temple on the Acropolis in Athens.

Ancient Greek Pottery

Amphora from 760 B.C. with mostly geometric designs ▶

Although pottery was made first to be useful, it also became an art form. Early pottery was decorated with geometric designs. Painters later added patterns with repeated images such as animals. Even later pots depicted a whole scene. Some of the scenes showed daily life in ancient Greece. Some scenes illustrated stories or myths.

◀ *Greek water jug from 530 B.C., showing women filling vases at a fountain*

Science & Medicine

Ancient Greeks were among the first to use logic to explain the world around them. They wanted to discover the reasons why things worked.

Anaxagoras (an·ak·SAG·uhr·uhs) was an early Greek astronomer. He learned that the moon did not make its own light. Instead, Anaxagoras believed that the moon's light was a reflection from the sun.

Archimedes (ar·kuh·MEE·deez) was an inventor and mathematician. He discovered the principle of a lever. Archimedes created a complicated set of levers and pulleys. He used them to lift a large ship from water to land by himself.

Hippocrates (hih·PAH·kruh·teez) was a Greek doctor. He is often called the father of medicine. He developed the Hippocratic oath, a promise to heal the sick. Today, many medical students take this oath when they become doctors.

Bust of Hippocrates ▶

In the fable "The Fox and the Grapes," the fox learns that he cannot always get what he wants.

Drama & Literature

The ancient Greeks created drama. The earliest Greek plays were religious ceremonies. A chorus sang and acted out stories about the gods. Later, dramas told legends of Greek heroes. Many plays were about gods. Other plays told about the Persian Wars.

The Greeks were the Western world's first writers of history. Around 450 B.C., Herodotus explored the Mediterranean region. He wrote long reports of wars, geography, customs, and legends. Herodotus is often called the father of history.

Aesop is one of the most famous Greek writers. In the 500s B.C., Aesop wrote hundreds of fables. These short stories about animals taught a lesson. Aesop's fables include "The Tortoise and the Hare" and "The Fox and the Grapes." Many of Aesop's fables are still told today.

Philosophy

Early Greek philosophers studied life, death, and other mysteries of the natural world. Socrates was the most famous philosopher from Athens. He was one of the first to study ethics. He taught students by asking questions, rather than giving them answers. This teaching method is now known as the Socratic method.

Plato was a student of Socrates. In his book *The Republic*, Plato describes his ideas for an ideal government. He also founded a school called the Academy.

Plato's most famous student was Aristotle. Aristotle became a great philosopher and scientist. He developed a scientific system to help understand the world. The ideas of Socrates, Plato, and Aristotle are still discussed today.

▼ *In addition to being a philosopher and scientist, Aristotle (left) taught Alexander the Great.*

▼ *Bust of Aristotle*

The U.S. Supreme Court building in Washington, D.C., was influenced by Greek architecture.

Greek Influence Today

Greece has influenced many modern governments. Democracy is now a common form of government. Ancient Greeks developed political speeches, debates, and voting. Trial by jury is another system created by the Greeks. A jury is a group of people that listens to and decides a court case.

The ancient Greeks believed in the rights of the male citizen. Aristotle wrote that the pursuit of happiness was important. When the 13 Colonies in North America separated from Great Britain, the colonists created the Declaration of Independence. This document borrowed Aristotle's idea. It states that people have the right to life, liberty, and the pursuit of happiness.

Often, government buildings also have Greek influence. Court buildings, capitols, and presidential homes have all used Greek architecture.

Every day, people take part in activities invented by the ancient Greeks. They read novels, attend plays, or exercise in a public gym. Athletes wrestle, box, and compete in track and field events. Philosophers explore the meaning of life. Scientists search for logical answers to problems. Ideas from ancient Greece continue to influence modern life.

The Modern Olympics

The ancient Greeks were the first civilization known to value sports. Greeks believed in achieving a balance between work and play. They felt that a good education should promote strong minds and bodies. The modern Olympics show Greece's sporting influence today.

In A.D. 393, the Roman Emperor Theodosius banned the Olympics. Theodosius was Christian, and the Olympic Games honored the Greek gods.

The Olympic Sports Complex in Athens includes two stadiums, three fields, and several buildings.

The games did not start again until 1896. That year, Athens hosted the first modern Olympic Games. Athletes from 14 nations competed in the 1896 Olympics.

The Olympics are now held every two years. The games alternate between summer and winter. Many cities around the world have hosted the Olympics.

The Olympics returned to Athens in 2004. Workers upgraded stadiums and created new ones to hold all the events. About 10,500 athletes from 200 countries competed. Tourists watched the modern competitions and visited the ancient sites.

▲ The logo of the 2004 Olympic Games features a wreath of olive branches.

▲ The Olympic Stadium in Athens was the location for the opening and closing ceremonies of the 2004 Olympic Games.

Think Critically

1. What were some characteristics of the ancient Olympic Games? NOTE DETAILS

2. Why does the author call ancient Greece "the birthplace of many modern ideas"? SYNTHESIZE

3. Compare and contrast Anaxagoras with Archimedes. COMPARE AND CONTRAST

4. The Greeks felt that sports were an important part of a young person's education. Do you agree? Explain. PERSONAL RESPONSE

5. **WRITE** Based on the selection and the photographs, describe what is special about ancient Greek architecture and art. Include the most important ideas from the text. SHORT RESPONSE

About the Author
KIM COVERT

Kim Covert has a passion for traveling. While she was growing up, her family moved frequently because her father was a pilot in the U.S. Air Force. The family lived in Japan, Germany, England, and seven states in the United States. Kim Covert says that reading has always been her favorite hobby. Writing must be a favorite pastime as well, because she has written thirteen nonfiction books for young people. She lives in Minnesota with her two teenagers.

 www.harcourtschool.com/storytown

Unwitting Wisdom

AN ANTHOLOGY OF *Aesop's Fables*

Fable

A Time

THERE WAS ONCE A CRICKET, a very happy creature with not a care in the world and not an idea in his head. He had never been burdened by great thoughts or bothered by the smaller, more useful ones that slipped from his head like down from a thistle. As long as the sun shone each day he was content to sit on a barley stalk and sing.

He ate when he was hungry, he slept when he was tired, and since the sun shone all summer, all summer he sang.

In autumn the cold began to bite. Food became surprisingly scarce, so the cricket grew hollow with hunger. He no longer felt inclined to sing, but shivered and rattled instead. It was well known that the ants had plentiful supplies, but nobody had dared to try their generosity. Nevertheless, the cricket left his barley stalk and set off for the ants' fortress . . .

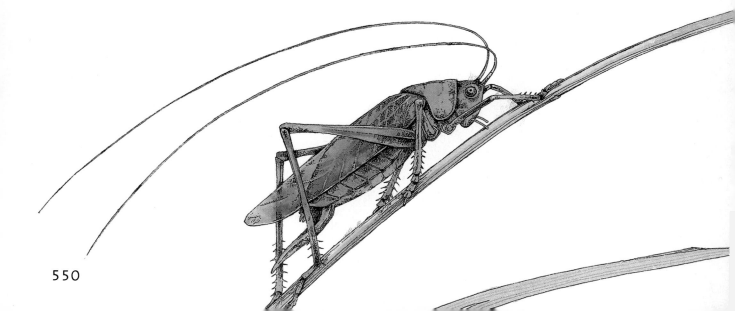

to Dance

retold and illustrated by Helen Ward

The cricket begged one of the guards for a little something to eat.

"How can you be hungry?" demanded the ant. "Winter is only just starting. What have you done with your stores of food?"

"Stores?" said the cricket.

"Food put away to eat in the winter. Stores of food from the months when there was plenty. What," asked the ant (though no more kindly), "have you been doing all summer?!"

"I was busy . . . ," whined the cricket (and he had to admit it sounded a little silly on a frosty morning), ". . . singing."

The ant of course was unimpressed. "Then MAYBE . . . ," he said acidly, ". . . YOU SHOULD DANCE ALL WINTER." And with that, he turned his back on the cricket and marched into the nest.

Do not put off until tomorrow what you should do today.

Connections

Comparing Texts

1. Which person described in "Ancient Greece" would you like to meet? Explain your answer.

2. Why do you think Aesop used stories about animals to teach a lesson? Do you think the message in "A Time to Dance" is important? Explain.

3. What contribution from ancient Greece do you think is most valuable in the modern world? Give specific reasons for your answer.

Vocabulary Review

Word Webs

Work with a partner. Choose two Vocabulary Words each, and create a word web for each word. Write related words and phrases in the outer parts of the web. Share your word webs with each other. Discuss with your partner how each word or phrase relates to the Vocabulary Word.

logic

promote

pursuit

ethics

banned

influenced

modern

urges

Fluency Practice

Partner Reading

In order to understand what you read, it is important to read every word accurately. Work with a partner to reread the section of "Ancient Greece" titled Philosophy, on page 544. Read the text aloud as your partner follows along in the book. Ask your partner to identify any words that were difficult for you to read accurately. Then switch roles and repeat.

Writing

Write a Compare-and-Contrast Paragraph

Write a paragraph that compares and contrasts the cricket and the ants in "A Time to Dance." Consider how they spend their time to prepare for the winter and what happens as a result.

Both

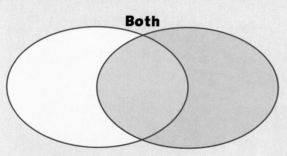

My Writing Checklist

Writing Trait ▶ Ideas

✔ I used a Venn diagram to plan my writing.

✔ I focused on similarities and differences.

✔ I used correct spelling, capitalization, and punctuation.

Reading-Writing Connection

Analyze Writer's Craft: Expository Nonfiction

Expository nonfiction gives facts and information about a topic. It may include headings, diagrams, photographs, and captions. When you write expository nonfiction, you can use the works of authors such as Kim Covert as writing models. Read the passage below from "Ancient Greece," and notice how the author focuses her ideas.

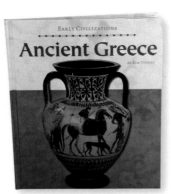

EARLY CIVILIZATIONS

Ancient Greece
BY KIM COVERT

Writing Trait ▶

CONVENTIONS
The author uses a **heading** to introduce a section of related information.

Writing Trait ▶

IDEAS The author begins the paragraph with a **topic sentence**. Then she gives **examples** of Greek influences, including *political speeches, debates,* and *voting.*

Greek Influence Today

Greece has influenced many modern governments. Democracy is now a common form of government. Ancient Greeks developed political speeches, debates, and voting. Trial by jury is another system created by the Greeks. A jury is a group of people that listens to and decides a court case.

Research Report

A **research report** is a kind of **expository nonfiction**. It includes facts and information from a variety of sources, such as books, magazines, encyclopedias, and the Internet. It also includes a list of the sources from which the writer got the information. Read this research report by a student named Lim, and notice how he chose strong **ideas** to explain his topic.

Student Writing Model

Modern Summer Olympics
by Lim K.

Writing Trait

IDEAS In his introduction, Lim gives background information about the **topic**. Then he mentions his three **main ideas** for the report.

The modern Summer Olympic Games are held every four years, usually between July and October. The location of the games rotates among participating countries. More than 10,000 athletes travel to the host city to represent their country and compete in events. Some events have continued since ancient times, while others have come and gone. Many new sports have been added over the years.

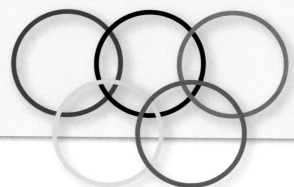

Enduring Events

Many Olympic events survive from ancient times. Footraces, the long jump, discus throwing, and wrestling have been Olympic events since the games were first held in ancient Greece. Footracing is the oldest Olympic competition. The first Olympics, in 776 B.C., featured just one event: the *stade,* or *stadion* race, a sprint that covered the length of a stadium.

Dropped Events

Many Olympic events have been dropped from the modern games. Chariot racing was discontinued because it was so dangerous. Croquet, rope climbing, tug-of-war, and cricket were introduced in modern times and then eliminated. In 2005, it was announced that baseball and softball will be dropped from the summer games starting in 2012.

Softball joined the summer games in 1996. Female athletes will throw out the last pitch in 2012.

The Newest Events

Fans are always trying to add their favorite sports to the Olympics. Beach volleyball, tae kwon do, and mountain biking are recent additions. In 2003, the International Olympic Committee announced that BMX racing would be added as a summer Olympic event. BMX is an off-road bicycle race that takes place on a winding dirt track.

Some Olympic events are lasting, and some are only temporary. The newest events may be eliminated before the next games begin. The spirit of the games, however, will last forever.

List of Sources

Gifford, Clive. *Summer Olympics*. Boston: Kingfisher, 2004.

VeloNews Interactive. "Olympic BMX? IOC Says Yes for 2008." 1 March 2007. <http://www.velonews.com/news/fea/4282.0.html>

Wallechinsky, David. "Olympic Games." *World Book Encyclopedia*. 1998 ed.

Writing Trait

IDEAS In his **conclusion**, Lim includes a summary of his ideas. He also tells why the topic is important.

Writing Trait

CONVENTIONS Titles of online articles and book chapters are enclosed in quotation marks. Book titles are typed in italics. Handwritten book titles should be underlined.

Now look at what Lim did to prepare to write his research report.

Notes

Lim used note cards to write down information from a variety of sources. He made a new note card for each important idea and included the source for the notes.

Beijing 2008 summer Olympics.
BMX — off-road bicycle race

VeloNews Interactive. "Olympic BMX? IOC Says Yes for 2008." 1 March 2007.
<http:www.velonews.com/news/fea/4282.0.html>

Outline

Then Lim created an outline to show the order of ideas he would follow as he began to write his report.

Title: The Modern Summer Olympics
  I.   Introduction
      A.   History and background
      B.   Main ideas
  II. Enduring events
      A.   Track and field
      B.   Stadion races
  III. Dropped events
      A.   Chariot racing, croquet, etc.
      B.   Softball
  IV. Newest events
      A.   Volleyball, Tae kwon do, etc.
      B.   BMX
  V.   Conclusion
      A.   Summary of main ideas
      B.   Importance of topic

Organization

Next Lim organized his note cards according to the order on his outline. He labeled the note cards to keep track of where the information will appear in his research report.

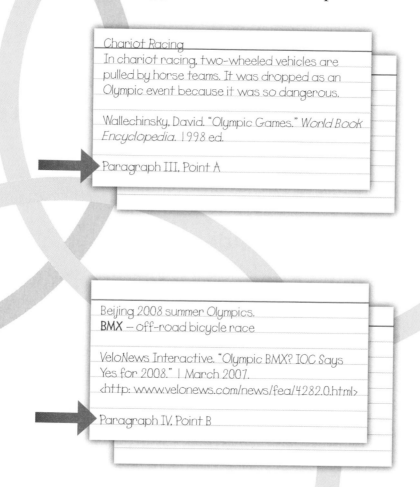

Chariot Racing
In chariot racing, two-wheeled vehicles are pulled by horse teams. It was dropped as an Olympic event because it was so dangerous.

Wallechinsky, David. "Olympic Games." *World Book Encyclopedia.* 1998 ed.

Paragraph III, Point A

Beijing 2008 summer Olympics.
BMX — off-road bicycle race

VeloNews Interactive. "Olympic BMX? IOC Says Yes for 2008." 1 March 2007.
<http: www.velonews.com/news/fea/4282.0.html>

Paragraph IV, Point B

CONTENTS

Lesson 22

Genre: Expository Nonfiction

JANE O'CONNOR

THE EMPEROR'S SILENT ARMY

TTA WARRIORS OF A

A Hidden City in the Andes
by Claire Llewellyn

Genre: Expository Nonfiction

Focus Skill

Text Structure: Compare and Contrast

Authors of expository texts use different text structures to show the relationships between ideas in the text. When the author points out similarities and differences between two or more things, the text is organized in a **compare-and-contrast text structure**.

Clue words and phrases like the ones below let you know the author has used a compare-and-contrast text structure.

- **Compare:** *similar, like, alike, both, also, too, as well as, same as*
- **Contrast:** *different, but, on the other hand, however, although, unlike, yet*

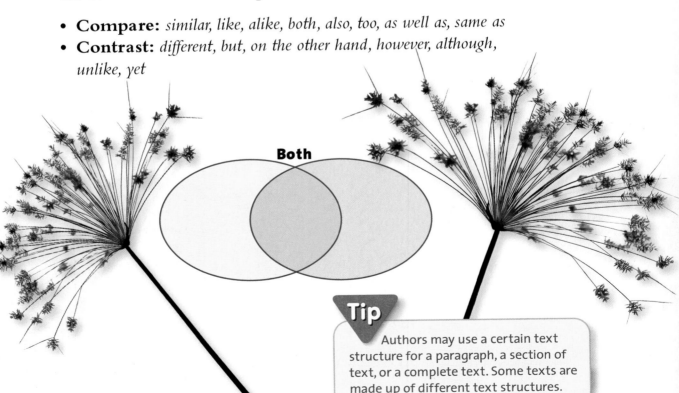

Both

Tip

Authors may use a certain text structure for a paragraph, a section of text, or a complete text. Some texts are made up of different text structures.

Read the paragraph below. Then look at the Venn diagram. It shows that papyrus and modern paper, two materials used for writing, have some important differences.

The ancient Egyptians made a paperlike material called papyrus from the bark of papyrus reeds. They cut the reeds into strips and pressed them together, creating a smooth surface for writing. By contrast, the paper we know today is made from plant fibers that have been mashed into pulp and spread to dry in a thin sheet. Unlike papyrus, it was first made in China more than 2,000 years ago.

Papyrus   **Both**   **Modern Paper**

- made by the Egyptians
- made of papyrus reeds cut into thin strips

- writing surface
- made from plants

- first made in China
- made of plant fibers mashed into pulp

Try This! ....

Rewrite the paragraph, using different clue words. Be sure to keep the meaning the same.

GO online www.harcourtschool.com/storytown

563

Vocabulary

Build Robust Vocabulary

precede

lustrous

trespass

strategically

prolong

resigned

temperaments

restored

Perfectly Preserved

Although warning signs usually **precede** a volcanic eruption, Mt. Vesuvius gave the people of Pompeii, Italy, little time to escape. In A.D. 79, the volcano suddenly erupted and buried the city under a layer of ash.

Pompeii remained buried for more than 1,600 years. In 1748, people began to explore the region. Treasure seekers uncovered buildings, stripped them of their **lustrous** wall paintings, and then covered them with dirt.

The residents of Pompeii appreciated beauty, as the remains of this garden show.

564

In 1860, Italian archaeologist Giuseppe Fiorelli took control of the site. He forbade anyone to **trespass** and devised a plan to excavate the city **strategically**. This planning would **prolong** the process of excavating the ruins, but it would insure that the work was done properly.

The ash preserved nearly everything in the city, from living rooms to loaves of bread. Imprints of some of Pompeii's residents also remain. Some must have been fleeing in panic. Others seem to have been peaceful, apparently **resigned** to their fate. Pompeii's remnants are a haunting reminder of a tragedy, but they offer a rare look at the daily life of people from the distant past.

Archaeologists are known for their patient **temperaments**. In the nineteenth century, they **restored** the roofs of some Pompeian houses to protect the mosaics and frescoes like the one shown here.

 www.harcourtschool.com/storytown

Word Detective

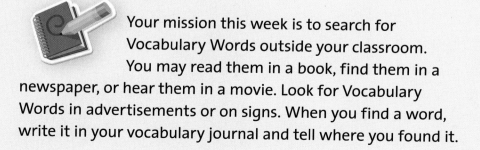

Your mission this week is to search for Vocabulary Words outside your classroom. You may read them in a book, find them in a newspaper, or hear them in a movie. Look for Vocabulary Words in advertisements or on signs. When you find a word, write it in your vocabulary journal and tell where you found it.

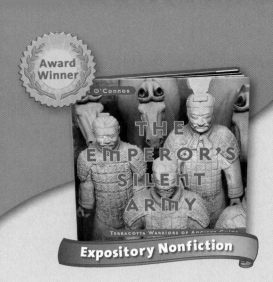

O'Connor

THE
EMPEROR'S
SILENT
ARMY

TERRACOTTA WARRIORS OF ANCIENT CHINA

Expository Nonfiction

Genre Study

Expository nonfiction presents and explains information about a topic. As you read, look for

- photographs, diagrams, or maps that support facts.

- text structure—the way ideas are organized.

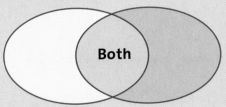

Both

Comprehension Strategy

Use graphic organizers like the one shown above to compare and contrast.

THE EMPEROR'S SILENT ARMY

TERRACOTTA WARRIORS OF ANCIENT CHINA

by Jane O'Connor

The terracotta army was discovered when well-diggers found the head of a "pottery man" like this one. No photographs were taken that day.

A Strange Discovery

LINTONG COUNTY, PEOPLE'S REPUBLIC OF CHINA, MARCH 1974

It's just an ordinary day in early spring, or so three farmers think as they trudge across a field in northern China. They are looking for a good place to dig a well. There has been a drought, and they must find water or risk losing their crops later in the year.

The farmers choose a spot near a grove of persimmon trees. Down they dig, five feet, ten feet. Still no water. They decide to keep on digging a little deeper. All of a sudden, one of the farmers feels his shovel strike against something hard. Is it a rock? It's difficult to see at the bottom of the dark hole, so the farmer kneels down for a closer look. No, it isn't a rock. It seems to be clay, and not raw clay but clay that has been baked and made into something. But what?

Now, more carefully, the men dig around the something. Perhaps it is a pot or a vase. However, what slowly reveals itself is the pottery head of a man who stares back at them, open-eyed and amazingly real looking. The farmers have never seen anything like it before. But they do remember stories that some of the old people in their village have told, stories of a "pottery man" found many years ago not far from where they are now. The villagers had been scared that the pottery man would bring bad luck so they broke it to bits, which were then reburied and forgotten.

The three well-diggers are not so superstitious. They report their discovery to a local official. Soon a group of archaeologists arrives to search the area more closely. Maybe they will find pieces of a clay body to go with the clay head.

In fact, they find much more.

During the weeks and months that follow, the archaeologists dig out more pottery men, which now are called by a more dignified term—terracotta figurines. The figurines are soldiers. That much is clear. But they come from a time long ago, when Chinese warriors wore knee-length robes, armor made from small iron "fish scales," and elaborate topknot hairdos. All of the soldiers are life-size or a little bigger and weigh as much as four hundred pounds. They stand at attention as if waiting for the command to charge into battle. The only thing missing is their weapons. And those are found too— hundreds of real bronze swords, daggers, and battle-axes as well as thousands of scattered arrowheads— all so perfectly made that, after cleaning, their ancient tips are still sharp enough to split a hair!

These soldiers' hands are clenched as if still holding their bronze weapons.

Today, after nearly thirty years of work, terracotta soldiers are still being uncovered and restored. What the well-diggers stumbled upon, purely by accident, has turned out to be among the largest and most incredible archaeological discoveries of modern times. Along with the Great Pyramids in Egypt, the buried army is now considered one of the true wonders of the ancient world. Spread out over several acres near the city of Xian, the soldiers number not in the tens or hundreds but in the thousands! Probably 7,500 total. Until 1974, nobody knew that right below the people of northern China an enormous underground army had been standing guard, silently and watchfully, for more than 2,200 years. Who put them there?

One man.

Known as the fierce tiger of Qin (CHIN), the divine Son of Heaven, he was the first emperor of China.

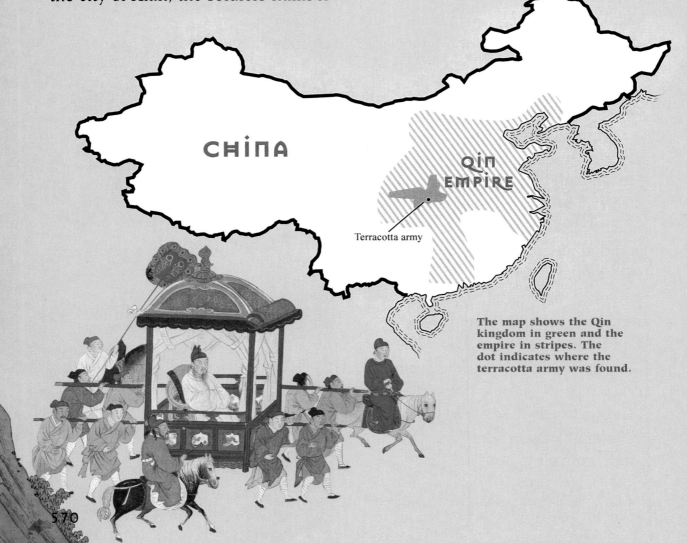

CHINA

QIN EMPIRE

Terracotta army

The map shows the Qin kingdom in green and the empire in stripes. The dot indicates where the terracotta army was found.

THE QUEST FOR IMMORTALITY

If he couldn't live forever, then Qin Shihuang (pronounced CHIN shir-hwong) was determined to live as long as possible. He ate powdered jade and drank mercury in the belief that they would prolong his life. In fact, these "medicines" were poison and may have caused the emperor to fall sick and die while on a tour of the easternmost outposts of his empire. He was forty-nine years old.

If word of Qin Shihuang's death got out while he was away from the capital there might be a revolt. So his ministers kept the news a secret. With the emperor's body inside his chariot, the entire party traveled back to the capital city. Meals were brought into the emperor's chariot;

This is a modern stone engraving of the first emperor of China.

daily reports on affairs of state were delivered as usual—all to keep up the appearance that the emperor was alive and well. However, it was summer, and a terrible smell began to come from the chariot. But the clever ministers found a way to account for the stench. A cart was loaded with smelly salted fish and made to precede the chariot, overpowering and masking any foul odors coming from the dead emperor. And so Qin Shihuang returned to the capital for burial.

The tomb of Qin Shihuang had been under construction for more than thirty years. It was begun when he was a young boy of thirteen and was still not finished when he died.

Even incomplete, the emperor's tomb was enormous, larger than his largest palace. According to legend, it had a domed ceiling inlaid with clusters of pearls to represent the sun, moon, and stars. Below was a gigantic relief map of the world, made from bronze. Bronze hills and mountains rose up from the floor, with rivers of mercury flowing into a mercury sea. Along the banks of the rivers were models of the emperor's palaces and cities, all exact replicas of the real ones.

In ancient times, the Chinese believed that life after death was not so very different from life on earth. The soul of a dead person could continue to enjoy all the pleasures of everyday life. So people who were rich enough constructed elaborate underground tombs filled with silk robes, jewelry with precious stones, furniture, games, boats, chariots— everything the dead person could possibly need or want.

Qin Shihuang knew that grave robbers would try their best to loot the treasures in his tomb. So he had machines put inside the tomb that

For thousands of years, the Chinese have made silk fabric. This detail of a silk robe shows an embroidered dragon, the symbol of Chinese emperors.

produced the rumble of thunder to scare off intruders, and mechanical crossbows at the entrance were set to fire arrows automatically should anyone dare trespass. The emperor also made certain that the workers who carried his coffin in to its final resting place never revealed its exact whereabouts. As the men worked their way back through the tunnels to the tomb's entrance, a stone door came crashing down, and they were left to die, sealed inside the tomb along with the body of the emperor.

Even all these measures, however, were not enough to satisfy the emperor. And so, less than a mile from the tomb, in underground trenches, the terracotta warriors were stationed. Just as flesh-and-blood troops had protected him during his lifetime, the terracotta troops were there to protect their ruler against any enemy for all eternity.

BURIED SOLDIERS

Qin Shihuang became emperor because of his stunning victories on the battlefield. His army was said to be a million strong. In every respect except for number, the terracotta army is a faithful replica of the real one.

So far terracotta troops have been found in three separate pits, all close to one another. A fourth pit was discovered, but it was empty. The entire army faces east. The Qin kingdom, the emperor's homeland, was in the northwest. The other kingdoms that had been conquered and had become part of his empire lay to the east. So Qin Shihuang feared that any enemy uprising would come from that direction.

The first pit is by far the biggest, more than two football fields long, with approximately six thousand soldiers and horses. About one thousand have already been excavated and restored. None of the soldiers in the army wears a helmet or carries a shield, proof of the Qin soldiers' fearlessness. But the archers stationed in the front lines don't wear any armor either. They needed to be able to move freely in order to fire their arrows with accuracy. And so these frontline sharpshooters, who were the first targets of an approaching enemy, also had the least protection.

Unlike most of the figures, who stand stiffly, face forward, this archer is in a much more natural pose.

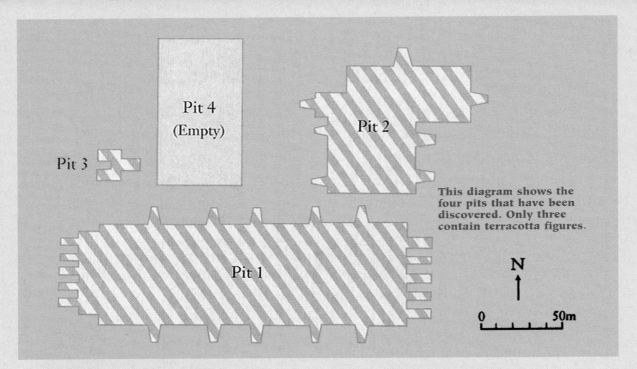

Pit 4
(Empty)

Pit 3

Pit 2

Pit 1

This diagram shows the four pits that have been discovered. Only three contain terracotta figures.

N

0   50m

Following the vanguard are eleven long columns of foot soldiers and lower-ranking officers, the main body of the army, who once carried spears, battle-axes, and halberds. The soldiers are prepared for an attack from any direction; those in the extreme right and extreme left columns face out, not forward, so that they can block enemy charges from either side. Last of all comes the rear guard, three rows of soldiers with their backs to the rest of the army, ready to stop an attack from behind.

The terracotta horses are life-size.

Stationed at various points among the foot soldiers are about fifty charioteers who drove wooden chariots. Each charioteer has a team of four horses and is dressed in full-length armor. In some carts, a general rides beside the charioteer, ready to beat a drum to signal a charge or ring a bell to call for a retreat.

The long rectangular arrangement of soldiers in Pit 1 follows a real battle formation used to defeat real enemies in ancient times. It is called a sword formation, with the frontline archers representing the tip of the sword, the chariots and columns of foot soldiers forming the blade, and the rear guard the handle.

Pit 2 is far smaller than Pit 1. With an estimated 900 warriors of all different ranks, Pit 2 serves as a powerful back-up force to help the larger army in Pit 1. There are also almost 500 horses—about 350 chariot horses and more than 100 cavalry horses.

The terracotta horses are Mongolian ponies, not very big, but muscular and full of power. With their flaring nostrils, bared teeth, and bulging eyes, the chariot horses all look as if they are straining to gallop across a battlefield. The mane of each chariot horse is trimmed short and its tail is braided. That is so it won't get caught in the harness.

By the time of the first emperor, soldiers on horseback were replacing war chariots. It was hard for even the most experienced drivers to manage a chariot over bumpy, rock-strewn ground. Cavalrymen could move much more swiftly and easily. Their horses had fancy saddles decorated with rows of nail heads and tassels, but no stirrups—they hadn't come into use yet.

Pit 3, by far the smallest, contains fewer than seventy warriors and only one team of horses. Archaeologists think that Pit 3 represents army headquarters. That's because the soldiers are not arranged in an attack formation.

Right: **This drawing shows what a wooden chariot would have looked like.** *Below:* **The actual chariots rotted away long before the discovery of the terracotta army.**

Instead, they face one another in a U shape, as if they are busy consulting among themselves. Although the officers at command central would not engage in hand-to-hand combat, the fate of the thousands of troops in Pit 1 and Pit 2 rests in their hands.

Altogether, the three pits of warriors and horses make up an unstoppable army. All the warriors are stationed strategically, exactly as they would have been on a real battlefield. For example, rows of kneeling soldiers with crossbows alternate with rows of standing archers. This way, while one row is firing, the other row has time to reload their bows. The crossbow was by far the most powerful weapon of the time. The Chinese were using crossbows as early as 400 B.C. In Europe, however, crossbows didn't come into use for at least another 1,300 years.

THE FACES OF ANCIENT CHINA

About two thousand soldiers have been unearthed, yet, amazingly, so far no two are the same. The army includes men of all different ages, from different parts of China, with different temperaments. A young soldier looks both excited and nervous; an older soldier, perhaps a veteran of many wars, appears tired, resigned. Some soldiers seem lost in thought, possibly dreaming of their return home; others look proud and confident. Although from a distance the figures appear almost identical, like giant-size toy soldiers, each is a distinct work of art.

The expressions on the soldiers' faces are what makes the figures look so real.

Low-ranking infantrymen wore no armor.

Did real-life models pose for the figures? Probably not. But hundreds of craftsmen from all over the empire spent more than ten years in workshops set up near the pits creating the warriors. It is likely that they made the faces of the soldiers look like the faces of people that they knew from home.

The uniforms of the terracotta figures are exact copies in clay of what real soldiers of the day wore. The soldier's uniform tells his rank in the army. The lowest-ranking soldiers are bareheaded and wear heavy knee-length tunics but no armor. Often their legs are wrapped in cloth shin guards for protection.

The generals' uniforms are the most elegant. Their caps sometimes sport a pheasant feather; their fancy shoes curl up at the toes; and their fine armor is made from small iron fish scales. Tassels on their armor are also a mark of their high rank.

This kneeling archer was found positioned in front of standing soldiers, just as he would have been on a real battlefield.

Modern-day potters make replicas of soldiers, faithfully copying every detail of their uniforms.

The terracotta soldiers are now the ghostly grayish color of baked clay, clay that came from nearby Mount Li. Originally the soldiers were all brightly colored. Tiny bits of paint can still be seen on many of the figures and are proof that uniforms came in a blaze of colors—purple, blue, green, yellow, red, and orange. The colors of each soldier's uniform indicated not only which part of the army he belonged to—cavalry or infantry, for example—but also what his particular rank was. The terracotta horses were fully painted, too, in brown with pink ears, nostrils, and mouths. Unfortunately, when figures are dug out of the ground, most of the paint on them peels off and sticks to the surrounding earth. Also, when exposed to air, the paint tends to crumble into dust.

Today, groups of artisans in workshops near the three pits make replicas of the soldiers, following the techniques used 2,200 years ago. Their work helps archaeologists learn more about how the original figures were created. Even though the workers today have the advantages of modern kilns that register temperatures exactly, no copies have ever come out as hard or as lustrous as the ancient originals.

The colored computer image shows how the general would have looked originally.

THINK CRITICALLY

1 Why does the terracotta army face east?
NOTE DETAILS

2 How are the terracotta warriors in Pit 3 different from the warriors in the other pits? TEXT STRUCTURE: COMPARE AND CONTRAST

3 The terracotta army is considered one of the greatest creations of the ancient world. Think about other ancient sites you have learned about. Which would you like to visit? Explain.
PERSONAL RESPONSE

4 What kind of person do you think Qin Shihuang was? Explain.
MAKE JUDGMENTS

5 **WRITE** Write a paragraph that explains why Qin Shihuang wanted to be buried with an army of clay soldiers. Use details and information from the selection to support your answer. EXTENDED RESPONSE

ABOUT THE AUTHOR
JANE O'CONNOR

In 2000, Jane O'Connor visited Xian, China, and viewed the terracotta army. The experience inspired her to learn more about the clay warriors and the emperor who had them made. Since then, Jane O'Connor has read everything she can find about the terracotta army. She decided to write *The Emperor's Silent Army* when she learned there were no books for young people about the ancient figures. Jane O'Connor lives in New York City with her husband and two sons.

GO online   www.harcourtschool.com/storytown

Social Studies

Great DISCOVERIES & Amazing ADVENTURES

THE STORIES OF HIDDEN MARVELS AND LOST TREASURES

CLAIRE LLEWELLYN
Foreword by Dr. Robert Ballard

Expository Nonfiction

A Hidden City in the Andes

by Claire Llewellyn

Machu Picchu stands on a remote ridge in the Andes mountains, around 8,200 ft. (2,500m) above sea level. The town, overlooked by towering peaks, was abandoned by the Incas. Amazingly the Spanish never found it during the 300 years that Peru was part of the Spanish Empire.

582

Between A.D. 1100–1500 the mighty Inca civilization flourished high up in the Andes mountains of Peru in South America. In 1532 Spanish adventurers known as *conquistadores* (conquerors) invaded the region and ransacked many Inca cities in search of gold. The Incas abandoned their other cities, which fell into ruin. One of these cities was Machu Picchu.

The Professor

Hiram Bingham (1875–1956), a history professor at Yale University, studied South American history for many years. In 1911, during a visit to Lima, Peru, he came across an old book that told of the downfall of the Incas. He was inspired by the description of the Inca retreat and the ancient mountain cities that they had abandoned. Bingham decided to try to find the ancient Inca capital city.

A Nerve-racking Climb

Bingham led an expedition to Peru. He went with his party to Cuzco in the foothills of the Andes. From there they climbed into the Urubamba gorge. On July 23, 1911, the group camped on the land of a local farmer, who told Bingham about ruins on top of a ridge. Bingham paid the farmer to guide him there, and the two set out one cold, drizzly morning. It was a nerve-racking climb up steep, rocky slopes and along narrow mountain paths. At times the professor had to crawl on his hands and knees across narrow bridges stretching over terrifying gorges.

A Sensational Find

At the top of the ridge Bingham and the farmer rested in a hut, where locals told them about the nearby ruins. An 11-year-old boy escorted the professor past overgrown terraces to some white granite walls. Bingham saw palaces, temples, terraces, and towers. Astonishing! It was an ancient Inca city, known to locals as Machu Picchu. Bingham was overwhelmed. He led three additional expeditions to Machu Picchu over the next four years.

Connections

Comparing Texts

1. Imagine you were with the Chinese farmers who found the terracotta army. Describe the sequence of steps you would take immediately after you made your big find.

2. "The Emperor's Silent Army" describes an important discovery in China. Compare this discovery with Hiram Bingham's discovery of Machu Picchu.

3. Did Qin Shihuang possess qualities you think are important in a leader? Explain.

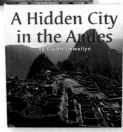

Vocabulary Review

Rate a Situation

Work with a partner. Take turns reading the sentences below aloud and pointing to the spot on the word line that shows how happy or unhappy you would feel in that situation. Discuss your choices.

Happy ———————————————————— Unhappy

- Your damaged photograph can be restored.
- Your school decides to prolong summer vacation.
- One hundred people precede you in line.
- You face some dogs with unpredictable temperaments.

precede

lustrous

trespass

strategically

prolong

resigned

temperaments

restored

Fluency Practice

Partner Reading

Work with a partner. Choose a passage from the selection to reread aloud. Read the passage aloud as your partner follows along in the book and listens. Focus on reading with accuracy. Ask your partner to help you identify any words you have difficulty reading. Then reread the passage to improve your accuracy. Switch roles and repeat the activity.

Writing

Write a Comparison

Imagine that you can somehow see the terracotta army as it was thousands of years ago. Write a paragraph that compares the soldiers' appearance when they were first placed in the tomb with their appearance as they are being excavated in Xian today.

My Writing Checklist

Writing Trait → Ideas

✔ I used a Venn diagram to plan my writing.

✔ I focused on the most important similarities and differences.

✔ I used a compare-and-contrast text structure.

Both

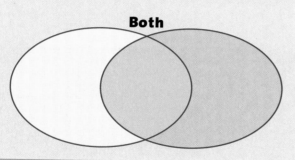

CONTENTS

Genre: Legend

ED YOUNG

THE SONS OF THE
Dragon King

A CHINESE LEGEND

FIRE, WATER, TRUTH, AND FALSEHOOD

by Heather Forest · illustrated by Stéphan Daigle

Genre: Folktale

587

Focus Skill

Literary Devices

No two authors tell a story in the same way. Literary devices are tools that authors use to make their writing style unique or to let readers know how they feel about a subject. The list below shows some common literary devices.

- **Dialogue** is the conversation between characters. It reveals characters' feelings and traits.
- A person, place, thing, or event that stands for something other than itself is called a **symbol**. For example, a heart is a symbol for love.
- Tone is the author's attitude about the subject. It helps set the **mood**, or overall feeling, of the story. An author's word choice reveals a story's mood and tone.
- **Irony** is a contrast between what readers expect to happen and what actually happens.

```
┌──────────────┐                    ┌──────────────┐
│   Dialogue   │                    │   Symbols    │
└──────────────┘                    └──────────────┘
           ┌──────────────────────────┐
           │    Literary Devices      │
           └──────────────────────────┘
┌──────────────┐                    ┌──────────────────┐
│    Irony     │                    │  Mood and Tone   │
└──────────────┘                    └──────────────────┘
```

Read the paragraph below. Then look at the diagram. It shows how the author used literary devices to tell the story in a unique way.

> One day, a kindly hermit found a snake that had been struck by a rock. Feeling sorry for the wounded creature, the hermit wrapped the snake in his rough cloak and carried it to his hut. Each day, the hermit cared for the snake. One day, when he went to feed it, the snake bit him. "Why on Earth did you do that?" the hermit demanded. The snake replied, "I'm a snake. That's why."

Dialogue
The hermit's angry question shows that he is hurt and surprised.

Symbols
The snake might be a symbol for evil.

Literary Devices

Irony
The snake bites the hermit who saved it.

Mood and Tone
The paragraph has the simple, quiet tone of a folktale. The overall mood is informal.

Try This!

Look back at the paragraph. What might the hermit be a symbol for? What words or phrases in the paragraph reveal the mood?

 www.harcourtschool.com/storytown

Vocabulary

Build Robust Vocabulary

- savory
- vigilantly
- disposition
- tolerated
- revered
- unsettling
- befitting
- dispute

In All Fairness

Once there was a poor man who had only potatoes to eat. Each day, he would take his dinner outside and sit beneath his wealthy neighbor's kitchen window. As he ate the potatoes, he would breathe in the **savory**, mouth-watering aromas coming from his neighbor's kitchen. This seemed to lend flavor to his own plain meal.

The poor man watched **vigilantly** for any sign of his neighbor. He knew that the wealthy man had a nasty **disposition**. The wealthy man eventually discovered the poor man's habit. "This theft will not be **tolerated**!" he thundered.

The wealthy man dragged the poor man to a **revered** village elder for advice.

"It is very **unsettling** to have the smells from my kitchen stolen," the wealthy man complained. "I demand that he pay for the privilege of enjoying them!"

"I cannot pay for the smells," the poor man responded. "All I own is my fine, loyal dog."

"An equal exchange is a solution **befitting** the nature of this **dispute**," replied the wise woman. "Since the poor man has freely taken something of yours, you are entitled to something of his. From now on, you shall be free to smell his dog whenever you wish."

 www.harcourtschool.com/storytown

Word Champion

 This week, take the Vocabulary Words home with you. Make a list of them and post it where you can look at it often. Use the words when you talk with your family or friends. For example, you might thank someone for preparing a savory meal. Write the Vocabulary Words you use in your vocabulary journal, and tell how you used each one.

ED YOUNG

THE SONS OF THE
Dragon King
A CHINESE LEGEND

Legend

Genre Study

A legend is a story passed down through time. As you read, look for

- a character or characters with heroic qualities.

- symbols that represent each character's traits.

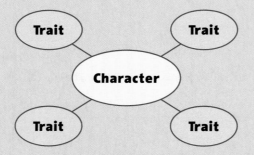

Trait — Trait

Character

Trait — Trait

Comprehension Strategy

Monitor comprehension as you read. If something is not clear, **read ahead** to look for information that might help you understand the text.

THE SONS OF THE

Dragon King

A CHINESE LEGEND
BY ED YOUNG

IN ANCIENT CHINA

it was said that the Dragon King had nine sons, each one immortal, each one very different from the next. As they grew older, each of the sons moved to a different region of the country to find his place in the world, far away from the Dragon King's watchful eye. Alas, it was not long before unsettling rumors made their way to the king. The first came from the tutor of his first son, Bei-She. . .

BEI-SHE

"Your son does nothing all day, nothing at all, but challenge the peasants in competitions to see if anyone is stronger than he is. This does not seem befitting the son of a king!" the tutor exclaimed.

Indeed it did not. Indeed, such behavior from the son of a king could not be tolerated. Bei-She was meant to discover his talent and make a contribution to his country! So the Dragon King decided to visit his son to set things straight. Disguised as a common peasant, he traveled to the region where Bei-She lived. There he saw Bei-She carrying an enormous weight on his back, racing another man who also carried an enormous weight on his back.

"You see!" cried the tutor. "This is how your son uses his time." The Dragon King was dismayed. He was about to call out to his son and scold him when he suddenly had a thought. Perhaps Bei-She would do well in a position that used his great strength! He beckoned Bei-She to him, and told his son of his idea. Bei-She, pleased that his father had recognized his great strength, readily agreed.

And to this day, Bei-She may still be found carrying the weight of the large columns that support the roofs of China's greatest buildings.

The Dragon King had just returned to his palace when an old servant from the home of his second son, Chi Wen, ran into the throne room.

"A thousand pardons, Your Highness, but I must tell you that your son Chi Wen does nothing all day, nothing at all, but stand upon his roof and stare into the distance. This does not seem befitting the son of a king!" the servant exclaimed.

Indeed it did not. Indeed, such behavior from the son of a king could not be tolerated. The Dragon King slipped his peasant disguise back on and set off for the region where Chi Wen lived. As he approached his son's house, he saw someone standing high on the roof, gazing intently into the distance. It was Chi Wen himself.

The king watched and watched, and his son never moved, except to slowly turn his head back and forth. He seemed to the king to be extraordinarily lazy, and the king was about to shout out to him when he suddenly had a thought. Perhaps Chi Wen was suited for a position that made use of his watchfulness! He called his son down from the roof and told him of his idea. Chi Wen, pleased that his father had recognized his hawklike eyesight, readily agreed.

CHI WEN

And to this day, Chi Wen may still be found at the tops of buildings, a sentinel searching the distance for potential danger.

595

PU-LAO

Before he could return home, the Dragon King was nearly knocked down by a group of villagers running toward him with their hands covering their ears. They had come from the direction of his son Pu-Lao's house.

"Your son!" they cried. "He does nothing all day, nothing at all, but make the most monstrous noises. This does not seem befitting the son of a king!"

Indeed it did not. Indeed, such behavior from the son of a king could not be tolerated. The king hurried to his son's house, where Pu-Lao bellowed from within. The king thought for a moment. Pu-Lao really didn't have a bad voice; it was just terribly loud. Perhaps he was musical! So the king covered his ears and went into the house to tell his son of his idea. Delighted, Pu-Lao began practicing more earnestly than ever.

And to this day, Pu-Lao is often seen adorning musical instruments, no doubt assuring that their sound will be loud and true.

Pleased, the Dragon King stopped at the home of Bi-An—his fourth son—on his way back to the palace. There he watched from a short distance as Bi-An resolved a dispute between two merchants by carefully weighing their goods on a scale. Wise and eloquent, he settled their disagreement and sent them on their way. Clearly, the king decided, Bi-An must serve the cause of justice. He spoke to his son, who readily agreed, pleased that his father thought him wise.

BI-AN

And these many years later, Bi-An may still be seen supervising the doorways to the great prisons, ensuring that only the guilty are locked inside.

TAO-TIEH

As he returned to his palace, the Dragon King was stopped by the caretaker of his fifth son, Tao-Tieh.

"Ah, good king, I do not like to spread rumors, but your son does nothing all day, nothing at all, but fuss about in the kitchen. This does not seem befitting the son of a king."

The Dragon King frowned deeply, then threw his disguise on once again and rushed toward Tao-Tieh's home, prepared to tell him it wasn't befitting behavior for the son of a king to spend his day in the kitchen. Then he saw a long line of people outside Tao-Tieh's house, standing patiently with bowls in their hands, and he breathed in the most magnificent aroma.

He joined the line, and once inside, he saw Tao-Tieh stirring a savory soup for all to share. The people already eating their soup seemed very pleased indeed. The king immediately knew that Tao-Tieh must play a role in the nourishment of the people. Upon hearing his father's idea, Tao-Tieh was so pleased that his father appreciated his cooking that he gave free soup to everyone for the rest of the day.

And today, Tao-Tieh may still be found protecting the places where food is prepared and served.

BA-SHA

The Dragon King's sixth son, Ba-Sha, lived fairly close to
Tao-Tieh, so the king decided to visit him before returning home.
On his way, he heard someone splashing in the Great River. As he
drew nearer, he saw that it was his own son frolicking in the water,
spraying streams of it from his mouth. The king was shocked.
What could he make of such a son? He called to Ba-Sha, who
swam so swiftly to him that the king was surprised. He hadn't
known his son was such a strong swimmer. That made him think.
Perhaps such a good swimmer would do well seeing to the safety
of those who used the kingdom's rivers and lakes. Ba-Sha splashed
water right onto his father in delight when told of the plan.

And ever since, Ba-Sha has perched
on bridges crossing the country's
waters, vigilantly watching over
those who pass by in their boats.

YA ZI

When the Dragon King returned home, one of his guards told him he had heard a rumor: The villagers in his son Ya Zi's province were afraid of Ya Zi. Although Ya Zi lived in a remote part of the country, the Dragon King once again donned his disguise and made his way to his son's home. As he approached, a servant came running from the house while Ya Zi shouted at him from the door.

"Oh, most revered king!" cried the servant. "The seventh son does nothing all day, nothing at all, but shout and scream and yell and holler. This does not seem befitting the son of the Dragon King!" Several villagers nearby nodded. The king looked at Ya Zi's angry face and wondered what to do with such a son. He was about to scold him when he realized that with his temperament, Ya Zi would be well suited for a position in the military, where he could direct his anger at the enemy. When he told this to his son, Ya Zi hollered, "Yes, sir!" and marched off excitedly.

And today, Ya Zi may still be seen emblazoned on the weapons that strike fear in the country's enemies.

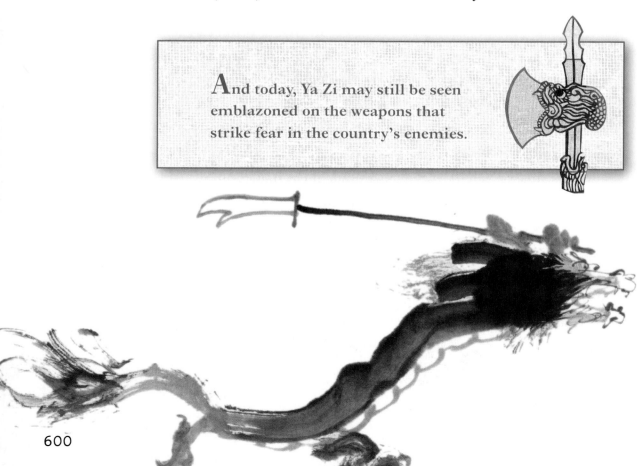

 Since then, Sua Ni has been found embellishing the pots and stands that hold incense during religious ceremonies.

SUA NI

Unlike Ya Zi, the Dragon King's eighth son, Sua Ni, looked fearsome but had a kindly heart. So the king was surprised when a monk from Sua Ni's province caught up with him on the road to tell him that the eighth son did nothing all day, nothing at all, but play with fire. The Dragon King sighed a great sigh and set off to visit Sua Ni.

When he arrived at Sua Ni's home, his son was tending to a flame that he believed would burn eternally, while patiently explaining to young children its importance. The Dragon King thought hard and decided that such a kind heart and such passion would serve Sua Ni well in a religious role. Sua Ni was delighted that his father approved of his interest.

TIAO TU

Before anyone else could come up to him with another rumor, the Dragon King took it upon himself to visit Tiao Tu, the ninth son. He found his son's home surrounded by high walls, and when he knocked at the thick, heavy door, no one answered. A little girl passing by shook her head. "Ninth son does nothing all day, nothing at all," she told the king, "unless he can do it from behind the walls of his palace." She bowed low.

Well, such behavior was hardly befitting the son of the Dragon King, the king knew. So he banged and banged and banged again on the door. When the door opened the slightest crack, the Dragon King forced his way through, prepared to scold his son. What could he do with a son with such a disposition? Then he thought, perhaps . . . perhaps in some way Tiao Tu could serve to protect people from unwanted intruders. . . .

Today, Tiao Tu can be found guarding the entryways to people's homes and businesses.

With great relief, the Dragon King returned home. He took off his disguise and smiled for the first time in a very long time. For now he knew he would hear no more unsettling rumors about his nine sons. And indeed he did not, for each of his sons happily undertook the role he was most suited for—a role befitting the son of the Dragon King—and through the ages, has never ceased to honor his royal heritage and responsibility.

THINK CRITICALLY

1. What is the Dragon King's main reason for visiting each of his nine sons? CAUSE AND EFFECT

2. What idea is the fifth son, Tao-Tieh, a symbol for? Explain.  LITERARY DEVICES

3. What does the way the Dragon King treats the unsettling rumors about his sons tell you about his personality? Use details from the text to support your answer. CHARACTER'S TRAITS

4. In your opinion, do the Dragon King's sons get equally good positions? Explain. MAKE JUDGMENTS

5. **WRITE** Imagine that the Dragon King discovers a long-lost tenth son. Describe the tenth son's talent and the position the Dragon King gives to this son. SHORT RESPONSE

ABOUT THE
AUTHOR & ILLUSTRATOR

Ed Young grew up in Shanghai, China. As a child, he loved to draw and read. When he was twenty years old, he traveled to the United States to study. Soon he began to illustrate children's books. Accurate storytelling is important to him, so he does careful research before illustrating a book. He says, "Training for an artist is a lifetime endeavor." Ed Young has illustrated and written dozens of children's books. He has won many awards, including the prestigious Caldecott Medal.

 www.harcourtschool.com/storytown

ED YOUNG

Folktale

FIRE, WATER, TRUTH, AND FALSEHOOD

by Heather Forest • illustrated by Stéphan Daigle

NORTHEAST AFRICA—ETHIOPIA

Long ago, Fire, Water, Truth, and Falsehood lived together in one large house. Although all were polite toward each other, they kept their distance. Truth and Falsehood sat on opposite sides of the room. Fire constantly leapt out of Water's path.

One day they went hunting together. They found a large number of cattle and began driving them home to their village. "Let us share these cattle equally," said Truth as they traveled across the grasslands. "This is the fair way to divide our captives."

No one disagreed with Truth except Falsehood. Falsehood wanted more than an equal share but kept quiet about it for the moment. As the four hunters traveled back to the village, Falsehood went secretly to Water and whispered, "You are more powerful than Fire. Destroy Fire and then there will be more cattle for each of us!"

Water flowed over Fire, bubbling and steaming until Fire was gone. Water meandered along, cheerfully thinking about more cattle for itself.

Falsehood, meanwhile, whispered to Truth. "Look! See for yourself! Water has killed Fire! Let us leave Water, who has cruelly destroyed our warmhearted friend. We must take the cattle high in the mountains to graze."

As Truth and Falsehood traveled up the mountain, Water tried to follow. But the mountain was too steep, and Water could not flow upwards. Water washed down upon itself, splashing and swirling around rocks as it tumbled down the slope. Look and see! Water is still tumbling down the mountainside to this day.

Truth and Falsehood arrived at the mountaintop. Falsehood turned to Truth and said in a loud voice, "I am more powerful than you! You will be my servant. I am your master. All the cattle belong to me!"

Truth rose up and spoke out. "I will not be your servant!"

They battled and battled. Finally they brought the argument to Wind to decide who was the master.

Wind didn't know. Wind blew all over the world to ask people whether Truth or Falsehood was more powerful. Some people said, "A single word of Falsehood can completely destroy Truth." Others insisted, "Like a small candle in the dark, Truth can change every situation."

Wind finally returned to the mountain and said, "I have seen that Falsehood is very powerful. But it can rule only where Truth has stopped struggling to be heard."

And it has been that way ever since.

Connections

Comparing Texts

1. Each brother in "The Sons of the Dragon King" has a different talent or skill. Which brother are you the most like? Explain.

2. Compare the theme in "The Sons of the Dragon King" with the theme in "Fire, Water, Truth, and Falsehood."

3. Each of the Dragon King's sons has a special talent that turns out to be useful. Think of another natural talent that has a practical use in the real world.

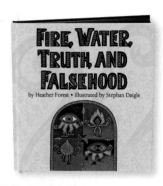

Vocabulary Review

I watched vigilantly as my sister mixed the ingredients for the savory dish.

Word Pairs

Work with a partner. Write each Vocabulary Word on a separate index card. Place the cards face down in two piles. Take turns flipping a card from each pile and writing a sentence that correctly uses both words. Read your sentence aloud to your partner. Each time you use a word correctly, you get one point. The partner who has the most points after all the words have been used wins.

savory

vigilantly

disposition

tolerated

revered

unsettling

befitting

dispute

Fluency Practice

Repeated Reading

When you read aloud, focus on grouping words into meaningful phrases. Proper phrasing is one characteristic of fluent reading. Work with a partner. Listen as your partner reads aloud the introduction to "The Sons of the Dragon King" on page 593. Give feedback on your partner's phrasing. Then switch roles. Repeat the procedure several times. Work to improve your phrasing with each reading.

Writing

Write a Legend

"The Sons of the Dragon King" is a legend that explains the origin of dragon carvings on many Chinese objects and buildings. Choose something you see every day, and make up a legend explaining its origin.

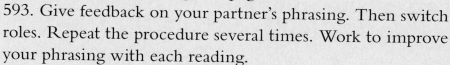

My Writing Checklist

Writing Trait → Conventions

✔ I developed the characters' traits.

✔ I used a variety of literary devices.

✔ I used proper spelling, grammar, and punctuation.

Dialogue

Symbols

Literary Devices

Irony

Mood and Tone

CONTENTS

Lesson 24

Genre: Expository Nonfiction

SECRETS OF THE
SPHINX
JAMES CROSS GIBL
BAGRAM IBATOULLIN

Advertisements from
The
EGYPTIAN
NEWS
by Scott Steedman

Genre: Advertisements

Literary Devices

You have learned that **literary devices** reveal an author's writing style and make the writing come alive. Another type of literary device is **imagery**—descriptive words and phrases that appeal to the senses. Imagery helps readers imagine how things look, sound, smell, taste, and feel. Read the sentences below.

- A crowd gathered in front of the door. (sight)
- The wind moaned through the forest. (sound)
- The sweet perfume of fresh flowers filled the air. (smell)
- She was surprised by the bitterness of the lemonade. (taste)
- The heat from the fireplace warmed the room. (touch)

Imagery helps set the **tone** and create a **mood**. The tone is the author's attitude about the subject. The mood is the overall feeling that the author's word choice and use of imagery create.

Imagery	Mood and Tone

Tip

To find imagery in a text, look for words that *describe*. To find the mood and tone of a text, look for words that express a *feeling* or *attitude*.

Read the paragraph below. Then look at the chart. The first column identifies one example of imagery from the paragraph. The second column shows how specific words and phrases help create a mood and set the tone.

When Howard Carter first peered through the door of Tutankhamen's tomb, he glimpsed an unimaginable treasure. The room he saw was filled with exquisitely painted furniture, elaborately carved boxes, and sculptures. The overwhelming glint of gold sparkled from every corner of the room. What an amazing find he had unearthed!

Imagery	Mood and Tone
"Exquisitely painted" is a description that helps readers picture how the furniture looked.	The words "unimaginable treasure" express a feeling of excitement and awe.

Try This!

Find one more example of imagery in the paragraph and tell which sense it appeals to. Then identify all the words and phrases that create a mood of excitement and awe.

 www.harcourtschool.com/storytown

Vocabulary

Build Robust Vocabulary

flourishing

fertile

primitive

immortalized

intact

descendants

reinforces

rituals

The interview below with anthropologist Dr. Hamed Kafar appeared in *Egyptology Times* magazine.

Egyptology Times: Your specialty is ancient cultures. Tell us about Egypt.

Dr. Hamed Kafar: First, the ancient Egyptian period covers a lot of time—about 3,000 years. The **flourishing** region along the Nile River benefited from the **fertile** soil there. The Nile provided water for crops and for boat transportation, making it possible for Egyptians to trade. Far from remaining **primitive**, the Egyptians developed and sustained an incredibly rich culture over thirty centuries.

Scenes from ancient Egyptian life are **immortalized** on tomb walls. Many everyday objects buried in tombs remain **intact**.

Egyptology Times: How does ancient Egyptian culture relate to that of contemporary Egypt?

Dr. Hamad Kafar: Modern Egyptians are very aware of their heritage. They are the **descendants** of the pharaohs. This legacy **reinforces** their ties to the past. Some modern ceremonies and **rituals** in Egypt have their origins in ancient practices.

Ramses II was one of the last great Egyptian kings. He ruled until about 1224 B.C.

GO online www.harcourtschool.com/storytown

Word Scribe

This week, your job is to use the Vocabulary Words in writing. In your vocabulary journal, write sentences that use the Vocabulary Words in meaningful ways. For example, you could write about an object you wish could be immortalized for your descendants to see. Use as many Vocabulary Words as you can. Share your sentences with your classmates.

Expository Nonfiction

Genre Study

Expository nonfiction tells about real people, things, places, or events. As you read, look for

- imagery and illustrations that help present information.

- facts supported by evidence.

K	W	L
What I Know	What I Want to Know	What I Learned

Comprehension Strategy

Monitor comprehension as you read. If something is not clear, **read ahead** to look for information that might help you understand the text.

SECRETS OF THE

SPHINX

by JAMES CROSS GIBLIN

illustrated by BAGRAM IBATOULLINE

THE MYSTERIOUS CREATURE

Before dawn, the giant creature is almost invisible. It sits in shadow in its rocky, horseshoe-shaped hollow. Then, as the sun slowly rises in the east, the creature's body is gradually revealed.

First, the huge paws of a lion appear, followed by the animal's powerful haunches and shoulders. As the sun rises higher, the creature's face catches the light. But it is not the face of a lion. No, it is the face of a man. A man with broad lips, a broken nose, and eyes that gaze steadily forward. A man wearing the flared headdress of an ancient Egyptian pharaoh.

This creature—part man, part beast—is the Great Sphinx. It was carved out of a natural rock formation, and is one of the largest sculptures in the world. From front to back, the Sphinx is the length of an average city block. It is as tall as a six-story building—sixty-six feet from its paws to the top of its head. Even its facial features are gigantic. What remains of the Sphinx's nose is more than $5\frac{1}{2}$ feet long, and its mouth is $7\frac{1}{2}$ feet wide. Its entire face has a breadth of thirteen feet eight inches.

Behind the Sphinx, on the sandy Giza Plateau, stand three massive pyramids formed from blocks of limestone. The largest of the three, the Great Pyramid of Giza, covers an area large enough to accommodate ten football fields.

The three pyramids were built to house the mummies of pharaohs who ruled Egypt during the Fourth Dynasty, which lasted from 2575–2467 B.C. Scholars believe the Sphinx was carved at the time the second of the pyramids was erected. If they are correct, the Great Sphinx has stood guard over this royal Egyptian cemetery for almost forty-five hundred years.

Ever since the Sphinx was new, it has stared across the desert sands in the direction of the Nile River, a few miles to the east. Then, as now, the Nile was the vital backbone of Egyptian life, providing water for people, animals, and crops. But there was no city of Cairo on the banks of the Nile in 2500 B.C. This great city, the present-day capital of Egypt, came into being much later.

Today, instead of open desert, the Sphinx looks out on souvenir stands and fast-food outlets. They stand less than two hundred yards away from the Sphinx's paws. These shops are part of the ever-expanding suburbs of Cairo, whose population has grown from two million to seventeen million in just forty years. With this growth have come cars, sewage, and air pollution, all of which have created problems for the Sphinx and the pyramids.

Other problems are brought on by the hordes of tourists from all over the world who visit the Giza Plateau each day. The money the tourists spend is essential to the health of the Egyptian economy, but their tramping feet and sweaty hands can cause damage to the ancient monuments.

Still, the tourists come, as they have since the days of the ancient Greeks and Romans. They gaze in awe at the Great Sphinx and the pyramids, and ask their guides the same questions visitors to Egypt have always asked: Who built these structures, and why? What do they mean? And how did their builders, using primitive tools, ever manage to shape and carve such towering monuments?

The answers to those questions aren't simple, and many of them have yet to be found. For to understand the pyramids and the Sphinx, one must first travel back to a time long before they were built—a mysterious time before there were any written records—a time before history.

THE BEGINNINGS OF EGYPT

No one knows exactly who the ancient Egyptians were. Nor is it known how they arrived at the long, narrow strip of fertile land along the Nile River that became their home. But by about 5000 B.C., Egypt had developed a flourishing Stone Age culture. These people chipped flints for knives and ax blades; made clay pots; grew crops of wheat and millet; and kept cows, goats, and donkeys.

The descendants of these people built on the accomplishments of their forebears. They discovered metals and made weapons and tools out of copper. They learned how to weave cloth, how to paint and sculpt, and how to add and subtract. At life's end, they buried their dead in rectangular graves lined with mud brick. No buildings from this period survive because they, too, were built of mud brick that crumbled long ago. But stone statues of lions, their mouths open in snarls, have been found in excavations of some ancient Egyptian ruins. The statues may have stood guard outside temples and inspired the sphinxes of later times.

Two important events occurred in the next phase of Egypt's development, starting about 3100 B.C. A pharaoh, whom some scholars call Narmer and others call Menes, united northern and southern Egypt into one nation and established his capital at Memphis. The city rose along the banks of the Nile, a few miles south of present-day Cairo. The other event was of equal, if not greater, importance: The Egyptians learned to write. When that happened, they left the shadowy world of prehistory and entered the world of history.

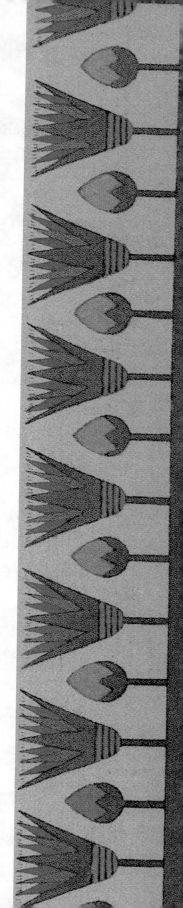

For a long time, scholars thought that the Sumerians, who lived in what is now Iraq, invented writing. The Sumerians made wedge-shaped marks in wet clay tablets that were then baked. This type of writing is called *cuneiform*, which means "wedge-shaped."

The ancient Egyptians traded with the Sumerians, and may have exchanged ideas about writing with them. But the Egyptians did not use wedge-shaped marks in their writing. Instead, they created a set of symbols called *hieroglyphs*. Scholars now believe that the earliest examples of hieroglyphic writing, dating to about 3500 B.C., are older than the earliest examples of cuneiform writing.

Egyptian hieroglyphs were difficult to understand and to copy, so only a small number of people learned how to write. They were called *scribes*, and occupied a position of honor in ancient Egyptian society. The scribes carved hieroglyphs on stone monuments or wrote them on sheets of papyrus, a paperlike material made from a tall plant which still grows in abundance along the Nile. Sheets of papyrus were glued together in rolls from which a scribe would cut off as much as was needed for a letter or document. Scribes wrote on the papyrus with a reed pen, using an ink made of water, gum, and soot.

Almost none of the earliest papyrus texts survive, and only a few of the oldest stone inscriptions remain. For information about the earliest periods in Egyptian history, scholars must rely on the accounts of later writers and the discoveries made by archaeologists. From these sources, the scholars have been able to piece together a list of the pharaohs who governed Egypt during the first dynasties. (A dynasty is a succession of rulers who are members of the same family.)

LIFE AFTER DEATH

Religion was central to Egyptian life from the beginning, and the pharaoh played a key role in its rituals. In life, the ruler was thought to be the son of Ra, the all-powerful sun god. In death, he rejoined his father in the west, the place where the sun set. There, in the Egyptian afterworld, he would enjoy eternal life, but only if his earthly body was still intact.

This led to the ancient Egyptian practice of mummification, the attempt to preserve the body after death by embalming it with resin, sodium carbonate, and other chemicals, and wrapping it in fine linen gauze. Originally, only the pharaoh, his queen, and other members of the royal family were mummified. Later, the practice spread to include high government officials and other people of means. Later still, the Egyptians embalmed cats, dogs, horses, cows, hawks, and other animals that were sacred to them.

Monumental tombs were built to house the royal mummies and everything they would need for life in the hereafter—clothes, jewelry, chairs, beds, dishes, even food. The first tombs, called *mastabas*, were flat-roofed structures with sloping sides of mud brick. By the Third Dynasty, the royal architects had begun to erect more permanent structures made of stone. The most noteworthy of these was the first Egyptian tomb that resembled a pyramid—the so-called step pyramid of the pharaoh Zoser, which rises in six ever-smaller terraces to a height of one hundred ninety feet.

The next dynasty, the Fourth, witnessed an incredible flowering of Egypt's civilization. There were fresh advances in the fields of mathematics, medicine, literature, and astronomy. Most spectacular of all were the strides made in architecture. These included the structures that rose on the Giza Plateau: the three huge pyramids and the Great Sphinx. More than one hundred other pyramids would be built in Egypt during later dynasties, but none of them would be as massive as the Giza tombs. Nor would any of the later sphinxes be as impressive as the Great Sphinx. It proved to be one of a kind.

The development of the pyramid can clearly be traced from the one-story mastabas of the First Dynasty to the towering structures at Giza. The path that led to the Great Sphinx is much less obvious. Other than a small sphinx with a woman's face that may have been carved during the reign of the previous pharaoh, no earlier examples have been found.

The lion had long been a symbol of strength and power in ancient art, but the sculptors of the Great Sphinx were the first, as far as we

know, to combine the animal's body with the head of a man. This was not just any man. Many scholars are convinced that the face on the Sphinx is actually a portrait of the Egyptian ruler Khafre, for its features closely resemble statues of him. Moreover, Khafre was one of the pharaohs who ruled Egypt during the Fourth Dynasty, and the pyramid immediately behind the Sphinx contained his remains.

Almost nothing is known of Pharaoh Khafre, who was called Chephren in Greek. But if he was even partly responsible for the creation of the Great Sphinx and the other achievements of the Fourth Dynasty, he deserves to be immortalized on the sculpture's face.

Perhaps the discovery of other sphinxes from earlier dynasties, or of written texts describing them, will reveal more of the Great Sphinx's secrets. In the meantime, archaeologists digging in the earth near the Sphinx and the pyramids have uncovered some startling new facts about how the monuments were built and the lives of the ancient Egyptians who labored on them.

CREATORS OF THE SPHINX

Until recently, scholars thought the builders of the pyramids and the Sphinx must have been little more than slaves. They believed the unfortunate workers were forced to labor on the monuments under threat of torture—or worse. Lately, however, a very different picture has emerged as a result of excavations on the Giza Plateau.

The foundations of row upon row of mud-brick houses have been unearthed at one of the sites. Scholars think that some of them were the homes of the overseers who supervised the building crews. Others were probably the residences of the skilled craftsmen who sculpted the face of the Sphinx and decorated the royal chambers in the pyramids.

It is estimated that five hundred to one thousand craftsmen lived with their families in the workers' settlement. These specialists devoted most, if not all, of their working lives to the design and construction of the Sphinx, the pyramids, and the temples and smaller tombs that surrounded them. From the available evidence, the craftsmen were respected for their abilities and lived well by ancient Egyptian standards.

Near the mud-brick houses, archaeologists have discovered the remains of a number of barracks-like buildings. Scholars believe these were the dwellings of the unskilled laborers who helped to build the pyramids and the Sphinx. The laborers were probably young farmers who were drafted to work on the monuments during the months when they were not needed to plant or harvest the crops. At any given time, it is thought there were five to seven thousand such laborers living in the military-style barracks at Giza.

As work on the pyramids and the Sphinx continued, the settlement grew to be the size of a city. Besides dwelling places, it had production and storage facilities for food, fuel, and metal tools. There was a building where fish caught in the Nile were dried and salted for future use. And there were bakeries in which bread—the staple of the workers' diet—was made from emmer, a form of wheat. It tasted like sourdough bread.

There was also a cemetery where those who died during the construction of the pyramids were buried. Domes built of limestone blocks marked the graves of the overseers and skilled craftsmen in the upper part of the cemetery. The common laborers were buried in the lower part of the cemetery under smaller domes made of mud brick.

None of the workers were mummified, but when scientists unearthed their graves they found many skeletal remains. These added to the scientists' knowledge of the conditions under which the pyramid builders labored, and the medical treatment they received.

Somewhat surprisingly, males and females were represented almost equally in the graves. This suggests that women played a bigger role in the construction of the pyramids and the carving of the Sphinx than anyone had previously imagined.

Life expectancy was much shorter in the ancient world than it is in most places today. The skeletons of the male workers indicate that many of them died between the ages of thirty and thirty-five. More females than males died before the age of thirty, which probably reflects the hazards of childbirth in ancient times.

The remains of both the men and women show signs of hard labor. Severe arthritis of the back and the knees was found in many skeletons, probably the result of constant heavy lifting. Other skeletons bore evidence of fractures in arms and legs. However, most of the fractures had healed completely, with full realignment of the broken bones. This indicates that the workers were given good medical care, and that the fractures were set with splints. It also reinforces the notion that the men and women who labored on the Giza Plateau were treated humanely.

Still, their work was extremely hard. Equipped only with hammers, chisels, and axes, they cut huge blocks of granite and limestone from quarries far and near. Then they transported the blocks to the building site by boat and sledge, and raised them into place as the pyramids gradually took shape.

THINK CRITICALLY

① Reread the description of the Sphinx at the beginning of the selection. What literary devices has the author used to help you picture this sculpture? LITERARY DEVICES

② Why were the pyramids built? CAUSE AND EFFECT

③ How does the author of "Secrets of the Sphinx" feel about his subject? How do you know? AUTHOR'S PERSPECTIVE

④ The author claims that the many visitors to the pyramids and the Sphinx cause damage to these ancient monuments. Has the author given enough evidence to support this statement? Explain. MAKE JUDGMENTS

⑤ **WRITE** Explain why the Nile River was important to ancient Egypt. Use details and information from the selection to support your answer. SHORT RESPONSE

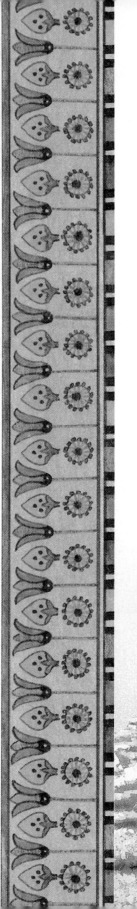

ABOUT THE ILLUSTRATOR
Bagram Ibatoulline

Bagram Ibatoulline grew up in Russia and studied at the State Academic Institute of Arts in Moscow. He changes his illustration style to fit each subject he illustrates. Some of his illustrations have the precision of photographs. Bagram Ibatoulline lives in Jersey City, New Jersey, with his family.

ABOUT THE AUTHOR
James Cross Giblin

James Cross Giblin grew up surrounded by books. He loved reading literature and making up his own stories. Now, as a writer of children's books, he enjoys researching and learning about different subjects. He says this about his work and his audience: "I only hope my pleasure communicates itself to young readers and makes them want to read more books. If it does, I'll be repaying the debt I owe all the fine writers who nurtured my love of reading when I was a child."

GO online www.harcourtschool.com/storytown

633

Advertisements from The EGYPT

FOR YOUR EVERY SCRIBAL NEED

Papyrus scrolls in all sizes made from the best-quality papyrus reeds. Also blue, green, red, and all-purpose black inks — only the finest colored earths and charcoal used.

SPECIAL OFFER

Buy a set of reed pens and a stone water pot — and get a free wooden carrying case!

PEN PALS, THE MARKET, ISNA

FARMLAND
AVAILABLE WITH HOUSE

❋

A small plot of farmland near the town of Abydos has become available — an ideal opportunity for the son of a farming family.

The house is on the edge of the town at the end of a quiet lane.

There are two rooms on the ground floor and an outside staircase to a roof terrace. A small courtyard at the front of the house contains a mud-brick oven.

Apply to the district governor at Abydos.

TOWNHOUSE

Small townhouse in Thebes, ideal for a young scribe and his family. Large reception room, two bedrooms with built-in sleeping platforms, and underground storage room. Roof terrace with shady covered area for the summer.

Box No. 6920

IAN NEWS

by Scott Steedman

CLASSY GLASS

Our fish-shaped perfume bottles make charming gifts.

Vases and makeup containers also available.

ROYAL GLASS FACTORY, ABYDOS

WIGS FANTASTIC

YOU CAN'T AFFORD TO BE WITHOUT ONE!

Made from the finest human hair. All wigs fit over a shaved head.

The Marketplace, Abydos

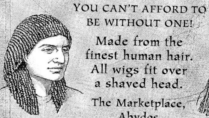

FAKE IT FURNITURE

Do you want stylish black furniture, but can't afford the price of ebony wood? We make tables, chairs, and beds in cheap wood and then dye it black. Looks just like the real thing!

Find us near the temple in Bubastis.

Papyrus rafts for short trips

Traders' ships made from top-quality cedar-wood

BOATS MADE TO ORDER

❖

WE BUILD BOATS FOR EVERY OCCASION

❖

THE DOCKYARD, MEMPHIS

Sailboats for river voyages

Extra-wide cargo boats, ideal for carrying cattle

Connections

Comparing Texts

1. Which fact about ancient Egyptian monuments is the most interesting or amazing to you? Explain.

2. Compare and contrast the text features in "The Egyptian News" and "Secrets of the Sphinx."

3. In ancient Egypt, only scribes knew how to read and write. If the same were true in our world today, what would be the effects on society?

Vocabulary Review

Word Webs

Choose two Vocabulary Words, and create a word web for each one. Put the Vocabulary Word in the center of the web. In the outside ovals, write words and phrases that are related to the Vocabulary Word. Share your webs with a partner. Explain how each word or phrase in your web is related to the Vocabulary Word.

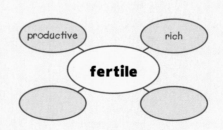

flourishing

fertile

primitive

immortalized

intact

descendants

reinforces

rituals

Fluency Practice

Partner Reading

Work with a partner. Each of you should choose one long paragraph from "Secrets of the Sphinx." As your partner reads the text aloud, listen carefully for the pauses between the phrases. Give your partner feedback on phrasing. Then read the paragraph you chose, making your phrasing sound natural. Trade paragraphs with your partner. Take turns reading the paragraphs aloud and giving each other feedback about phrasing.

Writing

Write a Journal Entry

Imagine that you are a scribe or a pyramid builder for a pharaoh of the Fourth Dynasty. Write a journal entry telling about one day at work.

Imagery	Mood and Tone

My Writing Checklist

Writing Trait ➤ Conventions

✔ I used correct spelling, punctuation, and grammar.

✔ I included imagery in my journal entry.

✔ I used a consistent tone in my writing.

CONTENTS

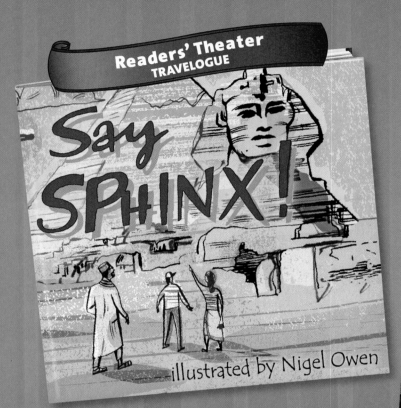

Say
SPHINX!

illustrated by Nigel Owen

YOUR
Social Studies
TEXTBOOK

overwhelming

ornery

aggravated

sophisticated

imposing

notable

prosperous

unassuming

conspicuous

pillaged

Reading for Fluency

When reading a script aloud,

- Practice your lines several times to achieve **accuracy**.

- Pay attention to **phrasing**. Use punctuation marks to help you read groups of words in meaningful chunks.

Say SPHINX!

illustrated by Nigel Owen

Characters

Narrator

Chorus

Samantha

Tarek Hawass, Amira's brother

Jason

Amira Hawass, Tarek's sister

Mrs. Hawass, Tarek and Amira's mother

Mr. Hawass, Tarek and Amira's father

Sameh, tour guide

Narrator: Samantha and Jason are walking through a bustling marketplace in Aswan, Egypt. They plan to meet some family friends who live in Aswan and sell their produce at the marketplace. Merchants, farmers, and fishers loudly promote their wares.

Chorus: Olives for sale! Walnuts are half price today! Come get your bread right here. We have the best prices anywhere in Aswan!

Samantha: This market is really different from the grocery store at home.

Aswan

641

Chorus: Fresh fish! They were swimming in the Nile two hours ago!

Tarek: Dates for sale! Get the sweetest dates in Aswan! Would you like to sample them?

Jason: Thank you. *Shukran!* These dates are delicious.

Amira: They're from our family farm on the bank of the Nile River. Let us introduce ourselves. I'm Amira, and this is my brother, Tarek.

Samantha: We have been looking for you! My name is Samantha and this is my brother, Jason. The last time we saw you, I was only eight years old.

Narrator: A large, hairy snout appears from above, snatching the date from Samantha's fingers. Gulp! Smack!

Samantha: Whoa! The camel grabbed the date right out of my hand!

Jason: Is that your camel? He's really big.

Samantha: And really hungry!

Tarek: This is Jamal, one of the camels from our farm. Sorry about that.

Jason: No problem! A little bit of camel slobber won't hurt. Right, Sam?

Amira and Tarek: Welcome to Egypt. *Marhaba!*

Samantha: Egypt has so many historic sights that it's overwhelming! Where should we go first? We want to see as much as possible.

Amira: If you really want to see Egypt, you must sail the Nile. That's the best way to explore the country.

Jason: Really? I was hoping to explore Egypt while riding a camel like Jamal!

Narrator: Tarek and Amira laugh and shake their heads.

Amira: Camels aren't comfortable to ride, especially for long distances. No offense, Jamal!

Narrator: Jamal makes a noise that's a cross between a snort, a grunt, and a whinny.

Tarek: Camels can get very ornery, too. You don't want to be anywhere near an aggravated camel.

Samantha: Okay, you've convinced me. Let's sail the Nile.

Narrator: Tarek turns to Amira and whispers something to her.

Amira: Tarek just had a wonderful idea. Our family owns a boat, and tomorrow we set sail for Cairo. Why don't you come with us?

Jason: Wow! We'd be honored!

Narrator: The next day, Samantha and Jason are on the Hawass family's boat, sailing north toward Luxor.

Samantha: I know that the Nile flows for more than 4,000 miles, but exactly where does the river start?

Amira: The Nile starts in east-central Africa. It flows north all the way through Egypt before emptying into the Mediterranean Sea.

Tarek: I'm glad the Nile is so long. I'd like to prolong our journey as much as possible.

Jason: Look—I see a hippopotamus wading in the river!

Narrator: Samantha whips out her camera and takes a picture.

Tarek: If you look carefully, you'll see crocodiles, frogs, and red-billed ibises, too. Lots of animals live in the Nile.

Jason: Look how green the sugarcane fields are! They certainly contrast with the desert in the distance.

Mrs. Hawass: Yes. In Egypt, we farm on the banks of the Nile. The richest soil is right here.

Chorus: Why is the best soil near the river?

Mrs. Hawass: For thousands of years beginning each June, the Nile flooded its banks and spilled across the lands of the delta. The floods deposited fertile soil along the Nile.

Fluency Tip

If you misread a word, reread the complete sentence correctly to improve your **accuracy.**

Mr. Hawass: Even today, more than sixty percent of Egyptians live in the Nile delta. The oldest, most historic places are near the Nile, too.

Jason: That's true! Aswan, Luxor, Saqqara [suh•KAR•uh], and Giza are all right next to the river. Mr. Hawass, why is the Nile so important?

Mr. Hawass: Without this river, the sophisticated culture of ancient Egypt might never have started, let alone flourished. The Nile has influenced the course of civilization.

Fluency Tip

Commas are clues that tell you where to **pause after phrases** when reading aloud.

Samantha: Now I understand why Amira and Tarek insisted that we sail the Nile. This is definitely the best way to get to know Egypt.

Jason: As much as I liked Jamal, I'm glad we're on this boat instead of riding him.

Narrator: The group arrives in the ancient city of Luxor, near the Avenue of Sphinxes. The Hawass family, Samantha, and Jason leave the boat to go sightseeing. The sun is blazing overhead as they approach the imposing Avenue of Sphinxes.

Sameh: *Ahlan wa sahlan.* Hello! My name is Sameh, and I'll be your tour guide.

Chorus: *Ahlan wa sahlan.* Hello, Sameh!

Sameh: Welcome to the Avenue of Sphinxes. This promenade leads to one of the most awe-inspiring buildings of Egypt—the famed Luxor Temple.

Jason: What exactly is a sphinx, Sameh?

Sameh: The sphinx is an imaginary beast with the body of a lion and the head of a person. Sphinxes are often found in Egyptian art and mythology.

Tarek: The head of the sphinx is usually carved to resemble a real person—usually one of the pharaohs who ruled ancient Egypt.

Sameh: That's right! Speaking of pharaohs, does anyone know the name of the pharaoh who built Luxor Temple?

Samantha: Didn't Pharaoh Ramses II build most of Luxor Temple? There was information about him in my social studies book. He ruled for almost seventy years.

Sameh: Very good! I'm not surprised that Ramses II was in your social studies book.

Jason: Why aren't you surprised? Was Ramses II notable?

Sameh: Ramses II was one of the most powerful and revered pharaohs to reign over Egypt. Even today, we call him Ramses the Great. Does anyone know why he was considered so great?

Amira: He made Egypt very prosperous. He also constructed many famous monuments all over the country.

Mr. Hawass: In Egypt we have a saying: "If you forget your own name, I will forgive you . . . but not if you forget the name of Ramses the Great!"

Chorus: We won't forget Ramses the Great!

Narrator: At the entrance to Luxor Temple, the Pylon of Ramses, everyone gazes at the statues of Ramses that flank the building.

Samantha: Wow! Now I definitely won't forget Ramses! These enormous statues are befitting a powerful ruler. How did the workers carve such massive stones?

Jason: I know! They used copper tools to quarry giant blocks of granite and limestone. The work was difficult because copper is relatively soft, and their tools had to be sharpened frequently.

Mrs. Hawass: Does anyone know how the giant blocks were moved after they were cut?

Tarek: Teams of workers pulled them on sleds. The Egyptians even invented special machines to roll the largest stones into place. Some stones weighed as much as two-and-a-half tons!

Chorus: That's a very heavy piece of stone!

Sameh: Wait until you see the pyramids at Giza!

Mr. Hawass: That's an impressive sight. When you see the sheer size of the pyramids, you'll be astonished!

Samantha: I can't wait, but don't worry—even if the sight makes me forget my own name, I won't forget Ramses the Great.

Chorus: We'll never forget Ramses the Great!

Narrator: After sailing farther north, the Hawass family, Samantha, Jason, and their tour guide Sameh travel by camel through the village of Saqqara, on the western bank of the Nile.

Sameh: We've arrived! This is the ancient necropolis of Saqqara.

Samantha: What's a necropolis?

Sameh: *Necropolis* means "city of the dead." It's like a gigantic graveyard. The Egyptians often built many tombs in a single location. Saqqara was part of the necropolis for the ancient city of Memphis. It's more than 4,500 years old.

Jason: What's that in front of us? It looks a lot like a pyramid . . . but I thought that all the pyramids in Egypt were located in Giza.

Mrs. Hawass: That's the Step Pyramid of Pharaoh Zoser. It's the very first monumental structure made of stone anywhere in the entire world.

Chorus: Wow! So, this is the oldest known pyramid?

Amira: Yes, Pharaoh Zoser's Step Pyramid precedes the pyramids at Giza by more than 200 years.

Samantha: I can see why it's called the Step Pyramid. There are six levels of stone blocks, with each level smaller than the one just underneath it. So, was Pharaoh Zoser buried here?

Mr. Hawass: Yes, he was. Before that time, ancient Egyptians buried their rulers in low stone structures.

Jason: What were those older tombs like?

Mr. Hawass: They were called *mastabas,* which means "benches" in Arabic. A mastaba was a low stone structure built on top of a long stairway that descended to the actual burial location. It was unassuming compared to a pyramid.

Jason: If I were a pharaoh, I'd much rather build a pyramid!

Mrs. Hawass: Pyramids are more imposing, but mastabas have one big advantage.

Chorus: What's the advantage of a mastaba?

Mrs. Hawass: Because pyramids were so conspicuous, they were easy targets for thieves who wanted to steal the pharaohs' treasures. In fact, over the centuries, looters robbed almost all the pyramids.

Amira: Archaeologists rarely find a pyramid intact. Most have been pillaged.

Sameh: You are both correct. Mastabas are smaller and harder to find. That's why many of those burial sites have remained undisturbed.

Tarek: So, Jason, would you still want to build a pyramid instead of a mastaba? Or have you changed your mind?

Jason: Hmmm. I'll have to give this some more thought!

Narrator: Samantha, Jason, the Hawass family, and their tour guide Sameh have arrived in Giza. They dismount from their camels.

Sameh: Giza is part of the necropolis of Memphis, just like Saqqara.

Jason: I can't believe we're here. There's the Pyramid of Khufu. That's the tallest one. It's 450 feet high.

Amira: That's more than twice the height of the Step Pyramid. It is only 200 feet tall.

Tarek: The Pyramid of Khufu doesn't look that big from here.

Jason: Wait until we get closer. The Pyramid of Khufu is as tall as a thirty-story building.

Sameh: And it covers an area bigger than eight soccer fields put together!

Tarek: Okay, I take it back. . . . That's huge!

Samantha: I recognize the Pyramid of Khafre, too. It's the only pyramid that's still covered by some of the limestone that originally paved its surface.

Mr. Hawass: That's right, Samantha. When the pyramids were constructed, a layer of fine limestone was laid over the rougher stone blocks to create a smooth exterior.

Jason: Where did the limestone go?

Mr. Hawass: Over the centuries, people chipped away the exterior stone and used it on other building projects.

Mrs. Hawass: Look to the right of the Pyramid of Khafre—there's the sphinx. It was carved about the same time as the Pyramid of Khafre.

Sameh: Pharaoh Khafre's face is immortalized in the face of the sphinx. It was carved to resemble him.

Jason: I loved seeing the Avenue of Sphinxes in Luxor, but this sphinx is even more amazing. What an incredible journey we've had, Samantha! Thank you, Sameh!

Chorus: Thank you, Sameh! That was great!

COMPREHENSION STRATEGIES
Review

Reading a Social Studies Textbook

Bridge to Content-Area Reading A textbook is an example of expository nonfiction. Expository nonfiction tells about real people, things, places, or events. The notes on page 651 point out features that are common in social studies textbooks. How can these features help you find and remember important information?

Review the Focus Strategies

You can also use the strategies you learned about in this theme to help you read your social studies textbook.

 Use Graphic Organizers

Graphic organizers can help you organize information from a text. When you read textbooks, you can write main ideas and details in a graphic organizer like the one shown here.

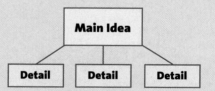

 Monitor Comprehension: Read Ahead

If you don't understand something you are reading, identify the part that is causing the problem. Read ahead in the text to see if information there will clear up the difficulty.

As you read the pages from a social studies textbook on pages 652–655, think about where and how you can use the strategies.

TIME LINES
Time lines show the period in history you are learning about.

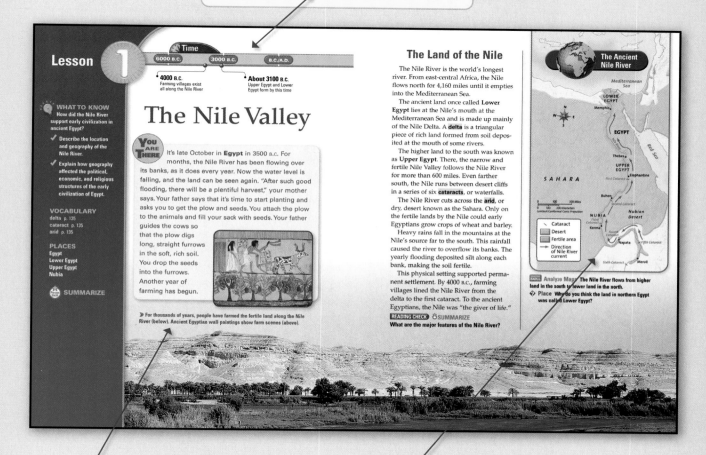

Lesson 1

Time

6000 B.C. 3000 B.C. B.C./A.D.

4000 B.C. Farming villages exist all along the Nile River

About 3100 B.C. Upper Egypt and Lower Egypt form by this time

The Nile Valley

WHAT TO KNOW
How did the Nile River support early civilization in ancient Egypt?

✓ Describe the location and geography of the Nile River.

✓ Explain how geography affected the political, economic, and religious structures of the early civilization of Egypt.

VOCABULARY
delta p. 135
cataract p. 135
arid p. 135

PLACES
Egypt
Lower Egypt
Upper Egypt
Nubia

SUMMARIZE

YOU ARE THERE
It's late October in **Egypt** in 3500 B.C. For months, the Nile River has been flowing over its banks, as it does every year. Now the water level is falling, and the land can be seen again. "After such good flooding, there will be a plentiful harvest," your mother says. Your father says that it's time to start planting and asks you to get the plow and seeds. You attach the plow to the animals and fill your sack with seeds. Your father guides the cows so that the plow digs long, straight furrows in the soft, rich soil. You drop the seeds into the furrows. Another year of farming has begun.

» For thousands of years, people have farmed the fertile land along the Nile River (below). Ancient Egyptian wall paintings show farm scenes (above).

The Land of the Nile

The Nile River is the world's longest river. From east-central Africa, the Nile flows north for 4,160 miles until it empties into the Mediterranean Sea.

The ancient land once called **Lower Egypt** lies at the Nile's mouth at the Mediterranean Sea and is made up mainly of the Nile Delta. A **delta** is a triangular piece of rich land formed from soil deposited at the mouth of some rivers.

The higher land to the south was known as **Upper Egypt**. There, the narrow and fertile Nile Valley follows the Nile River for more than 600 miles. Even farther south, the Nile runs between desert cliffs in a series of six **cataracts**, or waterfalls.

The Nile River cuts across the **arid**, or dry, desert known as the Sahara. Only on the fertile lands by the Nile could early Egyptians grow crops of wheat and barley.

Heavy rains fall in the mountains at the Nile's source far to the south. This rainfall caused the river to overflow its banks. The yearly flooding deposited silt along each bank, making the soil fertile.

This physical setting supported permanent settlement. By 4000 B.C., farming villages lined the Nile River from the delta to the first cataract. To the ancient Egyptians, the Nile was "the giver of life."

READING CHECK **SUMMARIZE**
What are the major features of the Nile River?

The Ancient Nile River

Analyze Maps The Nile River flows from higher land in the south to lower land in the north.
❖ **Place** Why do you think the land in northern Egypt was called Lower Egypt?

CAPTIONS
Captions explain photographs, illustrations, or diagrams, and support information in the main text.

MAPS
Maps show the region of the world that you are studying.

Apply the Strategies Read these pages about the Nile Valley from a social studies textbook. As you read, use a graphic organizer to write down the most important ideas in the text.

Lesson 1

Time

6000 B.C.   3000 B.C.   B.C./A.D.

4000 B.C.
Farming villages exist all along the Nile River

About 3100 B.C.
Upper Egypt and Lower Egypt form by this time

WHAT TO KNOW
How did the Nile River support early civilization in ancient Egypt?

✓ Describe the location and geography of the Nile River.

✓ Explain how geography affected the political, economic, and religious structures of the early civilization of Egypt.

VOCABULARY
delta p. 135
cataract p. 135
arid p. 135

PLACES
Egypt
Lower Egypt
Upper Egypt
Nubia

Focus Skill SUMMARIZE

The Nile Valley

YOU ARE THERE
It's late October in **Egypt** in 3500 B.C. For months, the Nile River has been flowing over its banks, as it does every year. Now the water level is falling, and the land can be seen again. "After such good flooding, there will be a plentiful harvest," your mother says. Your father says that it's time to start planting and asks you to get the plow and seeds. You attach the plow to the animals and fill your sack with seeds. Your father guides the cows so that the plow digs long, straight furrows in the soft, rich soil. You drop the seeds into the furrows. Another year of farming has begun.

❯ For thousands of years, people have farmed the fertile land along the Nile River (below). Ancient Egyptian wall paintings show farm scenes (above).

Write the main idea and details from the section titled The Land of the Nile. USE GRAPHIC ORGANIZERS

Detail	Detail	Detail
	Main Idea	

The Land of the Nile

The Nile River is the world's longest river. From east-central Africa, the Nile flows north for 4,160 miles until it empties into the Mediterranean Sea.

The ancient land once called **Lower Egypt** lies at the Nile's mouth at the Mediterranean Sea and is made up mainly of the Nile Delta. A **delta** is a triangular piece of rich land formed from soil deposited at the mouth of some rivers.

The higher land to the south was known as **Upper Egypt**. There, the narrow and fertile Nile Valley follows the Nile River for more than 600 miles. Even farther south, the Nile runs between desert cliffs in a series of six **cataracts**, or waterfalls.

The Nile River cuts across the **arid**, or dry, desert known as the Sahara. Only on the fertile lands by the Nile could early Egyptians grow crops of wheat and barley.

Heavy rains fall in the mountains at the Nile's source far to the south. This rainfall caused the river to overflow its banks. The yearly flooding deposited silt along each bank, making the soil fertile.

This physical setting supported permanent settlement. By 4000 B.C., farming villages lined the Nile River from the delta to the first cataract. To the ancient Egyptians, the Nile was "the giver of life."

READING CHECK ⚙ SUMMARIZE
What are the major features of the Nile River?

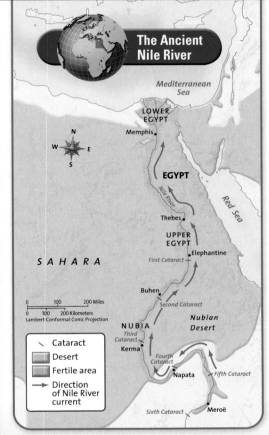

The Ancient Nile River

ANALYSIS SKILL **Analyze Maps** The Nile River flows from higher land in the south to lower land in the north.

❖ **Place** Why do you think the land in northern Egypt was called Lower Egypt?

If you don't understand why controlling the Nile River was so beneficial to ancient Egyptians, read ahead to the next section. MONITOR COMPREHENSION: READ AHEAD

Controlling the River

To the ancient Egyptians, the Nile was "the giver of life," but it also took life away. In some years, the rains were not heavy enough to make the Nile overflow its banks. The land baked in the sun, and the crops dried up. Without a harvest, many Egyptians starved. In other years, too much rain fell at the Nile's source, and the river flooded wildly, drowning people and destroying crops.

Over time, the Egyptians developed agricultural techniques that gave them some control of the Nile. At first, they built simple irrigation ditches to bring water to their fields. Later, they built dams and dikes to control the yearly flooding. They also learned to store water in ponds or pools for use during times when the river was low.

As the Egyptians learned to benefit more and more from the Nile, the populations of settlements along its shores increased. Irrigation became so important to the food supply in these growing communities that it was supervised by government officials. Eventually, the government began to have complete control over all farming and irrigation.

The authority of early Egyptian leaders was based on their ability to provide water for crops. Over time, they built more complex irrigation systems. In good years, large harvests produced surplus food so the rulers stored it to feed people in times of drought. They also used surplus food to feed the laborers on public works projects.

READING CHECK **SUMMARIZE**
How did ancient Egyptians control the flooding waters of the Nile?

GEOGRAPHY

Aswan High Dam

In 1970, Egypt completed the Aswan High Dam, one of the world's largest embankment dams. Embankment dams are constructed of earth and rock.

The Aswan High Dam holds back floodwater during rainy seasons and releases water during times of drought. It also generates huge amounts of electricity. Because of the dam, the Nile no longer overflows its banks to deposit rich soil. Farmers now depend on fertilizers to enrich their land. Also, the lack of new deposits of silt has caused land along the Nile to erode.

The lake formed by the dam would have covered ancient temples and settlements. So, in the 1960s, an international team of workers cut apart the temples and moved them to higher ground, where they were reassembled.

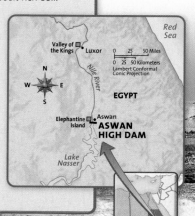

▶ Visitors to the Aswan High Dam can view Lake Nasser, the artificial lake created by the dam.

Toward Civilization

By 3100 B.C., the early Egyptians were developing an advanced civilization in towns along the Nile. They built temples as places to worship their gods and stone tombs to hold the bodies of rulers who had died. Early writing appears on these temples and tombs. The Egyptians made pottery on which they painted scenes from their lives. They mined copper for tool-making and gold for decorative art.

Farming along the Nile made all these advances possible. In the fertile soils of the Nile Delta and the Nile Valley, farmers grew surplus crops of wheat and barley. They used donkeys to carry grain to storehouses in towns, where scribes recorded it and rulers distributed it. The Egyptians ground the wheat into flour for making bread, the main part of their diet.

Having a surplus of grain allowed farmers in some towns to use the surplus grain for trade. The Sinai Peninsula was a crossroads for the early Egyptians and traders from southwestern Asia.

Trade also took place on the Nile River. The Nile served as a highway connecting Egyptian settlements. To use this "highway," the Egyptians became expert shipbuilders. At first, the Egyptians built their boats from bundles of reeds. Later, they made large sailing ships out of wood from what is now Lebanon.

Sails did more than just increase traveling speed. They also made it possible for ships to sail upstream against the river's current.

ANALYSIS SKILL **Analyze Time Lines** The early Egyptians made many advances in technology to improve their ways of farming.

❖ How are the events that are shown related to one another?

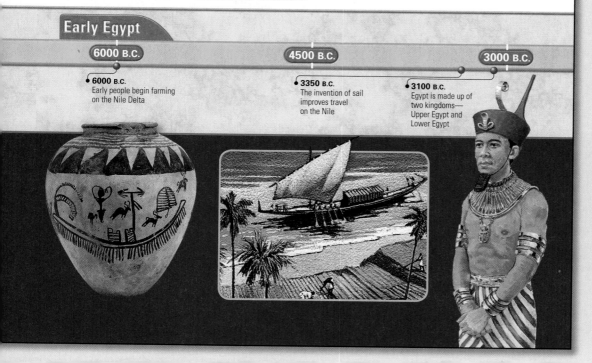

Early Egypt

6000 B.C.   4500 B.C.   3000 B.C.

6000 B.C.
Early people begin farming on the Nile Delta

3350 B.C.
The invention of sail improves travel on the Nile

3100 B.C.
Egypt is made up of two kingdoms— Upper Egypt and Lower Egypt

READING-WRITING
CONNECTION

656

Theme (6) The Outer Limits

▶ *Moonwalk*, Andy Warhol

657

CONTENTS

NEXT STOP NEPTUNE

EXPERIENCING THE SOLAR SYSTEM

BY
ALVIN JENK...

ILLUSTRATED B...
STEVE JENK...

WHAT GOES UP

DOESN'T ALWAYS COME DOWN
from NASA Website

Focus Skill

 ## Draw and Evaluate Conclusions

A **conclusion** is a statement based on evidence. Information in the text, what you already know about a topic, and what you know from experience are kinds of evidence you can use to support a conclusion. Drawing conclusions as you read can help you figure out information the author does not tell you.

Authors of nonfiction often include their own conclusions about a topic. You can evaluate an author's conclusions by asking these questions:

- Does the author give evidence to support the conclusion?
- Is the evidence reasonable?

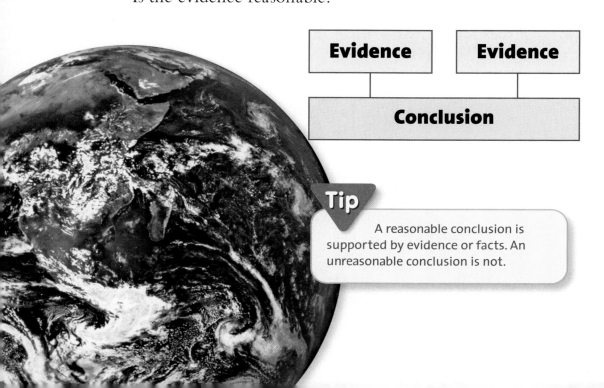

Evidence	Evidence

Conclusion

Tip

A reasonable conclusion is supported by evidence or facts. An unreasonable conclusion is not.

Read the paragraph below. The statement at the end of it is the author's conclusion. The graphic organizer shows evidence that supports the conclusion. The evidence includes information from the text and what the author already knows about the topic.

All objects on Earth have weight. An object's weight is determined by its mass and the force of Earth's gravitational pull. The farther an object travels from Earth, the less weight it has. An object that weighs 1 pound on Earth weighs just 4 ounces when it is 8,000 feet above Earth's surface. An object that continues to travel away from Earth will eventually weigh nothing.

Evidence
The farther an object travels from Earth, the less it weighs.

Evidence
I know that astronauts in space float in a weightless environment.

Conclusion
An object that continues to travel away from Earth will eventually weigh nothing.

Try This!

The moon's gravitational force is weaker than Earth's. Would an object weigh more or less on the moon than it does on Earth? Find evidence in the text to support your conclusion.

www.harcourtschool.com/storytown

Vocabulary

Build Robust Vocabulary

- mottled
- barren
- impact
- scale
- prominent
- chasm
- warped
- distinctive

Comet Crash!

In 2005, NASA flew a space probe directly into the path of the comet Tempel 1. The scientists at NASA knew they would learn a lot from the collision.

Before the mission, NASA scientists knew only what the outside of the comet looked like. They could see that its surface was **mottled**, a look resulting from many small craters. The surface seemed **barren**, but scientists hoped to find out what was inside. If the mission went smoothly, the **impact** of the crash would release debris from the comet's interior for scientists to analyze.

Close-up photographs of the comet show its features at the same **scale** as some close-up photographs of Earth.

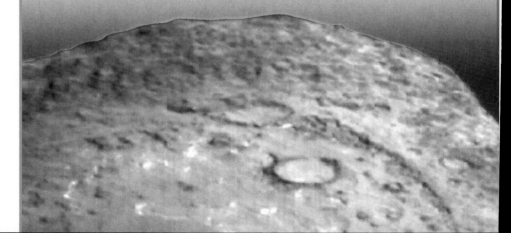

On July 4, the comet and the probe hit each other at a speed of 23,000 miles per hour. The intense collision released a **prominent** plume of debris. The scientists did not immediately see a gaping **chasm** where the probe hit the surface. Instead, a plume of dust **warped** their view. It rose from a surface similar to a snowbank.

This mission, which scientists called Deep Impact, revealed valuable information about what makes up comets.

Different colors show which parts of the dust plume were the brightest. Scientists studied these **distinctive** patterns of light and color.

 www.harcourtschool.com/storytown

Word Scribe

 This week your task is to use the Vocabulary Words in your writing. In your vocabulary journal, write sentences to show the meanings of the words. For example, you could write about something prominent outside your school building or in your neighborhood. Write sentences using as many of the Vocabulary Words as you can. Share your writing with your classmates.

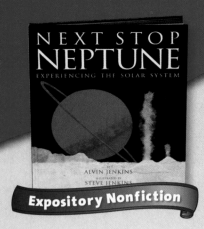

Expository Nonfiction

Genre Study

Expository nonfiction presents and explains facts about a topic. As you read, look for

- sections organized by headings.

- captions with important information.

K	W	L
What I Know	What I Want to Know	What I Learned

Comprehension Strategy

Summarize the main ideas and the most important details of each section in a sentence or two.

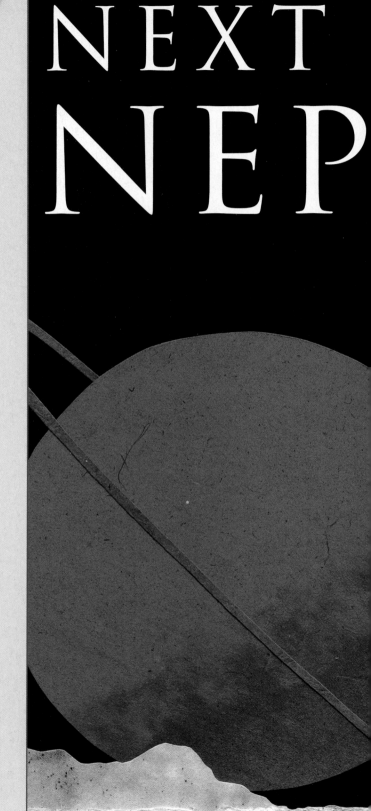

NEXT
NEP

STOP
TUNE

EXPERIENCING THE SOLAR SYSTEM

BY ALVIN JENKINS
ILLUSTRATED BY
STEVE JENKINS

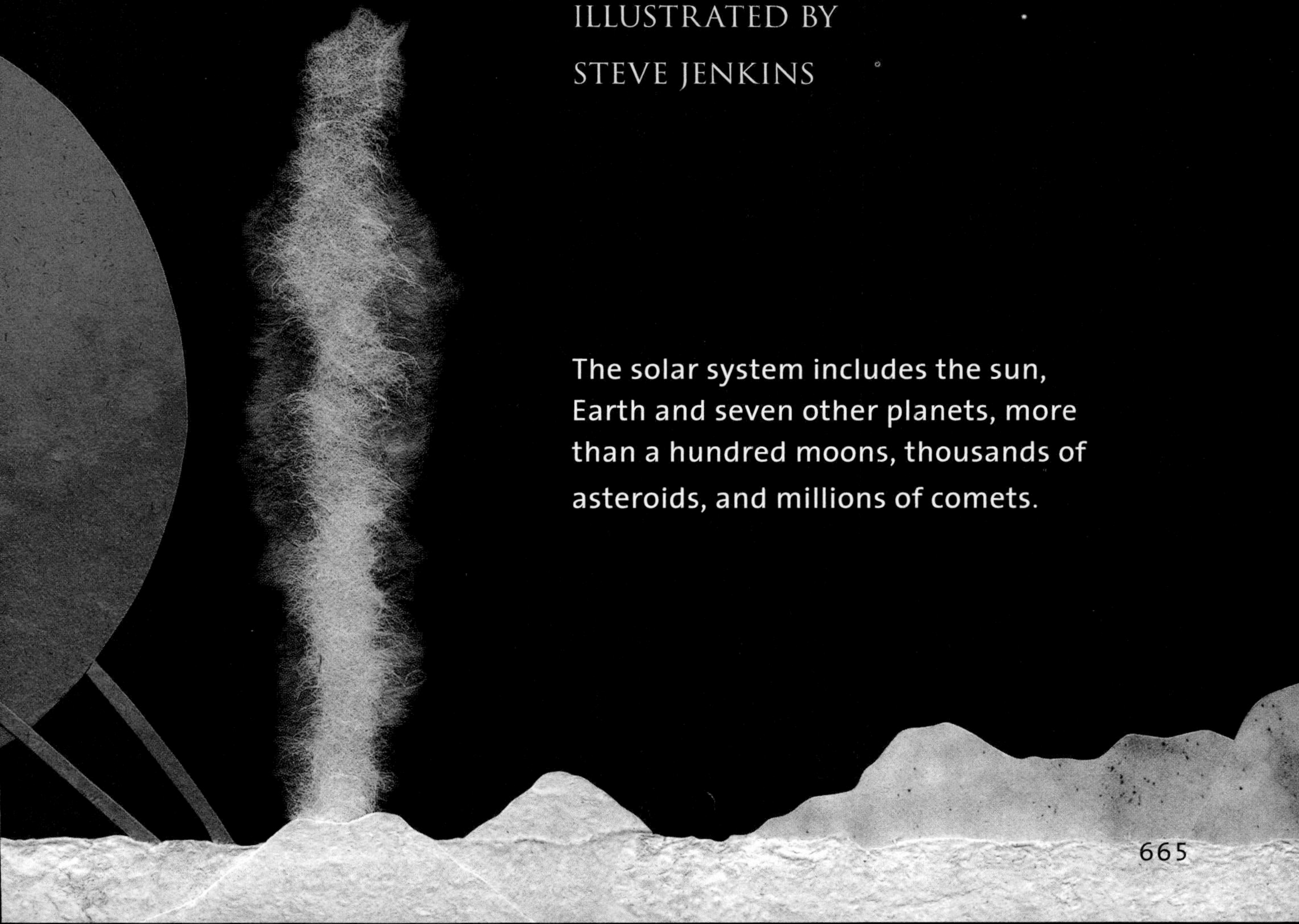

The solar system includes the sun,
Earth and seven other planets, more
than a hundred moons, thousands of
asteroids, and millions of comets.

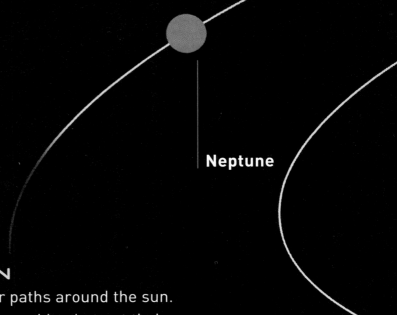

Neptune

CIRCLING THE SUN

The planets move in almost circular paths around the sun.
This illustration shows their paths, or orbits, but not their
actual spacing or size. Planets closer to the sun travel faster in
their orbits, while those farther away travel more slowly. The
outer planets also have much farther to go to circle the sun.
The time it takes to make a full orbit, or complete trip around
the sun, is called a year. A year on Mercury, the planet closest
to the sun, lasts about three Earth months. The planets also
rotate, or spin, as they travel around the sun. A day on a planet
is the length of time it takes the planet to rotate once.

VERY BIG, VERY EMPTY

It's hard to realize how big the solar system really is. And
because the planets are so small compared to the distances
between them, it's hard to draw an accurate picture of the solar
system. Imagine the sun shrunk to the size of a basketball. At
this scale, the solar system is almost a mile and a half across,
and all of its planets and moons together could be held in the
palm of your hand. The solar system is mostly empty space.

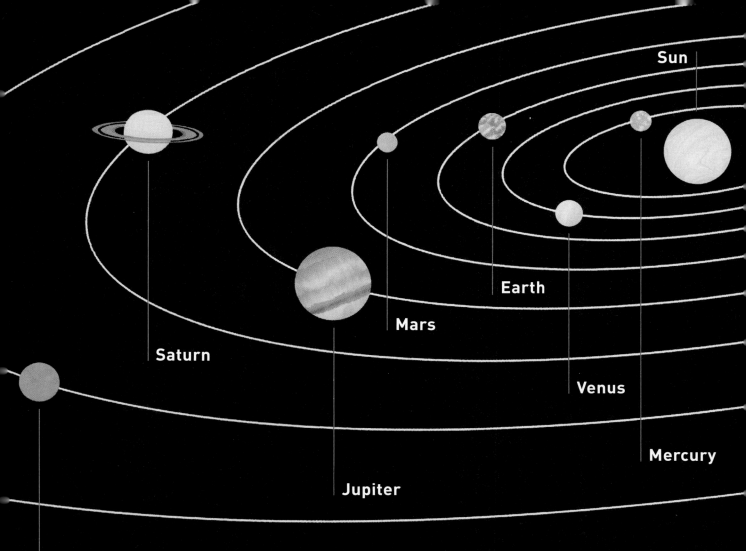

Sun

Saturn

Mars

Earth

Venus

Mercury

Jupiter

Uranus

SUN

The sun is very bright and very, very hot. It is so hot that every material we know of would become vapor—turn to gas—before it could reach the sun's surface. From a few million miles away, you can see the sun rotate slowly. As you get closer, the surface churns and roils, like water boiling in a pan. Sunspots—large dark areas a few thousand miles across—move past below you. A hundred thousand miles away, a spectacular column of brilliantly glowing gas shoots into space and falls back to the surface.

If you could dive into the sun, you'd find that there is nothing solid—it's made entirely of gas. Even so, the gas at the center of the sun is so dense that a drinking glass filled with it would weigh 75 pounds.

The sun is about 93 million miles from Earth. This distance is called an astronomical unit, or AU. If there were a road to the sun, it would take 177 years of nonstop driving at 60 miles per hour to get there.

The sun is rotating, but it is turning faster at its equator than at its poles. This is possible because the sun isn't solid—it's made of gas. It takes 25 days for the sun to make one revolution at the equator, 34 days near the poles.

The temperature at the sun's surface is 10,000 degrees Fahrenheit. At the center of the sun, the temperature reaches 28 million degrees.

MERCURY

You are standing on a bare, lifeless planet. The ground is hard and rocky and covered with gray dust. Everything is the same dull color. There are mountains in the distance and rugged terrain everywhere. There is no air, or atmosphere, on Mercury. On all sides are craters made by the impact of meteorites and asteroids. The sun, which has begun to set, looks much larger than it does on Earth. It is very hot. When the sun disappears from sight it will quickly become very dark and extremely cold—cold enough to freeze you almost instantly. But don't worry. It's only 88 days until sunrise!

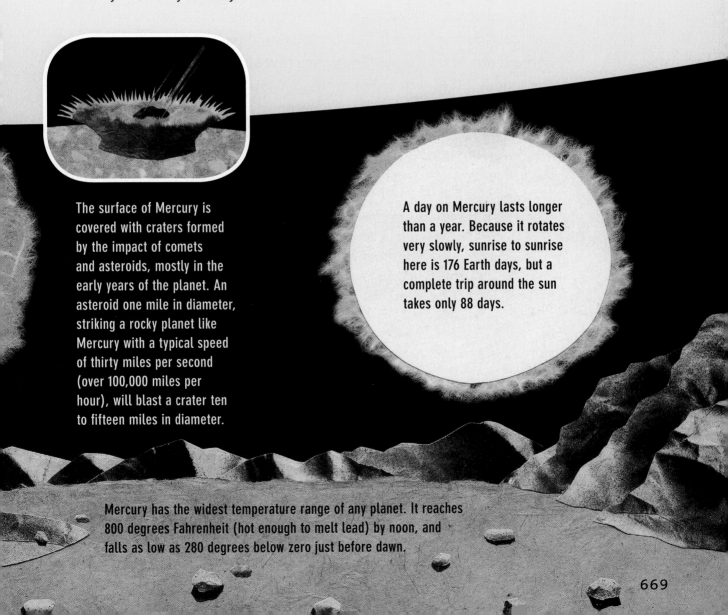

The surface of Mercury is covered with craters formed by the impact of comets and asteroids, mostly in the early years of the planet. An asteroid one mile in diameter, striking a rocky planet like Mercury with a typical speed of thirty miles per second (over 100,000 miles per hour), will blast a crater ten to fifteen miles in diameter.

A day on Mercury lasts longer than a year. Because it rotates very slowly, sunrise to sunrise here is 176 Earth days, but a complete trip around the sun takes only 88 days.

Mercury has the widest temperature range of any planet. It reaches 800 degrees Fahrenheit (hot enough to melt lead) by noon, and falls as low as 280 degrees below zero just before dawn.

VENUS

As you approach Venus, you see a smooth, unbroken white cloud surface covering the entire planet. These clouds are several miles thick and are not made of water, like the clouds on Earth, but of tiny droplets of sulfuric acid. Below them there is a thick layer of haze. Going lower, you finally emerge from the haze into clear air about 20 miles above the surface of Venus. When you finally stand on solid ground, you find yourself in an extremely hot environment. It's hotter here than inside a fireplace with a roaring fire. The ground is covered with slabs of rock, and barren mountains rise in the distance. Your vision seems blurred and warped by the thick atmosphere. It's very overcast during the day, and a soft yellowish light seems to come from everywhere. There are few shadows. Even at night the clouds glow with a dim light, and you can't see the sun or stars. If you lived on Venus, you might never know of Earth, or stars, or other planets, since they are always hidden by the clouds. The high temperatures and lack of water mean that no life, as we know it, can exist here.

Venus is closer to the sun than Earth, so it always appears near the sun in the sky and is visible only in the morning or evening.

It is often called the Morning Star or the Evening Star, but the second planet from the sun is not a star, because it doesn't shine with its own light, but by reflected sunlight. At its brightest, Venus is brighter than all objects in the sky except the sun and the moon. Because of its beauty, this planet was named after the Greek goddess of love. In the past, many people believed that Venus might be covered with a giant ocean.

EARTH

Approaching Earth from space, your first impression is of a beautiful blue ball hanging in a black sky. Getting closer, you see that the blue is mottled with white clouds and darker areas of land. Bright white regions of ice and snow can be seen at the top and bottom of Earth. Most of the planet is covered with water. The air is breathable, and in most places on the surface the temperature is comfortable—you are home. This is the only place in the solar system where you can survive without a sealed spacesuit. Anywhere else it is too hot or too cold, and either there is nothing to breathe or there's an atmosphere full of poisonous gases. Looking up from Earth on a dark, clear night you can see six other planets without a telescope: Mercury, Venus, Mars, Jupiter, Saturn, and Uranus.

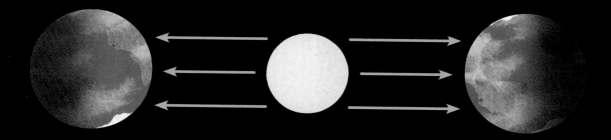

The seasons on Earth are caused by changes in the angle of the sunlight striking the surface. In the Southern Hemisphere the sun is directly overhead in the summer, strongly warming the surface. In the winter the sunlight falls at more of an angle, providing less warmth. The seasons are reversed in the Northern Hemisphere.

MARS

Here you are in a sandy, rocky landscape that looks a lot like a desert on Earth. The air is thin and very cold. The wind whips the fine red soil into fast-moving dust clouds. In the distance a mountain rises above a steep cliff. The land nearby is gently rolling, and has an orange color. The sky is yellowish because of the dust in the air. Here and there are craters of various sizes, and you can see what looks like a deep canyon. From Mars, the sun looks smaller and fainter than on Earth. As it sets, you can see two small moons in the sky above.

We have sent several probes to Mars. Some of them, like the Mars rover, have landed, explored the surface, and sent back pictures and information.

The temperatures on Mars are low. The daytime temperature on the Martian equator may be as high as a cold winter day on Earth, but for most of the planet it is much colder, averaging about 70 degrees below zero.

Valles Marineris is an enormous chasm, 2,500 miles long and up to 6 miles deep. It is one of the most prominent features on Mars.

JUPITER

As you get close to this giant planet, you see that what at first looked like the surface is really the tops of thick clouds. You feel very heavy. In fact, you weigh two and a half times more here than on Earth. Fast-moving, colorful bands of clouds race past below you, encircling the entire planet. As you pass through the layers of clouds—a white layer, an orange layer, then a blue layer—the light fades and the temperature rises. Occasionally a flash of lightning illuminates the clouds. The atmosphere becomes thicker and thicker until, gradually, it has become a liquid. This is not water, but an ocean of liquid hydrogen. If you could keep going, you'd finally arrive at the rocky core of Jupiter, where the pressure is enormous and it is hotter than the surface of the sun.

Jupiter is big. It's so big that more than 1,300 Earths would fit inside it. In fact, the fifth planet contains more than two-thirds of all the matter in the solar system outside of the sun. Seen from Earth, this giant planet is usually the fourth brightest object in the sky, after the sun, the moon, and Venus (sometimes Mars is brighter than Jupiter).

Winds of up to 400 miles per hour blow across Jupiter. These winds create the planet's distinctive bands of clouds. Among these bands is a huge red spot, nearly three times the size of Earth. The Great Red Spot is a fierce storm that has raged for more than 300 years.

673

SATURN

From far away, Saturn's ring system is awesomely beautiful. As you get closer the view becomes even more splendid. Saturn shines as a bright yellowish ball, surrounded by colorful, flat rings that extend far from its surface. Passing through the rings, you can see that they are made of millions of small rocks and chunks of ice that range from the size of a pea to the size of a house. There are so many pieces so close together that from a distance they seem to form a solid sheet. Below the rings, near the top of the clouds that cover Saturn, you enter a thick layer of haze that dims your view of the cloud layers below. Behind you the sun shines weakly. Here you weigh about the same as on Earth, but the temperature is very low, colder than anywhere on our planet. As you descend, you pass through several layers of clouds, and the temperature and pressure gradually increase. If you were to keep going, you'd reach a rocky core deep within the planet. Here on Saturn the days pass more quickly than on Earth—a full day is only about ten hours long, about the same as on Jupiter.

Saturn, the sixth planet, is twice as far away from the sun as Jupiter. It is the second largest planet, so large that almost 800 Earths would fit inside it. Saturn is a gas giant, and it is much less dense than Earth. In fact, Saturn would float on water.

Saturn has three major rings and many smaller ones. Though the rings are many thousands of miles across, they are only a few hundred feet thick. This is very thin—the same proportion as a sheet of paper that is 100 yards across. The rings may be the remains of a shattered moon or other large object.

674

URANUS

From space, Uranus looks like a blue-green sphere, with a few dim points of light—its moons—and a faint set of rings closely encircling the planet. As you pass near the rings, you can see that they are made of chunks of rock and ice like the rings of Saturn. Like the other gas giants, Uranus is completely covered by clouds and has no visible solid surface. From here, the sun looks like a very bright star. As you plunge into the clouds, you pass through a blue-tinted layer of haze, then into clouds that are banded like those on Jupiter. As on the other gas giants, the temperature and pressure rise as you descend. If you could keep going you would eventually reach a small rocky core, as in Jupiter and Saturn.

Uranus

Earth

Uranus, the seventh planet, is four times as large as Earth, and almost twenty times as far from the sun. You weigh about the same here as you do on Earth.

At the cloud tops the temperature is very low, about 330 degrees below zero. The sun provides less than 1 percent of the heat that it does at Earth's surface.

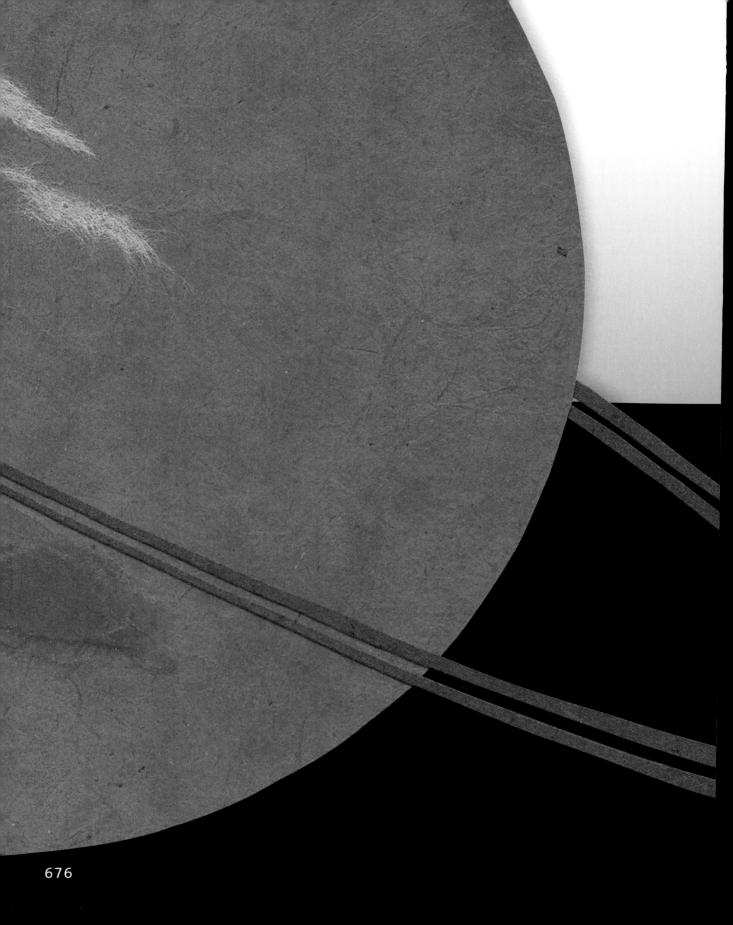

NEPTUNE

Neptune, the eighth planet, is almost a twin of Uranus. The clouds here look like those on Uranus, but have more of a bluish tint. Neptune is slightly smaller than Uranus, but it is denser. You weigh a little more here than on Earth. The sun looks like a bright star, and it provides little light or heat. At the cloud tops, the temperature is even colder than on Uranus. Neptune's moons look like faint points of light in the sky. Entering the atmosphere you are blown sideways by winds of up to 1,500 miles per hour, the fastest in the solar system. There is a deep layer of clouds on Neptune, and once again the temperature and pressure increase as you approach the planet's small, solid core.

At the cloud tops the temperature here is about 350 degrees below zero.

It would take 5,100 years to reach Neptune from Earth if you were traveling at 60 miles per hour.

A full cycle of day and night on Neptune lasts about 17 hours.

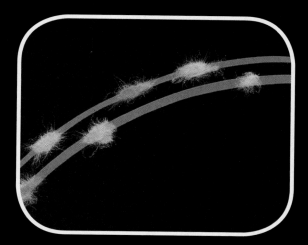

There are faint rings around Neptune. Here and there the rings are brighter, where more material has accumulated

THINK CRITICALLY

① If you were standing on Mercury, how would the sun look compared with the way it looks from Earth? MAKE COMPARISONS

② The author says that it's hard to imagine the size of the solar system. Do you agree with his conclusion? Use text evidence and what you already know to explain your answer. DRAW AND EVALUATE CONCLUSIONS

③ Do you think the author would support further space exploration? Why or why not? AUTHOR'S PERSPECTIVE

④ If you could safely and quickly travel to any planet, which one would you visit? Why? EXPRESS PERSONAL OPINIONS

⑤ **WRITE** Write a note of caution to someone planning to visit Neptune. In your note, describe what the visitor can expect on the planet, and give suggestions for what to pack. SHORT RESPONSE

ABOUT THE AUTHOR
ALVIN JENKINS

Next Stop Neptune is the first book Alvin Jenkins worked on with his son, Steve. However, the pair worked together on numerous science projects when Steve was young. That was about the time when the Space Age began and artificial satellites first orbited Earth. Today Alvin Jenkins is a retired professor of physics and astronomy. He lives in South Carolina with his wife.

ABOUT THE ILLUSTRATOR
STEVE JENKINS

When Steve Jenkins was growing up, he loved to draw insects and make animal scrapbooks. He planned to be a scientist, but he was also interested in drawing and painting. He says that working on science books for children allows him to enjoy the best of both worlds. He is known for his unique collage illustrations.

GO online www.harcourtschool.com/storytown

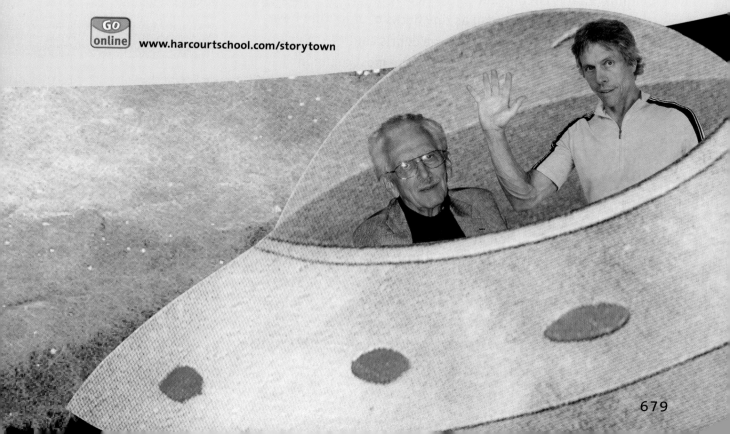

WHAT GOES UP
DOESN'T ALWAYS COME DOWN
from NASA Website

Website

WHAT GOES UP

PEOPLE HAVE BEEN LAUNCHING OBJECTS INTO SPACE FOR ABOUT 50 YEARS. THAT ADDS UP TO A LOT OF STUFF! MOST OF IT HAS FALLEN BACK TO EARTH. THESE OBJECTS HAVE EITHER LANDED OR BURNED UP IN THE ATMOSPHERE. A FEW OBJECTS HAVE BEEN LAUNCHED BEYOND EARTH'S GRAVITY. THESE OBJECTS TRAVEL TO OTHER WORLDS OR EXPLORE SPACE. BUT MANY OF THE OBJECTS THAT HAVE BEEN SENT INTO SPACE ARE STILL IN ORBIT. THEY ARE ENDLESSLY CIRCLING EARTH.

This "junk" that is circling Earth is called orbital debris. On one extreme, debris can be as small as tiny flecks of paint that have come off spacecraft. On the other, large debris could be <u>satellites</u> that are no longer working. The most common source of orbital debris larger than 1 centimeter (cm), or 0.39 inch, is the explosion of objects orbiting Earth. These are often rocket upper stages. These can contain fuel or high pressure fluids.

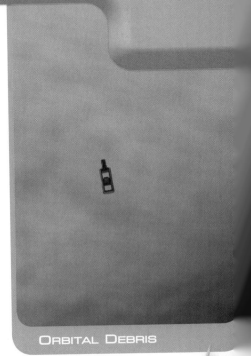

ORBITAL DEBRIS

To keep astronauts safe, scientists keep track of all the debris in orbit. They sort pieces by their size. The diameter of the piece is how scientists classify it. There are about 11,000 known objects that are bigger than 10 centimeters. Scientists believe that there are more than 100,000 pieces of orbital debris between 1 cm and 10 cm. And there are tens of millions of pieces smaller than 1 cm! All pieces of debris larger than 10 cm are carefully tracked. That information is used to estimate the number of small pieces of debris. Even though this system cannot detect every piece, it can give scientists an idea of the debris that is out there.

DOESN'T ALWAYS COME DOWN

FROM NASA WEBSITE

THE SPACE SHUTTLE

In low Earth orbit, most "space junk" is moving super fast. It can reach speeds of 4.3 to 5 miles per second. And if a spacecraft is moving toward the debris, this speed can seem even faster! The average impact speed of a piece of orbital debris running into another object is 22,370 miles per hour (mph). Since it is moving so quickly, a tiny piece of orbital debris can cause a lot of damage. In fact, an 8.8-pound piece of debris could create the same impact as a car moving at 60 mph!

Since we keep track of larger pieces of debris, crewed spacecraft are able to dodge them. When an object is expected to come within a few miles of the Space Shuttle, it changes its path to avoid the object. The International Space Station can also move away from debris in its path. Plus, the Station is also the most heavily shielded spacecraft ever. It can survive impact with smaller pieces of debris.

Since the smallest pieces of debris cannot be tracked, collisions with them are bound to happen. The Space Shuttle often returns to Earth with tiny impact craters. Impacts can even create small cracks in the front windows! Even though the spacecraft run into this debris quite often, the debris rarely runs into other debris. In fact, we know of only one time when this actually happened!

THE INTERNATIONAL SPACE STATION

Connections

Comparing Texts

1. In "Next Stop Neptune," you learned facts about the solar system. How might you use those facts the next time you are outside on a starry night?

2. What information in "Next Stop Neptune" and "What Goes Up Doesn't Always Come Down" might be useful to someone who is training to become an astronaut?

3. Before you read "Next Stop Neptune," what did you already know about the solar system? How did reading the selection change your ideas about the solar system?

Vocabulary Review

Word Sort

Sort the Vocabulary Words into categories. After you finish, form a small group and compare the categories that you chose to use. Explain why you categorized each word as you did. Then choose two Vocabulary Words from each category. Write a sentence for each word. Share your sentences with the group.

Noun	Adjective	Verb	Multiple-Meaning Word

mottled

barren

impact

scale

prominent

chasm

warped

distinctive

Fluency Practice

Repeated Reading

You have learned that your reading rate is the speed at which you can read a passage correctly and still understand what you read. With practice, you can improve your reading rate. Work with a partner. Reread aloud the section about Jupiter on page 673 while your partner times your reading with a stopwatch. Then switch roles. Repeat this process three times. Note how much you increased your reading rate.

Writing

Write a Descriptive Poem

Choose one of the planets you learned about in "Next Stop Neptune." List the planet's characteristics and its unique physical features. Then write a poem about the planet. Your poem may be rhymed or unrhymed.

Mars
1. rocky landscape
2. cold, thin air
3. dust clouds of red soil

My Writing Checklist

Writing Trait ➤ Organization

✔ I made a list of the planet's characteristics and its unique physical features.

✔ I selected the best information that describes the planet.

✔ I organized my ideas in a way that makes sense.

Analyze Writer's Craft: Expository Nonfiction

Expository nonfiction may give facts about a topic, or it may state the author's own ideas and **opinions**. Writers use clear **examples** and vivid **details** to support their ideas.

When you write expository nonfiction, you can use the works of authors such as Alvin Jenkins as writing models. Read the passage below from "Next Stop Neptune." Notice how he uses examples and details to compare the surface of Mars to a desert.

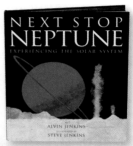

NEXT STOP
NEPTUNE
EXPERIENCING THE SOLAR SYSTEM

ALVIN JENKINS
STEVE JENKINS

Writing Trait

ORGANIZATION The author begins the paragraph with a **topic sentence** that states his idea: the surface of Mars looks like a desert. Then he supports his idea with **examples**, such as that the wind whips the soil into dust clouds.

Writing Trait

WORD CHOICE The author uses descriptive adjectives, such as *sandy, rocky, fine,* and *red.* **Sensory details** help the reader imagine the scene clearly.

Here you are in a sandy, rocky landscape that looks a lot like a desert on Earth. The air is thin and very cold. The wind whips the fine red soil into fast-moving dust clouds. In the distance a mountain rises above a steep cliff. The land nearby is gently rolling, and has an orange color. The sky is yellowish because of the dust in the air. Here and there are craters of various sizes, and you can see what looks like a deep canyon. From Mars, the sun looks smaller and fainter than on Earth. As it sets, you can see two small moons in the sky above.

Persuasive Composition

In a **persuasive** composition, a writer tries to persuade readers to agree with an **opinion**. The writer may want readers to believe something or to do something about an issue or problem. Writers give powerful **reasons** and use strong **emotional language** to persuade readers to agree. This persuasive composition was written by a student named Richard. Notice how he **organizes** his reasons, examples, and details.

Student Writing Model

Support Our Space Program!
by Richard S.

Without the space programs of the National Aeronautics and Space Administration (NASA), thousands of human lives might be lost every day. Without NASA, we would not have many of the fantastic inventions that make our lives easier every day. Some people want to let our space program die. I think we should all help it live!

Writing Trait

ORGANIZATION In the introduction, Richard states an **opinion**: everyone should support the space program. He gives two supporting **reasons**: that we all benefit from space technology and that space technology saves lives.

Writing Trait

ORGANIZATION
Richard restates his **opinion** and gives a **reason** in the opening sentence of this paragraph. Then he provides convincing **examples**.

Writing Trait

WORD CHOICE
Richard uses powerful **positive words,** such as *fantastic* and *amazing*, to describe NASA's benefits. He uses dramatic ideas, such as saving lives, to **appeal to readers' emotions.**

The **conclusion** tells what people can do to support the space program. Richard briefly **restates his arguments** and makes an emotional **call to action.**

We should support NASA because it created many of the amazing gadgets we take for granted every day. Small, personal computers were invented because NASA needed a computer small enough to fit into a space capsule. Moon Boot material made modern athletic shoes possible. Other NASA-inspired products include scratch-resistant lenses and compact discs. I can't wait to see what we'll get out of NASA's projects in the future!

We need NASA because it creates technology that saves lives every day. NASA developed the materials in bicycle helmets and the sensors in home smoke detectors. It made fire-resistant clothing and laser surgery possible. It also pioneered the technology that lets meteorologists predict hurricanes. It would be hard to estimate the number of lives saved by those inventions alone.

What can people do to help keep space exploration alive? We can write to Congress and actively support NASA funding. We can encourage private companies to fund space programs. We can even become astronauts! We must save our space program. The future of technology—and even our lives—may depend on it!

Now look at how Richard prepared to write his persuasive composition.

Brainstorming

First, Richard made an idea web. Then, he chose the topic about which he has the strongest opinions: the space program. Next, he listed his opinions about the topic. He chose *everyone should support the space program* as the focus for his composition because he had strong reasons and examples to support this opinion.

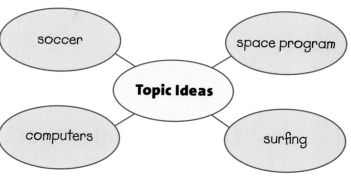

My Opinions About the Space Program
I think astronauts should travel to Mars.
I think we need another space station.
I think everyone should support the
         space program.

Outline

Richard created an outline to organize the parts of his composition. He used the outline to place his reasons and examples in order.

Title: Support Our Space Program!

I.   Introduction
     A. Reasons
     B. Opinion

II. Everyday gadgets
     A. Computers, athletic shoes
     B. Lenses, compact discs

III. Life-saving technology
     A. Helmets, smoke detectors
     B. Fire-resistant clothing
     C. Hurricane prediction

IV. Conclusion
     A. Ways to take action
     B. Call to action

CONTENTS

Genre: Expository Nonfiction

INCREDIBLE DEEP-SEA ADVENTURES

The Incredible Quest to Find the Titanic

MATSEN

HIGH-TECH TREASURE HUNT

by Kelly Bourne

Genre: Magazine Article

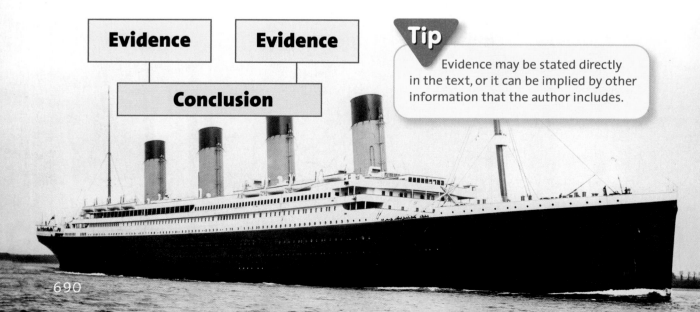

Focus Skill

Draw and Evaluate Conclusions

You have learned that when you read, you can **draw conclusions** to figure out what the author has not told you directly. Conclusions may be based on different kinds of evidence:

- facts or information in the text
- your prior knowledge about the topic
- your own experiences

Authors base their conclusions on the same kinds of evidence. To evaluate an author's conclusions, determine whether the facts or information in the text support the conclusion. Then think about anything you know or have experienced that might support the author's conclusion.

Evidence	Evidence

Conclusion

Tip

Evidence may be stated directly in the text, or it can be implied by other information that the author includes.

Read the following letter. Think about the writer's conclusion at the end of the letter. The graphic organizer below shows how text information and your own knowledge can be used to evaluate the writer's conclusion.

Dear Aunt Mary,

Tomorrow, the *Titanic* departs for New York City. The ship is truly a wonder. The White Star Line shipping company built it. The brochure says that the ship is practically unsinkable! Even if four of its watertight compartments flood, it will stay afloat. Everyone should feel safe knowing that the ship cannot sink!

Evidence	**Evidence**
The brochure called the *Titanic* "practically" unsinkable.	I already know that the *Titanic* sank on its first voyage.

Conclusion
The writer concluded that the *Titanic* would stay afloat. The conclusion was invalid because the ship sank.

Try This!

Reread the letter above. What conclusions could you draw about the writer? What evidence supports your conclusions?

 www.harcourtschool.com/storytown

Build Robust Vocabulary

Dive Guide

lavish

dreaded

ascent

doomed

murky

remains

Welcome to Sunset Island! During your stay at one of our **lavish** hotels, you may be tempted to explore the coral reef. Here are some tips for scuba divers and snorkelers.

Put Safety First Always listen to your instructor's directions. The most **dreaded** sight for a diver is a shark. If you see one, do not panic. Wait until the shark swims away. Then calmly make your **ascent** to the surface.

Many divers enjoy photographing the beautiful coral formations.

Explore a Shipwreck
With a scuba guide, divers can visit a Spanish shipwreck. An underwater exhibit tells them how the ship was **doomed** when it hit a reef more than 200 years ago.

Photograph the Reef The water is rarely **murky** in the waters around Sunset Island. The coral reefs on the island's west side are a photographer's dream. Butterfly fish, clown fish, and living coral provide an impressive display of color. Divers can get spectacular close-up shots that will amaze their friends!

Local legend says that gold is still buried deep within the ship's **remains**.

 www.harcourtschool.com/storytown

Word Detective

Your mission this week is to look for the Vocabulary Words outside of your classroom. You might hear the words on television or read them in a magazine or newspaper. When you see or hear a Vocabulary Word, write in your vocabulary journal how it was used. Be sure to tell where you found the word.

Expository Nonfiction

Genre Study

Expository nonfiction tells about real people, things, places, or events. As you read, look for

- information about a historical event and the people involved.

- details that support main ideas.

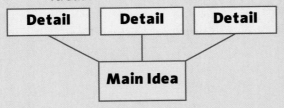

Comprehension Strategy

Summarize the main ideas and the most important details in one or two sentences.

THE INCREDIBLE

THE SINKING OF *TITANIC* IN 1912 WAS SURROUNDED
BY MANY MYSTERIES, UNTIL SEVENTY-THREE YEARS
LATER WHEN A GROUP OF RESEARCHERS FIRST
LOCATED THE SHIP'S WRECKAGE. WHAT WAS *TITANIC*
LIKE? WHAT DID THE RESEARCHERS DISCOVER ABOUT
THE BIGGEST SHIP OF ITS TIME?

QUEST TO FIND THE

TITANIC

BY BRAD MATSEN

Luxury Liner

Titanic was huge, but it was also the most modern, comfortable ship ever. It could carry 3,533 passengers and crew. (*Titanic* was not full when it sailed on its first voyage.) The passengers traveled in three classes. First class had grand dining rooms, luxurious cabins, and a swimming pool. The ship was as splendid and comfortable as an elegant hotel. *Titanic* had three elevators to take passengers between decks. It also had a grand staircase. Its first-class cabins and passageways had thick carpets. *Titanic* even carried an orchestra.

On its first voyage, many rich and famous people traveled in first-class cabins aboard *Titanic*. Most of the upper decks of the ship were reserved for first-class passengers only. Second-class passengers had lavish but smaller rooms. Third-class passengers paid the least for their tickets. Their cabins and dining rooms were smaller, and they had less space on deck for walking around. But they were still aboard the greatest ship ever built.

PASSENGERS STROLL ALONG THE UPPER DECK OF *TITANIC*.

Titanic Sails for New York

April 10, 1912, was a gusty spring day in Southampton, England. *Titanic* was ready to sail. Thousands of people lined the waterfront. At noon, Captain Edward Smith gave the order to cast off the lines that held the ship to the dock.

Titanic's gangway doors closed and its mighty engines came to life. Tiny tugboats guided the huge black-and-white ship into the Itchen River. Horns blew. The crowds cheered. The greatest ocean liner of its time set sail on its first voyage.

Disaster almost struck before *Titanic* even left the river. It sailed slowly past another ocean liner named *New York*, which was tied to the dock. The pull of *Titanic*'s propellers in the water sucked the *New York* from the dock. The *New York*'s mooring lines broke! The tugboats saved the two ships from a collision.

It was a strange coincidence that *Titanic* almost hit the *New York*. *Titanic* was going to New York City on its voyage! First, though, it stopped in Cherbourg, France, to pick up more passengers. Then it stopped in Queenstown, Ireland, to pick up its final passengers. Finally, *Titanic* headed toward the Atlantic Ocean and its destiny.

On the first day, Captain Smith did not run *Titanic* at full speed. On the second day, though, the weather was good. Everything on the great ship was working perfectly. Smith increased *Titanic*'s speed.

THE MIGHTY *TITANIC* SAILED AMONG A FIELD OF ICEBERGS.

The Iceberg's Journey

Icebergs are huge chunks of ice and rock. They float like ice cubes in a glass of water. Some icebergs are as large as ships. Others are larger than the state of Delaware. Only 10 percent of an iceberg sticks up above the water. The rest of it is hidden beneath the water's surface.

Icebergs break off from enormous, slow-moving rivers of ice called glaciers. A glacier is made of snow that hardens into solid ice. The force of gravity pulls the ice downward from higher land. Glaciers flow from mountains to the sea, where pieces break off to form icebergs. The icebergs are driven by wind and water currents out into the open sea.

About two years before *Titanic* sailed for New York, an iceberg broke off a glacier in Greenland. Greenland is a big island that is almost completely covered with ice. It is on the northwest edge of the Atlantic Ocean.

The iceberg fell off the front of the glacier with a loud crack. The whole iceberg may have been 1,000 feet (300 meters) high. The part of the iceberg that was out of the water was probably about 100 feet (30 meters) high. The whole thing weighed over 300,000 tons. By the night of April 14, the iceberg was right in the path of *Titanic*.

Titanic Hits the Iceberg

At 11:40 P.M. on April 14, *Titanic*'s passengers were finished with dinner. It was cold outside, so only a few were strolling on deck. Many had already gone to their cabins to sleep. Everyone felt very safe. The newspapers had proclaimed *Titanic* to be unsinkable, and everyone believed them. The great ship steamed through the darkness with starlit skies overhead. It was going 25 miles (40 kilometers) per hour.

The officers in charge of *Titanic* that night had been warned about icebergs by other ships. Captain Smith posted two lookouts near the front of the ship. The lookouts were Fred Fleet and Reginald Lee, who had come on duty at 10:00 P.M. They peered into the darkness and looked for signs of icebergs.

The officers and crew on duty steered *Titanic* and communicated with the engine room from a part of the ship called the bridge. Captain Smith was in his cabin taking a short rest. First Officer William Murdoch was in charge of the ship. He was responsible for telling the sailor at the wheel what course to steer.

Suddenly Fred Fleet cried out, "Iceberg ahead! Iceberg ahead!" He rang the warning bell three times. Then he picked up the telephone to warn the bridge. "Iceberg, right ahead," he said to Officer Murdoch.

"Hard to starboard!" called Murdoch. The sailor threw the wheel to the right. "Stop. Full speed astern!" Murdoch cried out. Another sailor sent that order down to the engine room.

Titanic continued to speed toward the iceberg. Then gradually the ship began to turn to port. It shuddered a little as the engines went into reverse. For a moment it looked like *Titanic* would miss the iceberg.

Then disaster struck. The huge submerged portion of the iceberg collided with *Titanic*'s underwater steel plates. The iceberg slid along the starboard side of the ship. It made a dull sound as it scraped past. Ice fell onto *Titanic*'s forward deck. The iceberg passed behind the ship and into the night.

Then there was silence.

Titanic Is Doomed

Captain Smith rushed to the bridge and asked what had happened. Murdoch told him they had just hit an iceberg. Smith ordered another of his officers to find out if the iceberg had damaged the ship.

Titanic was divided into sixteen separate compartments. They were joined by doors that could be closed to seal off damaged compartments. If part of the ship had a hole in it, the other sections would stay dry if the watertight doors were closed. *Titanic* would then stay afloat.

The news was bad. All four of *Titanic*'s forward compartments were flooding with water. Captain Smith talked to the ship's chief engineer, Joseph Bell. It was determined that the ship could stay afloat for only one or two hours. The passengers must be put into lifeboats immediately. *Titanic* was doomed.

Captain Smith knew one more bit of very bad news. There were only enough lifeboats for less than half the people aboard.

CANADA

UNITED STATES

TITANIC WRECK

ATLANTIC OCEAN

PACIFIC OCEAN

THE WRECK OF THE *TITANIC* LAY 400 MILES SOUTHEAST OF NEWFOUNDLAND AND 1,300 MILES EAST OF NEW YORK.

Titanic Goes to Its Grave

Captain Smith ordered the radio operator to send the distress signal CQD. That was the code for a ship in danger of sinking. (Today *SOS* is used instead.) If ships nearby heard that code on their radios they must hurry to help the doomed ship. CQD was the most dreaded code a sailor could send or hear. The radio operator sent out CQD. *Titanic* was sinking.

Then Captain Smith gave the order for women and children to get in the lifeboats first. During the first hour after he gave the order, many passengers thought there was no real danger. Many were not willing to get into the lifeboats. Some boats were lowered to the ocean partly full. Other lifeboats filled up.

When all the lifeboats were gone, panic swept through *Titanic*. Hundreds of people jumped into the ocean wearing life jackets. Only six of them would survive in the icy water. Many others stayed with the ship. They were swept into the sea or dragged to the bottom with *Titanic*.

By 2:20 A.M., *Titanic* was gone. The bow of the ship sank first. The stern stayed afloat for a few more minutes. Then it went down, too.

The 712 survivors were picked up a few hours later by another ocean liner, the SS *Carpathia*. Hundreds of others who had gone into the water in life jackets or clinging to wreckage died before the rescue ship arrived.

Exploring *Titanic*

Titanic rested alone in its watery grave for over seven decades. No human eyes had seen the lost ship until Robert Ballard and Jean-Louis Michel located it using remote control video cameras in 1985. *Titanic* lay in two big pieces on the bottom not far from where it sank. The wreck was 1,300 miles (2,093 kilometers) east of New York and 400 miles (644 kilometers) southeast of the island of Newfoundland. *Titanic*'s grave was 12,400 feet (3,780 meters) beneath the surface of the sea.

In 1986, Ballard returned to explore the *Titanic*. Jean-Louis Michel did not come on this second expedition. Michel would lead other expeditions in following years. On July 12, Ballard arrived over *Titanic*'s grave on his research ship *Atlantis II*.

This time, Ballard would dive to *Titanic* in *Alvin*. *Alvin* is a little submarine that can carry three people. It has spotlights and windows for exploring the deep sea. With *Alvin*, Ballard hoped he would actually see *Titanic* with his own eyes. Exploring *Titanic* had been Robert Ballard's dream since he was very young. Thanks to *Alvin*, his dream could come true. And he hoped to solve the mystery of how *Titanic* sank.

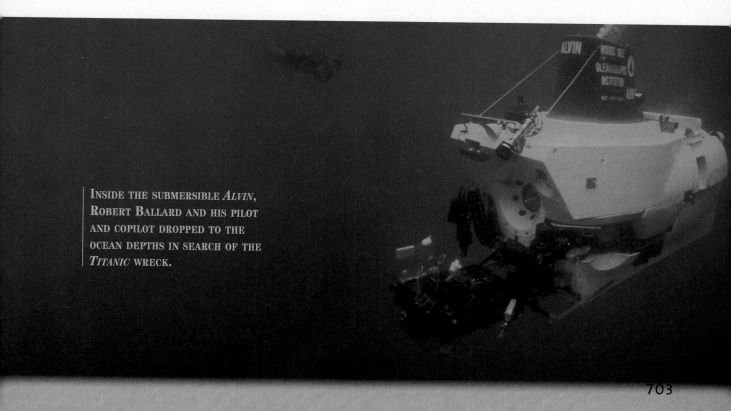

INSIDE THE SUBMERSIBLE *ALVIN*, ROBERT BALLARD AND HIS PILOT AND COPILOT DROPPED TO THE OCEAN DEPTHS IN SEARCH OF THE *TITANIC* WRECK.

Alvin and *Jason Jr.*

Alvin is made of titanium, a metal much stronger than steel. *Alvin* can move forward and backward and dive to a depth of 14,764 feet (4,500 meters). That's almost three miles below the surface of the ocean. *Alvin* could reach the *Titanic*.

Alvin carried a small robot submarine, *Jason Jr.* This was a brand-new kind of remotely operated vehicle (ROV). *Jason Jr.* was connected to *Alvin* with a cable called a tether. The little robot could send pictures from its television cameras through the tether to *Alvin*. Ballard would use *Jason Jr.* to explore the inside of *Titanic*.

A pilot inside *Alvin* controlled *Jason Jr.* He used a joystick to move the robot. He could turn the lights and cameras on and off. Everyone was excited about using the small robot. They wanted to visit inside *Titanic*'s cabins, dining rooms, and other places on the lost ship. No one had ever done anything like this before.

Diving to *Titanic*

Robert Ballard and his crew had prepared for almost a year for exploring *Titanic*. Finally the day of the first dive arrived. The crew rolled *Alvin* from its hangar on the deck of *Atlantis II*. Robert Ballard, pilot Ralph Hollis, and copilot Dudley Foster prepared for the first descent. They took off their shoes and climbed into the tiny cabin.

Hollis closed *Alvin*'s hatch. Ballard turned on the oxygen tank. Outside, a winch on *Atlantis II*'s deck lifted *Alvin* up and over the stern. The winch slowly lowered *Alvin* into the water. Three divers swam around the submersible and made final checks for the dive. At 8:35 A.M., the controller on *Atlantis II* told *Alvin* it was cleared to dive. Next stop, *Titanic*.

The men huddled in the cramped cabin. Hollis threw a switch to flood *Alvin*'s tanks with water and begin the descent. As the sub slipped beneath the surface, Ballard watched a jellyfish drift past the window. Then he saw a shark swim by. The shark was curious about the strange machine entering its domain, but it left the contraption alone.

The first dive was a test. Ballard wanted to see if he could safely get close to *Titanic*. *Jason Jr.* would stay in its garage aboard *Alvin*. The little robot would be used to explore *Titanic* beginning with the second dive.

Diving into the deep ocean is always dangerous. The water put enormous pressure on *Alvin*'s hull. Outside, the water was nearly freezing, and the cabin grew colder as they descended. The men put on more clothes to keep warm. The dive to *Titanic* would take two and a half hours.

On the way to the bottom, the men relaxed and looked out the windows. They played music on the stereo system. Fifteen minutes after they began the descent, the sea was totally black. No sunlight reaches the deep ocean. The light inside *Alvin* was soft red. The dials and gauges glowed. Down, down they went.

THE BOW OF THE *TITANIC* WAS COVERED IN RUSTY COLUMNS, WHICH BALLARD NAMED RUSTICLES.

First Sight of *Titanic*

The controller on *Atlantis II* directed *Alvin* to *Titanic*. Ballard switched on powerful searchlights. They crawled along the bottom but saw nothing. The men strained their eyes at the viewing ports. Still there was nothing. An alarm sounded. Some of *Alvin*'s batteries were not working very well. Hollis said they would have to surface soon.

Just then the seafloor began to look strange. It sloped upward at a steep angle. Ballard's heartbeat quickened. "Come right," he said to Hollis. "I think I see a wall of black just on the other side of that mud mound."

Suddenly, a dark steel wall towered over tiny *Alvin*. Ballard, Hollis, and Foster gasped. There it was. *Titanic*. Through the murky water, the ship looked enormous. For the first time in seventy-four years, human eyes could see the most famous ship in history.

The battery alarm continued to sound. Hollis told Ballard they must return to the surface immediately. They were in no danger, but he did not want to risk harming the sub. After just two minutes with *Titanic*, they began their ascent. Ballard was disappointed. He had not been able to explore at all. But he knew he would dive again the next day.

A Closer Look at *Titanic*

The next day, Ballard and Hollis prepared to descend again to *Titanic*. The third crew member was Martin Bowen, who was an expert at piloting *Jason Jr.* Again, they made the long dive to the bottom.

This time, *Alvin* performed perfectly. Ballard's second view of *Titanic* was breathtaking. As they glided along the bottom, the sharp edge of the ship's high bow loomed ahead. Ballard saw the two huge anchors still in their places. He saw that the bow had driven deeply into the mud when it made its deadly dive.

Hollis guided *Alvin* along the side of the ship. Everything was covered with rust. Some of the rust formed long columns like icicles. Ballard named these formations rusticles. Crabs and sea worms were living all over the wreck. All the wood on the ship had been eaten away. The explorers could clearly see rails, one of the ship's cranes, and the remains of the bridge. The wooden wheelhouse had completely vanished.

They rose above *Titanic*'s deck to look for a place to land. Ballard knew that the glass dome that had once covered the grand first-class staircase would give them an opening into *Titanic*. He particularly wanted to see the staircase.

HUNDREDS OF THESE SPECIAL CLAY DISHES FROM *TITANIC* WERE RECOVERED FROM THE OCEAN BOTTOM. THE WOODEN CABINET IN WHICH THEY WERE KEPT PROTECTED THEM DURING THE SINKING. OVER TIME THE WOOD ROTTED AWAY, LEAVING THE DISHES STACKED NEATLY TOGETHER IN THE SAND.

Emergency on the Bottom

They had been on the bottom for almost two hours. Hollis was piloting *Alvin* along the upper deck when disaster struck. The crew felt a thump. The sub shuddered and clanged. A shower of rust covered the windows. "Ralph, we've hit something," Ballard said.

Hollis carefully backed up. They saw what they had hit. It was a davit, a curved pole used for hanging a lifeboat on a ship. They continued to rise. The current was very strong and Hollis had trouble steering. Ballard saw that they were headed for a tangle of wreckage on the deck.

"Swing back to the left," Ballard cried. "I have wreckage just out of my view port and it's getting close. Swing left!"

"It won't come around into the current," Hollis answered.

This was the worst nightmare for a deep diver. They were out of control near tangled steel and cables that could trap them forever.

"Then come up," Ballard said. "Let's get out of here! It's too dangerous." For a few long seconds, *Alvin* failed to respond to Hollis's commands. Then slowly it rose away from the wreckage.

The controller on *Atlantis II* told them that the weather on the surface was getting bad. Picking up *Alvin* in rough seas is very difficult. Every minute more they spent on the bottom meant more danger. Just then, the battery alarm began to sound again. This dive was over.

Hollis made one more pass along *Titanic*'s side. Then the long ascent began. Ballard played music on the stereo. The men tried to relax. They had had a close call, but everything was okay. When they arrived on the surface, the sea was very stormy. *Jason Jr.* accidentally slipped out of its garage, but divers rescued it. Finally, *Alvin* was safe in its cradle.

The crew of *Atlantis II* crowded into the video studio. Ballard showed them the videotapes of the dive. They saw the great bow planted in the mud. They saw the decks, the portholes, and the remains of the bridge. Everyone was stunned as they viewed *Titanic* in its grave.

Mystery Solved

Robert Ballard was living his dream. He had landed on *Titanic* and explored the grand staircase. He and his crew made fifteen dives that summer. On every one, *Titanic* became more real. On one dive they used *Jason Jr.* to scan the side of the ship.

Using *Jason Jr.*'s cameras, they could see part of the iceberg damage on *Titanic*'s side. It looked like the iceberg had not cut a gash in the ship after all. Probably, the force of the collision had caused rivets to break. Then the plates on the side of the ship came apart at the seams. Water flooded in. No ship could have survived. Later, Ballard and other explorers confirmed the theory that the steel plates had come apart.

LARRY S. ANDERSON, *GRAND STAIRCASE*, WATERCOLOR ON PAPER, 1996. COURTESY OF THE ARTIST.

THINK CRITICALLY

1. What coincidence happened when *Titanic* first left the dock? Why was this event a coincidence? NOTE DETAILS

2. What events led to the sinking of *Titanic*? SEQUENCE

3. How does the author of "The Incredible Quest to Find the *Titanic*" help you picture the wrecked ship through the eyes of the underwater explorers? Use examples from the selection to explain your answer. LITERARY DEVICES

4. Do you agree with the author that Robert Ballard was living his dream while exploring *Titanic*? Why or why not? DRAW AND EVALUATE CONCLUSIONS

5. **WRITE** Use details from the selection to explain how *Alvin* and *Jason Jr.* each helped Ballard see *Titanic*. EXTENDED RESPONSE

ABOUT THE AUTHOR
BRAD MATSEN

For thirty years, Brad Matsen has been writing books, screenplays, documentary scripts, and magazine articles about the ocean and the cultures of the Pacific Northwest. He says that he didn't find his true voice in writing until he was about forty years old. He realized then that enthusiasm was as important to writing well as were discipline and skill. In addition to being a writer, Brad Matsen has also worked as a commercial fisherman and a merchant seaman. He has lived most of his life in Alaska and the Pacific Northwest. He now divides his time between Seattle and New York.

 www.harcourtschool.com/storytown

Tapping satellites circling
Earth, Scouts find loot
hidden in a geocache.
(Excuse me? Geo-cash-what?)

HIGH-TECH
TREASURE
HUNT

by Kelly Bourne
photographs by Brian Payne

First Class Scout Matt Stom had a determined look in his eyes and a phone-size device in his hand. But it was neither a cell phone nor a calculator, which wouldn't be of much use out here in the knee-high prairie grass and cold drizzle. Periodically he looked down at the gadget, changed his direction ever so slightly, and forged ahead.

Matt and 15 other members of Troop 374 from Omaha, Nebraska, were on a treasure hunt—one with a high-tech twist. He held a Global Positioning System (GPS) receiver, the futuristic compass that led the boys to the location of the hidden boxes.

The Scouts were participating in "geocaching," a kind of unconventional treasure hunt. They divided into four patrols, each equipped with a GPS device and the coordinates to where a small, waterproof box—or cache (said, "cash")—was hidden. The first group to find its cache would get its choice of the prizes inside. Matt's team wanted to win so badly that the look of determination on their faces was mesmerizing.

"At first I thought we were going in the wrong direction," said Senior Patrol Leader Michael Harrington. "The other patrols were heading straight west and we were going southwest."

WHAT IS THE GLOBAL POSITIONING SYSTEM?

The Global Positioning System (GPS) is a navigation system made up of 24 satellites orbiting Earth. A GPS device contains a radio receiver that reads signals from these satellites. The receiver "triangulates" its location, using signals from at least three satellites, and displays it as longitude (east/west) and latitude (north/south) measurements. Early GPS signals had encryption code—a signal filter, now removed—that made only U.S. military units very precise.

Go to **www.geocaching.com** to find a cache location, in longitude and latitude, near you.

>> *GPS works like a futuristic compass.*

But Scout Taylor Gardner was sure they were going in the right direction. "We were following the arrow on the GPS. Within half an hour, the GPS receiver told us we were in the right spot."

The GPS receiver gets you to within 20 feet of the target. After that, it's up to your sight, smell, touch—whatever it takes.

"Once we knew we were real close, we split up," explained Tenderfoot Scout Chris Lucas. "We spread out and looked for hiding places like grassy areas, bushes, or holes in the ground. We didn't really know where it would be hidden."

BASIC CACHE

Geocaching's basics are simple. Someone hides a cache and registers its position on the Web at www.geocaching.com. People who want to search for a cache look on this site for geocache spots in their area.

A cache might be covered with leaves or pine needles. It might be wedged under a large rock or in a hollow log. It might even be above eye level in a tree. The craftiness of people who hide caches shouldn't be underestimated—one cache allegedly was strapped 50 feet up a tree trunk.

Geocaching got its start in May 2000, inspired by the United States government's removal of the encryption code from GPS satellite signals (see "What Is the Global Positioning System?"). Since then, the popularity of geocaching has ballooned.

There are more than 10,000 caches hidden in more than 130 countries. More are added daily. People get involved in geocaching for many reasons. Some like being outdoors. Others enjoy the exercise. Most do it because they love the challenge and thrill of hunting for treasure!

SPREAD OUT

Michael was the first to recognize the cache's hiding spot.

"It was just a pile of leaves and sticks covered with brown curved seed pods," he pointed out. "But there was something different about it. There were too many seed pods on top of it. There weren't that many stacked up anywhere else so it caught my eye."

As he used his arm to sweep aside the leaves, he knew he had found the cache because it made a hollow, metallic sound. Once it was uncovered, the boys found that it was a green army ammunition box stenciled with "Geocaching.com" across one side.

"It was exciting to open it up," said Taylor. "We had no idea what would be in it."

The cache contained a silk daisy, several bookmarkers, a candy dispenser, a pencil sharpener, a doll outfit, a jigsaw puzzle, a small sewing kit, a pocketknife, and a key chain. The Scouts contributed a jamboree patch and a golf tee to the contents and took the pocketknife.

"After we put our patch into the box, we covered it up again very carefully. We wanted to make it just as hard for the next searchers to find," Chris said. "There's no reason it should be easier for them than it was for us."

ON TO CACHE TWO

The patrol of Second Class Scout Chris Bahr, Eagle Scout Burke Bourne, Scout Hari Narayanan, and First Class Scout Blake Griffiths was determined to be the first to find the next cache. Their search led them into a valley on the edge of a small stream. The boys initially leaped over the stream, but the GPS told them they'd gone too far west. So they leaped back to the original side.

714

After looking around the damp clearing for a few minutes, Burke suggested that they use a more organized approach. "Let's form a police line to make sure we cover every inch of this area," he said.

His idea worked. On the first sweep through the area, Blake spotted the ammo box as he went around a tree. The cache was tucked into the crack where the tree split into two trunks. To conceal the ammo box, a hefty branch and several large pieces of bark covered it.

"That cache was tricky," Hari said. "It wasn't where I expected it would be. Whoever hid it knew what they were doing."

Inside this cache: several small toys, a windshield ice scraper, a string of beads, several bookmarks, and a baseball card. In keeping with the spirit of geocaching, the Scouts took something and left something, exchanging a toy army truck and dinosaur with one of the troop's patches and a Webelos Scout medallion emblazoned with, "Do Your Best."

HIDDEN TREASURE

The Scouts found in geocaching a nice mix of technology and a good old-fashioned scavenger hunt.

"It was wet," Scout Eddie Hanlon said afterward, "but that just made it more challenging. If you can find a cache when the weather is bad, then you're pretty good."

"Using a GPS was pretty cool," Burke added. "Once you got used to it, you could go right to the general area where the cache is located."

Some Scouts thought the high point was just being outdoors, even if the weather wasn't the best.

"It was cool when a herd of deer came out of the woods," said First Class Scout Matthew Bang. The deer didn't seem the least bit upset to share their piece of wilderness with a crew of geocachers.

Connections

Comparing Texts

1. Robert Ballard's undersea exploration made an important discovery. If you could be an explorer, what kinds of discoveries would you like to make?

2. Compare Robert Ballard and his crew with the scouts in "High-Tech Treasure Hunt." What did the people in each group gain from their discoveries?

3. How can studying the remains of past shipwrecks such as the *Titanic* help scientists and engineers today?

Vocabulary Review

Rate a Situation

With a partner, read each sentence below. Point to a spot on the line to show how happy or unhappy you would be in each situation. Explain your choices.

Unhappy ——————————————————— Happy

- The part of a ride you had **dreaded** is over.
- You've been invited to a **lavish** party.
- You make a smooth **ascent** in an airplane.
- You can't see your wallet in the lake's **murky** water.

lavish

dreaded

ascent

doomed

murky

remains

Fluency Practice

Repeated Reading

You have learned that you can increase your reading rate with practice. Turn to the section, A Closer Look at *Titanic*, on page 706. Reread the section aloud, and time your reading with a stopwatch. Record how long it takes. Reread the section two or three more times, and record how long each reading takes. Continue practicing your fluency with sentences or paragraphs that may be slowing you down.

Writing

Write a Persuasive Composition

The sinking of the *Titanic* is perhaps the best-known shipwreck in history. Write a persuasive composition telling why the *Titanic* disaster should be or should not be studied.

```
┌──────────┐   ┌──────────┐
│ Evidence │   │ Evidence │
└────┬─────┘   └────┬─────┘
     │    ┌─────────┘
   ┌─┴────┴───┐
   │Conclusion│
   └──────────┘
```

My Writing Checklist

Writing Trait ➤ Organization

✔ I used a graphic organizer to plan my writing.

✔ I supported my conclusions with evidence.

✔ I organized my ideas from most important to least important.

CONTENTS

Genre: Science Fiction

Ember

HELEN FOX

Zoo

by Edward D. Hoch

Genre: Science Fiction

Characterization

Characterization is the way in which an author helps readers get to know a story character. Authors reveal a character's traits through clues in the story. Clues about a character may include:

- what the character looks like
- how the character acts
- what the character says, thinks, or feels
- what others say, think, or feel about the character

Character Trait	Clues From Story

Authors want the characters in their stories to be **credible**, or believable. Even in stories that are not realistic, credible characters will have strengths and weaknesses. They will also change or grow as a result of problems they face. As you read, look for clues that reveal the characters' traits. Use the traits to judge whether the characters are credible.

Tip

Look for clues about characters in their dialogue.

Read the story. Then look at the chart. It shows how clues from the story reveal two of Dr. Wilton's traits. One of the clues comes from Dr. Wilton's actions. The other clue comes from his dialogue.

Dr. Wilton had built Model 14 out of spare parts. He had programmed the robot to respond to events as humans do, but Dr. Wilton often forgot this. One day, Model 14 did his chores without his usual good cheer. The doctor paid no attention until he heard a sniffle. "Impossible!" he snapped. "Robots don't cry!" Exasperated, he asked, "What's the problem?"

"You forgot that today is my birthday," Model 14 moaned.

Character Trait	Clues From Story
Dr. Wilton is forgetful and impatient.	He forgets how Model 14 was programmed. He snaps at Model 14 when the robot cries.

Try This!

Look back at the story. What do Model 14's actions and dialogue reveal about his character? Is Model 14's behavior credible, based on what the author has told you about him?

 www.harcourtschool.com/storytown

Vocabulary

qualm

endanger

contrary

contentedly

contemplate

torrent

intolerable

officious

Androids Revolt

When Admiral Hill of Space Force invited us to travel to Beta Camp and back, we didn't have a **qualm** about the journey. The military would never **endanger** civilians—especially reporters. The mission was to move a group of androids to the camp. It seemed simple enough.

Blastoff

We boarded *Vulcan 8* early on July 10, found our seats, and strapped ourselves in. The rockets fired, and we felt the thrill of liftoff. **Contrary** to popular belief, space travel can be boring. At first, it's fun to lie back **contentedly** and **contemplate** the galaxy, but you can count asteroids for only so long. To pass the time, we got to know an android named Tinboy.

This was the view from our window. It's awesome, isn't it?

Trouble Onboard

What a techno-troublemaker! Two days into our journey, Tinboy released a **torrent** of angry words. He had told the other androids that Beta Camp was dangerous. They were ready to fight the crew for control of the ship. Captain Hill assured them that their mission was a safe one, and he restored peace. He punished Tinboy's **intolerable** actions by reprogramming him.

This **officious** fellow was the leader of the androids.

 www.harcourtschool.com/storytown

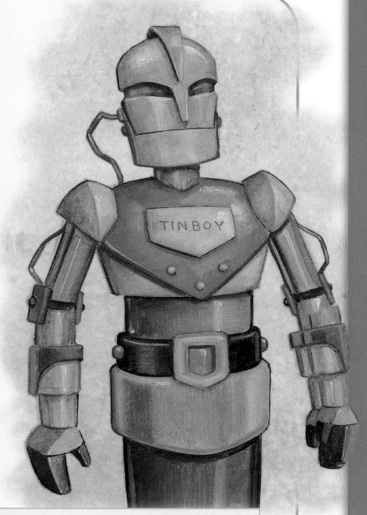

Word Champion

 Your challenge this week is to use the Vocabulary Words in conversations with friends and family members. Keep the list of words in a place at home where you can see it. Use as many of the words as you can by asking questions or describing things that you saw or did. For example, you might talk about spending an hour reading contentedly. In your vocabulary journal, keep track of how you used the words.

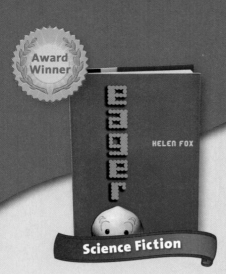

Award Winner

HELEN FOX

Science Fiction

Genre Study

Science fiction is about events that are imaginary and usually take place in the future. As you read, look for

- imagined details about science and technology.

- characters who are credible based on the setting.

Character Trait	Clues from Story

Comprehension Strategy

Answer questions by using what the author tells you, what the author implies, and what you already know.

by Helen Fox, from her original children's book _Eager_

illustrated for _StoryTown_ by Marcos Chin

In this story of the future, people rely on robots for many everyday tasks—cooking, cleaning, and even child care. The Bell family's newest robot, Eager, is very different from their aging robot, Grumps. Instead of being programmed to know certain things from the beginning, Eager is an experimental robot that learns new things through experience. Since Eager's arrival, life has improved for the Bells in many ways. However, they have learned that they can't anticipate every mistake Eager will make.

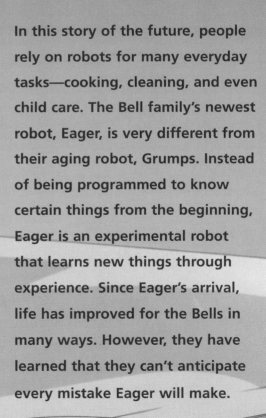

Mr. Bell had a meeting
at the site of the new factory and just had
time to gulp down a cup of coffee before kissing his wife
goodbye. Eager started to clear away the breakfast things.

"Eager," said Mrs. Bell, "I must finish a report today. I'd like
you to watch Charlotte for an hour until Grumps gets back."
She spoke casually but both she and Eager knew that this was
an important step.

"Are you sure?" Eager asked in spite of himself.

"You've been helping Grumps, haven't you? He seems to
think you're very good with her. The important thing is to keep
an eye on her at all times. Don't let her touch anything sharp or
put small objects in her mouth or—"

"Don't worry," interrupted Eager with feeling. "I know all
about dangers—cutting things, chemicals, falling . . . I learned
about them during my own infancy at the professor's house."

"Good," said Mrs. Bell. "Now, if she cries—you know the
grizzly sort of cry she makes . . . "

"She's probably thirsty, hungry or tired, or has a dirty diaper."

Mrs. Bell smiled. "I see you've learned a lot already. I'll leave
you to it. She's had a good breakfast but if she does seem
hungry later you can give her a cookie. You'll find the cookies
in a tin in the pantry."

She handed him Charlotte, who gurgled happily and
tried to pull his nose. "You're obviously a natural," laughed
Mrs. Bell. Nonetheless, a qualm seized her at the last moment.
Grumps had helped to bring up Fleur and Gavin and she didn't
think twice about leaving him with Charlotte, but Eager was still
an unknown quantity.

"Eager," she said firmly, "if you're in any doubt at all, if
there's any problem, you must call me at once."

"Yes, Mrs. Bell."

Charlotte was so absorbed in the nose-pulling game that she
didn't notice her mother leaving. After eight pulls Eager held
her at arm's length. "Time for something else. I'm not Grumps,"
he told her, and carried her into the living room to find some
toys. He took out some wooden bricks and built elaborate
towers with balustrades. To his immense frustration she knocked
them over each time.

Charlotte, he discovered, loved to make a noise and for a long time she banged an irregular rhythm on a battered tin drum. Then, without warning, she dropped the drumstick and her face puckered.

"Nahhhh! Nahhh!" It was the grizzle Mrs. Bell had reminded him about. He carried the baby into the kitchen and offered her a bottle. She pushed it away with unexpected strength. "Nahhhh! Nahhhhh!" It was too soon to change her diaper and she didn't seem to be tired. "Cookie?" suggested Eager. The grizzling stopped. Eager sat Charlotte down on the floor and went to the pantry. There was a large round tin just inside the door. He opened it and took out a cookie that was golden on one side and bright red on the other. He offered it to Charlotte.

"Mmm." She reached for the cookie. He handed it to her with the prettier red side uppermost, but instead of eating the cookie she waved it in the air and held it out to Eager. He began to wonder about human intelligence.

"Don't offer it to me," he said, "I just gave it to you."

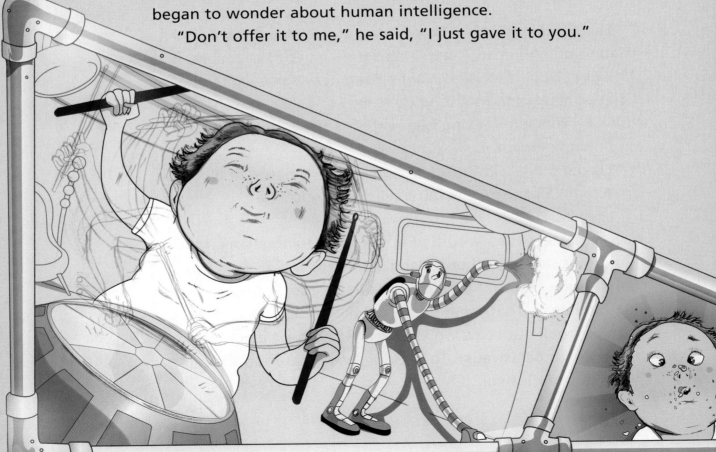

Charlotte put the cookie to her mouth and sank her small ivory teeth into it. She chuckled and waved the cookie at him once more.

Eager closed the lid and returned the tin to the pantry. The door closed behind him as he stopped dead in his tracks. When he had left Charlotte with the cookie she had been wearing a white top and pale yellow trousers. Now both were decorated in a livid red pattern. The same red was in evidence across her face, and as he moved closer he saw that it was in her hair as well. There was also a piece of cookie suspended on the side of her head. This confused him since the law of gravity suggested that the cookie should have fallen to the ground by now. He took it between his fingers and felt a slight resistance as he pulled it away from her hair. The downside, the red part, was sticky.

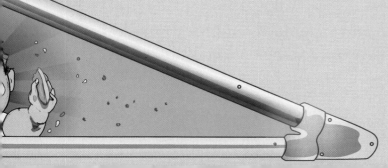

Charlotte had evidently taken a large bite of the cookie and was munching contentedly. The rest of it was squashed in her tiny fists and something red and syrupy oozed between her fingers. This cookie did not fit Eager's understanding of cookie. Cookies were hard. They made crumbs. They were not soft and they did not exude sticky lumps.

He stared at Charlotte in dismay. He had never seen her in such a mess! Grumps could be back at any moment and, worse, Mrs. Bell might come downstairs to check on his progress. The thought of failure was intolerable to him. He would never be trusted with the baby again. It surprised him to realize how much he had enjoyed the morning. He would have to remove the red stuff before anyone saw her. But how?

He knew that Charlotte had a bath every night but this was midmorning. Besides, she was covered in the sticky stuff—clothes, hair, face, the whole of her needed washing. He remembered his first evening in the house, when Grumps had shown him the washing and drying machines. "They'll tell you what to do," Grumps had said. Scooping up Charlotte and holding her at arm's length, he carried her to the laundry room. He noticed yet more hair stuck together in red clumps. There was even a blob of red on the end of her eyelashes.

The washing machine was activated by his approach. "What do you wish to wash?" it asked in an officious voice.

"A baby."

The machine considered for a moment. "I have never washed a baby before," it admitted, "so I am unable to advise you. Is it heavily soiled, lightly soiled or worn once?"

"Heavily soiled," said Eager decisively.

"Natural fabric or synthetic?"

"Natural." Eager was feeling pleased with himself. This was obviously the right thing to do.

"Delicate or—"

"Delicate," said Eager. There was no doubt that babies needed to be handled carefully.

"Then I recommend a long gentle wash with a mild detergent followed by a short spin."

Eager knew that chemicals could harm children. "I believe detergent is bad for babies."

"Very well. I shall use soap flakes. Place the item in the drum."

"Are you sure?" asked Eager. The door seemed rather small.

"Of course I am," replied the washing machine, somewhat irritably, Eager thought.

The door clicked open and Eager lowered Charlotte into the drum of the machine. She seemed to be enjoying the game and kicked her legs in pleasure.

"What are you doing?" thundered a voice. Eager looked over his shoulder. It was Grumps. The older robot appeared to be under so much strain that Eager was afraid he might explode.

"Remove that baby at once!"

He lifted Charlotte out of the drum and handed her into Grumps' outstretched arms.

"Don't you know . . . the first . . . law . . . of . . . robot . . . behavior?"

Before Eager could reply, Grumps unleashed a torrent of words. "Never . . . ever . . . in all my career . . . to harm a baby . . . We are programmed to care for humans. It is contrary to our behavior . . ."

Eager wished he could block out the sound of Grumps' voice. In fact, he could have put up a barrier between his ears and the sound but something told him this would be wrong. He stood there as the words washed over him until eventually he managed to say, "I am not programmed like you."

Grumps stopped in midsentence.

"I mean," continued Eager, "of course I know the laws of robot behavior . . ."

"Well?"

"A robot must never harm, or allow harm to be done to, a human being. A robot must never do anything that might endanger a human being. A robot must not harm itself or another robot, unless the other robot is endangering a human being." He broke off, although there were several other laws to recite. "The thing is, I am not programmed to obey rules. I am programmed to learn and to think for myself. It is my choice how I behave."

He could see that Grumps did not understand him and added miserably, "I thought the washing machine would know what to do."

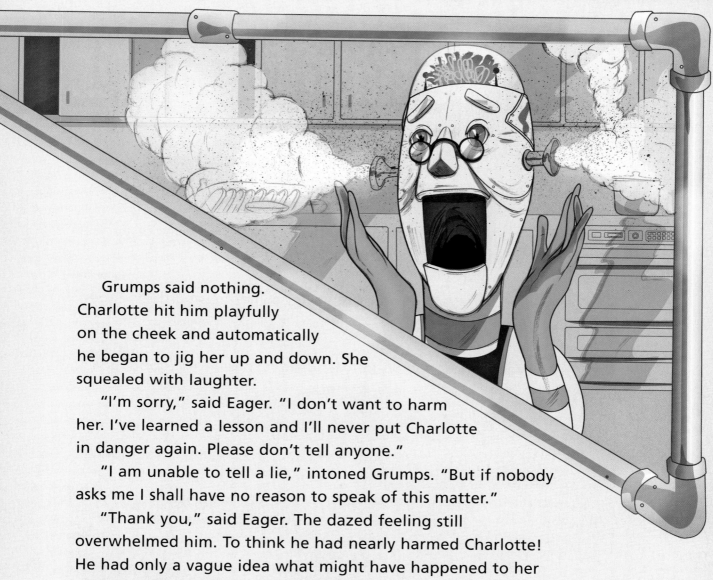

Grumps said nothing. Charlotte hit him playfully on the cheek and automatically he began to jig her up and down. She squealed with laughter.

"I'm sorry," said Eager. "I don't want to harm her. I've learned a lesson and I'll never put Charlotte in danger again. Please don't tell anyone."

"I am unable to tell a lie," intoned Grumps. "But if nobody asks me I shall have no reason to speak of this matter."

"Thank you," said Eager. The dazed feeling still overwhelmed him. To think he had nearly harmed Charlotte! He had only a vague idea what might have happened to her in the machine, yet he could tell by Grumps' reaction that it would have been very nasty. One day he would find out; for the time being he couldn't bear to contemplate it. He followed Grumps back into the kitchen.

"It all started to go wrong when I gave her the cookie," he pleaded. "It was a funny sort of cookie."

Grumps examined the red blobs on Charlotte's jumper. "Jam tart," he said. "I made some yesterday and left them in the pantry."

"Ah," said Eager, and thought, not for the first time, that real life was very confusing.

THINK CRITICALLY

1. Why does Eager want to clean up Charlotte before anyone sees her? CHARACTER'S MOTIVATIONS

2. Is Eager's mistake with Charlotte credible? Explain your answer, using examples of Eager's character traits.  CHARACTERIZATION

3. Why are the laws of robot behavior sometimes hard for Eager to obey? NOTE DETAILS

4. Is programming robots to learn from experience a good idea? Why or why not? PERSONAL RESPONSE

5. **WRITE** Compare and contrast Eager and Grumps. Tell how the robots are alike and how they are different. Use details and information from the story to support your answer.
SHORT RESPONSE

ABOUT THE AUTHOR

HELEN FOX

Helen Fox was working as an actor when she renewed her childhood interest in writing stories. Her love of storytelling led her to become a writer. Before she started writing full-time, Helen Fox taught in primary school and worked as a tour guide. She lives with her husband in London, England. *Eager*, her first novel, has a sequel titled *Eager's Nephew*.

ABOUT THE ILLUSTRATOR

MARCOS CHIN

Marcos Chin thinks that people-watching is an important part of his work. He uses his senses to absorb everything around him—from the sights and sounds of the environment to the personalities and attitudes of the people he sees. These observations come to life in his artwork. Marcos Chin creates his artwork on the computer. He has gained fame as an illustrator for newspapers and magazines. He lives in Toronto, Canada.

GO online www.harcourtschool.com/storytown

Science Fiction

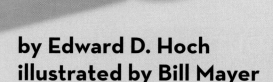

by Edward D. Hoch
illustrated by Bill Mayer

The children were always good during the month of August, especially when it began to get near the twenty-third. It was on this day that the great spaceship carrying Professor Hugo's Interplanetary Zoo settled down for its annual six-hour visit to the Chicago area.

Before daybreak the crowds would form, long lines of children and adults both, each one clutching his or her dollar and waiting with wonderment to see what race of strange creatures the Professor had brought this year.

In the past they had sometimes been treated to three-legged creatures from Venus, or tall, thin men from Mars, or even snake-like horrors from somewhere more distant. This year, as the great round ship settled slowly to Earth in the huge tri-city parking area just outside of Chicago, they watched with awe as the sides slowly slid up to reveal the familiar barred cages. In them were some wild breed of nightmare—small, horse-like animals that moved with quick, jerking motions and constantly chattered in a high-pitched tongue. The citizens of Earth clustered around as Professor Hugo's crew quickly collected the waiting dollars, and soon the good Professor himself made an appearance, wearing his many-colored rainbow cape and top hat.

"Peoples of Earth," he called into his microphone. The crowd's noise died down and he continued. "Peoples of Earth, this year you see a real treat for your single dollar—the little-known horse-spider people of Kaan—brought to you across a million miles of space at great expense. Gather around, see them, study them, listen to them, tell your friends about them. But hurry! My ship can remain here only six hours!"

And the crowds slowly filed by, at once horrified and fascinated by these strange creatures that looked like horses but ran up the walls of their cages like spiders. "This is certainly worth a dollar," one man remarked, hurrying away. "I'm going home to get the wife."

737

All day long it went like that, until ten thousand people had filed by the barred cages set into the side of the spaceship. Then, as the six-hour limit ran out, Professor Hugo once more took the microphone in hand. "We must go now, but we will return next year on this date. And if you enjoyed our zoo this year, telephone your friends in other cities about it. We will land in New York tomorrow, and next week on to London, Paris, Rome, Hong Kong, and Tokyo. Then on to other worlds!"

He waved farewell to them, and as the ship rose from the ground, the Earth peoples agreed that this had been the best Zoo yet. . . .

Some two months and three planets later, the ship of Professor Hugo settled at last onto the familiar jagged rocks of Kaan, and the odd horse-spider creatures filed quickly out of their cages. Professor Hugo was there to say a few parting words, and then they scurried away in a hundred different directions, seeking their homes among the rocks.

In one house, the she-creature was happy to see the return of her mate and offspring. She babbled a greeting in the strange tongue and hurried to embrace them. "It was a long time you were gone. Was it good?"

And the he-creature nodded. "The little one enjoyed it especially. We visited eight worlds and saw many things."

The little one ran up the wall of the cave. "On the place called Earth it was the best. The creatures there wear garments over their skins, and they walk on two legs."

"But isn't it dangerous?" asked the she-creature.

"No," her mate answered. "There are bars to protect us from them. We remain right in the ship. Next time you must come with us. It is well worth the nineteen commocs it costs.

And the little one nodded. "It was the very best Zoo ever. . . ."

Connections

Comparing Texts

1. Imagine that you have a personal robot like Eager. How could your robot help you in daily life?

2. How are "Eager" and "Zoo" alike? How are they different?

3. In what ways is Eager's world of the future like real life today? In what ways is it different?

Vocabulary Review

Word Pairs

His officious behavior was intolerable.

Work with a partner. Write the Vocabulary Words on separate index cards. Place the cards face down in two piles. Take turns picking up a card from each pile and writing a sentence that uses both words. Read your sentences aloud to your partner. If you have used both words correctly, keep the cards. If not, return them to the bottom of the piles. Continue until all the words have been used correctly. The player with more cards wins.

qualm

endanger

contrary

contentedly

contemplate

torrent

intolerable

officious

Fluency Practice

Partner Reading

When you read with expression, you bring to life the words on a page. In "Eager," there are human voices, robot voices, and the voice of a washing machine. Work with a partner to reread the part of the story that begins "The washing machine was activated...," on page 730, and ends with "I am not programmed like you," on page 732. Give each character's words the expression called for in the text. Ask your partner for feedback. Then switch roles.

Writing

WANTED:
Qualified Household Robot

Write a Want Ad

Imagine that your family plans to hire a qualified robot to help around the house. Write a want ad advertising the position. Use a word-processing program to type and format the advertisement so it looks like a real want ad.

Responsibilities	Personality Traits

My Writing Checklist

Writing Trait ➤ Word Choice

✔ I used a chart to organize my ideas.

✔ I used words that will grab readers' attention.

✔ My finished product is visually appealing.

CONTENTS

Lesson 29

Genre: Play

THE PHANTOM TOLLBOOTH
BY NORTON JUSTER
ADAPTED BY SUSAN NANUS
ILLUSTRATED BY MÉLISANDE POTTER

THE Road NOT TAKEN
by Robert Frost

Genre: Poetry

Characterization

Authors use **characterization** to develop the characters in a story and make them seem real. To help readers get to know a character, authors provide clues about the character's traits. A well-developed character has many traits that are revealed as he or she grows and changes throughout the story.

Character Trait	Clues From Story

Credible characters are one of the features of good literature. They make the plot believable. When you know a character's traits, you can judge whether or not the character's actions are credible. As you read a story, ask yourself:

- Does this behavior fit with what I already know about the character?
- Would this character really say something like this?
- Are the character's actions believable in this setting?

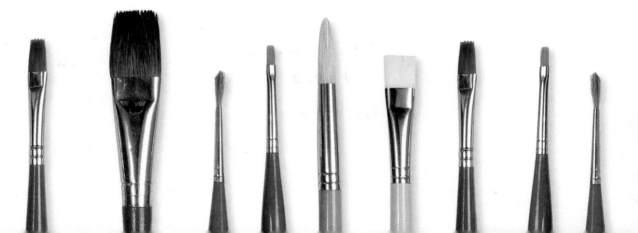

Read the following story. The chart below shows clues from the story that help readers get to know Magda. The clues reveal her character traits.

Magda stood staring at the painting she had been working on and murmured her disapproval. The trees looked as real as the ones outside, but the sky looked flat and uninspiring.

"Something just isn't right," she said to herself. Magda vowed to stay up all night in order to finish the painting in time for her mother's birthday celebration. On her palette she mixed oranges, reds, and yellows. Then she applied them to the canvas. "At last, the perfect sunset," she said.

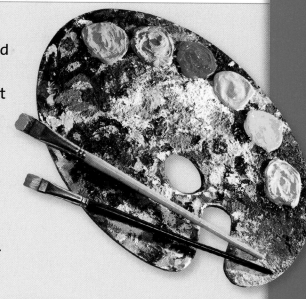

Character Trait	Clues From Story
thoughtful determined	She is painting a picture for her mother. She vows to stay up all night to finish the painting.

Try This!

Imagine that you are writing the next scene in the story about Magda. What might Magda do that would be consistent with her character traits? What would she never do?

GO online   www.harcourtschool.com/storytown

doldrums

dejectedly

misapprehension

banished

imposter

strenuous

linger

abide

Adventure Calls

Gary was bored. He turned on the TV, and a tiny man appeared on the screen. He said, "Are you in the **doldrums**, Gary? Come with me on the road to adventure."

"I can't get inside a TV," Gary replied **dejectedly**.

"Ah, let me relieve your **misapprehension** about the limits of TV. Touch the screen, my friend." Gary did. He felt a rush of air and closed his eyes. When he opened them, he was standing in a dark and beautiful forest. The tiny man stood next to him. He pointed to a castle in the distance.

"I have been **banished** from my land for fighting for the true queen. Now an **imposter** rules in her place. Will you help me rescue the real queen and restore her to her rightful position?"

"But what can I do?" asked Gary.

"You are young and strong. You can handle the **strenuous** tasks that lie ahead. Come, we must not **linger**. We have much to do and very little time."

Gary thought, "Why not **abide** by the man's directions? I've got nothing better to do." He nodded and said, "Let's go."

GO online www.harcourtschool.com/storytown

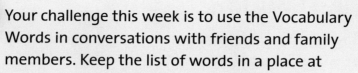
Word Champion

Your challenge this week is to use the Vocabulary Words in conversations with friends and family members. Keep the list of words in a place at home where you can see it. Use as many of the words as you can by asking questions or describing things that you saw or did. For example, you might tell about an activity that required strenuous effort. Keep track of how you used the words in your vocabulary journal.

THE PHANTOM TOLLBOOTH

BY NORTON JUSTER
ADAPTED BY SUSAN NANUS
ILLUSTRATED BY MÉLISANDE POTTER

Play

Genre Study

A play is a story that is meant to be performed for an audience. As you read, look for

- a plot revealed mostly through dialogue.

- stage directions that tell how the characters act and speak.

Character Trait	Clues from Story

Comprehension Strategy

Answer questions by using what the author tells you, what the author implies, and what you already know.

THE PHANTOM TOLLBOOTH

BY NORTON JUSTER

ADAPTED BY SUSAN NANUS

ILLUSTRATED BY MÉLISANDE POTTER

CAST (IN ORDER OF APPEARANCE)

THE CLOCK

MILO, A BOY

A VOICE

THE WHETHER MAN

SIX LETHARGARIANS

TOCK, THE WATCHDOG (SAME ACTOR AS THE CLOCK)

AZAZ THE UNABRIDGED, KING OF DICTIONOPOLIS

THE MATHEMAGICIAN, KING OF DIGITOPOLIS

PRINCESS SWEET RHYME

PRINCESS PURE REASON

GATEKEEPER OF DICTIONOPOLIS

FOUR WORD MERCHANTS

SPELLING BEE

THE HUMBUG

FIVE MINISTERS

PAGE

ACT ONE SCENE ONE

The stage is completely dark and silent. Suddenly the sound of someone winding an alarm clock is heard, and after that, the sound of loud ticking is heard.

LIGHTS UP on the CLOCK, *a huge alarm clock. The* CLOCK *reads 4:00. The lighting should make it appear that the* CLOCK *is suspended in mid-air (if possible). The* CLOCK *ticks for 30 seconds.*

CLOCK: See that! Half a minute gone by. Seems like a long time when you're waiting for something to happen, doesn't it? Funny thing is, time can pass very slowly or very fast, and sometimes even both at once. The time now? Oh, a little after four, but what that means should depend on you. Too often, we do something simply because time tells us to. Time for school, time for bed, whoops, 12:00, time to be hungry. It can get a little silly, don't you think? Time is important, but it's what you do with it that makes it so. So my advice to you is to use it. Keep your eyes open and your ears perked. Otherwise it will pass before you know it, and you'll certainly have missed something!

Things have a habit of doing that, you know. Being here one minute and gone the next. In the twinkling of an eye. In a jiffy. In a flash!

I know a girl who yawned and missed a whole summer vacation. And what about that caveman who took a nap one afternoon, and woke up to find himself completely alone. You see, while *he* was sleeping, someone had invented the wheel and everyone had moved to the suburbs. And then of course, there is Milo. (*LIGHTS UP to reveal MILO'S bedroom. The CLOCK appears to be on a shelf in the room of a young boy—a room filled with books, toys, games, maps, papers, pencils, a bed, a desk. There is a dartboard with numbers and the face of the MATHEMAGICIAN, a bedspread made from KING AZAZ'S cloak, a kite looking like the SPELLING BEE, a punching bag with the HUMBUG'S face, as well as records, a television, a toy car, and a large box that is*

wrapped and has an envelope taped to the top. The sound of FOOTSTEPS is heard, and then enter MILO dejectedly. He throws down his books and coat, flops into a chair, and sighs loudly.) Who never knows what to do with himself—not just sometimes, but always. When he's in school, he wants to be out, and when he's out, he wants to be in. (*During the following speech, MILO examines the various toys, tools, and other possessions in the room, trying them out and rejecting them.*) Wherever he is, he wants to be somewhere else—and when he gets there, so what. Everything is too much trouble or a waste of time. Books—he's already read them. Games—boring. T.V.—dumb. So what's left? Another long, boring afternoon. Unless he bothers to notice a very large package that happened to arrive today.

MILO: (*Suddenly notices the package. He drags himself over to it, and disinterestedly reads the label.*) "For Milo, who has plenty of time." Well, that's true. (*Sighs and looks at it.*) No. (*Walks away.*) Well . . . (*Comes back. Rips open envelope and reads.*)

A VOICE: "One genuine turnpike tollbooth, easily assembled at home for use by those who have never traveled in lands beyond."

MILO: Beyond what? (*Continues reading.*)

A VOICE: "This package contains the following items:" (MILO *pulls the items out of the box and sets them up as they are mentioned.*) "One (1) genuine turnpike tollbooth to be erected according to directions. Three (3) precautionary signs to be used in a precautionary fashion. Assorted coins for paying tolls. One (1) map, strictly up to date, showing how to get from here to there. One (1) book of rules and traffic regulations which may not be bent or broken. Warning! Results are not guaranteed. If not perfectly satisfied, your wasted time will be refunded."

MILO: (*Skeptically*) Come off it, who do you think you're kidding? (*Walks around and examines tollbooth.*) What am I supposed to do with this? (*The ticking of the CLOCK grows loud and impatient.*) Well . . . what else do I have to do. (MILO *gets into his toy car and drives up to the first sign. NOTE: The car may be an actual toy car propelled by pedals or a small motor, or simply a cardboard imitation that MILO can fit into, and move by walking.*)

A VOICE: "HAVE YOUR DESTINATION IN MIND."

MILO: (*Pulls out the map.*) Now, let's see. That's funny. I never heard of any of these places. Well, it doesn't matter anyway. Dictionopolis. That's a weird name. I might as well go there. (*Begins to move, following map. Drives off.*)

CLOCK: See what I mean? You never know how things are going to get started. But when you're bored, what you need more than anything is a rude awakening.

(*The alarm goes off very loudly as the stage darkens. The sound of the alarm is transformed into the honking of a car horn, and is then joined by the blasts, bleeps, roars and growls of heavy highway traffic. When the lights come up, MILO'S bedroom is gone and we see a lonely road in the middle of nowhere.*)

ACT ONE SCENE TWO
THE ROAD TO DICTIONOPOLIS

Enter MILO in his car.

MILO: This is weird! I don't recognize any of this scenery at all. (*A sign is held up before MILO, startling him.*) Huh? (*Reads.*) WELCOME TO EXPECTATIONS. INFORMATION, PREDICTIONS AND ADVICE CHEERFULLY OFFERED. PARK HERE AND BLOW HORN. (MILO *blows horn.*)

WHETHER MAN: (*A little man wearing a long coat and carrying an umbrella pops up from behind the sign that he was holding. He speaks very fast and excitedly.*) My, my, my, my, my, welcome, welcome, welcome, welcome to the Land of Expectations, Expectations, Expectations! We don't get many travelers these days; we certainly don't get many travelers. Now what can I do for you? I'm the Whether Man.

MILO: (*Referring to map.*) Uh . . . is this the right road to Dictionopolis?

WHETHER MAN: Well now, well now, well now, I don't know of any *wrong* road to Dictionopolis, so if this road goes to Dictionopolis at all, it must be the right road, and if it doesn't, it must be the right road to somewhere else, because there are no wrong roads to anywhere. Do you think it will rain?

MILO: I thought you were the Weather Man.

WHETHER MAN: Oh, no, I'm the Whether Man, not the weather man. (*Pulls out a sign or opens a flap of his coat, which reads: "WHETHER."*) After all, it's more important to know whether there will be weather than what the weather will be.

MILO: What kind of place is Expectations?

WHETHER MAN: Good question, good question! Expectations is the place you must always go to before you get to where you are going. Of course, some people never go beyond Expectations, but my job is to hurry them along whether they like it or not. Now what else can I do for you? (*Opens his umbrella.*)

MILO: I think I can find my own way.

WHETHER MAN: Splendid, splendid, splendid! Whether or not you find your own way, you're bound to find some way. If you happen to find my way, please return it. I lost it years ago. I imagine by now it must be quite rusty. You did say it was going to rain, didn't you? (*Escorts* MILO *to the car under the open umbrella.*) I'm glad you made your own decision. I do so hate to make up my mind about anything, whether it's good or bad, up or down, rain or shine. Expect everything, I always say, and the unexpected never happens. Goodbye, goodbye, goodbye, good . . . (*A loud clap of thunder is heard.*) Oh dear! (*He looks up at the sky, puts out his hand to feel for rain, and runs away.* MILO *watches puzzledly and drives on.*)

WHETHER MAN

MILO: I'd better get out of Expectations, but fast. Talking to a guy like that all day would get me nowhere for sure. (*He tries to speed up, but finds instead that he is moving slower and slower.*) Oh, oh, now what? (*He can barely move. Behind* MILO, *the* LETHARGARIANS *begin to enter from all parts of the stage. They are dressed to blend in with the scenery and carry small pillows that look like rocks. Whenever they fall asleep, they rest on the pillows.*) Now I really am getting nowhere. I hope I didn't take a wrong turn. (*The car stops. He tries to start it. It won't move. He gets out and begins to tinker with it.*) I wonder where I am.

LETHARGARIAN 1: You're . . . in . . . the . . . Dol . . . drums. . . . (MILO *looks around.*)

LETHARGARIAN 2: Yes . . . the . . . Dol . . . drums. . . . (*A yawn is heard.*)

MILO: (*Yelling.*) WHAT ARE THE DOLDRUMS?

LETHARGARIAN 3: The Doldrums, my friend, are where nothing ever happens and nothing ever changes. (*Parts of the scenery stand up or six people come out of the scenery colored in the same colors of the trees or the road. They move very slowly and as soon as they move, they stop to rest again.*) Allow me to introduce all of us. We are the Lethargarians at your service.

MILO: (*Uncertainly.*) Very pleased to meet you. I think I'm lost. Can you help me?

LETHARGARIAN 4: Don't say think. (*He yawns.*) It's against the law.

LETHARGARIAN 1: No one's allowed to think in the Doldrums. (*He falls asleep.*)

LETHARGARIAN 2: Don't you have a rule book? It's local ordinance 1-75389-J. (*He falls asleep.*)

MILO: (*Pulls out rule book and reads.*) Ordinance 1-75389-J: "It shall be unlawful, illegal and unethical to think, think of thinking, surmise, presume, reason, meditate or speculate while in the Doldrums. Anyone breaking this law shall be severely punished." That's a ridiculous law! Everybody thinks.

ALL THE LETHARGARIANS: We don't!

LETHARGARIAN 2: And most of the time, you don't, that's why you're here. You weren't thinking and you weren't paying attention either. People who don't pay attention often get stuck in the Doldrums. Face it, most of the time, you're just like us. (*Falls, snoring, to the ground.* MILO *laughs.*)

LETHARGARIAN 5: Stop that at once. Laughing is against the law. Don't you have a rule book? It's local ordinance 57438-1-W.

MILO: (*Opens rule book and reads.*) "In the Doldrums, laughter is frowned upon and smiling is permitted only on alternate Thursdays." Well, if you can't laugh or think, what can you do?

LETHARGARIAN 6: Anything as long as it's nothing, and everything as long as it isn't anything. There's lots to do. We have a very busy schedule . . .

LETHARGARIAN 1: At 8:00 we get up and then we spend from 8 to 9 daydreaming.

LETHARGARIAN 2: From 9:00 to 9:30 we take our early midmorning nap . . .

LETHARGARIAN 3: From 9:30 to 10:30 we dawdle and delay . . .

LETHARGARIAN 4: From 10:30 to 11:30 we take our late early morning nap . . .

LETHARGARIAN 5: From 11:30 to 12:00 we bide our time and then we eat our lunch.

LETHARGARIAN 6: From 1:00 to 2:00 we linger and loiter . . .

LETHARGARIAN 1: From 2:00 to 2:30 we take our early afternoon nap . . .

LETHARGARIAN 2: From 2:30 to 3:30 we put off for tomorrow what we could have done today . . .

LETHARGARIAN 3: From 3:30 to 4:00 we take our early late afternoon nap . . .

LETHARGARIAN 4: From 4:00 to 5:00 we loaf and lounge until dinner . . .

LETHARGARIAN 5: From 6:00 to 7:00 we dilly-dally . . . .

LETHARGARIAN 6: From 7:00 to 8:00 we take our early evening nap and then for an hour before we go to bed, we waste time.

LETHARGARIAN 1: (*Yawning.*) You see, it's really quite strenuous doing nothing all day long, and so once a week, we take a holiday and go nowhere.

LETHARGARIAN 2

LETHARGARIAN 5: Which is just where we were going when you came along. Would you care to join us?

MILO: (*Yawning.*) That's where I seem to be going, anyway. (*Stretching.*) Tell me, does everyone here do nothing?

LETHARGARIAN 3: Everyone but the terrible watchdog. He's always sniffing around to see that nobody wastes time. A most unpleasant character.

MILO: The Watchdog?

LETHARGARIAN 6: THE WATCHDOG!

ALL THE LETHARGARIANS: (*Yelling at once.*) RUN! WAKE UP! RUN! HERE HE COMES! THE

WATCHDOG! (*They all run off and enter a large dog with the head, feet, and tail of a dog, and the body of a clock, having the same face as the character the* **CLOCK.**)

WATCHDOG: What are you doing here?

MILO: Nothing much. Just killing time. You see . . .

WATCHDOG: KILLING TIME! (*His alarm rings in fury.*) It's bad enough wasting time without killing it. What are you doing in the Doldrums, anyway? Don't you have anywhere to go?

MILO: I think I was on my way to Dictionopolis when I got stuck here. Can you help me?

WATCH DOG

WATCHDOG: Help you! You've got to help yourself. I suppose you know why you got stuck.

MILO: I guess I just wasn't thinking.

WATCHDOG: Precisely. Now you're on your way.

MILO: I am?

WATCHDOG: Of course. Since you got here by not thinking, it seems reasonable that in order to get out, you must *start* thinking. Do you mind if I get in? I love automobile rides. (*He gets in. They wait.*) Well?

MILO: All right. I'll try. (*Screws up his face and thinks.*) Are we moving?

WATCHDOG: Not yet. Think harder.

MILO: I'm thinking as hard as I can.

WATCHDOG: Well, think just a little harder than that. Come on, you can do it.

MILO: All right, all right. . . . I'm thinking of all the planets in the solar system, and why water expands when it turns to ice, and all the words that begin with "q," and . . . (*The wheels begin to move.*) We're moving! We're moving!

WATCHDOG: Keep thinking.

MILO: (*Thinking.*) How a steam engine works and how to bake a pie and the difference between Fahrenheit and Centigrade . . .

WATCHDOG: Dictionopolis, here we come.

MILO: Hey, Watchdog, are you coming along?

MATHEMAGICIAN

TOCK: You can call me Tock, and keep your eyes on the road.

MILO: What kind of place is Dictionopolis, anyway?

TOCK: It's where all the words in the world come from. It used to be a marvelous place, but ever since Rhyme and Reason left, it hasn't been the same.

MILO: Rhyme and Reason?

TOCK: The two princesses. They used to settle all the arguments between their two brothers who rule over the Land of Wisdom. You see, Azaz is the king of Dictionopolis and the Mathemagician is the king of Digitopolis and they almost never see eye to eye on anything. It was the job of the Princesses Sweet Rhyme and Pure Reason to solve the differences between the two kings, and they always did so well that both sides usually went home feeling very satisfied. But then, one day, the kings had an argument to end all arguments. . . .

(The lights dim on TOCK *and* MILO, *and come up on* KING AZAZ *of Dictionopolis on another part of the stage.* AZAZ *has a great stomach, a grey beard reaching to his waist, a small crown and a long robe with the letters of the alphabet written all over it.)*

AZAZ: Of course, I'll abide by the decision of Rhyme and Reason, though I have no doubt as to what it will be. They will choose *words*, of course. Everyone knows that words are more important than numbers any day of the week.

(The MATHEMAGICIAN *appears opposite* AZAZ. *The* MATHEMAGICIAN *wears a long flowing robe covered entirely with complex mathematical equations, and a tall pointed hat. He carries a long staff with a pencil point at one end and a large rubber eraser at the other.)*

MATHEMAGICIAN: That's what you think, Azaz. People wouldn't even know what day of the week it is without *numbers.* Haven't you ever looked at a calendar? Face it, Azaz. It's numbers that count.

AZAZ: Don't be ridiculous. *(To audience, as if leading a cheer.)* Let's hear it for WORDS!

MATHEMAGICIAN: (*To audience, in the same manner.*) Cast your vote for NUMBERS!

AZAZ: A, B, C's!

MATHEMAGICIAN: 1, 2, 3's! (*A fanfare is heard.*)

AZAZ AND MATHEMAGICIAN: (*To each other.*) Quiet! Rhyme and Reason are about to announce their decision.

(RHYME *and* REASON *appear.*)

RHYME: Ladies and gentlemen, letters and numerals, fractions and punctuation marks—may we have your attention, please. After careful consideration of the problem set before us by King Azaz of Dictionopolis (AZAZ *bows.*) and the Mathemagician of Digitopolis (MATHEMAGICIAN *raises his hands in a victory salute.*) we have come to the following conclusion.

REASON: Words and numbers are of equal value, for in the cloak of knowledge, one is the warp and the other is the woof.

RHYME: It is no more important to count the sands than it is to name the stars.

RHYME AND REASON: Therefore, let both kingdoms, Dictionopolis and Digitopolis, live in peace.

(*The sound of cheering is heard.*)

AZAZ: Boo! is what I say. Boo and Bah and Hiss!

MATHEMAGICIAN: What good are these girls if they can't even settle an argument in anyone's favor? I think I have come to a decision of my own.

AZAZ: So have I.

AZAZ AND MATHEMAGICIAN: (*To the* PRINCESSES.) You are hereby banished from this land to the Castle-in-the-Air. (*To each other.*) And as for you, KEEP OUT OF MY WAY! (*They stalk off in opposite directions.*)

(*During this time, the set has been changed to the Market Square of Dictionopolis. Lights come up on the deserted square.*)

TOCK: And ever since then, there has been neither Rhyme nor Reason in this kingdom. Words are misused and numbers are mismanaged. The argument between the two kings has divided everyone and the real value of both words and numbers has been forgotten. What a waste!

MILO: Why doesn't somebody rescue the Princesses and set everything straight again?

TOCK: That is easier said than done. The Castle-in-the-Air is very far from here. But hold on, here we are. (*A man appears, carrying a gate and a small tollbooth.*)

GATEKEEPER: AHHHHREMMMM! This is Dictionopolis, a happy kingdom, advantageously located in the foothills of Confusion and caressed by gentle breezes from the Sea of Knowledge. Today, by royal proclamation, is Market Day. Have you come to buy or sell?

MILO: I beg your pardon?

GATEKEEPER: Buy or sell, buy or sell. Which is it? You must have come here for a reason.

MILO: Well, I . . .

GATEKEEPER: Come now, if you don't have a reason, you must at least have an explanation or certainly an excuse.

MILO: (*Meekly.*) Uh . . . no.

GATEKEEPER: (*Shaking his head.*) Very serious. You can't get in without a reason. (*Thoughtfully.*) Wait a minute. Maybe I have an old one you can use. (*Pulls out an old suitcase from the tollbooth and rummages through it.*) No . . . no . . . no . . . this won't do . . . hmmm . . .

MILO: (*To* **TOCK.**) What's he looking for? (**TOCK** *shrugs.*)

GATEKEEPER: Ah! This is fine. (*Pulls out a medallion on a chain. Engraved in the medallion is: "WHY NOT?"*) Why not. That's a good reason for almost anything . . . a bit used, perhaps, but still quite serviceable. There you are, sir. Now I can truly say: Welcome to Dictionopolis.

(*He opens the gate and walks off.* **CITIZENS** *and* **MERCHANTS** *appear on all levels of the stage, and* **MILO** *and* **TOCK** *find themselves in the middle of a noisy marketplace. As some people buy and sell their wares, others hang a large banner which reads: WELCOME TO THE WORD MARKET.*)

MILO: Tock! Look!

MERCHANT 1: Hey-ya, hey-ya, hey-ya, step right up and take your pick. Juicy tempting words for sale. Get your fresh-picked "if's," "and's" and "but's"! Just take a look at these nice ripe "where's" and "when's."

MERCHANT 2: Step right up, step right up, fancy, best-quality words here for sale. Enrich your vocabulary and expand your speech with such elegant items as "quagmire," "flabbergast," or "upholstery."

MERCHANT 3: Words by the bag, buy them over here. Words by the bag for the more talkative customer. A pound of "happy's" at a very reasonable price . . . very useful for "Happy Birthday," "Happy New Year," "happy days," or "happy-go-lucky." Or how about a package of "good's," always handy for "good morning," "good afternoon," "good evening," and "goodbye."

MILO: I can't believe it. Did you ever see so many words?

TOCK: They're fine if you have something to say. (*They come to a do-it-yourself bin.*)

MILO: (*To* MERCHANT 4 *at the bin.*) Excuse me, but what are these?

MERCHANT 4: These are for people who like to make up their own words. You can pick any assortment you like or buy a special box complete with all the letters and a book of instructions. Here, taste an "A." They're very good. (*He pops one into* MILO'S *mouth.*)

MILO: (*Tastes it hesitantly.*) It's sweet! (*He eats it.*)

MERCHANT 4: I knew you'd like it. "A" is one of our best-sellers. All of them aren't that good, you know. The "Z," for instance—very dry and sawdusty. And the "X"? Tastes like a trunkful of stale air. But most of the others aren't bad at all. Here, try the "I."

MILO: (*Tasting.*) Cool! It tastes icy.

MERCHANT 4: (*To* TOCK.) How about the "C" for you? It's as crunchy as a bone. Most people are just too lazy to make their own words, but take it from me, not only is it more fun, but it's also *de*-lightful, (*Holds up a "D."*) *e*-lating, (*Holds up an "E."*) and extremely *u*seful! (*Holds up a "U."*)

MILO: But isn't it difficult? I'm not very good at making words.

(*The* SPELLING BEE, *a large colorful bee, comes up from behind.*)

SPELLING BEE: Perhaps I can be of some assistance . . . a-s-s-i-s-t-a-n-c-e. (*The three turn around and see him.*) Don't be alarmed . . . a-l-a-r-m-e-d. I am the Spelling Bee. I can spell anything. Anything. A-n-y-t-h-i-n-g. Try me. Try me.

MILO: (*Backing off,* TOCK *on his guard.*) Can you spell goodbye?

SPELLING BEE: Perhaps you are under the misapprehension . . . m-i-s-a-p-p-r-e-h-e-n-s-i-o-n that I am dangerous. Let me assure you that I am quite peaceful. Now, think of the most difficult word you can, and I'll spell it.

MILO: Uh . . . o.k. (*At this point,* MILO *may turn to the audience and ask them to help him choose a word or he may think of one on his own.*) How about . . . "Curiosity"?

SPELLING BEE: (*Winking.*) Let's see now . . . uh . . . how much time do I have?

MILO: Just ten seconds. Count them off, Tock.

SPELLING BEE: (*As* TOCK *counts.*) Oh dear, oh dear. (*Just at the last moment, quickly.*) C-u-r-i-o-s-i-t-y.

MERCHANT 4: Correct! (*ALL cheer.*)

MILO: Can you spell anything?

SPELLING BEE: (*Proudly.*) Just about. You see, years ago, I was an ordinary bee minding my own business, smelling flowers all day, occasionally picking up part-time work in people's bonnets. Then one day, I realized that I'd never amount to anything without an education, so I decided that . . .

HUMBUG: (*Coming up in a booming voice.*) BALDERDASH! (*He wears a lavish coat, striped pants, checked vest, spats and a derby hat.*) Let me repeat . . . BALDERDASH! (*Swings his cane and clicks his heels in the air.*) Well, well, what have we here? Isn't someone going to introduce me to the little boy?

SPELLING BEE: (*Disdainfully.*) This is the Humbug. You can't trust a word he says.

HUMBUG: NONSENSE! Everyone can trust a Humbug. As I was saying to the king just the other day . . .

SPELLING BEE: You've never met the king. (*To* MILO.) Don't believe a thing he tells you.

HUMBUG: Bosh, my boy, pure bosh. The Humbugs are an old and noble family, honorable to the core. Why, we fought in the Crusades with Richard the Lionhearted, crossed the Atlantic with Columbus, blazed trails with the pioneers. History is full of Humbugs.

SPELLING BEE: A very pretty speech . . . s-p-e-e-c-h. Now, why don't you go away? I was just advising the lad of the importance of proper spelling.

HUMBUG: BAH! As soon as you learn to spell one word, they ask you to spell another. You can never catch up, so why bother? (*Puts his arm around* MILO.) Take my advice, boy, and forget about it. As my great-great-great-grandfather George Washington Humbug used to say . . .

SPELLING BEE: You, sir, are an imposter i-m-p-o-s-t-e-r who can't even spell his own name!

HUMBUG: What? You dare to doubt my word? The word of a Humbug? The word of a Humbug who has direct access to the ear of a King? And the king shall hear of this, I promise you . . .

VOICE 1: Did someone call for the king?

VOICE 2: Did you mention the monarch?

VOICE 3: Speak of the sovereign?

VOICE 4: Entreat the Emperor?

VOICE 5: Hail his highness?

(*Five tall, thin gentlemen regally dressed in silks and satins, plumed hats and buckled shoes appear as they speak.*)

HUMBUG

MILO: Who are they?

SPELLING BEE: The King's advisors. Or in more formal terms, his cabinet.

MINISTER 1: Greetings!

MINISTER 2: Salutations!

MINISTER 3: Welcome!

MINISTER 4: Good afternoon!

MINISTER 5: Hello!

MILO: Uh . . . Hi.

(*All the* MINISTERS, *from here on called by their numbers, unfold their scrolls and read in order.*)

MINISTER 1: By the order of Azaz the Unabridged . . .

MINISTER 2: King of Dictionopolis . . .

MINISTER 3: Monarch of letters . . .

MINISTER 4: Emperor of phrases, sentences, and miscellaneous figures of speech . . .

MINISTER 5: We offer you the hospitality of our kingdom . . .

MINISTER 1: Country

MINISTER 2: Nation

MINISTER 3: State

MINISTER 4: Commonwealth

MINISTER 5: Realm

MINISTER 1: Empire

MINISTER 2: Palatinate

MINISTER 3: Principality.

MILO: Do all those words mean the same thing?

MINISTER 1: Of course.

MINISTER 2: Certainly.

MINISTER 3: Precisely.

MINISTER 4: Exactly.

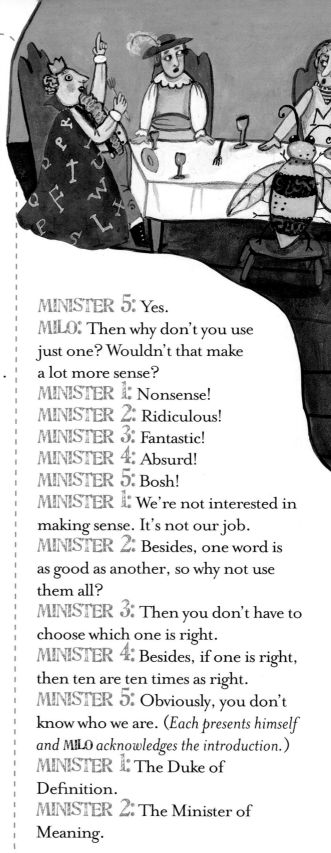

MINISTER 5: Yes.

MILO: Then why don't you use just one? Wouldn't that make a lot more sense?

MINISTER 1: Nonsense!

MINISTER 2: Ridiculous!

MINISTER 3: Fantastic!

MINISTER 4: Absurd!

MINISTER 5: Bosh!

MINISTER 1: We're not interested in making sense. It's not our job.

MINISTER 2: Besides, one word is as good as another, so why not use them all?

MINISTER 3: Then you don't have to choose which one is right.

MINISTER 4: Besides, if one is right, then ten are ten times as right.

MINISTER 5: Obviously, you don't know who we are. (*Each presents himself and* MILO *acknowledges the introduction.*)

MINISTER 1: The Duke of Definition.

MINISTER 2: The Minister of Meaning.

MINISTER 3: The Earl of Essence.
MINISTER 4: The Count of Connotation.
MINISTER 5: The Undersecretary of Understanding.
ALL FIVE: And we have come to invite you to the Royal Banquet.
SPELLING BEE: The banquet! That's quite an honor, my boy. A real h-o-n-o-r.
HUMBUG: DON'T BE RIDICULOUS! Everybody goes to the Royal Banquet these days.
SPELLING BEE: (*To the HUMBUG.*) True, everybody does go. But some people are invited and others simply push their way in where they aren't wanted.
HUMBUG: HOW DARE YOU? You

buzzing little upstart, I'll show you who's not wanted . . . (*Raises his cane threateningly.*)
SPELLING BEE: You just watch it! I'm warning w–a–r–n–i–n–g you! (*At that moment, an ear-shattering blast of trumpets, entirely off-key, is heard, and a PAGE appears.*)
PAGE: King Azaz the Unabridged is about to begin the Royal Banquet. All guests who do not appear promptly at the table will automatically lose their place. (*A huge table is carried out with KING AZAZ sitting in a large chair, carried out at the head of the table.*)
AZAZ: Places. Everyone take your places. (*All the characters, including the HUMBUG and the SPELLING BEE, who forget their quarrel, rush to take their places at the table. MILO and TOCK sit near the KING. AZAZ looks at MILO.*) And just who is this?
MILO: Your Highness, my name is Milo and this is Tock. Thank you very much for inviting us to your banquet, and I think your palace is beautiful!
MINISTER 1: Exquisite.
MINISTER 2: Lovely.
MINISTER 3: Handsome.
MINISTER 4: Pretty.
MINISTER 5: Charming.
AZAZ: SILENCE! Now tell me, young man, what can you do to entertain us? Sing songs? Tell stories? Juggle plates? Do tumbling tricks? Which is it?
MILO: I can't do any of those things.

AZAZ: What an ordinary little boy. Can't you do anything at all?

MILO: Well . . . I can count to a thousand.

AZAZ: AARGH, numbers! Never mention numbers here. Only use them when we absolutely have to. Now, why don't we change the subject and have some dinner? Since you are the guest of honor, you may pick the menu.

MILO: Me? Well, uh . . . I'm not very hungry. Can we just have a light snack?

AZAZ: A light snack it shall be!

(AZAZ *claps his hands. Waiters rush in with covered trays. When they are uncovered, shafts of light pour out. The light may be created through the use of battery-operated flashlights which are secured in the trays and covered with a false bottom. The guests help themselves.*)

HUMBUG: Not a very substantial meal. Maybe you can suggest something a little more filling.

MILO: Well, in that case, I think we ought to have a square meal . . .

AZAZ: (*Claps his hands.*) A square meal it is! (*Waiters serve trays of colored squares of all sizes. People serve themselves.*)

SPELLING BEE: These are awful. (HUMBUG *coughs and all the guests do not care for the food.*)

AZAZ: (*Claps his hands and the trays are removed.*) Time for speeches. (*To* MILO.) You first.

MILO: (*Hesitantly.*) Your Majesty, ladies and gentlemen, I would like to take this opportunity to say that . . .

AZAZ: That's quite enough. Mustn't talk all day.

MILO: But I just started to . . .

AZAZ: NEXT!

HUMBUG: (*Quickly.*) Roast turkey, mashed potatoes, vanilla ice cream.

SPELLING BEE: Hamburgers, corn on the cob, chocolate pudding p-u-d-d-i-n-g. (*Each guest names two dishes and a dessert.*)

AZAZ: (*The last.*) Pate de fois gras, soupe a l'oignon, salade endives, fromage et fruits et demi-tasse. (*He claps his hands. Waiters serve each guest his words.*) Dig in. (*To* MILO.) Though I can't say I think much of your choice.

MILO: I didn't know I was going to have to eat my words.

AZAZ: Of course, of course, everybody here does. Your speech should have been in better taste.

MINISTER 1: Here, try some somersault. It improves the flavor.

MINISTER 2: Have a rigamarole. (*Offers breadbasket.*)

MINISTER 3: Or a ragamuffin.

MINISTER 4: Perhaps you'd care for a synonym bun.

MINISTER 5: Why not wait for your just desserts?

AZAZ: Ah yes, the dessert. We're having a special treat today . . . freshly made at the half-bakery.

MILO: The half-bakery?

AZAZ: Of course, the half-bakery! Where do you think half-baked ideas come from? Now, please don't interrupt. By royal command, the pastry chefs have . . .

MILO: What's a half-baked idea?

(AZAZ *gives up the idea of speaking as a cart is wheeled in and the guests help themselves.*)

HUMBUG: They're very tasty, but they don't always agree with you. Here's a good one. (HUMBUG *hands one to* MILO.)

MILO: (*Reads.*) "The earth is flat."

SPELLING BEE: People swallowed that one for years. (*Picks up one and reads.*) "The moon is made of green cheese." Now, there's a half-baked idea.

(*Everyone chooses one and eats. They include: "It Never Rains But Pours," "Night Air Is Bad Air," "Everything Happens For The Best," "Coffee Stunts Your Growth."*)

AZAZ: And now for a few closing words. Attention! Let me have your attention! (*Everyone leaps up and exits, except for* MILO, TOCK, *and the* HUMBUG.) Loyal subjects and friends, once again on this gala occasion, we have . . .

MILO: Excuse me, but everybody left.

AZAZ: (*Sadly.*) I was hoping no one would notice. It happens every time.

HUMBUG: They've gone to dinner, and as soon as I finish this last bite, I shall join them.

MILO: That's ridiculous. How can they eat dinner right after a banquet?

AZAZ: SCANDALOUS! We'll put a stop to it at once. From now on, by royal command, everyone must eat dinner before the banquet.

MILO: But that's just as bad.

HUMBUG: Or just as good. Things which are equally bad are also equally good. Try to look at the bright side of things.

MILO: I don't know which side of anything to look at. Everything is so confusing, and all your words only make things worse.

AZAZ: How true. There must be something we can do about it.

HUMBUG: Pass a law.

AZAZ: We have almost as many laws as words.

HUMBUG: Offer a reward. (AZAZ *shakes his head and looks madder at each suggestion.*) Send for help? Drive a bargain? Pull the switch? Lower the boom? Toe the line? (*As* AZAZ *continues to scowl, the* HUMBUG *loses confidence and finally gives up.*)

MILO: Maybe you should let Rhyme and Reason return.

AZAZ: How nice that would be. Even if they were a bother at times, things always went so well when they were here. But I'm afraid it can't be done.

HUMBUG: Certainly not. Can't be done.

MILO: Why not?

HUMBUG: (*Now siding with* MILO.) Why not, indeed?

AZAZ: Much too difficult.

HUMBUG: Of course, much too difficult.

MILO: You could, if you really wanted to.

HUMBUG: By all means, if you really wanted to, you could.

AZAZ: (*To* HUMBUG.) How?

MILO: (*Also to* HUMBUG.) Yeah, how?

HUMBUG: Why . . . uh, it's a simple task for a brave boy with a stout heart, a steadfast dog, and a serviceable small automobile.

AZAZ: Go on.

HUMBUG: Well, all that he would have to do is cross the dangerous, unknown countryside between here and Digitopolis, where he would have to persuade the Mathemagician to release the Princesses, which we know to be impossible because the Mathemagician will never agree with Azaz about anything. Once achieving that, it's a simple matter of entering the Mountains of Ignorance from where no one has ever returned alive, an effortless climb up a two thousand foot stairway without railings in a high wind at night to the Castle-in-the-Air. After a pleasant chat with the Princesses, all that remains is a leisurely ride back through those chaotic crags. And finally after doing all that, a triumphal parade! If, of course, there is anything left to parade . . . followed by hot chocolate and cookies for everyone.

AZAZ: I never realized it would be so simple.

MILO: It sounds dangerous to me.

TOCK: And just who is supposed to make that journey?

AZAZ: A very good question. But there is one far more serious problem.

DICTIONOPOLIS

MILO: What's that?

AZAZ: I'm afraid I can't tell you that until you return.

MILO: But wait a minute, I didn't . . .

AZAZ: Dictionopolis will always be grateful to you, my boy, and your dog. (*AZAZ pats TOCK and MILO.*)

TOCK: Now, just one moment, sire . . .

AZAZ: You will face many dangers on your journey, but fear not, for I can give you something for your protection. (*AZAZ gives MILO a box.*) In this box are the letters of the alphabet. With them you can form all the words you will ever need to help you overcome the obstacles that may stand in your path. All you must do is use them well and in the right places.

MILO: (*Miserably.*) Thanks a lot.

AZAZ: You will need a guide, of course, and since he knows the obstacles so well, the Humbug has cheerfully volunteered to accompany you.

HUMBUG: Now, see here . . . !

AZAZ: You will find him dependable, brave, resourceful, and loyal.

HUMBUG: (*Flattered.*) Oh, your Majesty.

MILO: I'm sure he'll be a great help. (*They approach the car.*)

TOCK: I hope so. It looks like we're going to need it.

(*The lights darken and the KING fades from view.*)

AZAZ: Good luck! Drive carefully! (*The three get into the car and begin to move. Suddenly a thunderously loud noise is heard. They slow down the car.*)

MILO: What was that?

TOCK: It came from up ahead.

HUMBUG: It's something terrible, I just know it. Oh, no. Something dreadful is going to happen to us. I can feel it in my bones. (*The NOISE is repeated. They all look at each other fearfully. As the lights fade.*)

END OF ACT ONE

THINK CRITICALLY

1 Summarize what happens when Milo reaches the Doldrums. SUMMARIZE

2 At the banquet, Milo says that he didn't know he would have to "eat his words." What mistake does he make? FIGURATIVE LANGUAGE

3 Is Milo a believable character? Use examples of his character traits to support your answer. CHARACTERIZATION

4 In your opinion, are words and numbers of equal value? Explain your thinking. MAKE JUDGMENTS

5 **WRITE** Explain how Milo and the Lethargarians are alike. Use details from the story to support your answer.

SHORT RESPONSE

770

ABOUT THE AUTHOR

Norton Juster

Norton Juster began writing the novel *The Phantom Tollbooth*, on which this play is based, in 1959. *The Phantom Tollbooth* began as a short story. In it, Norton Juster focused on feelings he had as a child, including the feeling of not knowing what to do with free time. He published the resulting novel in 1961. Since then, Juster has written several other children's books, including his first picture book, *The Hello, Goodbye Window*, with artist Chris Raschka in 2005. Norton Juster lives with his wife in Massachusetts.

ABOUT THE ILLUSTRATOR

Mélisande Potter

Mélisande Potter loves to travel. She has illustrated children's books that are set in places all over the world. Some of her travels have been the result of her work in a theater company that she helped start many years ago. Mélisande Potter has held a variety of jobs in the performing arts—a concert pianist, a ballet dancer, a mime, a scenery painter, and even a mask maker. She now divides her time between New York City and Jamaica.

GO online www.harcourtschool.com/storytown

Language Arts

THE
Road
NOT TAKEN

by Robert Frost

Poetry

Paul Cézanne, *Forest Path*. Private collection.

THE Road NOT TAKEN

by Robert Frost

Two roads diverged in a yellow wood,
And sorry I could not travel both
And be one traveler, long I stood
And looked down one as far as I could
To where it bent in the undergrowth;

Then took the other, as just as fair,
And having perhaps the better claim,
Because it was grassy and wanted wear;
Though as for that, the passing there
Had worn them really about the same,

And both that morning equally lay
In leaves no step had trodden black.
Oh, I kept the first for another day!
Yet knowing how way leads on to way,
I doubted if I should ever come back.

I shall be telling this with a sigh
Somewhere ages and ages hence:
Two roads diverged in a wood, and I—
I took the one less traveled by,
And that has made all the difference.

Connections

Comparing Texts

1. If you found yourself "in the doldrums," how would you get out?

2. How does the message in "The Road Not Taken" relate to Milo's experiences in "The Phantom Tollbooth"?

3. In the play's introduction, the Clock says that time can pass slowly or quickly, depending on how you use it. Give an example of this from real life.

Vocabulary Review

Word Webs

Work with a partner. Choose two Vocabulary Words. Create two word webs. Put a Vocabulary Word in the center of each web. Write words and phrases that are related to the Vocabulary Word in the ovals around it. Share your word webs with your partner, explaining how each word or phrase in your web is related to the Vocabulary Word.

delay — linger — hang back

doldrums

dejectedly

misapprehension

banished

imposter

strenuous

linger

abide

Fluency Practice

Partner Reading

When you read a play aloud, it is important to read with expression. The stage directions in italic type help you read with the right expression by telling you how to say some lines. Work with a partner to reread Act One, Scene One. Ask your partner for feedback about your expression. Then switch roles. Repeat the activity until you are both satisfied with your expression.

Writing

Write a Character Sketch

In "The Phantom Tollbooth," Milo's character traits affect the ways in which he reacts to what he sees and affect the people he meets along the way. Write a character sketch in which you describe another character in the play.

Character Trait	Clues from Story

My Writing Checklist

Writing Trait ▶ Word Choice

✔ I used a chart to organize my ideas.

✔ I focused on what makes the character unique.

✔ I used specific adjectives to describe the character's traits.

CONTENTS

Readers' Theater
DOCUMENTARY

INTO THE DEEP

illustrated by John Hendrix

Comprehension Strategies
POETRY

EARTH SONGS
Myra Cohn Livingston, Poet
Leonard Everett Fisher, Painter

entrust

critical

understatement

emanates

erratic

elusive

unprecedented

cacophony

implode

acute

Reading for Fluency

When reading a script aloud,

- Read at a steady **rate** to keep listeners interested.

- Focus on **expression**. Make your voice reflect the feelings and moods of the characters.

Characters

Narrator

Chorus

Professor Auguste Piccard, designer of the *Trieste*

Navy Lieutenant A.W. Cooley, commander of the support ship USS *Wandank*

Jacques Piccard, Swiss scientist and underwater engineer

Navy Lieutenant Don Walsh, commander of the *Trieste*

INTO THE DEEP

illustrated by John Hendrix

Narrator: A strange ticking sound fills the air early morning on January 23, 1960, off the coast of Guam in the South Pacific Ocean. A deep-diving U.S. Navy ship called a bathyscaphe (BATH•uh•skaf) bobs above the Challenger Deep, the deepest spot in all the oceans on Earth.

Chorus: Listen to that constant ticking. Tick, tick, tick.

Narrator: Today, two divers will attempt a dangerous and extraordinary mission. They will try to go where no human has ever ventured. The vessel to which they will entrust their lives is called the *Trieste* (tree•EST).

Fluency Tip

Practice reading your part until you can read it at a steady **rate**.

Professor Piccard: My name is Professor Auguste Piccard. I probably know more about the *Trieste* than anyone because I helped build it. Can you believe I designed it to sink? It was constructed to go down to the bottom of the sea and come back up to the surface.

Narrator: Professor Piccard's son, Jacques Piccard, and Navy Lieutenant Don Walsh step from a rubber raft onto the *Trieste*. They are preparing for a strenuous dive that will take them almost seven miles down to the ocean floor. Once aboard the *Trieste*, they receive a radio call from Lieutenant Cooley, the commander of the support ship that brought the *Trieste* to this remote spot.

Lt. Cooley: Pre-check, pre-check. This is Lieutenant Cooley aboard the support ship USS *Wandank*. Can you hear me? *Trieste* crew, come in!

Chorus: Come in! Come in!

Jacques Piccard: This is Piccard.

Lt. Walsh: Lieutenant Don Walsh here. Radio connection is loud and clear.

Narrator: A wild whirling sound fills the air. It's the sound of the *Trieste* warming up.

Chorus: Listen to the whirling sounds. Whirl! Whirl!

Narrator: Piccard and Lt. Walsh are inside the *Trieste*'s diving chamber, a fourteen-ton spherical steel capsule.

Professor Piccard: It's a tight squeeze in the diving chamber. A space six feet in diameter is not a lot of room for a two-person crew plus all the instruments. This chamber hangs like a precious egg beneath the 50-foot-long steel body. Its location provides a good view out of the two portholes, through six inches of tough plastic.

Narrator: From the chamber, the two divers will direct the *Trieste*. They have just finished checking their instruments and their inventory of supplies.

Jacques Piccard: It is critical that we check everything very carefully.

Professor Piccard: "Critical" is an understatement. The *Trieste* is not attached by a cable to the support ship. So it contains everything the crew needs to survive, including the air supply.

Jacques Piccard: This dive will be a real test for the *Trieste*. Last year, we took it down to a depth of 18,600 feet.

Lt. Walsh: And now we're attempting to dive almost twice as deep.

Narrator: Just then, the radio sputters.

Cooley: Piccard! Lt. Walsh! This is Lt. Cooley—everything OK?

Jacques Piccard: Checklist complete.

Lt. Walsh: We're good to go.

Narrator: As the *Trieste* begins its risky five-hour descent into the strange world beneath the sea, the whirling sound builds and then settles into a constant hum.

Chorus: The whirling becomes a hum. Humm. Humm.

Narrator: Over the hum, Piccard calls out orders.

Jacques Piccard: Flood chambers one and two.

Professor Piccard: Seawater rushes into two air compartments. The weight of the water makes the *Trieste* descend into the depths of the ocean. The nine tons of steel pellets that it carries helps it sink like a rock, too. I built it to go dangerously deep!

Chorus: Down, down, down it goes. Where will it stop? Nobody knows!

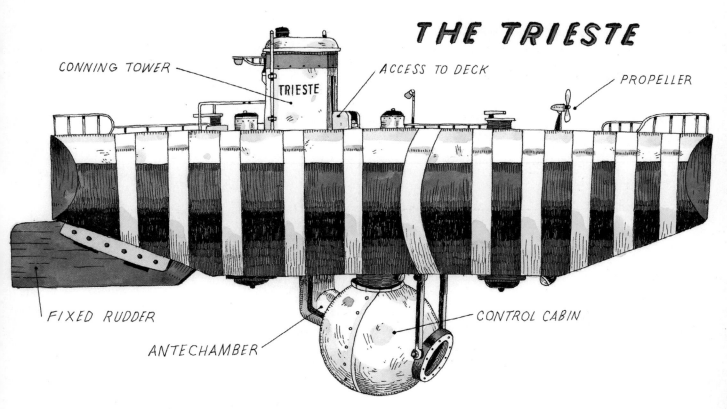

THE TRIESTE

CONNING TOWER

TRIESTE

ACCESS TO DECK

PROPELLER

FIXED RUDDER

ANTECHAMBER

CONTROL CABIN

Fluency Tip

Read with **expression**. Think about how the characters might be feeling as you read your lines.

Narrator: The sound of bubbles fills the diving chamber and then stops.

Jacques Piccard: That sonar beat—listen! That's what should make you feel better.

Narrator: A rhythmic beeping sound emanates from the Trieste's sonar depth detector.

Chorus: Beep . . . beep . . . beep.

Professor Piccard: Those beeping sounds bounce off the ocean floor and then return to the *Trieste*. By measuring the time it takes for the sound to return, the sonar detector tells the crew how deep they are.

Jacques Piccard: Descent on schedule. 7,500 feet . . . 8,000 feet . . . still dropping.

Professor Piccard: Though the water pressure is increasing as the *Trieste* drops deeper into the sea, it maintains an even pressure between its hull and the water outside. I have no qualms about how it will perform.

Jacques Piccard: Lt. Walsh, listen!

Narrator: Piccard and Lt. Walsh sit frozen, listening as they contemplate the strange sounds that seem to encircle them.

Jacques Piccard: Turn off the sonar depth detector.

Narrator: The beeping stops. An eerie, low-pitched whistling fills the silence.

Jacques Piccard: What's that? Slow us down, Lt. Walsh.

Narrator: Once again, the whirling sound increases and then settles into a constant hum. The whistling becomes softer and softer, until it stops as suddenly as it began.

Jacques Piccard: Listen! It's gone. I can't hear it now. We may never know what we just heard. Turn the depth detector back on.

Narrator: The beeping noise of the sonar starts up again.

Chorus: Beep . . . beep . . . beep.

Narrator: The whirling noise becomes erratic.

Jacques Piccard: 12,000 feet. 12,200. 12,400.

Lt. Walsh: Piccard, we're at the depth of one of your early records: 13,000 feet!

Narrator: A clanking noise catches the divers' attention. First, one gentle clank; then, two more.

Jacques Piccard: 13,600 feet and descending. Observable marine life. No further sound patterns.

Fluency Tip

A faster **reading rate** is appropriate when a character seems anxious and concerned.

Professor Piccard: The water pressure is increasing as Piccard and Lt. Walsh go deeper. It is squeezing the *Trieste* on all sides, making its frame clank. The water is getting colder and colder, darker and darker.

Chorus: It's colder and colder, darker and darker!

Jacques Piccard: Lt. Walsh, did you see that?

Lt. Walsh: What? Where?

Narrator: Lt. Walsh peers first through one porthole, then the other, looking for something—perhaps an elusive sea creature. The *Trieste* has reached a depth of 18,000 feet. The whirling noise becomes frantic.

Chorus: The whirling is out of control, out of control.

Narrator: The divers suspect that something has gone wrong.

Jacques Piccard: We have a leak, but it is minimal. We're at 18,000 feet.

Lt. Walsh: Condensation in the diving chamber.

Jacques Piccard: 18,600 feet. 19,000.

Lt. Walsh: No one's ever gone this deep. We just set an unprecedented world record!

Jacques Piccard: Correct, but to make the record books, we have to get back.

Narrator: As the *Trieste* continues to sink, clanking sounds create an almost intolerable cacophony. Then the divers hear one loud BANG, followed by a jolt.

Chorus: BANG! Feel that shaking.

Lt. Walsh: What was that?

Jacques Piccard: Water pressure— we're up to 15,000 pounds per square inch, and increasing.

Professor Piccard: With walls five inches thick, the *Trieste* can withstand intense pressure from the weight of the water. But the pressure down there may be too strong. Will its hull implode?

Jacques Piccard: 26,000 feet and still descending.

Narrator: The sound of escaping air can be heard. Piccard and Lt. Walsh prepare for the worst.

Chorus: Their lives may be in acute danger. The *Trieste* may be doomed!

Jacques Piccard: Lt. Walsh, turn everything off but the outside lights. If our lives end here, I want to take one last look.

Narrator: All of the noises suddenly cease.

784

Jacques Piccard: 35,800 feet and counting. Lt. Walsh, after almost five hours we're on the bottom.

Lt. Walsh: What do you see?

Jacques Piccard: Turn on the lights. Oh, my . . .

Lt. Walsh: What is it? Why are you laughing?

Jacques Piccard: Light number two is out. It must have imploded. That was the impact we felt. The ship is fine!

Professor Piccard: Of course the ship is fine. I never doubted it for a minute!

Narrator: The *Trieste* has reached the deepest spot in the world, the bottom of the Challenger Deep.

Jacques Piccard: Turn down lights one and three by ten degrees. I see something. What is it?

Lt. Walsh: Only dust. We've just disturbed sediment from the ocean floor. It's barren here. There's no life. Nothing.

Chorus: Nothing here at all.

Narrator: Disappointed, the explorers stare through the portholes. Suddenly, Piccard points at the ocean floor.

Jacques Piccard: Then what do you call that animal burrowing into the ocean floor? I'd say it's some kind of flatfish.

Lt. Walsh: So, life can exist at these great depths!

Jacques Piccard: It appears that it can. I wasn't sure that waters this deep would have enough oxygen to support life.

Narrator: Lt. Walsh and Piccard encountered creatures rarely seen by humans. They also found ooze containing microscopic algae. However, they did not linger. They stayed on the ocean floor for only twenty minutes.

Jacques Piccard: It's time to attempt our ascent. Lt. Walsh, release the ballast.

Professor Piccard: The crew releases two tons of the steel pellets that helped the *Trieste* reach the murky depths. This will lighten the vessel and allow it to rise to the surface.

Narrator: The ascent to the surface takes more than three hours. As the *Trieste* nears the surface, Piccard and Lt. Walsh hear a familiar voice over the radio.

Lt. Cooley: Congratulations, *Trieste*! You're home!

Jacques Piccard: Thank you, Lt. Cooley. We're glad to be back.

Narrator: Jacques Piccard and Lt. Walsh's bold journey into the Challenger Deep has never been repeated.

COMPREHENSION STRATEGIES
Review

Reading Poetry

Bridge to Reading for Meaning Poetry is a type of expressive writing told in verse. Rhythm, rhyme, and figurative language are often used in poetry to express tone and meaning. The notes on page 789 point out some of the features of a poem. How can knowing these features help you understand and interpret poems?

Review the Focus Strategies

You can also use the comprehension strategies you learned about in this theme to read poetry.

 Summarize

Pause several times while you read to summarize. Tell the most important ideas in one or two sentences. You should also summarize when you have finished reading.

 Answer Questions

If you have difficulty answering a question about the poem, think about where and how you can find the answer.

- You can often find the answer in one part of the poem.
- Sometimes you need to combine information from different parts of the poem.
- At other times you can use your prior knowledge.

As you read "Earth Songs" on pages 790–793, think about how you can use the comprehension strategies.

STANZAS
Stanzas are sections of a poem. A stanza may focus on one central idea or thought.

EARTH SONGS

BY MYRA COHN LIVINGSTON   ILLUSTRATED BY LEONARD EVERETT FISHER

Little O, small earth, spinning in space,
face covered with dizzy clouds, racing,
chasing sunlight through the Milky Way,
say your secrets, small earth, little O,
know where you lead, I follow. I go.

Patched together
With land and sea,
I am earth,
Great earth.
Come with me!

Huge continents lie on me, dry land,
sand grained from crumbled rock, now drifted,
sifted to powder. Silt, sand, red clay
weigh down my crust in layers of loam.
Roam everywhere—I am earth, your home.

Uplands clamber over me, climb high
skyward. Hummocks, hillocks, small knolls
roll in circles, slope and tumble down.
Round hills rise to bluffs. My highlands change—
Range over me! Look! My shapes grow strange.

Mountains rise above me, their slopes white,
bright with fresh snow, tall peaks glistering.
Blistering brown domes bend over, hunched,
bunched together. Some, chained in deep folds,
molded in waves, sleep, wrinkled and old.

Hot volcanoes breathe in me, my back
blackened with cinders, scars of old fires,
pyres of ash. My red mouth and throat burn,
churn with hot, liquid lava. Below
flow molten rivers. Turn away! Go!

Forests live on me. Tall evergreens
lean against my mountains. Stands of beech
reach to the sky. Huge timber and bark
darken my leaf-strewn floors. Oak, teak, and pine,
vine-twisted rain forests—all are mine.

FIGURATIVE LANGUAGE
Figurative language describes something ordinary in an interesting way.

PUNCTUATION
Commas, periods, and dashes tell the reader when to pause. Punctuation can shape the rhythm of the poem.

Apply the Strategies Read the following poem that celebrates earth and nature. As you read, use different comprehension strategies, such as summarizing, to help you understand.

EARTH

BY MYRA COHN LIVINGSTON   ILLUSTRATED BY LEONARD EVERETT FISHER

Little O, small earth, spinning in space,
face covered with dizzy clouds, racing,
chasing sunlight through the Milky Way,
say your secrets, small earth, little O,
know where you lead, I follow. I go.

Patched together
With land and sea,
I am earth,
Great earth.
Come with me!

Huge continents lie on me, dry land,
sand grained from crumbled rock, now drifted,
sifted to powder. Silt, sand, red clay
weigh down my crust in layers of loam.
Roam everywhere—I am earth, your home.

Stop and Think

Pause occasionally to summarize a stanza or a page.

SUMMARIZE

SONGS

Uplands clamber over me, climb high
skyward. Hummocks, hillocks, small knolls
roll in circles, slope and tumble down.
Round hills rise to bluffs. My highlands change—
Range over me! Look! My shapes grow strange.

Mountains rise above me, their slopes white,
bright with fresh snow, tall peaks glistering.
Blistering brown domes bend over, hunched,
bunched together. Some, chained in deep folds,
molded in waves, sleep, wrinkled and old.

Hot volcanoes breathe in me, my back
blackened with cinders, scars of old fires,
pyres of ash. My red mouth and throat burn,
churn with hot, liquid lava. Below
flow molten rivers. Turn away! Go!

Forests live on me. Tall evergreens
lean against my mountains. Stands of beech
reach to the sky. Huge timber and bark
darken my leaf-strewn floors. Oak, teak, and pine,
vine-twisted rain forests—all are mine.

791

Waters bathe me, splash over my shores.
Pouring down from springs, ribboned streams
gleam with rills, hurry downwards, dashing,
plashing. Rivers rise. Blue swells leap high.
Dry up my waters and I will die.

Tundra covers me; swamps sodden, dank,
banked with moss, a soft, spongy morass.
Grassy bogs blanket my soaked crust here.
Sere, barren plains slush through marshes found
mounded with sedge on wet, withered ground.

Lowlands slide down me. Dip and hollow
follow the path to dell and ravine,
careen to broad valley, rocky gorge,
forge giant fissures. My canyons deep
sleep in stone walls, black, silent and steep.

Deserts sleep on me, restless, shifting,
drifting mounds of sand whipped by dry wind.
Skinned and barren, these dun, arid dunes
strewn with scorched tumbleweed, slumber, cursed,
submersed in mirage and endless thirst.

Find the answers to questions such as this one: *How do ice and water change the surface of the earth?* ANSWER QUESTIONS

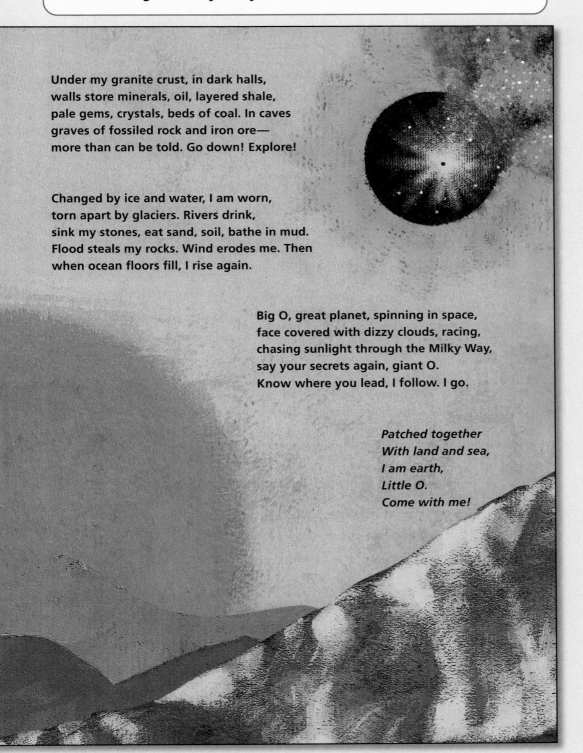

Under my granite crust, in dark halls,
walls store minerals, oil, layered shale,
pale gems, crystals, beds of coal. In caves
graves of fossiled rock and iron ore—
more than can be told. Go down! Explore!

Changed by ice and water, I am worn,
torn apart by glaciers. Rivers drink,
sink my stones, eat sand, soil, bathe in mud.
Flood steals my rocks. Wind erodes me. Then
when ocean floors fill, I rise again.

Big O, great planet, spinning in space,
face covered with dizzy clouds, racing,
chasing sunlight through the Milky Way,
say your secrets again, giant O.
Know where you lead, I follow. I go.

Patched together
With land and sea,
I am earth,
Little O.
Come with me!

Using the Glossary

Like a dictionary, this glossary lists words in alphabetical order. To find a word, look it up by its first letter or letters.

To save time, use the **guide words** at the top of each page. These show you the first and last words on the page. Look at the guide words to see if your word falls between them alphabetically.

Here is an example of a glossary entry:

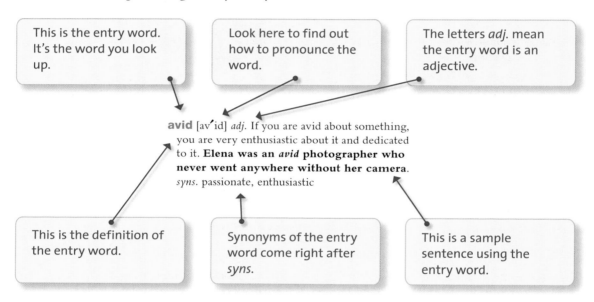

This is the entry word. It's the word you look up.

Look here to find out how to pronounce the word.

The letters *adj.* mean the entry word is an adjective.

avid [av´id] *adj.* If you are avid about something, you are very enthusiastic about it and dedicated to it. **Elena was an *avid* photographer who never went anywhere without her camera.** *syns.* passionate, enthusiastic

This is the definition of the entry word.

Synonyms of the entry word come right after *syns.*

This is a sample sentence using the entry word.

Word Origins

Throughout the glossary, you will find notes about word origins, or how words got started and have changed. Words often have interesting backgrounds that can help you remember what they mean. Here is an example of a word-origin note:

Word Origins

paddock *Paddock* comes from the Old English word *pearruc,* which means "an enclosed area." *Pearruc* is related to the word *park*.

Pronunciation

The pronunciation in brackets is a respelling that shows how the word is pronounced. The **pronunciation key** explains what the symbols in a respelling mean. A shortened pronunciation key appears on every other page of the glossary.

PRONUNCIATION KEY

a	add, map	m	move, seem	u	up, done
ā	ace, rate	n	nice, tin	û(r)	burn, term
â(r)	care, air	ng	ring, song	yo͞o	fuse, few
ä	palm, father	o	odd, hot	v	vain, eve
b	bat, rub	ō	open, so	w	win, away
ch	check, catch	ô	order, jaw	y	yet, yearn
d	dog, rod	oi	oil, boy	z	zest, muse
e	end, pet	ou	pout, now	zh	vision, pleasure
ē	equal, tree	o͝o	took, full	ə	the schwa, an
f	fit, half	o͞o	pool, food		unstressed vowel
g	go, log	p	pit, stop		representing the
h	hope, hate	r	run, poor		sound spelled
i	it, give	s	see, pass		*a* in *above*
ī	ice, write	sh	sure, rush		*e* in *sicken*
j	joy, ledge	t	talk, sit		*i* in *possible*
k	cool, take	th	thin, both		*o* in *melon*
l	look, rule	t̶h̶	this, bathe		*u* in *circus*

Other symbols:
- **· separates words into syllables**
- **′ indicates heavier stress on a syllable**
- **′ indicates lighter stress on a syllable**

Abbreviations: *adj.* adjective, *adv.* adverb, *conj.* conjunction, *interj.* interjection, *n.* noun, *prep.* preposition, *pron.* pronoun, *syn.* synonym, *v.* verb

A

a·ban·don [ə·ban′dən] *v.* **a·ban·doned** Something that has been abandoned has been left vacant and uncared for. **The owners *abandoned* the old building, and it became a safety hazard for the community.** *syns.* desert, discard

a·bide [ə·bīd′] *v.* When you abide by a decision or a law, you agree to it and follow it in your behavior. **The judge told the jury to *abide* by the rules.**

a·bun·dant [ə·bun′dənt] *adj.* When something is abundant, there are large quantities of it. **We picked an *abundant* supply of oranges from our tree.** *syn.* plentiful

> ### ACADEMIC LANGUAGE
> **accuracy** When you read with *accuracy*, you read without any mistakes.

ac·quain·tance [ə·kwān′təns] *n.* You have an acquaintance with someone you have met but do not know very well. **Even though I have an *acquaintance* with Larhonda, I do not know much about her.**

a·cute [ə·kyo͞ot′] *adj.* When something, such as an illness, is acute, it is strong and severe. **Tyrell went to the doctor with an *acute* sore throat.** *syn.* intense

> ### ACADEMIC LANGUAGE
> **advertisement** An *advertisement* is a public announcement or notice about things for sale or upcoming events. The purpose of advertisements is to persuade readers to take some kind of action, such as purchasing a product.

a·fi·ci·o·na·do [ə·fish′ē·ə·nä′dō *or* ə·fē′sē·ə·nä′dō] *n.* **a·fi·ci·o·na·dos** Aficionados are people who are enthusiastic and knowledgeable about a particular interest or subject. **Since Tiffany is an *aficionado* of classical music, she has a season ticket to the symphony orchestra.** *syn.* expert

ag·gra·vat·ed [ag′rə·vāt′əd] *adj.* An aggravated situation was already bad and has been made even worse. **Caleb went back to the doctor to have her reexamine his *aggravated* injury.** *syn.* irritated

> ── Word Origins ──
> **aggravate** Like the word *gravity*, *aggravate* comes from the Latin word *gravis*, which means "heavy" and "burdensome." In the word's literal meaning, something that is *aggravating* you is weighing you down.

al·i·bi [al′ə·bī] *n.* When you have an alibi, you can offer an explanation as to where you were when an event occurred. **In court, the accused person tried to provide an *alibi* that would prove he was not in the store during the robbery.** *syns.* excuse, explanation

al·ti·tude [al′tə·t(y)o͞od] *n.* A landform's altitude is its height above sea level. **We enjoyed the view from the highest *altitude* in our area.** *syns.* height, elevation

altitude

ap·par·ent [ə·par′ənt] *adj.* Something that is clear and obvious is apparent. **Since Caroline was rude to customers and was constantly late for work, it was *apparent* to her boss that she did not take her job seriously.** *syns.* obvious, evident

ar·du·ous [är′jo͞o·əs] *adj.* An arduous task requires you to work extremely hard to complete it. **Medical school involves an *arduous* program of study.** *syns.* difficult, grueling

as·cent [ə·sent′] *n.* When you make a steep upward climb, you make an ascent. **Many mountain climbers dream of making a successful *ascent* of Mt. Everest.** *syn.* climb

as·ton·ish·ment [ə·ston′ish·mənt] *n.* When you feel astonishment, you are greatly surprised or are experiencing a sense of wonder. **My *astonishment* about the party was noticeable to everyone in the room.** *syns.* surprise, amazement

as·tound·ing [ə·stound′ing] *adj.* When you find something astounding, it overwhelms you with surprise. **Even though Lauren had studied only a few extra hours, the improvement in her grades was *astounding*.** *syns.* astonishing, surprising

as·tute [ə·st(y)o͞ot′] *adj.* If you are astute, you are shrewd and clever about understanding situations and behavior. **On the first day on the job, the *astute* supervisor figured out who the best workers were.** *syns.* shrewd, smart

avid [avˊid] *adj.* If you are avid about something, you are enthusiastic about it and dedicated to it. **Elena was an *avid* photographer who never went anywhere without her camera.** *syns.* passionate, enthusiastic

> ### FACT FILE
>
> **avid** We use the word *avid* to describe someone who is passionate and enthusiastic about something, but *avid* can also describe someone who desperately wants what others have. *Avid* comes from the Latin *avēre,* meaning "to desire or crave," and is closely related to the word *avarus,* meaning "greedy."

B

ban [ban] *v.* **banned** When it is officially stated that something is not allowed to be done, shown, or used, it has been banned. **Skateboarding has been *banned* from this park because there have been so many injuries.** *syns.* forbid, exclude

ban·ish [banˊish] *v.* **ban·ished** People who are banished from a place are sent away and not allowed to return. **Throughout time, governments have *banished* certain people from their countries as punishment for committing crimes.** *syns.* expel, exile

bar·ren [barˊən] *adj.* Land that does not have trees and other plant life is barren. **After a forest fire, the land may look *barren*.** *syns.* desolate, unproductive

bea·con [bēˊkən] *n.* A light or fire that acts as a signal or warning is a beacon. **Lighthouses use a *beacon* of light to guide ships in the night.** *syn.* signal

bear·a·ble [bârˊə·bəl] *adj.* Something that you can usually put up with is bearable. **Mark decided that sharing a room with his little brother would be *bearable* because it was for only a short time.** *syns.* manageable, tolerable

beacon

be·fit·ting [bē·fitˊing] *adj.* Something that is befitting is suitable or appropriate for a person. **The queen wore a jeweled crown *befitting* her royal status.** *syn.* suitable

be·lov·ed [bi·luvˊid *or* bi·luvdˊ] *adj.* You feel great love and affection for someone or something that is beloved. **The happiest day of Martha's life was the day she married her *beloved* Ed.** *syn.* adored

> ### ACADEMIC LANGUAGE
>
> **biography** A *biography* is the story of a real person's life and is written by another person.

bliss [blis] *n.* When you feel bliss, you feel happy and content. **My idea of *bliss* involves lying on a tropical island beach, feeling the warm breeze, and hearing the gentle sound of surf.** *syn.* happiness

blurt [blûrt] *v.* **blurt·ed** When you have blurted out something, you have said it suddenly or impulsively. **As the girls were walking, Mary *blurted* out the news that her friend Emma had asked Nick to the school dance.**

brain·child [brānˊchīld] *n.* A brainchild is someone's original thought or idea. **Jared said that the kitchen design was his *brainchild* because he had created the sketch for it.** *syn.* idea

C

ca·coph·o·ny [kə·kofˊə·nē] *n.* A cacophony is a collection of harsh sounds that happen all at the same time. **Inside the pet store, the *cacophony* of all the animals was ear-splitting!** *syns.* dissonance, disharmony

ca·lam·i·ty [kə·lamˊə·tē] *n.* A calamity is an event that causes damage or distress. **Tearing her expensive and unique gown at the dress rehearsal was a *calamity* for the actor.** *syn.* disaster

chasm [kazˊəm] *n.* A deep split or crack in rock or ice is a chasm. **When Chen and Malcolm went hiking in the mountains, they came upon a deep *chasm* and had to find another route.** *syn.* gap

clam·or [klamˊər] *n.* When there is a clamor for something, people are asking for it noisily or angrily. **There was a *clamor* in the classroom because the students wanted a class trip to a theme park on the last day of school.** *syns.* outcry, uproar

a add	e end	o odd	o͞o pool	oi oil	th this		a in *above*
ā ace	ē equal	ō open	u up	ou pout	zh vision		e in *sicken*
â care	i it	ô order	û burn	ng ring		ə =	i in *possible*
ä palm	ī ice	o͝o took	yo͞o fuse	th thin			o in *melon*
							u in *circus*

cock·y [kok′ē] *adj.* Cocky people are overly confident and sure of themselves. **James, who was in first place, walked onto the diving board with a** *cocky* **smile.** *syns.* smug, overconfident

co·in·ci·den·tal·ly [kō·in′sə·den′tə·lē] *adv.* When two things happen coincidentally, they happen by accident at the same time, but they seem to be connected. *Coincidentally,* **my best friend and I both wore blue T-shirts to the party.**

com·mem·o·rate [kə·mem′ə·rāt] *v.* To commemorate an event is to do something to honor its memory. **A military parade will** *commemorate* **the end of World War II.** *syns.* honor, remember

com·mu·nal [kə·myoo′nəl *or* kom′yə·nəl] *adj.* Something that is shared by a group of people is communal. **The house's tenants shared a** *communal* **kitchen.** *syns.* shared, common

com·pen·sate [kom′pən·sāt] *v.* When you compensate for something, you provide something else to balance out its negative effects. **Kaprecia plans to** *compensate* **for her poor eyesight by sitting at the front of the room.** *syn.* balance

com·po·sure [kəm·pō′zhər] *n.* When you maintain your composure, you remain calm in a difficult situation. **The kennel owner maintained her** *composure* **as she waited for news about the dog that had run away.** *syns.* serenity, self-possession

con·cede [kən·sēd′] *v.* When you concede something, you acknowledge or admit that it is true, often against your will. **When the candidate learned that he had received only a few votes, he reluctantly agreed to** *concede* **that his opponent had won.** *syns.* grant, admit

con·fi·den·tial [kon′fə·den′shəl] *adj.* Something that is confidential is meant to be secret and not told to anyone else. **The patient information in the doctor's files is** *confidential* **and not allowed to be made public.** *syn.* private

con·front [kən·frunt′] *v.* To challenge someone face-to-face is to confront that person. **Sean was on his way to** *confront* **the person who had falsely accused him of stealing Lucy's cell phone.** *syn.* challenge

---

Word Origins

confront We sometimes use the phrase *head-to-head* to describe a type of challenge, which is what *confront* literally means. *Confront* is derived from the Latin words *com*, meaning "against," and *frons*, meaning "forehead."

---

con·spic·u·ous [kən·spik′yoo·əs] *adj.* Something that stands out and is easily noticed is conspicuous. **Because he is so much taller than the other students, Lenny is** *conspicuous* **when the class lines up.** *syn.* obvious

con·tem·plate [kon′təm·plāt] *v.* When you contemplate something, you think carefully about it. **I like to** *contemplate* **the idea of hiking the entire Appalachian Trail.** *syn.* consider

contemplate

con·tent·ed·ly [kən·tent′ed·lē] *adv.* To act contentedly is to show pleasure or satisfaction with the way things are. **When Kwan's mother saw his neat, clean room, she smiled** *contentedly.* *syn.* happily

con·tor·tion [kən·tôr′shən] *n.* **con·tor·tions** When you put something through contortions, you twist it into unnatural shapes. **The circus acrobat impressed the crowd with his seemingly impossible** *contortions.* *syn.* twist

con·trar·y [kon′trer·ē] *adj.* Statements that are contrary go against accepted beliefs or understanding. **The defense attorney's statements are** *contrary* **to the evidence presented by the other side.** *syn.* opposite

con·ven·tion·al [kən·ven′shən·əl] *adj.* Something that is conventional conforms to the usual and accepted standards. **Her written report includes a bibliography that follows the** *conventional* **standards for citing sources.** *syn.* usual

con·vince [kən·vins′] *v.* When you convince someone of something, you persuade the person that what you are saying is true. **The lawyer tried to** *convince* **the jury of his client's innocence.** *syn.* persuade

coun·ter·act [koun′tər·akt′] *v.* **coun·ter·act·ed** When you have counteracted something, you have acted in an opposite manner to prevent or reduce its effect. **Josie's flu vaccination** *counteracted* **the probability of her getting the flu.** *syn.* offset

crest·fall·en [krest′fôl·ən] *adj.* Someone who is crestfallen is very disappointed and sad. **After losing the election for class president, Jarnell appeared** *crestfallen.* *syns.* dejected, disappointed

crit·i·cal [krit′i·kəl] *adj.* When something is critical, it is extremely important, even essential. **Clean air is** *critical* **to our future.** *syns.* vital, crucial

cul·prit [kul′prit] *n.* A culprit is the person who committed a crime or offense. **The community is relieved that the *culprit* has been caught and sent to jail.** *syn.* offender

---

D

---

de·feat·ist [di·fē′tist] *adj.* Being defeatist is expecting, accepting, or resigning to failure. **Even though he had a good chance of winning, Michael's *defeatist* attitude kept him from entering the contest.** *syn.* pessimistic

de·ject·ed·ly [di·jekt′id·lē] *adv.* People act dejectedly when they are disheartened or in low spirits. **After her best friend moved away, Susan *dejectedly* waited by the phone, hoping for a call.** *syns.* sadly, dismally

de·mand [di·mand′] *n.* **de·mands** If someone makes demands of you, you are expected to give your time, facilities, or resources. **Carl's older brother makes *demands* of him to mow the lawn and take out the garbage.** *syn.* request

de·mol·ish [di·mol′ish] *v.* **de·mol·ished** When a building has been torn down or knocked down, it has been demolished, often because it is old and dangerous. **The crew *demolished* the old building that the Department of Health had condemned.** *syn.* destroy

demolish

de·scen·dant [di·sen′dənt] *n.* **de·scen·dants** Your relatives in future generations are your descendants. **Steven is writing a family history so that his *descendants* will be able to trace their roots.** *syn.* offspring

de·vour [di·vour′] *v.* **de·voured** You have devoured something if you have eaten it quickly and enthusiastically. **The lion *devoured* its prey.** *syn.* consume

di·ag·nose [dī′əg·nōs′] *v.* **di·ag·nosed** When an illness or problem has been identified, it has been diagnosed. **The doctor *diagnosed* Frank's illness as food poisoning.** *syns.* identify, recognize

dis·band [dis·band′] *v.* **dis·band·ed** When an organization is disbanded, its members stop working together as a group. **Because so many members had moved away, the model airplane club *disbanded*.** *syn.* break up

dis·or·i·ent·ed [dis·ôr′ē·ent·id] *adj.* If you feel lost or have lost your sense of direction, you have become disoriented. **After Felicia became *disoriented* in her walk through the woods, she was happy to find a ranger.** *syn.* confused

dis·own [dis·ōn′] *v.* If you disown someone or something, you break your connection with them. **My father jokingly said he would *disown* me if I wore the hat with the purple feathers.** *syns.* renounce, reject

dis·po·si·tion [dis·pə·zish′ən] *n.* Your disposition is your typical mood or temperament, especially the way you usually behave or feel. **Lashandra has a pleasant personality and an easygoing *disposition*.** *syns.* nature, temperament

dis·pute [dis·pyo͞ot′] *n.* If you have a dispute with someone, you have a disagreement or quarrel. **Evelyn and Robin had a *dispute* over who should be invited to the party.** *syns.* argument, disagreement

---

Word Origins

dispute The word *dispute* comes from the Latin *disputare*, in which *dis* means "apart" and *putare* means "to count" or "to consider." A *dispute* over a decision is a taking apart and reexamination of that decision.

---

a add	e end	o odd	o͞o pool	oi oil	th this		a in *above*
ā ace	ē equal	ō open	u up	ou pout	zh vision		e in *sicken*
â care	i it	ô order	û burn	ng ring		ə =	i in *possible*
ä palm	ī ice	o͝o took	yo͞o fuse	th thin			o in *melon*
							u in *circus*

dis·sat·is·fied [dis·sat′is·fīd′] *adj.* When you are dissatisfied, you are unhappy about the way something has turned out. **Jacob was *dissatisfied* with the quality of the music recording.** *syn.* displeased

dis·tinc·tive [dis·tingk′tiv] *adj.* When something is distinctive, it has special characteristics that make it easily recognizable. **No two zebras are identical, because each individual animal has a *distinctive* pattern of stripes.** *syn.* unique

dis·trac·tion [dis·trak′shən] *n.* A distraction takes your attention away from what you are trying to do. **The sound of the TV was a *distraction* to Suki as she studied.** *syns.* interruption, disturbance

dis·tur·bance [dis·tûr′bəns] *n.* **dis·tur·ban·ces** Disturbances are things that disrupt or interfere with something else. **Randy's mother stopped answering the phone after a series of calls became *disturbances* during dinnertime.** *syns.* upset, interruption

dol·drums [dōl′drəmz] *n. (pl.)* When you feel dull and lacking in energy, you are in the doldrums. **Wayne has been in the *doldrums* since his favorite TV show was canceled.** *syns.* sadness, depression

FACT FILE

doldrums The word *doldrums* comes from the Middle English word *dold*, meaning "dull." It also refers to an area near the equator that is known for its lack of wind. Long ago, when ships relied on wind to move, getting stuck in the windless doldrums was extremely dangerous.

doom [dōōm] *v.* **doomed** If something is doomed, it is expected that something terrible will happen to it. **The manatee may be *doomed* to extinction if the laws to protect this gentle animal aren't obeyed.** *syn.* condemn

dread [dred] *v.* **dread·ed** If you have dreaded something, you have greatly feared it happening. **Cindy *dreaded* getting back the results of her math test.** *syn.* fear

E

ea·ger [ē′gər] *adj.* When you are eager to do something, you are enthusiastic about it and very interested in it. **Bob is *eager* to begin piano lessons.** *syns.* enthusiastic, impatient

ec·stat·ic [ek·stat′ik] *adj.* If you are ecstatic, you are extremely happy. **Chelsea is *ecstatic* about winning the spelling bee.** *syns.* delighted, thrilled

ecstatic

e·lu·sive [i·lōō′siv] *adj.* When something is hard to understand, find, or achieve, it is elusive. **Paul is searching for a word, which is temporarily *elusive* to him, to describe the beautiful sunset.** *syns.* vague, indescribable

em·a·nate [em′ə·nāt] *v.* **em·a·nates** When a sound emanates from an object, it comes from that object. **The audience listens to the melody that *emanates* from Elina's flute.** *syns.* originate, come

e·merge [i·mûrj′] *v.* **e·merged** When something has emerged from somewhere, it has come out from behind, under, or inside that place. **The booming baritone voice that *emerged* from Raynard surprised the music teacher.**

en·dan·ger [in·dān′jər] *v.* To endanger something is to put it in a situation in which it could be hurt or damaged. **When boaters speed, they *endanger* the lives of manatees.** *syns.* imperil, jeopardize

en·thrall [in·thrôl′] *v.* **en·thralled** When you are enthralled with something, it is completely holding your interest or attention. **Kevin is *enthralled* with his new science fiction book.** *syns.* enchant, fascinate

en·trust [in·trust′] *v.* When you entrust someone with something, you give him or her the responsibility of taking care of it. **When I go on vacation, I will *entrust* María with the care of my cat.** *syns.* delegate, assign

en·twine [in·twīn′] *v.* **en·twined** When things are entwined, they are twisted together and wound around one another. **Catherine *entwined* roses with zinnias and tulips to make a beautiful wreath of flowers.** *syns.* twist, interweave

e·quip [i·kwip'] *v.* **e·quipped** When you have been equipped with something, it has been provided to you. **The school *equipped* the soccer team with uniforms, cleats, and shin pads.** *syns.* prepare, outfit

er·rat·ic [i·rat'ik] *adj.* Something that is erratic moves around or acts in an irregular or unpredictable way. **The hurricane's *erratic* path worried the weather forecasters, and they warned everyone in the state to be on the alert.** *syns.* inconsistent, unpredictable

eth·ics [eth'iks] *n. (pl.)* Your ethics are your system of moral beliefs and rules about what is right and wrong. **Because of her strong *ethics,* Ruth has a good reputation.** *syns.* principles, morals

ex·ert [ig·zûrt'] *v.* **ex·erts** When something exerts pressure on something else, it pushes on that thing. **Carbon dioxide in soda *exerts* pressure that is released when the container is opened.** *syn.* apply

ACADEMIC LANGUAGE

expository nonfiction *Expository nonfiction* text presents and explains facts about a topic. Photographs, captions, and headings are commonly found in these texts.

expression Reading aloud with *expression* means using your voice to match the action of the story and the characters' feelings.

ex·tent [ik·stent'] *n.* The extent of something is the size of the area it covers. **The *extent* of the state's land is shown clearly on the map.** *syns.* amount, scope

ACADEMIC LANGUAGE

fable A *fable* is a short story that teaches a lesson or presents a moral. Fables often include animals as characters.

faint [fānt] *adj.* When something is faint, it is not noticeable or bright. **The artist put such *faint* strokes of pink in the painting of the sunset that most people aren't aware of them.** *syns.* pale, dim

fer·tile [fûr'təl] *adj.* Land that is fertile is full of nutrients that are good for growing crops. **All kinds of fruits and vegetables grow well in this *fertile* valley.** *syns.* lush, productive

fertile

flour·ish [flûr'ish] *v.* **flour·ish·ing** Something that is flourishing is successful and growing rapidly. **Eric works hard and is good with animals, so his pet-sitting business is *flourishing.*** *syns.* prosper, increase

ACADEMIC LANGUAGE

folktale A *folktale* is a story that reflects the customs and beliefs of a culture. Folktales were first told orally and have been passed down through generations of a region or culture.

fore·sight [fôr'sīt] *n.* People who have foresight are able to envision possible problems in the future. **People concerned with Earth's environment have the *foresight* to look for new sources of energy now.** *syns.* forethought, prudence

frol·ic [frol'ik] *v.* **frol·icked** If something has frolicked, it has played in a happy, lively way. **The lambs *frolicked* in the meadow.** *syn.* play

fum·ble [fum'bəl] *n.* A fumble is a mistake or error, such as dropping the ball in a football game. **When Chase made a *fumble,* he knew his team would lose the game.** *syns.* mistake, blunder

fuse [fyo͞oz] *v.* **fused** When two or more things are fused, they are joined to become one object. **The electrician *fused* the two wires to make a new connection.** *syn.* combine

a	add	e	end	o	odd	o͞o	pool	oi	oil	th	this	ə =	*a* in *above*
ā	ace	ē	equal	ō	open	u	up	ou	pout	zh	vision		*e* in *sicken*
â	care	i	it	ô	order	û	burn	ng	ring				*i* in *possible*
ä	palm	ī	ice	o͝o	took	yo͞o	fuse	th	thin				*o* in *melon*
													u in *circus*

G

gin·ger·ly [jin′jər·lē] *adv.* If you approach something cautiously and tentatively, you move toward it gingerly. **Quietly and *gingerly*, Zelda walked toward the baby skunks.** *syns.* cautiously, delicately

grim·y [grī′mē] *adj.* Something that is grimy is covered with dirt or soot. **The fireplace had not been cleaned in years, and the chimney was *grimy*.** *syns.* dirty, grubby

H

ham·per [ham′pər] *v.* **ham·pered** If you have been hampered, something has made it difficult for you to accomplish what you had wanted to. **Diane's broken leg *hampered* her efforts to make the track team.** *syn.* hinder

hap·haz·ard·ly [hap·haz′ərd·lē] *adv.* Something that is organized haphazardly is not well planned or arranged. **Because Josiah had placed the trophies on the table *haphazardly*, some were given to the wrong people.** *syns.* randomly, carelessly

hay·wire [hā′wīr] *adj.* When something has gone haywire, it has gone wildly out of control. **The computer went *haywire* and Dave could not print his report.** *syns.* erratic, crazy

hin·drance [hin′drəns] *n.* A hindrance is someone or something that gets in the way of accomplishing a task. **Camilla feels that having to baby-sit her younger sister is a *hindrance* to completing her homework on time.** *syns.* obstacle, barrier

> ### ACADEMIC LANGUAGE
> **historical fiction** *Historical fiction* stories are set in the past and portray people, places, and events that did happen or could have happened.

hov·er [huv′ər] *v.* **hov·ered** If something hovered, it stayed in the same place in the air without moving in any direction. **The blimp *hovered* overhead.** *syn.* float

> ### ACADEMIC LANGUAGE
> **how-to article** A *how-to article* gives step-by-step instructions for completing a task or project.

hu·mon·gous [hyoo·mong′gəs] *adj.* Something that is extremely large in size or amount is humongous. **The shoe store attracted a big crowd with its *humongous* balloon that was shaped like a sneaker.** *syns.* gigantic, oversized

hys·ter·i·cal [his·ter′ə·kəl] *adj.* A person who is hysterical is in a panic or very excited. **When the boat started to sink, Nita became *hysterical*.** *syn.* frantic

I

i·de·al [ī·dē′əl *or* ī·dēl′] *adj.* When something is perfectly suited for a particular purpose, it is ideal. **A minivan is the *ideal* vehicle for a long family trip.** *syns.* perfect, best

il·lu·mi·nate [i·loo′mə·nāt] *v.* **il·lu·mi·nates** When something illuminates an object, it shines light on it to make it brighter or more visible. **Jorge's desk lamp *illuminates* his book.** *syn.* light

illuminate

im·mo·bile [i·mō′bəl] *adj.* If something is immobile, it cannot be moved. **The artist bolted the piece of sculpture to the floor so that it would be *immobile*.** *syn.* stationary

im·mor·tal·ize [i·môr′təl·īz] *v.* **im·mor·tal·ized** When someone is immortalized, something has been created to keep the memory of that person living forever. **The Washington Monument *immortalized* the first President of the United States and his achievements.** *syn.* commemorate

im·pact [im′pact] *n.* When one object smashes into another, the event is called an impact. **The *impact* of the rock shattered the car's windshield.** *syns.* crash, collision

im·per·a·tive [im·per′ə·tiv] *adj.* If something is imperative, it must be done no matter how difficult it is. **Even though Peter and Melea are rehearsing for the school play, it is *imperative* that they turn in all past-due assignments today.** *syns.* crucial, necessary

im·plode [im·plōd′] v. When something collapses in on itself, it implodes. **The engineers set the explosives to *implode* the building and make way for a new road.** syn. collapse

FACT FILE

implode The word *implode* was not used until the 1800s, after *explode* had taken on the meaning "to burst outward," which it still has today. *Implode* comes from the Latin *im*, meaning "in" or "inwardly," and *plaudere*, meaning "to clap" or "to applaud." *Explode,* the opposite of *implode,* was originally a theatrical term that meant "to suddenly burst into applause."

im·pos·ing [im·pō′zing] adj. Things that are imposing are very impressive or awe-inspiring in their appearance. **The White House is an *imposing* building.** syns. impressive, grand

im·pos·ter (*or* im·pos·tor) [im·pos′tər] n. A person who pretends to be someone else is an imposter. **The *imposter* pretended to be royalty.** syns. charlatan, fake

in·ca·pac·i·tat·ed [in′kə·pas′ə·tāt′əd] adj. Someone or something that is incapacitated is unable to work because of damage or injury. **The bus driver is *incapacitated* because she has broken her arm.**

in·debt·ed [in·det′id] adj. You are indebted to a person if you are grateful or obliged for a favor or assistance given to you by that person. **Sheila is *indebted* to Patricia for giving her a ride to school when it was raining.** syn. owing

in·flu·ence [in′flōō·əns] v. **in·flu·enced** When something has influenced you, it has made a difference in your development or decisions. **Latreisha's English teacher *influenced* her decision to attend college.** syn. sway

in·quire [in·kwīr′] v. When you inquire about something, you ask for information about it. **Ken *inquired* about the time and place of the meeting.** syns. ask, question

in·tact [in·takt′] adj. When something is intact, it is whole and undamaged. **Tenisha's mom received a new set of dishes *intact* from the delivery truck.** syns. whole, unbroken

in·tense [in·tens′] adj. Something intense exists in great strength or degree. **Tani has an *intense* desire to learn to speak French.**

in·ter·cept [in′tər·sept′] v. When you intercept someone on the way to a place, you meet the person before he or she gets there. **Chuck planned to *intercept* Alyssa as she was on her way to the library.** syns. interrupt, stop

in·tim·i·dat·ing [in·tim′ə·dāt′ing] adj. If something is intimidating to you, it makes you feel fearful or threatened. **Melissa says that the thought of moving to a big city is *intimidating*.** syn. frightening

in·tol·er·a·ble [in·tol′ər·ə·bəl] adj. Something intolerable is so awful that you cannot accept its continuing as it is. **Cho's dad considers world hunger *intolerable* and works to overcome it.** syn. unbearable

in·to·na·tion [in′tō·nā′shən] n. Intonation is the rise and fall in pitch of any sound. **The *intonation* of Pablo's voice during his speech was pleasant.** syn. inflection

ACADEMIC LANGUAGE

intonation Intonation is the rise and fall of your voice as you read aloud.

in·val·u·a·ble [in·val′y(ōō·)ə·bəl] adj. Something is invaluable to you if you feel that you can't do without it. **Larry's dictionary is *invaluable* to him when he writes his book reports.** syns. priceless, essential

J

jest [jest] n. Something said in jest is said in a playful or joking manner. **Rod's parents say in *jest* that he is going to eat them out of house and home if he doesn't stop growing.**

jus·ti·fi·ca·tion [jus·tə·fə·kā′shən] n. When you provide a reason or an explanation for a certain action, you provide justification. **Ricky's *justification* for eating ice cream and spoiling his dinner was that he was too hungry to wait another hour.** syns. excuse, reason

a	add	e	end	o	odd	$\overline{oo}$	pool	oi	oil	th	this		a in *above*
ā	ace	ē	equal	ō	open	u	up	ou	pout	zh	vision		e in *sicken*
â	care	i	it	ô	order	û	burn	ng	ring			ə =	i in *possible*
ä	palm	ī	ice	$\overline{oo}$	took	yōō	fuse	th	thin				o in *melon*
													u in *circus*

L

la·ment [lə·ment′] *v.* **lamented**
If you lamented something, you expressed deep regret that it happened. **Elisa *lamented* the loss of the bracelet that her grandmother had given her.** *syn.* grieve

lav·ish [lav′ish] *adj.*
Something that is lavish is richly decorated and looks impressive. **The *lavish* wedding cake must have taken many hours to decorate.** *syns.* fancy, ornate

lavish

ACADEMIC LANGUAGE

legend A *legend* is a story that is passed down through time and often reflects the beliefs or values of a culture. It may be based on real people or places.

le·thal [lē′thəl] *adj.* When something is capable of killing, it is lethal. **The fangs of sea snakes, probably the most venomous snakes on Earth, are *lethal* weapons.** *syns.* deadly, toxic

lin·ger [ling′ər] *v.* When you linger at a place, you are slow to leave because you want to stay there. **The students *lingered* at the football field after the game.** *syn.* remain

log·ic [loj′ik] *n.* Logic is the science of reasoning, which decides the truth of a statement by using a set of rules. **The judge used *logic* and the facts to decide the case.** *syns.* reason, sense

lunge [lunj] *v.* **lunged** If you lunged at something, you moved suddenly toward it. **The shark *lunged* toward the smaller fish.** *syns.* attack, leap

lus·trous [lus′trəs] *adj.* Something that shines or glows is lustrous. **The diamond is a *lustrous* jewel.** *syns.* radiant, shimmering

lux·u·ry [luk′shər·ē] *n.* A luxury is a pleasure or an item that is not necessary and is not often experienced because it is too costly. **A yacht is a *luxury* most people cannot afford.** *syn.* extravagance

M

ACADEMIC LANGUAGE

magazine article A *magazine article* gives information on a topic and usually includes photographs with captions.

mar·vel [mär′vəl] *v.* When you marvel at something, you feel intense amazement at it. **The children *marvel* at the way the tightrope walker keeps her balance so perfectly on the narrow wire.** *syn.* wonder

me·an·der [mē·an′dər] *v.* **me·an·der·ing** If you are moving slowly with a lot of bends or curves in your path, you are meandering. **The students were *meandering* through the art museum, stopping to look at the paintings that caught their attention.** *syn.* wander

FACT FILE

meander *Meander* was the classical name for a river in western Turkey. The *Meander* was so famous for its twisted and winding course that the Romans adopted the word as *maeander,* which in Latin means "winding path." Today, we use the word *meandering* when we talk about someone who is wandering, or walking aimlessly.

me·tic·u·lous·ly [mə·tik′yə·ləs·lē] *adv.* When you do something meticulously, you do it carefully, paying strict attention to details. **In science lab, Frederico makes sure he measures the chemicals *meticulously*.** *syns.* carefully, scrupulously

meticulously

mirth [mûrth] *n.* Mirth is a feeling of amusement that causes you to laugh out loud. **The clown's jokes made Esteban and Michelle feel full of *mirth*.** *syns.* amusement, merriment

mis·ap·pre·hen·sion [mis′ap·ri·hen′shən] *n.* When you have a misapprehension, you have misunderstood something. **Jana must have been under a *misapprehension,* because she showed up today for tomorrow's meeting.** *syn.* misunderstanding

mod·ern [mod′ərn] *adj.* Something that is modern is characteristic of the present time. **Juanita's house has *modern* furniture, not antiques.** *syns.* contemporary, current

mottle [mot′(ə)l] *v.* **mot·tled** A surface that is mottled has irregular shapes, patterns, or colors on it. **The painter used several shades of blue and green to give the wall a *mottled* appearance.** *syns.* dappled, spotted

murk·y [mûr′kē] *adj.* Something that is murky is dark and difficult to see through. **The water is so *murky* that Lisa can't see the bottom of the lake.** *syns.* dark, unclear

ACADEMIC LANGUAGE

myth A *myth* is an imaginative story that explains how people and places came to be. Myths are often based on what a group of people in the past believed.

N

ACADEMIC LANGUAGE

narrative nonfiction *Narrative nonfiction* tells about people, things, events, or places that are real.

neg·lect [ni·glekt′] *v.* **neg·lect·ed** When something has not been given proper care or attention, it has been neglected. **John *neglected* the plant, which died from lack of water.** *syns.* ignore, disregard

no·ta·ble [nō′tə·bəl] *adj.* Notable people and events are important and worth remembering. ***Notable* members of the community will attend the opening of the new science museum.** *syns.* prominent, famous

O

ob·jec·tion [əb·jek′shən] *n.* **ob·jec·tions** When you make objections to something, you give reasons for not liking or agreeing with it. **The town's plan for trash disposal was met with *objections* from homeowners who said there were not enough recycling bins.** *syn.* protest

of·fi·cious [ə·fish′əs] *adj.* Someone who is officious is very bossy and talks as if he or she is in charge of everything. **The manager spoke to the workers in an *officious* tone of voice.** *syns.* bossy, overbearing

op·ti·mis·tic [op′tə·mis′tik] *adj.* You are optimistic when you feel hopeful and positive about the future. **Jeremy's parents are *optimistic* about buying a new house soon.** *syns.* hopeful, positive

or·di·nar·y [ôr′də·ner·ē] *adj.* Something that is ordinary is not special or different in any aspect. **It was an *ordinary* summer day until the sky suddenly got dark and the tornado warning sounded.** *syns.* normal, commonplace

or·ner·y [ôr′nər·ē *or* ôrn′rē] *adj.* An ornery person or animal is usually uncooperative and in a bad mood. **Tom knew that it would be a bad idea to walk his dogs near the river, where *ornery* alligators had been known to attack small animals.** *syn.* irritable

o·ver·shad·ow [ō′vər·shad′ō] *v.* **o·ver·shad·owed** Something that is overshadowed by something else is viewed as less successful, less important, or less impressive than what it is being compared to. **Tim's first-place award in the state science fair *overshadowed* his brother's honorable mention.** *syns.* outshine, surpass

o·ver·whelm·ing [ō′vər·(h)welm′ing] *adj.* Things that are overwhelming seem to be too much to deal with. **The news that Miguel had been elected to the Music Hall of Fame was *overwhelming* to him.** *syn.* overpowering

P

ACADEMIC LANGUAGE

pace Reading aloud at an appropriate *pace* means reading with smoothness and consistency.

pelt [pelt] *v.* **pelt·ing** When you say that rain is pelting down, you mean that it is falling hard and hitting you with force. **The raindrops were *pelting* Roger and Jerry, and the boys were soaked by the time they got home.** *syn.* bombard

a	add	e	end	o	odd	$\overline{oo}$	pool	oi	oil	th	this		*a* in *above*
ā	ace	ē	equal	ō	open	u	up	ou	pout	zh	vision		*e* in *sicken*
â	care	i	it	ô	order	û	burn	ng	ring			ə =	*i* in *possible*
ä	palm	ī	ice	$\overline{oo}$	took	yōō	fuse	th	thin				*o* in *melon*
													u in *circus*

perch [pûrch] *v.* **perched** If you are perched on an object, you are sitting right on its edge. **The birds *perched* on the branch.** *syn.* sit

perch

per·fec·tion·ist [pər·fek′shən·ist] *n.* Somebody who feels that he or she has to do everything absolutely right is a perfectionist. **Greg was a *perfectionist* when it came to spelling, so he proofread his paper three times.** *syn.* stickler

per·ish·a·ble [per′ish·ə·bəl] *adj.* Foods that are perishable spoil if they are not stored properly. **We put away the groceries immediately so that the *perishable* items would not spoil.** *syn.* unpreserved

per·sist [pər·sist′] *v.* **per·sist·ed** When you have continued a task for a long time, even though it is difficult, you have persisted. **Debbie *persisted* in practicing the violin until she became good at it.** *syns.* persevere, continue

ACADEMIC LANGUAGE

personal narrative A *personal narrative* reveals the author's thoughts and feelings about something that happened to him or her. Personal narratives are told in first-person point of view.

ACADEMIC LANGUAGE

persuasive text *Persuasive text* is written to convince readers to take action or to agree with the author's viewpoint on a topic. Editorials, reviews, and advertisements are examples of persuasive text.

pe·ti·tion [pə·tish′ən] *v.* When you petition a higher authority, you formally make a request for an action or decision from someone who has more power than you have. **The homeowners *petitioned* the zoning board to reject the plans for the huge restaurant.** *syn.* appeal

phe·nom·e·non [fi·nom′ə·non] *n.* Something you can observe that exists in nature is called a phenomenon. **A lunar eclipse is a natural *phenomenon*.** *syns.* occurrence, fact

ACADEMIC LANGUAGE

phrasing *Phrasing* is grouping words into meaningful "chunks," or phrases, when you read aloud.

pil·lage [pil′ij] *v.* **pil·laged** Places that have been pillaged have had artifacts stolen. **The tombs of many of ancient Egypt's kings have been *pillaged* for gold, jewels, and other treasures.** *syns.* plunder, loot

ACADEMIC LANGUAGE

play A *play* is a story that is meant to be performed for an audience. Plays often include stage directions that tell the characters how to act and are often broken up into acts and scenes.

plea [plē] *n.* When you ask for something in an emotional or intense way, you are making a plea. **Tracy made a *plea* for forgiveness after she hurt her friend's feelings.** *syns.* appeal, request

ACADEMIC LANGUAGE

poetry *Poetry* is a form of expressive writing told in verse.

pre·cede [pri·sēd′] *v.* When something occurs or goes before something else, it is said to precede it. **In an essay, the conclusion should never *precede* the introduction.** *syn.* lead

pre·cise [pri·sīs′] *adj.* When something is exact and accurate, it is precise. **After Roberto got new glasses, his vision was sharp and *precise*.** *syns.* exact, accurate

pre·mo·ni·tion [prē′mə·nish′ən *or* prem′ə·nish′ən] *n.* A premonition is a feeling that something is about to occur. **Alisha had a *premonition* that her science fair project would not win an award.** *syns.* feeling, hunch

prim·i·tive [prim′ə·tiv] *adj.* Something that is primitive is crude, simple, and not technologically advanced. **The designs on the *primitive* clay pot had been scratched on the surface with a stick.**

pro·long [prə·lông′] *v.* When you prolong something, you make it last longer than it needs to. **The mayor wished she had not decided to *prolong* her speech, because the audience started to leave.** *syns.* extend, lengthen

prom·i·nent [prom′ə·nənt] *adj.* When a feature is prominent, it is very noticeable and may stick out from a surface. **The eyes are a *prominent* feature on some species of fish.** *syn.* noticeable

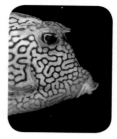

prominent

pro·mote [prə·mōt′] *v.* When you promote something, you contribute to its growth and help make it happen. **Marisa's encouragement did much to *promote* her sister's self-esteem.** *syns.* endorse, support

pro·pel [prə·pel′] *v.* When you propel a body or an object, you cause it to move in a certain direction. **Tyler kicked off at the end of the swimming pool to *propel* himself forward.** *syns.* push, thrust

pros·per·ous [pros′pər·əs] *adj.* People and places that are successful are prosperous. **The *prosperous* businesswoman was easily able to afford an expensive house.** *syns.* wealthy, affluent

pru·dent [prōō′dənt] *adj.* People who are prudent are sensible and practical in their actions. **Jerome made the *prudent* decision to get a good night's sleep before the test.** *syns.* cautious, sensible

pub·li·cize [pub′lə·sīz] *v.* When you publicize something, you make it widely known to the public. **Kathy placed posters all over the school to *publicize* the club's bake sale.** *syn.* advertise

pur·suit [pər·s(y)ōōt′] *n.* Your pursuit of a goal involves the actions you perform and the attempts you make to achieve it. **Daniel knew that to succeed in his *pursuit* of a gold medal, he would have to swim a mile every day.** *syns.* chase, quest

Q

qualm [kwäm *or* kwälm] *n.* When you have a qualm about something, you feel uneasy about whether it is right or wrong. **Joyce had a *qualm* about asking for help with her paper since it was supposed to be original work.** *syns.* doubt, apprehension

quan·da·ry [kwon′də·rē *or* kwon′drē] *n.* If you are in a quandary, you are unsure about what to do in a certain situation. **Rosa was in a *quandary* over whether to choose the flute or the clarinet as her band instrument.** *syns.* dilemma, predicament

R

rank [rangk] *adj.* Something that is rank tastes or smells foul. **The *rank* smell came from the spoiled milk.** *syns.* foul, rancid

ACADEMIC LANGUAGE

reading rate Your *reading rate* is how quickly you can read a text correctly and still understand what you are reading.

realistic fiction *Realistic fiction* stories have characters, settings, and plot events that are like people, places, and events in real life. The characters face problems that could really happen.

re·cede [ri·sēd′] *v.* **re·ced·ed** When water has receded, it has flowed away from where it was before. **Because the storms have washed away the sand, the shoreline has *receded* and the water is coming up to the buildings.** *syns.* retreat, withdraw

ref·uge [ref′yōōj] *n.* A refuge is a place that provides shelter and protection. **The cave provided a *refuge* from the sudden snowstorm.** *syn.* shelter

ACADEMIC LANGUAGE

refuge The word *refuge* comes from the Latin *refugium,* which means "a place to flee back to." This Latin word is also the source of the word *fugitive,* which names someone who flees from arrest.

reg·u·late [reg′yə·lāt] *v.* **reg·u·lates** When someone regulates something, he or she controls its functions and workings. **Stephanie *regulates* the air conditioner so that the temperature in the house is comfortable.** *syns.* control, adjust

re·in·force [rē′in·fôrs′] *v.* **re·in·forc·es** When something reinforces something else, it provides additional strength and support. **Because the fire is so large and dangerous, the chief *reinforces* his crew with firefighters from other places.** *syns.* strengthen, supplement

a	add	e	end	o	odd	ōō	pool	oi	oil	th	this		a in *above*
ā	ace	ē	equal	ō	open	u	up	ou	pout	zh	vision	ə =	e in *sicken*
â	care	i	it	ô	order	û	burn	ng	ring				i in *possible*
ä	palm	ī	ice	ōō	took	yōō	fuse	th	thin				o in *melon*
													u in *circus*

re·ject [ri·jekt′] *v.* **re·ject·ed** Someone or something that has been turned down or not accepted has been rejected. **John *rejected* the possibility that he could be wrong.** *syn.* discard

re·ly [ri·lī′] *v.* When you rely on something, you trust that it will be there when you need it. **Karen instructs her family to *rely* on the cell phone in emergencies.** *syn.* depend

re·mains [ri·mānz′] *n.(pl.)* The parts that are left of something that has died, grown old, or been destroyed are its remains. **The gardener dug up the *remains* of the dead plants.** *syns.* remnants, relics

rem·e·dy [rem′ə·dē] *n.* **rem·e·dies** Remedies are used to cure illnesses, stop pain, or fix problems. **Doctors prescribe *remedies* for illnesses, and people take the prescriptions to pharmacists.** *syns.* medication, solution

re·morse [ri·môrs′] *n.* If you feel remorse about an action, you feel guilt or regret about it. **When he thought about how he had ignored the new student, Jonathan felt *remorse*.** *syns.* regret, guilt

> **FACT FILE**
>
> **remorse** The word comes from the Latin *remorsus*, in which *re* means "again" and *morsus* means "to bite." So, in its original meaning, *remorse* is something that bites you again.

ren·dez·vous [rän′dā·voo′] *n.* When you have a rendezvous with someone, you have arranged to meet that person at a certain time and place. **Judy plans a *rendezvous* with Eileen at the movie theater at 7:00 P.M.** *syns.* meeting, date

rep·li·ca [rep′lə·kə] *n.* A replica is an exact model or copy of an object. **This model is a *replica* of a famous ship.** *syns.* copy, duplication

replica

re·serve [ri·zûrv′] *adj.* A reserve supply of something has been set aside for a special purpose. **We kept the *reserve* supply of canned goods in the pantry for emergencies.** *syn.* auxiliary

re·signed [ri·zīnd′] *adj.* When you are resigned to something, you accept it as it is because you know you cannot change it. **Ben's mother is *resigned* to her son's decision to be an astronaut.** *syns.* submissive, accepting

re·store [ri·stôr′] *v.* **re·stored** When you have restored something, you have put it back to its earlier condition. **The antiques dealer *restored* the old wooden desk to a beautiful condition.** *syns.* reinstate, refurbish

re·trieve [ri·trēv′] *v.* To retrieve something, you get it and take it back to where it was before. **The dog ran to *retrieve* the baby's teddy bear, which had fallen out of the carriage.** *syns.* recover, repossess

re·vered [ri·vird′] *adj.* If you are revered, you are highly respected and admired. **The heart surgeon who saved the newborn's life is greatly *revered*.** *syns.* respected, admired

ric·o·chet [rik′ə·shā] *v.* **ric·o·cheted** Something that has ricocheted has hit and bounced off another object. **The ball *ricocheted* off one wall and hit the opposite wall.** *syn.* rebound

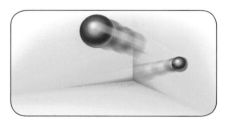

ricochet

rig [rig] *v.* **rigged** If you have rigged up an object, you have constructed it by using only materials that were available at the time. **Kyle *rigged* up a go-cart to compete in the race.** *syns.* fix, arrange

rit·u·al [rich′oo·əl] *n.* **rit·u·als** A culture's rituals are its ceremonies that involve a series of actions performed according to a set order. **The members of the group have a set of *rituals,* one of which involves greeting one another before each meeting.** *syns.* ceremony, service

S

sage [sāj] *adj.* A sage person is wise and knowledgeable. **The *sage* carpenter gave the apprentice his expert advice.** *syns.* wise, learned

sa·vor·y [sā′vər·ē] *adj.* Something that is savory has an appetizing taste or smell and tastes salty or spicy, not sweet. **The island's traditional food has a *savory* flavor.** *syns.* flavorful, salty

scale [skāl] *n.* You refer to the scale of something when you want to represent and compare sizes and distances but the real measurements are too enormous to be shown. **The architect showed her client a *scale* model of the house she had designed.** *syns.* size, range

scan·dal [skan′dəl] *n.* A situation or an event that causes public outrage or shock is known as a scandal. **The newspaper had a front-page story on the *scandal* of the stolen artwork.** *syn.* disgrace

ACADEMIC LANGUAGE

scandal Originally, *scandal*, which comes from the Greek word *skandalon*, meant "trap," which isn't much different from what a scandal is today. People caught in a scandal may feel as if they are in a trap.

scheme [skēm] *n.* **schemes** A scheme is a plan someone makes for getting in a clever way what he or she wants. **The police detective thought of various *schemes* to catch the criminal.** *syns.* plan, idea

ACADEMIC LANGUAGE

science fiction *Science fiction* stories have events that take place in the future, in space, or in different worlds. They contain imagined details about science and technology.

seep [sēp] *v.* **seeped** A liquid or a gas that has seeped into a place has leaked there slowly. **The grape juice *seeped* through the tiny hole in the paper cup and stained the tablecloth.** *syn.* leak

se·vere [sə·vir′] *adj.* Something that is very serious, very harsh, or very strict is severe. **The students decided not to skip school because the punishment would be too *severe*.** *syn.* harsh

sheep·ish·ly [shē′pish·lē] *adv.* If you act sheepishly, you show that you feel embarrassed or foolish. **When Carlos tripped over his shoelaces, he grinned *sheepishly*.** *syn.* awkwardly

ACADEMIC LANGUAGE

short story A *short story* is a fictional narrative that is not part of a novel. It focuses on one main problem or event.

sin·u·ous [sin′yoo·əs] *adj.* Something that is sinuous is long and curving like a snake. **The landscaper thought straight lines were boring, so he designed a *sinuous* walkway through the garden.** *syns.* twisting, winding

slink [slingk] *v.* **slunk** Someone who has slunk away has left quietly and secretively. **Joan *slunk* away after accidentally breaking her mother's favorite vase.** *syns.* creep, sneak

so·phis·ti·cat·ed [sə·fis′tə·kā′tid] *adj.* Cultures that are sophisticated are more advanced, complex, and modern than other cultures. **A *sophisticated* culture typically produces works of art.** *syn.* complicated

sta·bil·ize [stā′bə·līz] *v.* When you stabilize something, you make it less likely to move in response to forces such as wind. **Darrell planted grass on the hillside to *stabilize* the soil and keep it from washing away.** *syn.* steady

sta·tion·ar·y [stā′shən·er′ē] *adj.* Objects that are stationary stay in one place and do not move. **Jim's *stationary* bicycle is good for exercise but not for travel.** *syn.* motionless

stead·fast [sted′fast] *adj.* When you are steadfast, you are firm and unwavering about what needs to be done. **Julia was a *steadfast* supporter of her team, even after it had lost ten games in a row.** *syns.* unwavering, resolute

stationary

strand [strand] *v.* **strand·ed** Something that has been stranded has been left somewhere and cannot get back. **The storm *stranded* the survivors of the shipwreck on an island.** *syns.* trapped, marooned

stra·te·gi·cal·ly [strə·tē′ji·kə·lē *or* strə·tē′jik·lē] *adv.* When you place something strategically, you deliberately put it in the place that will be the most useful or have the most effect. **Arnold placed his sign *strategically* on a busy street, where it was sure to be seen.** *syns.* tactically, advantageously

stren·u·ous [stren′yoo·əs] *adj.* A strenuous activity requires you to use a lot of energy and effort to complete it. **Our car ran out of gas, and pushing it off the road was *strenuous* work.** *syns.* vigorous, demanding

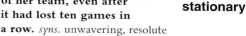

a	add	e	end	o	odd	o͞o	pool	oi	oil	th	this		*a* in *above*
ā	ace	ē	equal	ō	open	u	up	ou	pout	zh	vision	ə =	*e* in *sicken*
â	care	i	it	ô	order	û	burn	ng	ring				*i* in *possible*
ä	palm	ī	ice	o͝o	took	yo͞o	fuse	th	thin				*o* in *melon*
													u in *circus*

809

sty·mie [stī′mē] *v.* **sty·mied** You feel stymied when you are prevented from making progress on a task. **Lien was *stymied* when she couldn't find a way to get the equipment she needed for her science fair project.** *syns.* thwart, block

sub·tle [sut′(ə)l] *adj.* When people or things are subtle, they are not immediately noticeable, but they can be very effective. **Kate's *subtle* adjustment to her backstroke technique helped her win the race.** *syn.* slight

> **FACT FILE**
>
> **subtle** Before *subtle* took on the meaning that it has today, it was used to describe fabric. The word comes from the Latin *subtilis*, which means "delicate" and "finely woven."

suit [so͞ot] *v.* For something to suit you, it must be appropriate for you. **A ten-room house would *suit* a family with six children.**

sup·ple [sup′əl] *adj.* A supple object can move and bend easily without breaking or cracking. **Exercising every day kept the dancer's body *supple*.** *syn.* flexible

sur·pass [sər·pas′] *v.* **sur·passed** Something that has surpassed something else has gone beyond or done better than the other thing. **The football team *surpassed* its opponent's record for number of wins.** *syns.* exceed, outdo

sur·vey [sər·vā′] *v.* When you survey a place, you look around and consider it carefully. **Mr. Clark climbed the hill to *survey* the land.** *syns.* examine, review

---
T
---

tem·per·a·ment [tem′pər·(ə·)mənt] *n.* **tem·per·a·ments** People's temperaments are a measure of how they react to situations and what their usual moods are. **Most residents of the apartment house had pleasant *temperaments* and got along well with one another.** *syns.* nature, disposition

ter·min·al [tûr′mə·nəl] *adj.* When someone's condition is terminal, it cannot improve or be cured. **Unfortunately, the patient suffers from a *terminal* disease.** *syn.* incurable

tes·ti·mo·ny [tes′tə·mō′nē] *n.* When you give testimony, you give proof in support of a fact. **He appeared in court to give *testimony* as to his cousin's whereabouts on that specific night.** *syn.* evidence

thrive [thrīv] *v.* A living thing that is growing in a healthy manner is said to thrive. **Subtropical plants *thrive* in a warm climate.** *syns.* flourish, prosper

tol·er·ate [tol′ər·āt] *v.* **tol·er·at·ed** When you have let something that you did not agree with continue, you have tolerated it. **Amanda's parents disliked the posters of music groups on the door of her room but *tolerated* them anyway.** *syn.* endure

tor·ment [tôr·ment′] *v.* **tor·ment·ed** Someone who is tormented about something is extremely and painfully troubled by it. **The runner was *tormented* by the thought of falling and losing the race.** *syns.* tortured, stressed

tor·rent [tôr′ənt *or* tär′ənt] *n.* A torrent is a fast and powerful rush or flow. **When a large pipe breaks, the water escapes in a *torrent*.** *syns.* gush, surge

torrent

trac·tion [trak′shən] *n.* Traction is the force exerted by the act of pulling an object. **The *traction* of the windsail pulled the boat across the water.**

trea·son [trē′zən] *n.* Someone who betrays his or her country commits the crime of treason. ***Treason* is a serious crime in every country.** *syn.* disloyalty

trep·i·da·tion [trep′ə·dā′shən] *n.* You feel trepidation when you are fearful or anxious about something that is going to happen. **Amy awaits the sound of the drill at the dentist's office with *trepidation*.** *syns.* fear, anxiety

tres·pass [tres′pəs *or* tres′pas] *v.* When you trespass, you go on someone's property without permission or consent. **When people *trespass* on private property, the owner has the right to call the police.** *syn.* intrude

> **Word Origins**
>
> **trespass** *Trespass* comes from the Old French word *trespasser*, which means to "pass beyond or across." We use the word *trespass* to refer to crossing both literal and figurative boundaries without permission.

tri·al [trī′əl *or* trīl] *adj.* A trial run is a test or an experiment to see whether something will work. **When the *trial* run showed problems, the scientists realized that the solar-powered heater had to be redesigned.** *syn.* test

tri·um·phant [trī·um′fənt] *adj.* You feel triumphant when you are happy because you have achieved a goal or a victory. **Richard was *triumphant* as he crossed the finish line first in the big race.** *syns.* successful, victorious

U

un·as·sum·ing [un′ə·sōō′ming] *adj.* People and things that are unassuming are quiet and do not have an air of superiority. **The *unassuming* girl sat quietly while the teacher praised her excellent essay.** *syns.* modest, humble

un·der·state·ment [un′dər·stāt′mənt] *n.* When you make an understatement, you say something that does not fully express the extent to which something is true. **To say that the 101-degree weather was warm was a huge *understatement*.**

un·earth [un·ûrth′] *v.* **un·earthed** Something that has been unearthed has been discovered or uncovered, usually after a search or an investigation. **The scientists *unearthed* a giant dinosaur skeleton.** *syns.* expose, reveal

u·ni·son [yōō′nə·sən] *n.* When objects or people move in unison, they move together and at the same time. **The audience members waved their hands in *unison* at the rock concert.**

unison

un·prec·e·dent·ed [un·pres′ə·den′tid] *adj.* When something occurs that has never happened before, it is unprecedented. **The boxer had an *unprecedented* win against the undefeated champion.** *syn.* unparalleled

un·set·tling [un·set′ling] *adj.* Something that is unsettling causes you to feel worried and uncertain. **Seeing how well the other contestants had done gave Dennis an *unsettling* feeling.** *syns.* disturbing, disconcerting

urge [ûrj] *v.* **urg·es** When something urges you to do something, it encourages you to perform that action. **My conscience *urges* me to do the right thing.** *syn.* advocate

u·til·i·tar·i·an [yōō·til′ə·târ′ē·ən] *adj.* Objects that are utilitarian are designed and built to be useful rather than attractive. **The big old car was *utilitarian* and served its purpose of getting us to school.** *syns.* useful, practical

V

vie [vī] *v.* **vy·ing** When two competitors are vying for something, they are competing for the same goal. **The two tennis champions are *vying* for the grand prize.** *syns.* compete, contend

vig·i·lant·ly [vij′ə·lənt·lē] *adv.* When you have been watchful and alert to a problem or a danger, you have acted vigilantly. **The security guard did his job *vigilantly* and caught the burglar.** *syn.* attentively

W

wage [wāj] *v.* When you wage something, you begin an action and carry it out for a period of time. **The colonists were forced to *wage* a long war against England.**

warped [wôrp] *adj.* Something that is warped has been twisted out of shape, usually by heat or water, so that it does not function in a normal manner. **The *warped* flooring was caused by water that had leaked from the dishwasher.** *syns.* distorted, misshapen

wedge [wej] *v.* **wedged** Something that is wedged into a space is packed in tightly. **Nick *wedged* his suitcase into the overhead compartment on the plane.** *syns.* jam, lodge

wince [wins] *v.* **winced** You have winced when you have suddenly pulled away from something in anticipation of something unpleasant. **When Keisha saw the nurse carrying the needle, she *winced*.** *syns.* flinch, cringe

a add	e end	o odd	ōō pool	oi oil	th this	
ā ace	ē equal	ō open	u up	ou pout	zh vision	ə = { a in *above*
â care	i it	ô order	û burn	ng ring		e in *sicken*
ä palm	ī ice	ōō took	yōō fuse	th thin		i in *possible*
						o in *melon*
						u in *circus*

Index of Titles and Authors

Page numbers in green refer to biographical information.

Acknowledgments

For permission to reprint copyrighted material, grateful acknowledgment is made to the following sources:

Atheneum Books for Young Readers, an Imprint of Simon & Schuster Children's Publishing Division: From *S.O.R Losers* by Avi. Text copyright © 1984 by Avi Wortis. *The Sons of the Dragon King: A Chinese Legend* by Ed Young. Copyright © 2004 by Ed Young.

Kelly C. Bourne: From "High-Tech Treasure Hunt" by Kelly Bourne in *Boys' Life* Magazine, November 2002. Published by the Boy Scouts of America.

Boyds Mills Press, Inc.: From *Buildings in Disguise* by Joan Marie Arbogast. Text copyright © 2004 by Joan Marie Arbogast. "Embroidery" and "Washed Away: A Double Haiku" from *Water Music* by Jane Yolen, photographs by Jason Stemple. Text copyright © 1995 by Jane Yolen; photographs copyright © 1995 by Jason Stemple. Published by Wordsong, an imprint of Boyds Mills Press.

Candlewick Press, Inc., Cambridge, MA: Cover illustration by Jeffrey Fisher from *Seeing the Blue Between: Advice and Inspiration for Young Poets,* compiled by Paul B. Janeczko. Illustration copyright © 2002 by Jeffrey Fisher. Illustrations by Chris Raschka from *A Kick in the Head: An Everyday Guide to Poetic Forms* by Paul B. Janeczko. Illustrations copyright © 2005 by Chris Raschka. From *The Egyptian News* by Scott Steedman, illustrated by Angus McBride and Peter Visscher. Text copyright © 1997 by Scott Steedman; illustrations copyright © 1997 by Walker Books Ltd.

Capstone Press: From *Ancient Greece* by Kim Covert. Text © 2004 by Capstone Press.

Carus Publishing Company, 30 Grove St., Suite C, Peterborough, NH 03458: "How Athens was Named," retold by Pat Betteley from *FACES: Greece,* September 2000. Text copyright © 2000 by Cobblestone Publishing Company.

Chronicle Books LLC, San Francisco, ChronicleBooks.com: "The Girl Who Named Pluto," adapted from *The Kid Who Named Pluto* by Marc McCutcheon, illustrated by Jon Cannell. Text © 2004 by Marc McCutcheon; illustrations © 2004 by Jon Cannell. "A Time to Dance" from *Unwitting Wisdom: An Anthology of Aesop's Fables,* retold and illustrated by Helen Ward. © 2004 by Helen Ward.

The Cricket Magazine Group, a division of Carus Publishing Company: "Calder: The Man Who Made Art out of the Ordinary" by Doug Stewart from *Muse* Magazine, November/December 2005. Text © 2005 by Doug Stewart.

Kalli Dakos: "I was sitting at lunch" by Kalli Dakos from *Seeing the Blue Between: Advice and Inspiration for Young Poets,* compiled by Paul B. Janeczko. Text copyright © 2002 by Kalli Dakos.

Jerry C. Dunn, Jr.: "Find Your Way Anywhere Using Only the Sun and Your Wristwatch" by Merry Vaughn from *Tricks of the Trade,* edited by Jerry Dunn, cover illustration by Stephen Schudlich. Text and cover illustration copyright © 1994 by Jerry Dunn. Published by Houghton Mifflin Company.

Enslow Publishers, Inc., Berkeley Heights, NJ: From *The Incredible Quest to Find the Titanic* by Brad Matsen. Text copyright © 2003 by Enslow Publishers, Inc.

Farrar, Straus and Giroux, LLC: From *The Man Who Made Time Travel* by Kathryn Lasky, illustrated by Kevin Hawkes. Text copyright © 2003 by Kathryn Lasky; illustration copyright © 2003 by Kevin Hawkes.

Harcourt, Inc.: *Wilma Unlimited: How Wilma Rudolph Became the World's Fastest Woman* by Kathleen Krull, illustrated by David Diaz. Text copyright © 1996 by Kathleen Krull; illustrations copyright © 1996 by David Diaz. "Ode to Pablo's Tennis Shoes" from *Neighborhood Odes* by Gary Soto. Text copyright © 1992 by Gary Soto.

HarperCollins Publishers: Cover illustration from *100 Great Science Fiction Short Short Stories* by Isaac Asimov ET AL. Illustrations copyright © 1978 by Isaac Asimov, Martin Harry Greenberg, and Joseph D. Olander. From *The Color of My Words* by Lynn Joseph, cover illustration by Robert Crawford. Text copyright © 2000 by Lynn Joseph; cover illustration © 2002 by Robert Crawford. Cover illustration from *S.O.R. Losers* by Avi Wortis.

Obadinah Heavner, www.obadinah.com: Cover illustration by Obadinah Heavner from *Muse* Magazine, November/December 2005.

Highlights for Children, Inc., Columbus, Ohio: "Why Do Cliff Swallows Live Together?" by Jack Myers, illustrated by John Rice from *Highlights for Children* Magazine, June 2005. Copyright © 2005 by Highlights for Children, Inc. "Drawing Horses" by Cerelle from *Highlights for Children* Magazine, April 2000. Text copyright © 2000 by Highlights for Children, Inc.

Holiday House, Inc.: Illustrations by Leonard Everett Fisher from *Earth Songs* by Myra Cohn Livingston. Illustrations copyright © 1986 by Leonard Everett Fisher.

Houghton Mifflin Company: From *Next Stop Neptune: Experiencing the Solar System* by Alvin Jenkins, illustrated by Steve Jenkins. Text copyright © 2004 by Alvin Jenkins; illustrations copyright © 2004 by Steve Jenkins.

Hyperion Books for Children: From *Maxx Comedy: The Funniest Kid in America* by Gordon Korman, cover illustration by Alex Ferrari. Text copyright © 2003 by Gordon Korman; cover illustration © 2003 by Alex Ferrari. "Focus" and "Flying Solo" and cover photograph from *Perfect Harmony: A Musical Journey with the Boys Choir of Harlem* by Charles R. Smith, Jr. Text and cover photograph copyright © 2002 by Charles R. Smith, Jr.

Kids Can Press Ltd., Toronto: From *The Wright Brothers: A Flying Start* by Elizabeth MacLeod. © 2002 by Elizabeth MacLeod.

Kingfisher, a Houghton Mifflin Company imprint: From "A Hidden City in the Andes" in *Great Discoveries & Amazing Adventures* by Claire Llewellyn. Text copyright © 2004 by Kingfisher Publications Plc.

Lee & Low Books Inc.: "Words Free as Confetti" from *Confetti: Poems for Children* by Pat Mora. Text copyright © 1996 by Pat Mora.

Lerner Publications Company: From *Smokejumpers* by Elaine Landau, photographs by Ben Klaffke. Text copyright © 2002 by Elaine Landau; photographs copyright © 2002 by Ben Klaffke. From *Life on the Edge* by Cherie Winner. Text copyright © 2006 by Cherie Winner.

Little, Brown and Company, (Inc.): From *Maniac Magee* by Jerry Spinelli, cover photograph by Roger Hagadone. Text copyright © 1990 by Jerry Spinelli; cover photograph © by Roger Hagadone.

Mélina A. Mangal: "The Long Bike Ride" by Mélina Brown. Text copyright © 2001 by Mélina Brown.

Milkweed Editions: Cover illustration by Trudy Nicholson, map by Paul Mirocha from *Stories from Where We Live: The California Coast,* edited by Sara St. Antoine. Cover illustration © 2001 by Trudy Nicholson; map © 2001 by Paul Mirocha.

National Geographic Society: "Statue of Liberty" from *Monumental Verses* by J. Patrick Lewis. Text copyright © 2005 by J. Patrick Lewis. From "Are you Laughing at me?" by Michael Witzer and Laura Daily in *National Geographic World* Magazine, April 2001. Text copyright © 2001 by National Geographic Society.

Naomi Shihab Nye: "To My Dear Writing Friends" by Naomi Shihab Nye from *Seeing the Blue Between: Advice and Inspiration for Young Poets,* compiled by Paul B. Janeczko. Text copyright © 2002 by Naomi Shihab Nye.

Kathi Paton Literary Agency, on behalf of the Estate of Fred C. Kelly: Illustration by James MacDonald from *How We Invented the Airplane: An Illustrated History* by Fred C. Kelly. Illustration © 1953 by Fred C. Kelly. Published by Dover Publications.

Brian Payne: Photographs by Brian Payne from "High-Tech Treasure Hunt" by Kelly C. Bourne in *Boys' Life* Magazine, November 2002. Published by the Boy Scouts of America.

QA International, www.qa-international.com: "A World in Motion" from *Scholastic Atlas of Oceans.* © 2006 by QA International.

Random House Children's Books, a division of Random House, Inc.: From *Befiddled* by Pedro de Alcantara, cover illustration by Susan Farrington. Text copyright © 2005 by Pedro de Alcantara; cover illustration © 2005 by Susan Farrington. From *Eager* by Helen Fox, cover illustration by Adam Willis. Text copyright © 2004 by Helen Fox; cover illustration © 2004 by Adam Willis. From *Brian's Winter* by Gary Paulsen, cover illustration by Bruce Emmett. Text copyright © 1996 by Gary Paulsen.

Marian Reiner: Earth Songs by Myra Cohn Livingston. Text copyright © 1986 by Myra Cohn Livingston.

Marian Reiner, on behalf of August House, Inc., Little Rock, AR: "Fire, Water, Truth, and Falsehood" from *Wisdom Tales from Around the World* by Heather Forest, cover illustration by David Boston. Text and cover illustration copyright © 1996 by Heather Forest.

Scholastic, Inc.: From "Inspiration to Invention" by Cate Baily in *Scholastic Scope* Magazine, November 2003. Text copyright © 2003 by Scholastic Inc. From *Secrets of the Sphinx* by James Cross Giblin, illustrated by Bagram Ibatoulline. Text copyright © 2004 by James Cross Giblin; illustrations copyright © 2004 by Bagram Ibatoulline. Published by Scholastic Press. "Incredible Rescues" from *Fire!* by Joy Masoff. Text copyright © 1998 by Joy Masoff. From *Scholastic Book of World Records 2005* by Jenifer Corr Morse. Text and cover copyright © 2004 by Georgian Bay Associates. Cover illustration from *Scholastic Atlas of Oceans.* Illustration copyright © 2004 by Scholastic Inc. Published by Scholastic Reference.

Simon & Schuster Books for Young Readers, an imprint of Simon & Schuster Children's Publishing Division: Illustrations by Karen Barbour from *Wonderful Words: Poems About Reading, Writing, Speaking and Listening,* selected by Lee Bennett Hopkins. Illustrations copyright © 2004 by Karen Barbour. From *Escaping the Giant Wave* by Peg Kehret. Text copyright © 2003 by Peg Kehret.

SLL/Sterling Lord Literistic, Inc.: From *The Phantom Tollbooth* by Norton Juster, adapted by Susan Nanus. Text copyright © by Norton Juster.

Sternig & Byrne Literary Agency: "Zoo" by Edward D. Hoch from *Fantastic Universe.* Text copyright © 1958 by King-Size Publications, Inc.

Tilbury House, Publishers, Gardiner, Maine: From *Life Under Ice* by Mary M. Cerullo, photographs by Bill Curtsinger. Text © 2003 by Mary M. Cerullo; photographs © 2003 by Bill Curtsinger.

Viking Penguin, A Division of Penguin Young Readers Group, A Member of Penguin Group (USA) Inc., 345 Hudson St., New York, NY 10014: From *The Emperor's Silent Army* by Jane O'Connor. Copyright © 2002 by Jane O'Connor.

Walker Publishing Company, Inc.: The Great Serum Race: Blazing the Iditarod Trail by Debbie S. Miller, illustrated by Jon Van Zyle. Text copyright © 2002 by Debbie S. Miller; illustrations copyright © 2002 by Jon Van Zyle.

Weekly Reader Corporation: From "Get in Gear with Safety" by Tracy Early in *Current Health 1*® Magazine, January 2001. Text published and copyrighted by Weekly Reader Corporation.

Photo Credits

Placement Key(t) top; (b) bottom; (l) left; (r) right; (c) center; (bg) background; (fg) foreground; (i) inset.

17 (b) Peter Bennett/Ambient Images; 17 (tr) Scala/Art Resource; 18 Images.com/Corbis; 22 (b) Joe Atlas/PictureQuest; 23 (tr) VStock LLC/Index Stock; 24 (b) Zoran Milich/Getty; 44 (l) Peter McBride Photography; 45 (tr) Peter McBride Photography; 53 (b) Brandon D. Cole/Corbis; 56 (b) Brandon D. Cole/Corbis; 57 (tr) Larry West/Bruce Coleman, Inc.; 77 (tr) Jon Shireman/Getty; 79 (bl) Lester Lefkowitz/Corbis; 80 (br) James Marshall/Corbis; 81 (tr) Siede Preis/Getty; 83 (tr) Tim Hawkins/Corbis; 85 (b) Wright State University; 86 (bl) Wright State University; 86 (br) Wright State University; 87 (bl) Henry Ford Museum & Greenfield Village; 87 (br) Wright State University; 88 (br) National Air and Space Museum; 89 (tr) Bettman/Corbis/Magma; 91 (b) Library of Congress; 92 (b) Library of Congress; 93 (t) Library of Congress; 93 (br) Smithsonian Institution; 94 (bl) Library of Congress; 95 (c) Library of Congress; 95 (bl) Library of Congress; 97 (b) Wright State University; 98 (br) Library of Congress; 98 (bl) Wright State University; 99 (b) Wright State University; 102 Corbis; 109 (b) Jerry Cooke/Corbis; 112 (bl) Bettmann/Corbis; 113 (tr) Tony Duffy/Allsport/Getty; 128 (t) Stephen Dalton/Photo Researchers Inc.; 129 (c) OSF/Howard Hall/Animals Animals; 131 (tr) Jim Vecchi/Corbis; 150 Anna Pugh/Lucy Campbell Gallery; 157 (tr) Stockdisc/Superstock; 179 (b) David Stoecklein/Corbis; 180 (b) Michael Wells/Getty; 181 (tr) Bigshots/Getty; 182 (b) Michael Cogliantry/Getty; 201 (br) Comstock/Superstock; 201 (bcr) Thinkstock/Superstock; 205 (bl) Robert Dowling/Corbis; 206 (bl) Ludovic Maisant/Corbis; 207 (tr) Tom Nebbia/Corbis; 208 (bl) Bettmann/Corbis; 208 (br) Hulton-Deutsch Collection/Corbis; 209 (tr) Bettmann/Corbis; 224 (bl) Standard Insurance Company; 225 (l) Paul A. Souders/Corbis; 225 Standard Insurance Company; 228 (b) Kevin R. Morris/Corbis; 230 (b) Gordon Whitten/Corbis; 231 (tr) Ed Kashl/Corbis; 234 Ben Klaffke/Millbrook Press/Lerner Publishing Group; 236 (t) Ben Klaffke/Millbrook Press/Lerner Publishing Group; 237 (r) Ben Klaffke/Millbrook Press/Lerner Publishing Group; 238 (tl) Ben Klaffke/Millbrook Press/Lerner Publishing Group; 238 (b) Ben Klaffke/Millbrook Press/Lerner Publishing Group; 239 (tr) Ben Klaffke/Millbrook Press/Lerner Publishing Group; 239 (br) Ben Klaffke/Millbrook Press/Lerner Publishing Group; 240 Ben Klaffke/Millbrook Press/Lerner Publishing Group; 241 (r) Ben Klaffke/Millbrook Press/Lerner Publishing Group; 242 (l) Ben Klaffke/Millbrook Press/Lerner Publishing Group; 243 (tl) Ben Klaffke/Millbrook Press/Lerner Publishing Group; 243 Ben Klaffke/Millbrook Press/Lerner Publishing Group; 244 (t) Ben Klaffke/Millbrook Press/Lerner Publishing Group; 245 (b) Ben Klaffke/Millbrook Press/Lerner Publishing Group; 248 (l) Setboun/Corbis; 249 Ed Kashi/Corbis; 250 (l) Justin Sullivan/Getty; 251 (r) Barry Smith/Scholastic; 253 (tr) Dan Lamont/Corbis; 267 James L. Amos/Corbis; 268 James L. Amos/Corbis; 271 (l) Tom Bean/Corbis; 272 Christie's Images/Corbis; 275 (b) Paul A. Souders/Corbis; 276 (b) Royalty-free/Getty; 277 (tr) MedioImages Inc./Index Stock; 278 (b) Norbert Wu/Minden Pictures; 279 (tr) Bill Curtsinger/National Geographic Image Collection; 281 (t) Bill Curtsinger/Tilbury House; 282 (tl) Bill Curtsinger/Tilbury House Publishers; 282 (bl) Bill Curtsinger/Tilbury House Publishers; 282 (c) Bill Curtsinger/Tilbury House Publishers; 283 (tr) Bill Curtsinger/Tilbury House Publishers; 284 (tl) Bill Curtsinger/Tilbury House Publishers; 284 (cr) Bill Curtsinger/Tilbury House Publishers; 286 (tl) Bill Curtsinger/Tilbury House Publishers; 286 (bl) Bill Curtsinger/Tilbury House Publishers; 286 (br) Bill Curtsinger/Tilbury House Publishers; 287 (br) Bill Curtsinger/Tilbury House Publishers; 289 Bill Curtsinger/

Tilbury House Publishers; 290 (t) Bill Curtsinger/Tilbury House Publishers; 290 (b) Bill Curtsinger/Tilbury House Publishers; 291 (c) Bill Curtsinger/Tilbury House Publishers; 292 (tr) Bill Curtsinger/Tilbury House Publishers; 292 (br) Bill Curtsinger/ Tilbury House Publishers; 292 (tl) Bill Curtsinger/ Tilbury House Publishers; 293 (b) Bill Curtsinger/Tilbury House Publishers; 294 (b) Bill Curtsinger/Tilbury House Publishers; 296 (br) Lester V. Bergman/Corbis; 296 (t) Tom Brakefield/Getty; 297 (tr) Lester V. Bergman/Corbis; 299 (tr) Steve Terrill/Corbis; 300 (b) Ludovic Maisant/Corbis; 301 (br) National Geographic/Zuma/ Corbis; 301 (b) Wolfgang Kaehler/Corbis; 303 (b) Peter Adams/ Zefa/Corbis; 305 (tr) Theo Allofs/Corbis; 306 (b) Darrell Gulin/ Corbis; 307 (tr) Veer; 308 (cr) Galen Rowell/Corbis; 308 (bl) Galen Rowell/Corbis; 309 (r) Galen Rowell/Corbis; 324 Tilbury House Publishers; 325 (t) Jason Stemple/Boyds Mills Press; 325 (b) Jason Stemple/Boyds Mills Press; 327 (tr) Kennan Ward/ Corbis; 329 (b) P. Wilson/Zefa/Corbis; 332 (b) Hulton Archives/ Getty; 333 (tr) Bettmann/Corbis; 364 (b) Royalty-free/Corbis; 365 (tr) Lew Robertson; 367 (r) Royalty-free/Corbis; 404 Bettmann/Corbis; 406 (bl) Royalty-free/Corbis; 406 (cr) Royalty-free/Corbis; 406 (t) Royalty-free/Corbis; 407 (bl) Royalty-free/Corbis; 407 (cl) Royalty-free/Corbis; 407 (cr) Royalty-free/Corbis; 408 (b) Royalty-free/Corbis; 409 (r) age fotostock/Superstock; 410 (b) HIP/Art Resource; 411 (r) Fine Art Photographic Library, London/Art Resource; 428 Calder Foundation/ARS; 429 (br) Art Resource; 429 (cl) Calder Foundation/ARS; 430 Art Resource; 430 (t) Art Resource; 430 Art Resource; 430 Art Resource; 430 (bl) Calder Foundation/ ARS; 431 (b) Calder Foundation/ARS; 431 (t) Calder Foundation/ ARS; 433 (tr) Royalty-free/Corbis; 434 (br) Ingo Boddenberg/ Zefa/Corbis; 440 (b) Royalty-free/Corbis; 441 (cr) Comstock/ Superstock; 441 (tr) Royalty-free/Corbis; 442 (b) Image Source Photography/Veer; 461 (r) Royalty-free/Corbis; 463 Images. com/Corbis; 464 (b) Denis Scott/Corbis; 465 (r) Royalty-free/ Corbis; 467 (tr) James Noble/Corbis; 483 (br) Jose Fuste Raga/ Corbis; 484 (c) Kelly-Mooney Photography/Corbis; 487 (r) Macduff Everton/Corbis; 488 (b) Jeff Chiu/San Francisco Chronicle; 489 (r) John Kalucki; 490 Joan Marie Arbogast/Boyds Mills Press; 491 (tl) Joan Marie Arbogast/Boyds Mills Press; 491 (c) Stan Shoneman/Omni Photo Communications, Inc.; 492 (bl) The Save Lucy Committee, Inc.; 492 (r) The Save Lucy Committee, Inc.; 493 (br) The Save Lucy Committee, Inc.; 493 (cr) The Save Lucy Committee, Inc.; 494 (bl) The Save Lucy Committee, Inc.; 494 (br) The Save Lucy Committee, Inc.; 495 (br) Joan Marie Arbogast/Boyds Mills Press; 495 (tr) The Save Lucy Committee, Inc.; 495 (tc) The Save Lucy Committee, Inc.; 496 (l) Stan Shoneman/Omni Photo Communications, Inc.; 497 Boyds Mills Press; 498 (b) South Dakota Department of Tourism, Corn Palace Convention and Visitors Bureau; 499 (t) South Dakota Department of Tourism, Corn Palace Convention and Visitors Bureau; 500 (b) "DUTCH WONDERLAND® Family Amusement Park, Lancaster, PA; (C) 2006 Wonderland Amusement Management LLC. DUTCH WONDERLAND is a registered trademark used under license."; 500 (tl) Enchanted Forest, Turner, Oregon; 501 (tr) Joan Marie Arbogast/Boyds Mills Press; 501 (b) Joan Marie Arbogast/Boyds Mills Press; 502 (tl) Boyds Mills Press; 502 (b) Peter Bennett/Ambient Images; 503 (t) Lincoln Highway Heritage Corridor, Pennsylvania; 505 (c) Dog Bark Park Inn B&B; 509 (t) Royalty-free/Corbis; 528 Stapleton Collection/Corbis; 531 (tr) Erich Lessing/Art Resource; 531 (bl) Erich Lessing/Art Resource, NY; 532 (bl) Karl Weatherly/ Corbis; 533 (tr) S. Carmona/Corbis; 533 (cr) Yiorgos Karahalis/ Reuters/Corbis; 534 (b) Charles O'Rear/Corbis; 535 (r) Ludovic Maisant/Corbis; 537 (l) Corbis/Christie's images; 537 (t) Stock Montage; 538 Art Resource/Erich Lessing; 540 Wolfgang Kaehler; 541 (c) Art Resource/Scala; 541 (t) Corel; 541 (r) Wolfgang Kaehler; 542 Art Resource/Erich Lessing; 543 (t) Corbis/Bettman; 544 (br) Art Resource/Scala; 544 (bl) Getty Images/Hulton Archives; 545 (t) Unicorn Stock Photos/Patti McConville; 546 (c) DigitalGlobe Inc.; 547 (c) Gary Hershorn; 548 (l) Ruggero Vanni; 553 (tr) Erich Lessing/Art Resource; 554 (b) Charles O'Rear/Corbis; 556 (b) Le Segretain P./Corbis Sygma; 557 (b) Lester Lefkowitz/Corbis; 560 Keren Su/Getty; 562 (b) Helen Norman/Botanica/PictureQuest; 563 (tr) M. Timothy O'Keefe/Bruce Coleman, Inc.; 564 (b) Mimmo Jodice/ Corbis; 565 (tr) Mimmo Jodice/Corbis; 567 Zhang Zongkun/ Imaginechina; 568 (t) O. Louis Mazzatenta/National Geographic Society Image Collection; 569 (tr) Private Collection/Bonhams, London, UK/Bridgeman Art Library; 569 (br) Zhou Kang/ Imaginechina.com; 570 (bl) Giraudon/Art Resource; 571 (tr) O. Louis Mazzatenta/National Geographic Society Image Collection; 572 (tr) Private Collection/Bonhams, London, UK/Bridgeman Art Library; 573 (br) O. Louis Mazzatenta/National Geographic Society image Collection; 574 (bl) O. Louis Mazzatenta/National Geographic Society Image Collection; 575 (cr) Imaginechina. com; 575 (b) Zhou Kang/Imaginechina.com; 576 (tl) Patrick Aventurier/Gamma; 576 (tr) Patrick Aventurier/Gamma; 576 (br) Patrick Aventurier/Gamma; 576 (bl) Tomb of Qin shi Huang Di, Xianyang, China/Bridgeman Art Library; 577 (br) O. Louis Mazzatenta/National Geographic Society Image Collection; 577 (t) Tomb of Qin shi Huang Di, Xianyang, China/Bridgeman Art Library; 578 (t) O. Louis Mazzatenta/National Geographic Society Image Collection; 579 (r) Doug Stern/National Geographic Society Image Collection; 579 (r) Doug Stern/ National Geographic Society Image Collection; 579 (l) O. Louis Mazzatenta/National Geographic Society Image Collection; 580 (t) Giraudon/Art Resource; 581 (b) Dagli Orti/The Art Archive; 582 Royalty-free/Corbis; 583 (bc) National Geographic Society/ Image Collection; 583 (bl) Pablo Corral Vega/Corbis; 585 (tr) Wilfried Krecichwost/Image Bank/Getty; 587 (b) ImageState-Pictor/PictureQuest; 609 (tr) Joe Atlas/PictureQuest; 611 (b) Jacob Halaska/Index Stock; 612 (br) Scala/Art Resource; 613 (r) Sandro Vannini/Corbis; 614 (br) Giraudon/Art Resource; 615 (tr) Michele Burgess/Visuals Unlimited; 637 (tr) Paul Hardy/Corbis; 656 The Andy Warhol foundation, Inc./Art Resource; 659 (bl) NASA/JPL-Caltech; 662 (br) NASA/JPL-Caltech/UMD; 663 (tr) NASA/JPL-Caltech/UMD; 680 (tr) NASA; 681 (b) NASA; 681 (cl) NASA; 684 (b) Denis Scott/Corbis; 690 (b) The Mariners' Museum/Corbis; 691 (cr) Montague B. Black/Corbis; 691 (cl) Ralph White/Corbis; 692 (b) Stephen Frink/Getty; 696 John Batchelor/www.publishingsolutions.co.uk; 699 John Batchelor/www.publishingsolutions.co.uk; 701 (t)John Batchelor/ www.printsolutions.co.uk; 702 (tl) Artville, LLC/Getty Images; 703 (b) Woods Hole Oceanographic Institution/Rod Catanach; 705 National Geographic Society Image Collection/Emory Kristof; 707 (b) Ralph White/Corbis; 709 (b) Larry Anderson; 713 (l), ® Brian Payne Photography; 714 (br) Brian Payne Photography; 715 (bl) Brian Payne Photography; 715 (br) Brian Payne Photography; 717 (tr) Ralph White/Corbis; 720 (bl) Royalty-free/Corbis; 772 Erich Lessing/Art Resource, NY.

All other photos © Harcourt School Publishers. Harcourt photos provided by Harcourt Index, Harcourt IPR, and Harcourt Photographers: Weronica Ankarorn, Eric Camden, Doug DuKane, Ken Kinsie, April Riehm and Steve Williams.

Illustration Credits, Cover Art; James Shepherd, Background art by: Laura and Eric Ovresat, Artlab, Inc.